INTREPID PIONEERS

to dalia
I do hope you find
of interest
warm regards

Isabelle

To my husband Ivor Seddon for his overwhelming love, kindness and support and to my daughters Sophia and Anya Broido who have followed their passions and are determined and independent women.

INTREPID PIONEERS

Jewish Women in the Public Arena

ISABELLE SEDDON

VALLENTINE MITCHELL
LONDON • CHICAGO

First published in 2024 by Vallentine Mitchell

Catalyst House,
720 Centennial Court,
Centennial Park, Elstree WD6 3SY, UK

814 N. Franklin Street,
Chicago, Illinois,
IL 60610 USA

www.vmbooks.com

Copyright © 2024 Isabelle Seddon

British Library Cataloguing in Publication Data:
An entry can be found on request

ISBN 978 1 80371 048 8 (Paper)
ISBN 978 1 80371 049 5 (Ebook)
ISBN 978 1 80371 050 1 (Kindle)

Library of Congress Cataloging in Publication Data:
An entry can be found on request

Contents

Acknowledgements

With utmost gratitude to Professor Tony Kushner for his unbelievable encouragement, support and tremendous patience. He is truly inspirational.

My appreciation goes to Jennifer-Craig Norton for her invaluable and generous input.

My thanks go to Karen Robson, Head of Archives and Special Collections, University of Southampton Library and to the Parkes Institute, University of Southampton for all their help and assistance.

Foreword

At my alma mater, South Hampstead High School, one of the Girls' Day School Trust schools that turn out to have produced many of the women in this excellent volume, the school song, sung rarely but always at Prizegiving, was from Ben Sirach/Ecclesiasticus: "Let us now praise famous men, and our fathers that begat us......" (Ecclesiasticus 44.1). It seemed extraordinary even then that a girls' school should have this as its song of choice – it does so no longer – but it makes the obvious point to us all that even a school committed to educating girls so that they could do anything in any career they wished put men first, and could not see that another song might have been more suitable! Yet many of the women featured in this volume will have been encouraged and helped by their fathers and other men who wanted to see a level playing field, and real opportunities for women, and in some cases they took over their fathers' role and made an even greater mark on the world.

These were women who were successful against the odds – hence being described as intrepid pioneers. Whether discussing the Jewish Labour women MPs who were so targeted by antisemites in the Corbyn years of the Labour Party – Luciana Berger, Ruth Smeeth, Margaret Hodge, Louise Ellman – or the women rabbis who had to fight to be recognised as equals to the men in many congregations, or the women in media who needed to be especially committed and resolute to get where many men had arrived more easily, most of these women had tough journeys....... And this book tells their stories and allows the reader to celebrate success and share in admiration, and even sometimes wonder.

It also provides an important historical background. Jewish women were just as ambitious, even if without the opportunities, back in the nineteenth century as they are now. And the wealthy female philanthropists and educators did an extraordinary job, insufficiently remembered or even recognised. They too were pioneers. That includes various Rothschild women, some of whom are discussed in this book, and who now have their own 'biography' in Natalie Livingstone's 'The Women of Rothschild', Anna Maria Goldsmid, who helped found West London Synagogue, University

College London and University College Hospital, but who is rarely studied or even mentioned these days, the great Lily Montagu and her sisters Marion Montagu and Netta Franklin, and many many others whose contribution is all too often forgotten.

And when it comes to politics there were the great radicals, such as Minnie Lansbury, discussed in this volume. But there were also the social reformers and politicians, such as Miriam Moses, founder of the Brady Girls' Club in 1925 (to be a club as important as the Brady Boys' Club founded by Lady Charlotte Rothschild, Mrs Arthur Franklin and Mrs N S Joseph back in 1900). Miriam Moses became a long-standing Liberal party councillor, taking over her father's seat, and first woman Mayor of Stepney to boot. Along with Henrietta Adler, another pioneer, she condemned the anti-immigrant (read anti-Jew) housing policies of the Municipal Reform Party in 1932. Miriam Moses gets a chapter here, but her longtime collaborator on social issues, Henrietta Adler, does not. Adler, daughter of a Chief Rabbi, served on the London County Council, and became its vice chair. In being a London County Councillor, she was joined by many other Jewish women, often now forgotten, such as Helen Bentwich (Labour, and daughter of Mrs Arthur Franklin), Leah L'Estrange Malone, whose husband was an MP, and Eleanor Nathan, who chaired the LCC for a year..... All these women, many of whom have not yet been the subjects of a proper biography, made huge contributions. It is to Isabelle Seddon's great credit that she marks the contributions of the early pioneers, as well as those who have done sterling work in more recent years.

But it's not just politicians and rabbis. Seddon discusses doctors and scientists, campaigners, media presenters and lawyers. And, of course, agony aunts. I loved this section and learned a great deal from it. I had not known that the two most famous (and Jewish) agony aunts in the United States, Ann Landers and Abigail van Buren, were in fact identical twin sisters Esther and Pauline Friedman (Eppie and Popo), though their reach was nationwide, syndicated coast to coast, and Ask Ann Landers was an advice column that ran for half a century. But Seddon then focusses on two British Jewish agony aunts, Claire Rayner and Marje Proops both of whom I knew reasonably well, and she writes of them with such respect and affection, but makes such important points about their roles, that I was considerably moved. She asks the rhetorical question as to why Jewish women become so popular as agony aunts. Neither Rayner nor Proops started out that way. Claire Rayner was a nurse, Marje Proops a more regular journalist. Seddon quotes Claire Rayner saying that "It may spring from an urgent desire to meddle, to stick your nose into other people's business.' I am not convinced that sticking one's nose into other people's business is uniquely Jewish, but I do wonder whether the traditional sitting at a table on Friday nights, discussing the week, asking questions- nosiness – and analysing and advising, all in a family setting and often led by women, may have been a factor in their way of approaching problems. And Proops' amazing capacity for getting on with everyone, everyone's best friend, was extraordinary, and lies at the heart of her success. She was friends with grandees, in the Hofjude, court Jew, style, but a loyal companion and support for the ordinary and the oppressed when times got tough.

All these women's stories make for fascinating reading. I look forward to Seddon's next volume, on the writers and artists and actors amongst Jewish women. And I hope she will then think about a third, a volume that tracks the history of these women's forerunners, largely unremembered, who set the scene and made these women's lives and careers possible. There's yet another great story to be told, but we have much to relish right here.

Baroness Julia Neuberger DBE

Introduction

The twentieth century was a momentous time for women when major changes in women's status occurred both in the Jewish community and society as a whole. Beginning with the women's suffrage movement and women's voting rights, the political participation and engagement of women expanded in the years that followed. Links were forged between women's workforce participation and their active involvement in public affairs. Women's liberation movements reached across age, class and racial barriers to forge new policy demands. In short, it was an exciting time during which women came to the forefront in many diverse fields. The subsequent chapters will explore the lives of Jewish women who made their mark in the public arena. In order to appreciate the great strides they made, it is necessary to look at the position of Jewish women in British society in the previous century. In spite of limitations, they contributed to all aspects of Jewish history, if often excluded from the mostly male-produced records of the times.

From 1656, when Jews were allowed to resettle in Great Britain, the Anglo-Jewish community benefited from a relative tolerance towards minorities as well as general economic and political developments. Great Britain offered a haven to Jewish immigrants and Jews prospered, became British and participated in the wider culture of the urban middle classes. The status of Jewish women was affected both by larger social mores and by the nature of the Anglo-Jewish community. The community was comprised initially of Sephardim (Jews of Spanish and Portuguese descent) followed by a later wave of Ashkenazim (Jews of German and East European in origin). Though most were poor, a wealthy elite emerged among the Sephardim. Among recently arrived immigrants, Jewish women worked in shops and market stalls, alone or with their husbands. In time, Jews of both Sephardi and Ashkenazi origin acculturated and moved into the middle classes with many Sephardim entering the upper classes. When they became middle class, largely in the nineteenth century, they adopted prevalent bourgeois values and women generally withdrew from the marketplace. Like other middle-class women they devoted themselves to their households.[1]

Although Jews had prospered during the nineteenth century, new Jewish immigrants from Eastern Europe who came after the assassination of Tsar Alexander II in 1881 through to the start of the First World War in 1914 were mainly impoverished. It is estimated at the height of this migration, between 100,000 and 150,000 immigrants settled permanently in Britain. They sought to escape the poverty, fear of pogroms and oppressive conditions of life under the Tsarist regime in Russia. The majority settled in London's East End, but substantial numbers also settled in the industrial towns of the provinces such as Manchester, Leeds, Liverpool and Glasgow, and found work as tailors, cabinet makers, furriers and shoemakers. Their arrival was greeted with mixed feelings by members of the established Anglo-Jewish community, who were well integrated into British society and highly sensitive to prevailing attitudes in the majority society. They felt threatened by the presence of so large and visible an immigrant population which might place at risk their position in British society.[2]

It was this elite group that set the standard within the Jewish community. For them it was not religious learning which held the key to status and power but rather wealth and prestige in the eyes of the wider society, especially in the eyes of the English upper middle classes on whose goodwill their own position depended and from whom the models for their norms and values were derived. There was a close identity of interest between the Jewish establishment and the liberal upper middle classes who saw the established Jews as conforming to and exemplifying their own standards of hard work, sobriety and philanthropy. The acceptance of the established Anglo-Jewish community to their host society was perceived as conditional and heavy pressure was exerted on the immigrant Jews to become acculturated as quickly as possible.[3]

The existing Jewish community did not want the immigrants to become a public burden and established numerous charitable institutions, which created opportunities for women. In 1884, for example, the Jewish Board of Guardians created the Ladies' Conjoint Visiting Committee, which provided advice and financial assistance to poor Jews. Like many other middle-and upper-class women, they accepted the notion of 'domestic feminism' that expanded women's roles into the larger society, accepted responsibility for improving the situation of less fortunate Jewish women and helped them meet the expectations of the society at large. The established Jewish community promoted Anglicisation among immigrant women via their children and communal services.[4]

In nineteenth-century England, a key distinction (in theory if not in practice) was drawn between the arenas of the public and private, the workplace and the home, the former being a male province and the latter a female domain. As more generally among the middle classes, women in the established Anglo-Jewish community were assigned the role of preserving the sanctity of the home and family.

Life and the community upheld the Victorian ideal of separate roles for men and women. Girls' education emphasised practical domestic skills in preparation for married life. Women were expected to stay in the home and not work. Even in the home, women's activities were limited as most middle- and upper-class families employed servants. Victorian society saw the woman as the spiritual guardian of the home and this role was enhanced for Jewish women by the domestic rituals expected of them in religious law.[5] 'In the established Anglo Jewish community the role of women more or less mirrored that which was found at society at large'.[6]

Jewish Immigrant Women

The rigid demarcation between home and work primarily reflected a middle-class household. For working-class women 'home and work' did not represent incompatible or mutually exclusive options and women engaged in many different forms of paid work.[7] This was especially true of immigrant Jewish women who had a tradition of working in Eastern Europe where the stated ideal was for the man to study while the woman dealt with earthly concerns which extended from housekeeping and childcare to breadwinning. Religious learning brought social status and respect, amongst the wealthy as amongst the poor. It brought practical power and political influence since it was traditionally one of the main criteria for membership to the community council which controlled every aspect of community life and served as the government agent, levying taxes. In this context it was acceptable and even desirable for women to work as breadwinners because this enabled their husbands to gain religious, social and material advantages.[8]

In England, however, it was expected that all women ceased work after marriage. The middle-class vision of married women's withdrawal from paid employment was an unattainable ideal for most Jewish immigrants. Initially these women had to work as poorly paid artisans as their husbands often could not earn enough to support a family. Some ran shops and market stalls or worked in sweat shop industries based in the home. Evidence suggests that in the space of one generation, Jewish immigrant women began to remain more at home.[9] The definition given to the role of Jewish women was underwritten by the attitude of the host society and the nature of the relationship between the community and that society. The confinement of the Jewish woman to the domestic sphere, in accordance with the ideals of the English middle classes, was used to express and communicate the respectability and acceptability of the Jewish community. The identity of a community, and consequently the way in which its woman's roles are defined, is shaped in part by its response to the society in which it is located.[10]

In Rickie Burman's interviews with women from Manchester who were born between 1890 and 1910, a major change in a woman's economic role became apparent. Interviewees emphasised that for their generation it was not the rule but the custom for a Jewish wife to stay home and look after her home and her husband and not go out to work. As historian Catherine Hall found in her study on married women in Birmingham in the 1920s and 1930s, for this generation the domestic idyll was not simply accepted as an ideal; it was enacted in practice. It became more common for men to manage the household economy while their wives' concerns become more narrowly focused upon the physical and emotional needs of their husband and children and the creation of comfort in the home. Burman notes that such a transition following migration did not happen immediately but by the 1920s, the statement that 'Jewish women are seldom allowed by their husbands to go out to work after their marriage',[11] was becoming increasingly accurate. Increased prosperity and a decline in family size meant that the once crucial economic contribution of women was often no longer required. By refraining from paid work, women increased the level of domestic comforts of their husband and children and also furthered the status of the family by demonstrating that the husband earned sufficient income to keep the wife at home. This was by no means coincidental, for the children of Jewish immigrants were coming under pressure from the established Anglo-Jewish community to conform to the values and behavioural norms of the English middle classes.[12]

Burman points out that the change in women's economic role did not necessarily occur overnight. While a large proportion of the interviewees who were mainly children of immigrants or immigrants who came to England at an early age do not appear to have worked after marriage, some of their mothers were economically active and would work if their husbands fell ill and would try and earn a living from home, such as buttonholing and selling sweets. The strong independent woman of the East European *shtetl* (village) did not disappear completely. A minority of Jewish women continued to carve out careers for themselves in the market trade. Nevertheless, in general, Jewish women seem to have moved towards a situation of greater economic dependency and a more exclusively domestic orientation.[13]

Education

Girls' formal education had been generally neglected in the eighteenth and nineteenth centuries. Middle class parents were generally not as committed to separate Jewish schools for their children, fearing they encouraged a sense of exclusiveness, and were even less concerned with education for girls. Middle-class and wealthier families educated girls at home or in private schools. Few, however, objected to separate schools for the poor. Some 'respectable' poor girls attended the Ashkenazi-founded trade school of the Jews' Hospital, established in 1807. Girls studied moral values their teachers thought appropriate, along with domestic skills such as knitting, washing, ironing and cooking that prepared them to become domestic servants in Jewish homes. The Jews' Free School, founded in 1817, also provided poor girls, as well as boys, with an elementary general and religious education. In 1846, a girls' school connected to Westminster Jews' Free School opened and philanthropic support was given because of fear of missionary influences on children. [14] Anna Maria Goldsmid (1805-1889), born into a wealthy Ashkenazi family, was an advocate of women's education and emancipation, helped to establish the girls' school.[15]

Anna Maria's career in advocacy for Jewish education, especially for women, began in 1839 with a call to British Jewry to increase at-home religious instruction to mothers by providing accessible instructional materials. Her appeal to mothers as instructors proved immensely influential. In her later years she devoted herself to the national issue of teacher training. She believed there were too few 'normal schools' for the training of teachers to serve the developing national education system. She edited a Prussian educational code as a mode for English educational reform, contacted educational reformer Mark Pattison and endowed a trust for a school.[16]

Jewish women, among them Lady Louisa Goldsmid (1819-1908) and Fanny Hertz (1830-1908), played a prominent part in the movement for women's education in the second half of the nineteenth century. Louisa Goldsmid, who was also born into a privileged Anglo-Jewish family and was the sister-in-law of Anna Maria Goldsmid,[17] was one of the founders of Girton College, Cambridge, the first residential college for women in the

UK (1869) and her involvement meant that Jewish women gained admission to the university alongside Christian women.[18] After the establishment of Girton College, Goldsmid continued to take an active interest in the women's education movement. Hertz was the founder of the North of England Council for Promoting the Higher Education of Women and the Mechanics' Institute for Women in Bradford, one of the first in England. Born in Hanover, Germany, to a diamond merchant, she moved to London as a young child. She married her cousin, mill owner and yarn merchant William David Hertz, and their Bradford home served as a meeting place for artists, thinkers and radicals.

To evaluate the work of Goldsmid and Hertz one must look at the causes of the nineteenth century movement for women's education. They were mainly social and economic. The education of a middle-class girl was directed solely to one aim, that of obtaining a husband. If a girl failed to get married and her father was not in a position to maintain her, the only socially approved way of earning a living was for her to become a governess. No special training was expected as long as she herself had received an education of a lady. As there were far more governesses than situations available to them, their salaries were very low. The Governesses Benevolent Institute was founded to improve their position and it was concluded that one way to solve the problem was that the work of a governess be raised to that of a profession, to give every middle-class girl the opportunity of becoming a teacher, so that she could resort to a profession if the need should arise. The Institute founded Queens College, Harley Street in 1848, a school for girls and women above the age of 12 and an educational centre for governesses. It had an immense influence on women's education and helped create the pattern of the girls' grammar school which developed in the second half of the nineteenth century. Among the members of the Ladies Committee was Lady Louisa Goldsmid, her mother-in-law Isabel Goldsmid and sister-in-law Anna Maria Goldsmid who were all involved in Jewish education and part of the Langham Place Circle, a network of philanthropic and activist women. Louisa devoted herself to working towards women's admission into university examinations. In 1862 her name appeared on a pamphlet which set forth reasons why London University should admit women to university examinations on the same terms as men.[19]

Whereas Louisa Goldsmid was concerned with the extension of women's education in the south of England, Fanny Hertz played an important part in the north, and in particular Bradford. Hertz was a proponent of women's education, in particular working-class women who were not eligible to study in Mechanics' Institutes and founded the Bradford Mechanics Institute for Working Women. As her work aroused much interest, she was among the first women to be selected to address a Social Science Congress in 1859. She advocated education for its own sake and believed that any human being, whatever his or her station in life, had a right to benefit from a liberal education. In addition to her activities for female working-class education, she founded the Bradford Ladies Educational Association in 1868, which raised funds to found Bradford Girls Grammar School. She accepted reading, writing, arithmetic and needlework as a core for female education and rejected that education should be designed to prepare women 'for the duties of wives and mothers, of mistresses and servants' and advocated for a broader curriculum. She represented Bradford on the North of England Council for promoting the higher education of women in England. The Council instituted local lectures for women and prepared the way for university extension which was started as an experiment by Cambridge University in 1873. She was a passionate believer in education for all women and girls, not just streamlining learning towards the upper spheres of society. 'Both women worked hard and successfully for a cause, which although unpopular in their lifetime, eventually changed the whole position of society'.[20]

Philanthropy

For those women who did not go out for work, there was the possibility of becoming involved in philanthropic work. The involvement of individual Jewish women in philanthropy may be traced back to 1662 when a number of women are known to have worked as volunteers in charitable schools established by the community.[21] During the nineteenth century, an important responsibility for social welfare lay with voluntary agencies. It was largely the philanthropists who supplied new hospitals, financed research and established libraries and parks. Facilities provided by the state were largely supplementary to their efforts. Victorian Jewry excelled in the variety and quality of their charitable bodies. Their principal objective was to help the poor provide for themselves rather than to have to continue to rely on benefits. It was mainly the Jewish aristocracy and upper middle classes who provided these welfare agencies with financial support and leadership, led by families such as the Rothschilds, Montagu, Montefiore and other leaders of the community. Due to their ties of marriage, this elite group of Jewish families, whose wealth was derived from the fields of banking and finance, was known as the 'The Cousinhood'.

In 1840 Lady Louise Rothschild initiated the first independent Jewish women's philanthropic associations, the Jewish Ladies Benevolent Loan Society and the Ladies Visiting Society. Like other nineteenth century Anglo-Jewish philanthropic organisations, these associations were strongly influenced by the methods of the non-Jewish Charity Organisation Society, established by Octavia Hill. They sought to replace selective acts of individual benevolence, which might encourage charitable dependence, with an organised approach that aimed to assist those in need and to foster a spirit of independence through thrift and self-help. A Ladies Conjoint Visiting Committee was set up in London in 1882 under the auspices of the Jewish Board of Guardians, the community's leading charitable body that had been established in 1859 as a centralised agency. Other developments under the Board of Guardian auspices were a needlework training scheme (1885), Mothers Meetings (1896) in which mothers learnt to sew and received instruction on the care and feeding of infants and the Sick Room Help Society (1898).[22] Like many Victorians, Charlotte de Rothschild (1819-1884) believed that the poor needed training, education and refinement as well as financial assistance. She inaugurated Sabbath Schools, supported the Workroom of the Jewish Board of Guardians, started an Invalid Kitchen in 1858 and was President of the Ladies Benevolent, Loan and Visiting Society. In the same vein, Lady Louisa (Montefiore) de Rothschild (1821-1910) supported numerous Jewish charities, sponsored evening classes to teach reading, writing and arithmetic to working class girls and was active in the management of the Jewish Free School, where she provided eyeglasses and knew many children by name. Like many philanthropists of the day, she favoured personal acquaintance with the poor.[23] Such programmes were an important example of the types of interaction between young immigrant women and middle-class native Jews and their values.

Jewish Association for the Protection of Girls and Women

The Jewish Association for the Protection of Girls and Women (JAPGAW) was founded in 1885 by Constance Rothschild Battersea (1843-1931). The issue of 'white slavery' as the sex traffic in women was known, was a major political concern and critics highlighted the role of Jews as pimps and prostitutes. In the period of mass immigration, many men travelled ahead of other family members and women regularly moved to England on their own. Travel was precarious. Upon arrival some women found themselves deserted by husbands and some were tricked and ended up as prostitutes.

In late nineteenth-century Britain, participation in organisations such as the JAPGAW offered women leadership opportunities and influence in communal decision making. The JAPGAW worked closely with Christian anti-trafficking groups, coordinated rescue opportunities and sponsored Charcroft, a home for unmarried mothers. Battersea's election in 1901 as president of the National Union of Women Workers was seen within the Jewish community as a sign of social acceptance.

The report for the year 1925 stated their ongoing objectives including providing cheap and comfortable lodgings with board for working girls and assisting them in in finding respectable work and situations; protecting Jewish girls and women from evil influences and from lives of suffering, slavery and degradation; visiting girls and befriending them in their situations; providing a home where girls and women could live in safety whilst their cases were being tried in court; sending agents to railway stations and docks to meet unprotected girls and placing them in safety and cooperating with societies and institutions having similar objectives. In 1925, 1,231 cases were dealt with by the Association.[24]

The 1902 Conference of Jewish Women

Like their non-Jewish counterparts, middle-class Jewish women used charitable endeavours to occupy their own time in a productive way and to achieve a sense of self-worth and significance. For some women, philanthropy represented an escape route from the formality of middle-class family life and an outlet for self-expression. At the same time, compassion and a desire to improve the position of working-class Jewish women were important motives.[25] It was ironic that as a result of their charity work, they gained increasing acceptance in public life and a growing desire for change in their unequal position in society.[26] As the nineteenth century drew to its close, women still had no parliamentary voting rights. Women were still largely perceived as domestic creatures and second-class citizens. By the time of Queen Victoria's death in 1901 some progress had been made with improving their status in society. By moving into philanthropy, women stepped out of the private sphere of the home and began to move into the public arena. In a world that was divided between public and private, this was of considerable importance.[27] Philanthropy led to more links with other organisations outside the Jewish community.

The 1902 Conference of Jewish Women served as a showcase for the philanthropic endeavours of Jewish women. The aim of the event was to meet and discuss matters concerning the spiritual, social and moral welfare of the community and to interchange information regarding the various methods of community work in London and the provinces.[28] Women heard papers on rescue and prevention work related to white slavery, philanthropy, religion, girls' clubs and mothers' meetings. Attended by Millicent Garrett Fawcett, leader of the National Union of Women's Suffrage Societies, the conference associated itself with England's woman's movement.

For these women, philanthropy played an important role in securing for women a sphere of independent action outside the immediate domestic environment. By 1902, middle-class women of the Anglo-Jewish community enjoyed a greater deal of personal freedom than the preceding half century and were beginning to secure a degree of representation in communal affairs. Through their involvement the women were gaining confidence and organisational experience; they were forging links with other women, Jewish and non-Jewish, pursuing charitable work outside the home and becoming aware of their abilities. The very holding of the conference, gathering over 800 Jewish women from all over the country, was a public statement of their achievements in a sphere outside the domestic environment and expressed for the first time a sense of unity and solidarity among Jewish women nationwide. Although political demands were not made at this stage, feminist consciousness was rising and several women who figured prominently at the conference later became active in the Jewish League for Women's Suffrage.[29]

Jewish League for Women's Suffrage

Jewish women became involved in the feminist movement in the 1890-1914 period and campaigned both for equality within the Jewish community and for national women's suffrage.[30] Their confidence had grown as a result of their increasing involvement in charitable work and in 1912 the Jewish League for Women Suffrage (JLWS) came into being, as the community's equivalent for suffrage set up by other groups.[31] The JLWS was modelled on Christian leagues such as the Catholic Women Suffrage Society and the Friends (Quaker) League for Women Suffrage. 'Jewish women led lives similar and parallel so those of their Christian peers. Like them they were loyal to the denomination in which they had been raised. Initiatives outside the familial home were often shaped by their religious formation and undertaken with the support of extensive kinship networks.'[32]

JLWS was the only Jewish women's organisation in England – indeed the world – devoted exclusively to obtaining both national and Jewish suffrage for women.[33] It had two primary goals: earning the right to vote nationally and to vote in their own synagogues. It was led by prominent members of Anglo-Jewry and developed links with secular women's suffrage societies at both national and international levels. It was the first Jewish organization to link Judaism with suffrage and redefined the concept of Anglo-Jewish womanhood to include secular, religious and communal feminist goals. Its executive council featured upper-middle class Anglo Jewry who occupied positions within the suffrage movement, such as Henrietta 'Netta' Franklin, the daughter of Samuel Montagu (Baron Swaythling), a wealthy banker and member of Parliament, who served as President of the National Union of Women's Suffrage Societies (NUWSS).[34]

In 1913, the League's entry in the *Suffrage Annual and Women's Who Who* stated that 'it was felt by a great number that a Jewish League should be formed to unite Jewish suffragettes of all shades of opinions, and that many would join a Jewish League where otherwise they would hesitate to join a purely political party'. The League was non-party.[35] The JLWS organised their own lectures with prominent speakers on subjects that included the economic status of women and the legal aspect of women's suffrage. For Jewish women suffrage became 'a vital symbol of their social acceptance as Englishwomen as well as of their political, religious and communal emancipation'.[36]

The JLWS were not afraid to show their religious affiliation and wore their own badge which had a purple surround with a pale blue centre and a Star of David in the centre. A quotation 'it is the joy of the righteous to do justice' was written in Hebrew.[37] Most suffragists wanted to retain their Jewish identity. Both religious and secular suffrage organisations made it possible for them to do so.[38] They gained admission to English feminist organisations and created a distinctively Jewish woman's movement with its English counterpart.[39] Through their activism they improved communication and coordination between the Jewish community and secular agencies.

Union of Jewish Women

The formation of the Union of Jewish Women (UJW) which emerged out of the 1902 Conference of Jewish women was an important milestone. It was the first national organisation in the United Kingdom run entirely by Jewish women and brought together women from different social, religious and intellectual backgrounds. The objective was to promote the social, moral and spiritual welfare of Jewish women and to bring about practical cooperation between them throughout the country. The *Jewish Chronicle* commented that the establishment of the UJW had shown many the ability with which Jewish women could organise and carry through a large and novel scheme. The UJW gave Anglo-Jewish women their first taste of real political power in national, religious and communal life. Initially its membership consisted mainly of family members of the Jewish aristocracy. However, they did not work on a one-to-one basis with the beneficiaries of their efforts but rather saw themselves as an organisation working for the welfare of educated women or girls who had fallen on hard financial times. They sought to promote women's professions by providing funds, mainly in the form of loans, to young women and girls to enable them to train for and find suitable employment, as teachers, nurses and other skilled trades.[40]

As early as 1913, the Union expanded its mandate to include international feminist goals: equal employment, improved living conditions and political and religious rights for working class as well as middle-class women. After the First World War and the rising influence of the middle and working classes, the Union started to train Jewish women as social workers, dentists and even policewomen. It added affiliate social service organisations concerned with Jewish women and children such as rest homes for mothers and babies and holiday homes for children of the working classes. In 1919, the UJW became the first women's organisation to send representatives to the Jewish Board of Deputies. Gradually the Union's leadership changed. In the early annual reports there were nine titled ladies on their list of vice-presidents; by 1970 there were just three. The formation of the UJW was a significant communal milestone and marked the beginning of the leadership of women in the Jewish community from aristocratic hands into the control of the expanding middle classes. It provided a precedent for the public involvement of women in major office.[41]

League of Jewish Women

The League of Jewish Women (LJW), a welfare organisation, was founded in May 1943 and reflects the changing status of women in the general community, the Jewish community and in the welfare services. Though it did not seek it, like many women's twentieth-century organisations, the LJW became an involuntary element in the women's liberation movement, fighting for equality of the sexes.

In June 1938, in order to prepare for the dislocation that would inevitably be caused to the civil population if war would break out, the Home Secretary called on Stella Isaacs, the Marchioness of Reading, to form a voluntary service of women that would be attached to local authorities and by 1942 more than one million women had been mobilised. Whilst the leadership of the Women's Voluntary Service (WVS) tended to upper-class ladies, the majority of members were middle-class middle-aged housewives. From the outset they became heavily committed to the war effort and helped organise the mass evacuation of women and children, ran canteens and helped with hospital services. Many Jewish women who were already working for the UJW and Jewish organisations such as Bnai Brith and Wizo joined the WVS. A conference was held in 1943, which found that there was a need to combine the 'service' element of Jewish charitable organisations into a single fellowship. The *Jewish Chronicle* said a clear objective of the conference was to revitalise Jewish women by awakening in them a sense of communal responsibility and ensuring that they all took an intelligent interest in affairs.[42]

The outbreak of the Second World War marked an important revival in the fortunes of the women's movement in Britain. It provided them with further opportunities to demonstrate that, like men, they were capable of making an important contribution to the national war effort. By 1943, an estimated 8 million women had been conscripted into the wartime workforce to replace male workers. The end of the war sent many of them back to their homes, but women had now become a firm and integral part of the labour market. The LJW aimed to unite in one organisation Jewish women in Britain of every shade of opinion; to intensify their sense of responsibility to the Jewish community and the community generally; to make contributions to solving problems confronting the Jewish community generally and to encourage the formation of local groups throughout the country.

The Association of Jewish Friendship Clubs for the elderly were set up under the joint auspices of the LJW and the United Synagogue Welfare Committee. The clubs formed rapidly and synagogues, whatever their denomination, began to feel that their purpose was not complete without having a senior citizens' club held on their premises and subsequently 121 clubs were established. The friendship clubs' growth was directly linked with the high efficiency with which LJW organised the work. These clubs were one of LJW's most important achievements. Other aspects were important: the variety of work undertaken; the creation of a large body of Jewish women who were given an additional rounded education, beyond their formal education, helping to make them articulate, confident and informed on local, national and international matters and enabling them to play an important role in the Jewish and wider community.[43]

Early Presidents such as Lady Hartog (1943-47), Esther Samuel (1947-52), Miss Hilda Schlesinger (1952-57) and Lady Rose Henrique (1957-61) were women from 'The Cousinhood'. Henrique was 'the last of the old brigade'. Control was passing to the new, ever expanding middle class. Rosa Freedman (1961-64) was the first of the new guard presidents and ending the era of benign patronage. The presidents that followed her, President Phoebe White (1970-73) and Sybil Brown (1979-82) came from East End backgrounds.[44] The Cousinhood ladies could never have imagined that babies born in Mother Levy's, a charity they supported financially and helped on the ward, would one day be Presidents of the League. By this time, a candidate's opportunity to take office did not depend on her financial situation but on her ability.

During the time of Sybil Brown's tenure, the League's work included running friendship clubs, luncheon clubs, meals on wheels, serving tea in Strangeways Prison, taking part in an army exercise in case the bomb fell, chauffeuring people who needed hospital treatment, helping disabled children with riding lessons and working with women of other faiths. Work carried out included hospital visitation, welfare of the aged, parties and outings for children, and clothing parcels. In the 1954 annual report it was claimed that that JWL was already operating a miniature welfare state helping those in need from childhood to old age. It was at that time agreed to start training classes in committee procedure, public speaking and becoming a group officer. In 1957, the League was invited to help in a pilot project working with a medical team in psychiatric hospitals, believed to be the first time a voluntary organisation was involved in such work.[45]

By the end of the 1980s, there were 70 groups and 5,000 members. Services included helping at 51 children's hospitals, baby clinics and playgroups weekly; 42 general hospitals; cooking and serving 115,000 meals at day centres and luncheon clubs per year; family and bereavement counselling; delivering annually 83,000 meals on wheels to the housebound; assisting weekly at 57 units for physically handicapped; visiting 113,000 housebound people annually, transporting 4,000 people annually to hospitals, day centres and friendship clubs and assisting at 21 psychiatric hospitals. Throughout its history LJW has been affiliated with more than 100 other organisations and in 2005 there were 32 affiliates that included Age Concern, Breast Cancer, the British Association of Counselling, Citizens Advice Bureau and the National Council of Women of Great Britain. The latter was established in 1895 and its aims were to monitor legislation, represent women's opinions and concerns to Parliament and systematically follow them up. It provided specialist knowledge on issues such as violence against women, migration and asylum and was UJW's chief affiliate.[46]

The Association of Jewish Women's Organisations

The Association of Jewish Women's Organisations (AJWO) was formed in 1965 and was a landmark in the history of Jewish women's organisations in England. In 1964, Vera Braynis, President of the League of Jewish Women, presented the idea at a meeting of the Board of Deputies of British Jews. She believed that the time had come for other Jewish women's organisations to seek similar representation at the Board and to further establish a communal forum of women in the community to work together on matters of collective concern. She arranged a meeting to explain the mutual benefits of such a forum and invited all the main Jewish women's organisations in Britain to participate. The idea was that this new umbrella organisation, embracing the major Jewish women's organisations, would provide 'a forum to promote unity and understanding among Jewish women of all shades of opinion, encouraging them to deliberate on matters of common interest and concern. It would urge representation on communal bodies, act as a source of information and make public statements and/or take common action if necessary'. AJWO has been involved with a host of campaigns in the community and was in the forefront of the Soviet Jewry Campaign in the 1970s. Many of its members participated in the March of Silence in 1971 and supported the formation of the National Council for Soviet Jewry.[47]

The above shows the great strides made by Jewish women during the twentieth century. The following chapters will highlight their achievements in a wide range of professions and occupations and look at how their Jewish history and background impacted and contributed to their success. As Jewish women's involvement in many fields can be traced back to the struggle for women's rights, the first chapter will look at Jewish women campaigners of the late twentieth century whose work carried on the legacy of the suffragettes and who championed the oppressed, victims of trauma, persecution and abuse, and the forgotten and overlooked both Jewish and non-Jewish. Following this, an examination of the careers of two Agony Aunts, whose Jewish backgrounds and sensibilities helped make them uniquely able to offer help to those in need of advice and guidance. Continuing with figures associated with journalism and broadcasting, the next chapter focuses on Jewish women in the media, chronicling their struggles as outsiders – both as women and as Jews – to establish themselves as serious journalists in a male dominated profession. The next three chapters each feature women who similarly had to battle for their places in the heavily male professions of law, medicine and science, their gender even more than their religious heritage presenting challenges to their attainment of success and achievement. The final two chapters follow the lives of prominent Jewish women, religious leaders and politicians, who, like their sisters in other professions, faced headwinds related to gender and in the case of politicians, often vicious antisemitism.

Issues of gender link these women's experiences across a range of public activities and professions, as do themes related to Jewishness, social status, education and cross-cultural heritages. Historical Jewish persecution, including the Holocaust, is one of the factors that ties many of these highly accomplished and civic minded women together and along with the legacies of immigrant and refugee backgrounds, motivated and inspired them to make their mark in British culture, society and politics.

1

Campaigners

It was not until the late nineteenth century that anything like a true women's movement began to emerge in England. A group of women known as 'the ladies of Langham Place', after one of their early meeting places, organised campaigns around issues such as women's urgent need for better education and for increased possibilities of employment, as well as the improvement of the legal position of married women. In the course of the nineteenth century the vote gradually became central to feminist demands. It was seen as important both symbolically (as a recognition of women's rights to full citizenship) and practically (as a necessary way of furthering reforms and making practical changes in women's lives).[1]

Organised campaigns for the right for women to vote began to appear in the 1860s. When Parliamentary Reform was being debated in 1867, John Stuart Mill proposed an amendment that would have given the vote to women on the same terms as men, but this was rejected and as a result the campaign gained momentum after this. In 1897 the National Union of Women's Suffrage Societies (NUWSS) was formed under the leadership of Millicent Fawcett, the first national movement with women's rights in mind.

In 1903 the 'votes for women' campaign became energised by the creation of the Women's Social and Political Union (WSPU). Founded in Manchester by Emmeline Pankhurst and her daughters, the WSPU aimed to wake the nation to the cause of women's suffrage through 'deeds not words'. The decision to relocate the headquarters of the WSPU to London in 1906 transformed the movement and the fight to win the vote became a highly public and at times violent struggle.[2]

The word "suffragette' was first used in 1906 by the *Daily Mail* to describe women campaigning for the right to vote, referring to the militant activist suffragists who favoured direct action and to distinguish them from the suffragists who favoured working through constitutional change.[3] The WSPU burst onto the streets of London at a time when women played little part in public life. The Pankhursts stimulated a spirit of revolt that directly challenged this exclusion. By taking their campaign to the streets the suffragettes attracted maximum publicity for their cause and became recognisable by their purple, white and green colours. Street processions were announced by brass bands playing marching songs. The move to the political heart of the nation enabled suffragettes to maintain a constant presence in Whitehall, petitioning Downing Street, heckling MPs and chaining themselves to government buildings. Over 1,000 suffragettes received prison sentences for their activism where their protests continued as hunger strikes. The authorities responded with brutal force feeding.[4]

From 1912 the WSPU shifted the focus of its campaign to attacks on property and the disruption of public life with window smashing and attacks on works of art. The outbreak of the First World War brought an immediate suspension of action and they devoted themselves into supporting the war effort. Yet through their challenge in taking their campaign to the streets they had gained confidence and independence and their work eased the way for women to take a more active and public role during the war. This role was finally acknowledged with the grant of the parliamentary vote to propertied women over the age of thirty in 1918. In 1928 another law was passed lowering the voting age for women down to twenty-one years in accordance with male enfranchisement.

Middle-class Jewish women became involved in the feminist movement in the 1890-1914 period and campaigned both for equality within the Jewish community and for national women's suffrage.[5] The Anglo-Jewish campaigners, like those of the NUWSS, were from the middle and upper echelons of society. The confidence of middle-class women was growing as a result of their increasing involvement in public life through charitable work. The Jewish League for Women Suffrage (JLWS) came into being in 1912, the community's equivalent of suffrage set up by other groups.[6] Religious differences appear not to have been a barrier and the JLWS was modelled on Christian leagues such as the Church League (Anglican), the Catholic Women Suffrage Society and the Scottish Church League.

JLWS was the only Jewish women's organisation in England – indeed the world – devoted exclusively to obtaining both national and Jewish suffrage for women. It had two primary goals: earning the right to vote nationally and earning the right to vote in their own synagogues. Jewish religious practice was overwhelmingly male-oriented and women were not allowed a role in synagogue management nor in synagogue ceremonies.[7] It was led by prominent members of Anglo-Jewry and developed links with secular women's suffrage societies at both national and international levels. It was the world's first Jewish organisation to link Judaism with suffrage and redefined the concept of Anglo-Jewish womanhood to include secular, religious and communal feminist goals. Its survival and acceptance in class conscious Britain was because its executive council featured upper-middle class Anglo-Jewry who had already occupied positions within the suffrage movement, such as Henrietta 'Netta' Franklin, the daughter of Samuel Montagu, a wealthy banker and Member of Parliament. Netta served as president of the NUWSS in 1916 and 1917 and many female members of the clan into which she had married were active members.

The League had its own banner and were not afraid to show their religious affiliation. They wore their own badge which had a purple surround with a pale blue centre and a Star of David in the centre. A quotation 'it is the joy of the righteous to do justice' was inscribed in Hebrew.[8] Many suffragists wished to retain their Jewish identity. Both religious and secular suffrage organisations made it possible for them to do so. There was no conversion agenda on the part of the Christian leagues.[9] They gained admission to English feminist organisations and created a distinctly Jewish women's movement with its English counterpart.[10]

The struggle of the suffragettes became known as 'first wave feminism' that focused on equal rights for women, the fight for women's right to vote and changes in the law around marriage, employment and education. What is termed 'second wave feminism' emerged after the Second World War. In 1947 a commission on the status of women was established by the United Nations and two years later it issued a Declaration of Human Rights which both acknowledged that men and women had 'equal rights as to marriage, during marriage and at its dissolution' as well as women's entitlement to 'special care and assistance' in their roles as mothers.[11] The second wave of feminism is usually demarcated from the 1960s to the late 1980s. It was a reaction to women returning to their roles as housewives and mothers after the end of the Second World War when the men, who had left the workforce to join the defence forces, had returned and taken back their jobs. Women were expected to quietly resume their lives as loyal and subjugated wives. The 'second wave' focused on both public and private injustices.

Much like the suffragettes before them, the activists of this wave, the Women's Liberation Movement of the 1960s-80s, realised that it was deeds, not words that would win the day. They discovered that they would need to employ shock tactics in their fight, which largely focused on gaining equality in the workplace, in the family and for rights over their bodies.

Women had been meeting in London since 1969; some had been involved in protesting against the war in Vietnam and helping American deserters; other women emerged from traditional left-wing groups from the student movement. Perhaps the most distinctive element in the new movement was its organisation: women met in small groups, some locally based, and others were later formed to discuss specific issues or work for particular causes.[12]

This emerging group of women were ready to fight for equality. Women still earnt less than men. They were expected to give up work when they got married or became pregnant; to settle down and be good housewives. Their campaigns included giving support to a night cleaners' campaign for better pay and conditions and to a strike by women machinists at the Ford Dagenham plant who earnt less than men in equivalent work. To see any effective change they had to get organised and be more than a little bit daring. This included disrupting the 1970 Miss World contest at the Albert Hall, London by pelting the stage, hosts and participants with flour bombs, tomatoes and stink bombs in protest of the way it objectified women and, in 1971, 4,000 women took to London's streets for the first Women's Liberation march. They waved washing lines and chanted 'one, two, three, four, we want a bloody damn sight more!' They descended on Downing Street to hand over a petition which called for the government to meet their four demands: equal pay; equal educational and job opportunities; free contraception and abortion on demand and free 24-hour nurseries.[13]

This spirit, determination and the importance of performance and visibility and boldness in the public sphere was mirrored by a group of middle-class suburban Jewish housewives who campaigned for Soviet Jewry. Other women featured in this chapter are Helen Bamber who fought for human rights and Ursula Owen, a pioneering member of the Women's Liberation Movement.

Women's Campaign for Soviet Jewry – The 35's

The British campaigns on behalf of Soviet Jewry in the 1970s were dominated by the Women's Campaign for Soviet Jewry which was more commonly known by its nickname the '35's'. The 35's were formed in the context of a growing sense of frustrated at the perceived lack of support for persecuted Soviet Jewry from the established bodies in Britain, such as the Board of Deputies of British Jews. Those involved were Jewish housewives who developed a professional expertise; hardheaded yet compassionate, they wept tears of sorrow and tears of joy. Their effectiveness was due to their total dedication to the cause of Soviet Jewry, passionately motivated by the 'never again' rationale.[14]

Jews had lived in Russia and its neighbouring countries since the sixteenth century. Following the assassination of Tsar Alexander II in 1881, many emigrated. After the Bolshevik Revolution in 1917 some Soviet Jews embraced Bolshevism in the hope that the Revolution would bring the promised freedom, equality and ease the burden of their lives and stamp out the antisemitism which was endemic there. During the civil war that followed the Revolution 150,000 Jews were massacred by both the Red and White armies. Following the civil war came Lenin's 'use of terror' policy which led to the murder of the leaders of the religious, educational, cultural and Zionist organisations that were responsible for Soviet Jewish life. The Lenin terror was replaced from 1934-1953 by the Stalin regime. Stalin was determined to eradicate what remained of Jewish life within the Soviet Union and from 1948 onwards there were purges against writers and artists.

Although Stalin's death in 1953 might have lessened the excesses of the secret police, persecution against Jews continued. They were met with discrimination and there was great difficulty in obtaining positions in places of higher learning. Through a gradual process, Jewish religious and secular institutions disappeared in order to silence the Jews. When a Jew applied for an exit visa, life became even more intolerable. They were branded as traitors and were invariably dismissed from their jobs and were fortunate if they could find very menial jobs as a caretaker or cleaner. If they were unable to find work they were accused of parasitism (it was illegal to be unemployed), they encountered KGB harassment, mysterious attacks in the street, arrests were made, and they were imprisoned on trumped up charges.

The 1967 Six Day War stirred up the emotions of the Soviet Jews. The euphoria which followed the Israeli victory together with the increasing antisemitism and anti-Zionism were the catalysts for the desire not only to learn about their religious and historical heritage but to emigrate to Israel. Margaret Rigal, co-chairperson of the 35's group explains that all their lives they had remained hidden as Jews and now they wanted to come out in the streets and talk to other Jews about this miraculous Israeli victory. They applied to leave the Soviet Union in order to live as Jews and they were refused. They considered that if they continued to make a noise and were supported by the West they could be let out.[15] They became known as 'refuseniks' – Jews who had applied to leave the Soviet Union but were refused the necessary exit visas by the Soviet authorities.

A former air pilot Mark Dymshitz, so frustrated by his inability to get suitable employment after he had applied for an exit visa, devised a plot. He, together with other Jewish activists, bought all the tickets on a small aircraft, intending to tie up the pilot, leave him at Leningrad airport and fly the plane to Sweden, in order to get to Israel. Unfortunately, they were betrayed and were captured in June 1970 and charged with attempting to leave the country illegally. Two of them were sentenced to death and the others received long prison sentences. This aroused Jewish consciousness both within and outside the Soviet Union. Amelie Jakobovits, wife of the British Chief Rabbi, led a protest march organised by members of the Association of Jewish Women's Organisations to the Soviet Embassy in London. This was an early intimation of the unsuspected activist potential of Jewish women. After worldwide protests, organised virtually overnight, the death sentences were commuted. Pressure from the outside world had an impact and, encouraged by this, the campaign on behalf of Soviet Jewry gained momentum which in turn encouraged the activists in the Soviet Union who increased their efforts despite the consequences as they now knew they were being supported by the outside world.[16]

Support for Soviet Jewry in Britain began in the mid-1960s. The students, the Board of Deputies of British Jews and a number of individuals were then contributing to what was to develop into a dynamic and influential movement. The earliest organisation actively involved in support of Soviet Jewry was started by the Universities Committee for Soviet Jewry (UCSJ) which played a role in organising demonstrations, petitions and letter writing. In February 1969, a crowd of 10,000 marched from Speakers Corner, Hyde Park to the Soviet Embassy. With the passage of time the work of the UCSJ gradually diminished and was largely replaced by that of the Women's Campaign for Soviet Jewry.[17]

Igo Rager, in charge of Soviet Jewish affairs at the Israeli Embassy London (1971-73) thought that British Jewish housewives would be a great force to use in a campaign supporting Soviet Jewry owing to the spare time that they had available and that women activists could be a good gimmick. He approached women's organizations to help lead such an endeavour and the Women's Campaign for Soviet Jewry was formed. Their actions went on to play a significant part in the emigration of thousands of refuseniks and their activism had an impact on the collapse of the Soviet Union itself.

Throughout the 1970s the 35's developed a reputation for outlandish demonstrations on behalf of the refuseniks. Their demonstrations were reliant on the group's utilisation of imagery and symbolism through which they drew attention to their cause. The organization's first event was on May Day 1971, a 24-hour vigil and hunger strike to highlight the plight of Raiza Palatnik, an imprisoned refusenik from Odessa, Ukraine.[18]

Raiza Palatnik was always conscious of her Jewish background and constantly looked for opportunities to identify herself with her Jewish roots. After graduation from the Moscow Institute of Librarians she found it impossible to find work commensurate with her qualifications and this together with the continued antisemitic campaigns led her to consider emigrating to Israel and to locate her relations there. She was arrested in December 1970 and in June 1971 was sentenced to two years imprisonment where her life was one of brutality and neglect. She suffered a heart attack for which she received no medical care. Her sister was allowed to leave for Israel and once there vowed to do all she could to bring about Raiza's release. The campaign began to gain momentum in Britain and the United States.[19]

Igo Rager approached three women whom he considered would contribute greatly to the campaign – Joan Dale, Doreen Gainsford and Barbara Oberman. He presented a proposition to them. As Raiza was 35 years old, he wanted them to find 35 women who would demonstrate on her behalf. This was the start of a new movement. The 35 women, dressed in black, gathered outside the Soviet Embassy with a large banner bearing the slogan 'KGB stop torturing Raiza Palatnik' and with the intention to deliver a petition to the wife of the Soviet ambassador calling on her to use her influence to help. Doreen Gainsford recalled that they were lucky that there were no security gates in those days and, as it was before the days of mass demonstrations, the press were interested in them. They were, after all, an unusual group – Jewish housewives from the north west London suburbs. There was a telephone box nearby and Gainsford constantly rang every newspaper, television and radio station and told them that they were a group of 35 women demonstrating for the release of a 35-year-old woman and that they intended to stay for 35 hours outside the embassy (although in truth it was to be 24 hours). When she heard that a man on the *Daily Telegraph* news desk say 'it's those 35's again', the name for the movement was born. It became an important part of their identity and appeared prominently in their publications and demonstration banners. For several weeks following the demonstration, the 35's took a letter to the wife of the Soviet ambassador every day apart from the Sabbath, but as it became increasingly difficult to gain entry the deliveries became weekly and then were posted. At an international amnesty press conference in London in November 1975, Raiza Palatnik said it was public awareness of her suffering that led to the improvement of her prison conditions and brought about her early release.[20]

Throughout the 1970s the 35's utilised an array of symbolism and humour in their demonstrations to draw attention to the plight of the refuseniks. One symbol that was repeatedly used was that of a 'prisoners' banquet' where prominent figures would be invited by the organisation to take part in a meal of the type that the refusenik would receive daily in

1. Petitioning for Soviet Jews (Courtesy of the Archives & Special Collections, Southampton University)

prison. Actress Ingrid Bergman attended a banquet where she ate a meal of watery cabbage soup, a potato, a lump of black bread, an ounce of raw cod and a lump of sugar. The meal was a replica of the type of meal being eaten by refusenik Sylva Zalmanson during her imprisonment. By connecting the meal to an individual, the 35's were using strong imagery to present a refusenik's experience in a very authentic manner and this was more effective than merely accounts of life in the Soviet Union that were being published.

Other demonstrations by the 35's were stage invasion of public events where Soviet cultural delegations of artists or athletes were performing. Their demonstrations were designed to catch the eyes of those present as well as the media. These included rushing on to Crystal Palace's football ground just before a match against visiting Russian team Leningrad Zenit in November 1972 which disrupted the proceedings and coming on stage at the London Coliseum where the Georgian State Dance Company were

2. Sharansky Protest at Wembley Arena, early 1980s (Courtesy of the Archives & Special Collections, Southampton University)

performing in 1973 and opening umbrellas with the phrase 'USSR Stop Antisemitism' emblazoned upon them. During a June 1974 performance of the Bolshoi Ballet's Swan Lake, also at the London Coliseum, those attending the performance were greeted by nearly 200 policemen on duty and demonstrators with banners calling out 'KGB stop persecuting the Jews'. There were repeated interruptions to the ballet which ranged from individuals standing up and vocalising their protest against the Soviet regime to a 'high pitch whine' from a device inside a discarded chocolate box. Throughout their demonstrations in the 1970s the 35's intended to attract as much media attention as possible. Their relationship with the press was pivotal to their campaigns. Many national newspapers reported on both their demonstrations and the position of the individual refuseniks that the group were working to support, such as Raiza Palatnik and Sylva Zalmanson.[21]

On a number of occasions, the 35's hosted refuseniks who had been granted exit visas during which they created a media spectacle to attract attention to their guests and the campaign. In February 1972 the 35's invited Katia Palatnik, who had campaigned in the Soviet Union for the release of her sister Razia, to join them in London for two weeks. Katia was granted an exit visa unexpectedly the previous month and the 35's believed this was a result of the difficulties that she was causing the Soviet authorities by her communication with the West, who were then using the information to publicise the abuses being carried out. It was a sign that their campaigns were having an effect on the Soviet authorities. Upon her arrival in Britain, Katia was met at the airport by the 35's who presented her with 35 white roses which was described by *The Guardian* as a 'floral reception'. The media were drawn not only to Razia's case, but to the others still being persecuted in the Soviet Union with information about their treatment that included daily interrogations, long periods of solitary confinement and antisemitic harassment whilst being detained in a labour camp. In the early 1970s knowledge of the refuseniks was very limited among the British public and as a result the 35's focused their attention on raising awareness of the persecution of Soviet Jewry through their novel demonstrations. By the end of the decade the Soviet Jews' plight was well known and there was a need to shift the target of the campaign's work from the general public to those in position of power and to persuade those with political influence to pressurise the Soviet authorities to cease their abuse.[22]

The 35's based at their central London office became known as the group 'frontliners' who dealt with the day to day running of the organisation. In 1978 there were 36 frontliners and 150 people who could be called upon to attend demonstrations at short notice. The frontliners' tasks included reading newspapers to collate stories of interest and press cuttings which created records on individual refuseniks that were used in campaigns. Other 35's groups were established around the country, with particularly active groups in Liverpool, Leeds and Bournemouth, and the London office coordinated the affiliated groups. Members from the London office visited the groups regularly to supply information and give encouragement. The groups worked closely with London but were autonomous. Each group devised its own campaigns and was instrumental in achieving extensive coverage both in the local newspapers and radio stations. By the late 1970s there were 19 groups in Great Britain.[23] Regional groups were of great benefit as appeals to individual members of Parliament carried more weight if they came from a group of constituents rather than a single appeal from London. They organised their own local demonstrations, such as the one in Liverpool in 1979 that was reported in the *Liverpool Weekly News,* whereby there was a teddy bears' picnic to mark the international year of the child with six of the children having bears called Misha (the symbol of the Russian Olympic Games) demanding 'this year in Jerusalem'.[24]

In June 1978 the London office began distributing a newsletter to regional groups and other activists with details of the latest refusenik cases and reports on demonstrations and forthcoming events. The Circulars contained a great deal of information but were amateurish in style compared to publications produced by other groups in this period. They were poorly photocopied, had low quality images and press articles photocopied straight from the original without any formatting. They were produced at low cost so information could be spread as widely and cheaply as possible. They also referred to the refuseniks by their first name which gave it a very personal style, and this was in contrast to other publications of the period. This approach shows the emotional nature of the 35's efforts, working for individuals that they considered friends rather than more abstract figures. Despite the stylistic flaws, the Circulars contained a high level of information on the refuseniks that was of great help to activists.[25]

While the group had initially made a name for themselves by their outlandish demonstrations, by the late 1970s their campaigns were underpinned by reliable and accurate information. They were recognised as experts on the refusenik issue and were respected by journalists and politicians for having the most up-to-date information. There were occasions when they staged innovative demonstrations, but these were used more sparingly and when they wished to be seen by Soviet visitors, British politicians or strategy makers. One occasion was in September 1979 when delegates attending the Trades Union Congress conference in Liverpool were 'haunted by the plight of Ida Nudel and Vladimir Slepak, in the form of ghostly 35's'. After this demonstration, six trade union leaders from the conference appealed directly to the Soviet authorities for their release and a petition signed by hundreds of delegates was sent to Brezhnev. This new strategy was used during the 1980 Olympic Games in Moscow. Discussions about British athletes boycotting the games made the event a media spectacle and this provided the 35's with an opportunity to highlight the plight of the refuseniks in the national and international press.[26]

The 35's continued to lobby individuals in position of political power and attaining support of Members of Parliament added weight to their activism. Groups such as the All-Party Parliamentary Committee for the Release of Soviet Jewry and the Parliamentary Wives for the Release of Soviet Jewry were formed. Many MPs repeatedly raised the plight of the refuseniks in Parliament in the late 1970s and early 1980s. The 35's were intent on getting the attention of senior government ministers. Prime Minister Margaret Thatcher was deeply concerned about the human rights violations in the Soviet Union and was a supporter of the 35's efforts. During her meeting with Mikhail Gorbachev at Chequers in 1984, shortly before his rise to power, she reputedly raised the issue of the refuseniks and criticised the constraints placed on Jewish emigration to Israel. Throughout Thatcher's time in office the 35's did all they could to develop a relationship with her. Thatcher also benefited from her links with the 35's as she was able to get from them the latest information available regarding the refuseniks which was of use to government officials. This indicated that Thatcher considered their material to be accurate and reliable which reflects the reputation that the group had attained. Her support was shown when a sack of 35's postcards, which normally would have been refused by the Soviet Embassy, were sent via Downing Street. Thatcher's backing would have raised the 35's profile in the eyes of the Soviet authorities and the realisation that the 35's campaign could not be ignored.

During the 1980s the group were seen as experts on information regarding the refusenik situation. In an article in *The Times* dated 29 April 1985 that reported on the transfer of Iosif Begun to a Moscow jail, the newspaper referred to the 35's as its sole source of evidence and this was reiterated in an article in November 1985. In the early 1970s the group used gimmicks to get themselves heard but by the mid-1980s they had the respect of the media.[27]

Activists affiliated to the 35's gave up vast amount of time and resources to the refusenik cause, supporting individuals in the Soviet Union that they had never met. Their efforts were borne out of the frustration of the inaction of others. The personal risks taken by many 35's and the amount of effort and time that they put into their work necessitated a great sense of altruism. They felt a duty to stand up against the persecution of the refuseniks with whom they shared a common religious faith. In comparison to other activists in Britain working to support dissidents in the Soviet Union, the 35's developed strong emotional bonds with those they were supporting. A great trust developed between the two sides that was beyond that of a friendship and more like close family relations.

Mark Hurst questions why there was such a commitment towards the refuseniks and that the reason needs to be placed into the wider historical context of the twentieth century. Jews were subjected to great persecution throughout their history, most notably in the Tsarist pogroms in Russia and the Holocaust. The persecution of the refuseniks was part of a long lineage of antisemitism in Russia. The efforts of the 35's filled the void in public knowledge about the persecution of the refuseniks in the Soviet Union. They did not want the same situation regarding the lack of information in Britain about the Holocaust in the 1930s and 1940s. Throughout the 35's activism there were references to the broader antisemitic persecutions during the twentieth century. They considered there was the potential to prevent another tragedy that could be compared to the Holocaust. The organisation's activity should be seen as both a reaction to The Holocaust and an attempt to halt further persecution in the Soviet Union. Some scholars have identified the increased awareness and understanding of the Holocaust as having an impact on human rights activism in the 1970s. The 35's and their activism highlights the post-war idealism of human rights that was evident in the 1948 Universal Declaration of Human Rights. The antisemitism in the immediate post war period did not lead to the formation of Soviet Jewry groups that were created in the 1970s. The impact of the 35's greatly increased once détente weakened in the late 1970s and human rights became an important issue in international relations.[28]

The names of four women have been synonymous with that of the 35's: In the beginning Barbara Oberman and Doreen Gainsford focused on getting media attention, highlighting the plight of the refuseniks as an important political issue. Once the dissidents' plight had become mainstream news and both Gainsford and Oberman had emigrated to Israel, Rita Eker and Margaret Rigal took the 35's in a different direction, focusing on getting the attention of those in power. Oberman had always been troubled by the realisation that more could have been done for the Jews of Germany prior to the Second World War. In 1970 after hearing a talk by a refusenik she knew she had to act. Jewish organisations that she contacted were against any form of public demonstration. Shunned by the establishment she canvassed friends. 'I was severely criticised for using such tactics'. She explained that she was a member of a respected north-west London Jewish family and mixed in respectable Anglo-Jewish circles. Family members were not too happy'.

Gainsford dedicated her life to Soviet Jewry from 1971-78. 'We were women, we were attractive'. No opportunity was missed for a demonstration or campaign with an 'impact'. When an engineer lost his job and was forced to become a street cleaner, the 35's swept the streets of London. When a doctor was accused of poisoning a child, the 35's wheeled a hospital trolley down Regent Street. The 35's needed courage, particularly in the early years. Intimidation, insults and criticism were commonplace and frightening to these inexperienced women. Gainsford was summoned to a meeting of heads of Jewish organisations and told after their second 1971 demonstration that if they made too much noise about Soviet Jewry, they would create antisemitism in the country. This was the attitude of much of Anglo-Jewry at the time and it was to the credit of these women that by their fortitude and imagination they raised the consciousness of the community regarding the plight of Soviet Jewry. The work was not without risks. Gainsford was arrested in Helsinki and deported from Belgrade. [29] After the collapse of the Soviet Union, BBC journalist John Snow wrote to them and commended them for showing such courage and foresight which helped bring the regime to an end.[30]

The 35's campaigned for human rights as did Helen Bamber who was renowned for her lifetime pursuit to help those who had faced the worst of kind of humanity.

Helen Bamber (1925-2014)

Helen Bamber OBE was a psychotherapist and human rights activists who

3. Helen Bamber OBE in attendance for JOURNEY Art Installation against Human Trafficking for Sex Industry, Washington Square Park, New York, NY 10 November 2009 (Everett Collection/Alamy Stock photo) Photographer Kristin Callahan

worked with people who had suffered torture, trafficking, slavery, the effects of war and other forms of extreme cruelty. Over almost 70 years she helped tens of thousands of victims to confront the horror and brutality of their experiences. It was her belief that through restoring dignity to those who have suffered atrocity, we find dignity and humanity in ourselves.[31]

Bamber was born in London on 1 May 1925 to Louis Balmuth and Marie Badger. Her father was born in America in 1887 and her mother in Britain and both her parents' families came from Poland. Her father gave her very little information on place names and dates; the family history was a sealed box. He, together with his parents and three brothers, moved to England in 1895. He told her that life had been hard for him in America and that he could not go out on the streets in the summer because he had no shoes, and the sidewalk was too hot under his bare feet.[32]

Bamber grew up in Amhurst Park, north-east London in 'quite a splendid house' that even had a billiards room. This was largely paid for by her uncle Michael who described himself as a 'merchant' and had made a lot of money. Amhurst Park was an area where Jewish immigrants moved to from the East End when they had become more prosperous. The Balmuths were a noisy, divided, family. Relations between the siblings were close and abrasive. Bamber remembers vicious disputes in Yiddish, French and English. 'They were clever and all of them were good linguists. But they quarrelled about everything, each other, their politics and their partners'. For her the extended family was a battleground. Her maternal grandparents lived just off Mare Street in Hackney, also in a large house. Her grandfather was a barber who by the mid-1920s owned a chain of hair salons. Around 1936 the Balmuth family fell on harder times and her uncle was no longer so successful. Bamber and her parents moved to a small house in Stamford Hill. Her parents had an unhappy arranged marriage; they were extremely ill matched, and their quarrels never abated.[33]

Strong beliefs in human rights pervaded the household. Even before Hitler's electoral victory in January 1933 her father had become convinced that fascism was a threat. In contrast to some of his contemporaries he had a literal belief in the imminence of war and extermination. He never relaxed. He wrote incessantly alone in his room every night. He wrote on ethics, religion, fascism and violence.

> He was obsessional but visionary in the way he saw that it would spread and destroy so much. And I have to admit that I lived in some terror because of this. By the time I was nine or ten I was certain that when war came, and if the Germans came to this country, my family

and I would be eliminated. Much of my childhood after 1933 was overshadowed by the fear of grey German figures in polished boots coming as it were, up the garden path.

During the day Louis Balmuth was an accountant, working for a metal supply firm that had connections in Germany and which Bamber thinks enabled him to help Jews inside the Nazi state and to get money and people out.[34] 'He did a great deal to bring to the notice of MPs and others what was going on in Nazi Germany. But it was difficult to get people to listen. Even within the Jewish community there was a tendency to deny'.[35]

Her father shared his fears with his daughter. 'He told me too much, made no attempt to protect me. As the situation became worse in Germany, he would tell me more and more. At night he read sections of *Mein Kampf* to me or translated articles by Goebbels from the Nazi press.[36] Her mother was a total contrast. She was fun and loving and disappointed by her life and her husband.[37] 'It was an extremely unhappy marriage', Bamber recalls. Her father was obsessed with Goebbels' manipulation of language and was preoccupied with the fate of refugees. Her mother preferred to bake profiteroles.[38] She grew up in a tense, secretive environment, sharing the burden of her father's increasing preoccupation with the fate of European Jewry. As the Fascists grew more powerful and Mosley's Blackshirts marched through London's East End, she watched a strange procession of refugees and Zionist agents file through her home.[39]

In her late teens Bamber found work as a secretary and administrator to the National Association of Mental Health which treated returning soldiers and airmen. There she gained considerable insight into trauma. In 1945 Helen responded to a call for volunteers to help survivors of Nazi concentration camps. At the age of 20 she joined the Jewish Relief Unit under the auspices of the United Nations Relief and Rehabilitation Administration to enter the recently liberated Bergen-Belsen concentration camp in Germany where she worked for two years. 'There was nothing at times that I could do for the survivors, other than to listen and bear witness to the rasping out of their story'. Many were to die, but all she could say was 'your story will be told, I will be your witness'. Bearing witness and refusing to be a bystander remained themes throughout her life's work. On her return to Britain in 1947, Helen was appointed to the Committee for the Care of Children from Concentration Camps and became responsible for 722 orphaned children who had survived Auschwitz. During the next eight years she trained to work with disturbed young adults and children while in close liaison with the Anna Freud clinic. She became one of the founding members of the National Association for the Welfare of Children in Hospital that established the practice of allowing a mother to remain with her young child.

In 1947 she married Rudi Bamberger, a German Jewish refugee who was born in Nuremberg in 1920 and who later anglicised his name to Bamber. She acknowledged the irony that even though she had helped thousands of victims of torture, she had not been able to help her own husband. As a child he had seen his father beaten to death by German storm troopers; his mother perished with most of his family in the camps. He was so deeply scarred by his own past that he found it difficult to relate to his wife's comparatively fortunate upbringing and they found it impossible to discuss the Holocaust. They divorced in 1970 although they remained friends until he died.[40]

Bamber joined Amnesty International shortly after its inception in 1961. She chaired the British section's first medical group, which developed a systematic approach to documenting the physical and psychological injuries arising from state-sponsored torture around the world. She found that documenting injuries alone was not enough and that survivors of human rights abuses and their families were also in desperate need of support to overcome what had happened to them. She began providing therapy, alongside a team of doctors, to deal with the aftermath of trauma, during which people became haunted, unable to trust others and debilitated by flashbacks and nightmares. In Latin America she worked with the 'disappeared' and tortured in Chile, Argentina and Nicaragua.[41]

In 1985 Helen founded the Medical Foundation for the Care of Victims of Torture, initially with a grant from the UN Voluntary Fund, operating out of two rooms in an abandoned hospital in north London with one part time assistant. From these small beginnings it grew into a centre staffed by more than 100 professionals, full time and volunteer, treating more than 2,500 survivors a year.[42] Bamber had started the Foundation in response to a call from British doctors who said they did not have time to deal with the complexities of torture survivors coming to the UK or to 'listen to their silences'.[43] The Foundation offered physiotherapy, psychotherapy, counselling and creative therapy, such as music, art and movement. Evidence of torture was documented and passed on to organisations such as the British Medical Association. Such evidence was also used to support applications for political asylum. It offered some care to Holocaust survivors and former inmates of Japanese prisoner of war camps.[44] Bamber explains that 'it is the memory which is most difficult to eradicate, especially seeing someone tortured. That is far worse than their own torture. Children are sometimes tortured too, to bring pressure on their parents. Parents are tortured in front of their children'. Yet despite the stories of so much cruelty and suffering, Bamber was bolstered by seeing the reward of people recover, taking 'great hope' from the young Holocaust orphans she worked with at the beginning of her career. 'They managed to overcome unbelievable adversity, lead good lives and make a contribution to their society'.[45]

Bamber pioneered a treatment approach aimed at achieving what she termed 'creative survival'. It was her view that therapy in isolation was not sufficient. If a person's recovery following atrocity was to be sustained, then it was necessary for that person to also feel safe. She combined legal protection and the prevention of social deprivation with therapy and rehabilitation as the cornerstones of care for those whose lives had been shattered. She explained:

> One cannot give therapy if a person does not feel safe, if there is no food or roof over your head. The rehabilitative aim is centred on the purpose of freeing victims from a form of bondage through which the torturer ensures that his interventions will last over time.

Her approach was considered ahead of its time.

Helen Bamber remained at the helm of the Medical Foundation for almost 20 years. In 2005, in response to changing patterns of global violence and an increasingly hostile political landscape, she and Michael Korzinski founded the Helen Bamber Foundation. The new Foundation had a broader remit and included not only torture survivors but those who had suffered other forms of human rights violations, including those brutalised by criminal gangs, trafficked for labour or sexual exploitation, or kept as slaves by profiteers or families, who often sought international protection but continued to be dehumanised as liars, cheats or asylum seekers. Bamber's ability to speak the truth to those in power and represent those who she considered the most marginalised was a rare and inspiring quality that earned her great respect. Sir Geoffrey Bindman, lawyer and specialist in human rights, said 'she ranks high among the outstanding humanitarians of our time'. In recognition of her work Helen was named European Woman of Achievement in 1993 and made an OBE in 1997.[46]

Her background affected her views and involvement with the disadvantaged throughout her life. At a meeting at the New North London Synagogue to explain the work of UK Jewish Aid and International Development in helping to set up a camp for several thousand Kurdish refugees on the Turkish-Iraqi border, Bamber said that the plight of the

Kurds reminded her of stories that her father told her of pogroms against Russian Jews. 'The descriptions of the torture and humiliation of Kurds in Iraq and Turkey, of crops being destroyed and cattle burnt is so similar'.[47] At a cross community meeting held under the auspices of the Jewish Emergency Aid appeal in respect of the Kosovo refugee crisis, Bamber told those present that in terms of the aid effort, Jews must not be passive bystanders.[48] For Bamber, the desire to be more than a bystander was the galvanising force in her life. She became a tireless campaigner, fighting for mothers to be allowed to stay with their sick children in hospital, an end to medical research on unknowing patients and the release of prisoners of conscience.[49]

In 1993 Bamber went to Israel to testify on behalf of a Palestinian prisoner who she determined had been tortured. Whilst studying his case, she sat for an hour wearing a hood like the one officers had put over the prisoner's head whilst he was interrogated. She gagged and felt panicked. She said it had hurt her to accuse Israel, the state founded by Jews, of torture. Yet it was the memory of the Holocaust that propelled her lifelong mission to help those that had undergone torture. She remembered arriving at Bergen-Belsen after piles of bodies had been buried. A strange sickly smell lingered. It reminded her of geraniums. She asked what it was. 'Death', someone said. She kept geraniums in pots on the terrace of her London home 'for no reason that she can really articulate: the need to forget, the wish to remember'.[50]

Bamber's experience of hearing about the Holocaust in her childhood had a profound effect on her life and galvanised her into taking action and caring for those who had suffered trauma. She campaigned for 'the outsider' as did Ursula Owen.

Ursula Owen (1937 -)

Ursula Owen has been a significant figure in the worlds of literature and free expression since the 1970s. As a pioneering feminist and co-founder of the Virago publishing house which promotes the work of forgotten and undiscovered women writers, Owen has enjoyed a rich and satisfying career. As a publisher and editor she has championed the outsider. She has faced professional rancour and personal turbulence but her combative stance clashes with the need to fit in, stemming from her early experience of fleeing the Nazis.[51]

Owen was born in Oxford in 1937 to Emma Boehm and Werner Sachs who were born in Frankfurt into prosperous Jewish families already highly

4. Ursula Owen (Courtesy of the Association of Jewish Refugees)

assimilated into bourgeois German life.[52] It was with incredible foresight that she and her brother Peter were born in England. Her mother had travelled from Berlin to Oxford to give birth to Owen as she had done in the case of Peter's birth in 1933 in Leeds. She had been warned by a family friend in 1933, just after Hitler came into power, that this would be an advisable course of action. In both cases Emma stayed for six weeks with family members and then returned to Germany. Owen's father was a chemical engineer and together with his cousin ran a company that prepared metal used in the manufacture of armour piercing bullets that was forcibly taken over by the Nazis. Her parents received exit papers to leave in July 1938.[53] The children were left with their grandparents Hans and Lotte Sachs but as the situation in Germany deteriorated, her parents panicked and the family's German maid, who was not Jewish and the only one who could cross the border, brought the children to Holland. Their father was waiting for them and from there they flew to England with their British passports and an exit visa that said, 'single journey only'.[54]

The family lived in Putney, an affluent suburb in south-west London. Owen's family were extremely lucky as they came out of Germany with many possessions, including a Bechstein piano, fine china, crockery and silver. As a young child she was so diffident, always apologising for her existence. She was a very shy, quiet and conformist child. Anxious and melancholy.[55] At home her parents spoke only German while she was made to answer in English. Her father established a successful metal company that helped the British war effort by supplying non-ferrous metals and alloys to the British steel industry. He was famous for his organisation and his temper. Her mother was a talented violinist and at home they played chamber music with her father on flute, brother on cello and Owen on piano. Both parents clung to their guttural accents and German mannerisms while urging their daughter to become a model English rose, despite her dark features. 'They never made the slightest attempt to be English themselves.'[56] Although her parents decided to settle where few Jews were living their closest friends during the war were fellow Jewish refugees. She explains that 'they remained utterly themselves. They never tried to be what they were not. They converted to Christianity and you could argue that was partly an assimilatory thing to do but it was also linked to their support for the Christian opposition to Hitler in Germany. They did want us to be English which in a way was understandable. They wanted us to belong.'[57]

She attended Putney High School where she became deputy head girl, captain of the hockey team, star pianist and won a place at St Hugh's College, Oxford University. Yet she continued to doubt herself. Her sister Ruth, seven years her junior, recalls 'she was slightly anxious about things, always wanting to make things safer'. She was anxious about her mother, who developed severe mental illness in her early 40s. She was diagnosed as schizophrenic and spent years in and out of psychiatric institutions. Despite her achievements, Owen continued to feel like a failure at school. She saw herself as a 'good' girl rather than a bright girl. She sensed that her father with his wealth and academic accomplishments, was disappointed in her. Ruth comments:

> There were always these expectations that she would do well and she was weighed down by them. You have to remember that my parents were in their mid-30s when they moved here and they wanted the very best for their children. There was an anxiety, a need to know that their children were going to be all right.[58]

The young Owen tried always to be good – a good daughter, good at school and playing the piano, anxious not to upset her mother whose mental illness became increasingly disturbing. She seems always to have felt conflicted: longing to please, to be assimilated, to belong. It was only when she reached

Oxford that she became more confident. 'Hungry for ideas, I began to try and make sense of the world; I began to think'. Owen recalls how she was in a daze by the time she got to Oxford to study medicine. Her mother was so ill and she was terrified she would inherit her sickness. She felt she was shallow, without an opinion to her name. University transformed her. It was the time of the 1956 Hungarian Revolution and the Suez Crisis. She suddenly found herself stimulated by students taking to the streets to protest. 'Within six weeks I was radicalised'. She made friends with a small group of women, discovered socialism and for the first time in her life felt worthwhile.[59]

Just before graduating the group discussed what they wanted to do with their lives. There was a choice – to be good (to work and do good deeds) or to be happy (to marry and have children). Her three friends dedicated themselves to goodness, while Owen whispered that she wanted to be happy. She became engaged to fellow student Robert Owen, a socialist historian, and they married soon after graduation. Meanwhile, Ursula gave up on medicine and qualified as a social worker, then as a psychiatric social worker.

> I'm sure I became a psychiatric social worker partly to try and deal with the whole mental illness thing. I was deeply preoccupied with it until I was about 40, which was about the age that my mother started to get ill. I was afraid of getting mentally ill. I think I really grappled with it, and one of the ways that I did was to plunge myself into a mental hospital.[60]

Regarding her marriage, she thought she would be a wife with some talents and some abilities. Although she would work, she would fundamentally be a wife and mother; that would be her main role in life. 'It was the late 1950s. I come from a generation where that was perfectly normal'. She accompanied Roger when he worked abroad. They spent a year each in New York, Cairo and Beirut. She was liberated by New York where people were trying all sorts of things without necessarily being good at them. 'Until then I'd always felt that if you didn't have a first from Balliol, and especially if you weren't a man, you weren't encouraged to try things'.[61] She taught English in Cairo, was a market researcher in New York and tried sculpting in Lebanon. It was in Cairo that she thinks she probably began to think seriously about women's position, their lives as handmaidens to men's lives, the barriers to their freedom.[62]

In the 1950s, if people asked you what you were going to do you answered in terms of what your husband would do. My friends and I assumed we would fit our working lives around what our husbands did and we didn't mind.

In Owen's case she had difficulty having children which perhaps left her freer to choose her own path. Eighteen months after she and her husband adopted a baby daughter – Kate – she left the marriage. She moved to Tufnell Park in north London, where she still lives, with her daughter. She joined a weekly north London women's liberation group which included feminist theorist and historian Sheila Rowbotham and went into publishing.

> I always wanted relationships with men and to have children but slowly I realised that marriage 24/7 wasn't what I liked or was good at. It was painful not getting pregnant and although my father was authoritarian and controlling, something about him gave me the confidence to feel I could go out there into the marketplace and try things.[63]

Owen became very much part of the women's liberation movement which gave her wings, helped her to understand how many of her anxieties had sprung from living in what was then a man's world. She learnt to campaign about abortion, family allowances, sex workers, childcare, support for night-shift cleaners and victims of rape. She went to Greenham Common and she talked into the night. 'Too much talk, Mum', said her little daughter, 'too much talk'.[64]

Owen's publishing career began at Frank Cass in the early 1970s, where she learnt on the job. A reviewer lambasted her first efforts as 'the worst edited book I have ever read' but she was mentored by a female colleague. Owen made her name in publishing when she was in her late 30s. In 1973, together with Carmen Callil, she became the founding director of Virago Press, the influential feminist publisher of Maya Angelou, Angela Carter and Margaret Atwood and out of print books by neglected writers that included Antonia White, Rosamund Lehman and Rebecca West. It was an exciting time as Virago became a rival to commercial publishers and tapped into an audience for feminist writing. Owen remained a director until Virago was sold to Little Brown in 1996. 'The 1960s were exciting but it was almost all about men. Men, not women, wrote their memoirs, but we wanted to change that. It was as exciting as all enterprises that involve passion and ideas are'.[65] There were no men on the editorial staff and virtually all the books published were by women. 'At that time we were probably the only two feminists in publishing'. Virago electrified the book world in the 1970s and at its peak provided a platform for previously unknown or silenced voices.[66]

Virago, with its distinctive green-spined paperbacks dominated the independent bookshops in the late 1970s and 80s. It became as much a widely recognised brand name as Penguin. Identifying, rediscovering and celebrating writers it created a new enthusiastic readership. Owen recalls that in the early days booksellers reported how people just came in to ask for the latest Virago book.[67] Virago had a big impact in all sorts of ways.

> The idea of making feminist books a commercial success was unusual. What happened was that we and other feminist publishers began to show it was possible. Then eventually the bigger publishers saw that they sold.

Owen feels proud to have played a part in championing feminist literature like Margaret Atwood and less prominent writers. 'We did academic books, commissioned from young women who hadn't even got to the first step on the academic ladder and now they are all professors'.[68] She adds that 'you could not have asked for more joyousness or pleasure from people asking about the existence of Virago. People would come up to me and say "oh my God, it's changed my life". It was extraordinary really. Young women just felt their lives had been changed by it'.[69]

Yet success made for conflict. There were arguments with feminists who thought Virago was too corporate, too middle class and too expensive. There were arguments with some feminists who did not think that women's writing should be confined to a ghetto. And there were arguments between themselves. By the late 1970s there were already tensions between Owen and Callil which intensified over the next five years. In 1982 Callil left to become managing director of Chatto & Windus, and Virago was taken over by the Cape, Chatto and Bodley Head group. Owen and Harriet Spicer became joint managing directors of Virago. Virago regained its independence after five women (Owen, Callil, Spicer, Alexandra Pringle and Lennie Goodings) completed a management buyout in 1987. Three years later Owen left and became a non-executive director. Finally, in 1995 after a bitter row, Virago was sold to Little, Brown.[70]

After leaving Virago in 1990 Owen was appointed director of the Paul Hamlyn Fund and cultural policy advisor to the Labour Party. The Fund was established to promote and develop Labour's cultural policies under the Shadow Arts Minister Mark Fisher in the run up to the 1992 general election. She advised them on the presentation of their ideas and published books reflecting the Party's cultural policy.

In 1993 she became editor and chief executive of Index on Censorship, an organization campaigning for freedom of expression which produces a quarterly magazine. It was founded by Stephen Spender in 1972. In the days when show trials were held in the USSR, dissidents sought the support of the West. It transpired that the prisoners of conscience did not receive the telegram signed by Auden, Cecil Day Lewis and Stephen Spender for months. Spender decided to take matters further and the magazine was started in 1972. It supports free expression, publishing distinguished writers from around the world, exposing suppressed stories and providing an international record of censorship. Owen is a founder trustee of Free Word, a centre for literature, literacy and free expression in London. Free Word was conceived in 2004 and Owen took it from an idea to concrete reality, finding the funding from the Norwegian foundation Fritt Ord that supports freedom of expression and a free press, to buy a building for the centre in Farringdon Road, London.

Throughout her career, Owen has not been afraid to challenge convention. This could be due to the fact that she has always considered herself an outsider. A very English German, a very Jewish Christian, a radical in a conservative world. Owen has often wanted to belong, to be quietly accepted. At the same time, part of her has always laughed, or scowled, in the face of convention.[71] Owen is a curious kind of immigrant in that she was British born. She was a toddler when the family left Germany for good, settling in Putney, deliberately avoiding the capital's traditional Jewish pockets of community life.[72]

Most Jews who fled Nazi Germany came away with little to say that was positive about their former home, but this was not the case for Owen. 'It's quite common that people don't talk about terrible things, but the thing about our upbringing was we were brought up with lots of good stories about Germany'. She explains that 'we were a relatively lucky family in the sense not many people died in the camps. Two or three relatives, but we were not brought up to feel this fear and loathing'. After the war her father, by then established in the British metal trades, returned to Germany in 1945 to survey the state of the country's industry. 'He had some difficult encounters and says in letters home "here they are, the Germans again thinking it's nothing to do with them" but he doesn't go on about it. He was someone who felt you just had to get on and do the next thing'.[73]

Like many German Jews the family were not observant but the fallout of their enforced migration to Britain in 1939 would reverberate down the years. Owen was desperate to belong. Her affluent south London upbringing was bounded by post war restrictions on young women, a controlling father and a mother who spent long periods in institutions. 'My family was never religious yet they felt themselves to be Jewish and the war made them feel even more so. Even though they converted to Anglicanism they thought of themselves as Jews'.[74]

It was important to her parents that their children should be integrated into English life. North London, where many Jewish refugees had settled, was not in their eyes the route to assimilation.

Her parents had been interested in the Christian opposition to Hitler and had heard Dietrich Bonhoeffer[75] and Martin Niemoller[76] preach. Upon arriving in England they joined the Anglican Church and their children were christened. Christianity continued to mean something to her parents for the rest of their lives but Owen felt unengaged with Anglicanism, unlike her brother and sister who were drawn to the Christian community.

But for her parents being Jewish remained an integral part of their identity and it continued to be the way they described themselves to themselves and to other people. She reflects that in Germany in the 1930s her parents would have seen themselves as Isaac Deutscher's 'non-Jewish Jew'– solidarity with the persecuted, feeling the pulse of Jewish history, supporting the security and self-respect of the Jews. And culturally they lived lives as German Jews which for then had a distinctive though unreligious quality. 'We as children growing up in England learned a lot about the place of Christianity in our cultural life, much of it at school and from our peers. Jewish cultural, imbibed from our parents and other relatives was always separated from the Jewish religion'.[77]

Yet at times their newly adopted religion did not come naturally. The family celebrated Christmas in a rather grimly organised German fashion with none of the spontaneity that Owen's friends enjoyed.[78] Although her parents converted to Anglicanism, they remained culturally German Jewish with their emphasis on music and distinct culinary habits. Owen and her siblings were encouraged to embrace English life and all of them married out of the faith. 'My parents wanted us to assimilate because they wanted us to have as easy a life as possible'. [79] As Owen notes, it is a hole in her life that she has always regretted. 'I had no education in the Jewish religion at all and the first Seder I attended was with my ten-year-old granddaughter in 2003. I wish now I'd made an effort to learn more'.[80]

Labour MP Mark Fisher comments that 'she is deeply shaped by her past. Her attempts to assimilate and become English affected her almost as much as the external events of the past. There is a permanent tension of wanting to conform and be part of something and yet her critical intelligence always pulls her away from that. She wants to be invited to the party and have the right not only not to go but to criticise it if she does turn up. The tension between these two things make her curious, provocative and delightful.'[81]

Owen has come to terms with being two different people. When she was in her 40s she went back to Berlin to the house where she had lived. It had been bombed and was now a laboratory. She stood by the building and found herself weeping.

> It was something about being in the place where you first were. If you're exiled you don't have that. You can't touch the place where you came from. I don't feel very English. I never have. I used to feel myself as an outsider and then I discovered that most people do. Most people do for this reason or that. I did discover gradually, slowly, and that was partly because of the context of the world we were living in that it was quite a good place to be, in the margins. I certainly would say that being an outsider has huge advantages, so long as you can get over the anxiety about it.[82]

It was the first time that she had dug into her roots and she realised the enormous decisions that her young parents had to make. She tried so hard to belong as a child and to believe that she was English despite the fact that at home her life was totally German in terms of food, music and culture. 'When I got to Berlin I started to be able to acknowledge that I was both.'[83] With regard to assimilation she considers that 'people are quite scornful about assimilation. I think a lot of Jews felt that assimilation, the desire for German Jews to assimilate, was partly responsible for what happened. That they kidded themselves that they were part of the society when they were not'. [84]

She now sees assimilation as not succumbing to the dominant culture. 'My experience was that you had one culture, you had the other culture and you accepted some of it and accepted some of your own'. Her identity is mixed. 'I still feel Jewish. I still feel quite German, I still feel quite English'. With age her lifelong search for belonging has dissipated; she is finally at peace with herself.[85] Today she embraces her multitudes – Judaism, Christianity, Englishness, Germanness, her desire for permanence, her fear of petrification. She says it's a long time since she felt she was on probation in England but of course, as a daughter of Jewish refugees she is still an outsider.[86]

Conclusion

The women featured above all came from middle-class suburban backgrounds and whether they worked collectively, as in the case of the 35's, or individually, their spirit of campaigning could be seen as an indirect result of the Holocaust. The 35's activism was both a reaction to the Holocaust and determination to prevent another tragedy. Research has shown that the increased awareness and understanding of the Holocaust had an impact on human rights activism in the 1970s.[87]

Helen Bamber's father was obsessed with the situation that European Jews were facing during the 1930s. He shared his fears with his daughter and she recalled that he told her too much and made no attempt to protect her. It was therefore not surprising that she volunteered to help survivors of the concentration camps and that experience propelled her to campaign for those who had suffered trauma.

Although Ursula Owen was not part of a Jewish community and was brought up as a Christian in south London, it was her parents' experience of fleeing Germany and wanting their children to become totally assimilated, that shaped her life as she grappled with being considered English and at the same time feeling an outsider. Undoubtedly this contributed to her campaigning for those who did not have a voice.

2

Agony Aunts

From ugly spouses and corset wearing dilemmas to sex and relationship problems, people have spent the last 300 years turning to advice columns for help. In 1691 publisher John Dunton invited readers of *The Athenian Mercury* to send in questions on a range of topics that would be answered by experts. He decided that his readers' own dramas were more interesting than politics and current innovation was that they could do so anonymously and this has remained a feature of problem pages ever since. Dunton's advice column was a great success and subscribers asked advice on subjects ranging from animal husbandry and politics to manners and courtship. The growth of the middle classes in the Victorian era increased the boom. The upwardly mobile were greatly concerned with good manners and turned to the advice of agony aunts believing they were authorities on good taste. The flappers of the 1920s were young women known for embracing a lifestyle viewed by many at the time as outrageous. They were portrayed as sexually liberated, confident young women but when it came to the opposite sex, they were often quite ignorant, and they would write to the agony aunts for help. During the Second World War agony aunts were frequently asked to help distraught readers who confessed to affairs whilst their husbands were away.[1]

Until the 1960s, sex before marriage was seen as an evil that could potentially cause a woman to risk everything. With the introduction of the Pill, women gained unprecedented control over their fertility and lives. Marjorie Proops, who was for many years the most famous and popular agony aunt in Britain, writing the 'Dear Marje' column in the *Daily Mirror*, led the way by talking with a newfound directness about sex.[2] Tabitha Carey considers that the original role of the advice column was to uphold strict moral standards and keep women dutifully on the straight and narrow, which was largely defined by men. The big change in the 1970s was that the aunts stopped scolding women for their own unhappiness and began to sympathise and question. Carey considers that agony aunts helped women to negotiate women's liberation. They were refreshingly frank, after decades when only genteel questions could be published and columnists would respond privately, in plain brown envelopes, to anything as shocking as a gynaecological problem.[3]

Proops was the doyenne of agony aunts, who were trusted to interpret their readers' worries. Hilary Freeman, the *Jewish Chronicle's* agony aunt considers why Jewish women are such great nurturers – a critical quality for an advice columnist. 'You don't have to be Jewish to be an agony aunt but it certainly helps.' She cites the Jewish agony aunts Proops, Clare Rayner who had columns in teenage magazines and the *Sun* and Irma Kurtz from *Cosmopolitan* magazine. Freeman suggests the reason why Jews are so over-represented in the agony aunt trade is that it may be a legacy of the centrality of the strong matriarchal figure to Judaism – this person who imparts the knowledge and looks after everybody. Judaism goes through the mother and the mother has always had a very important role in terms of education, nurturing children and looking after the family. She also points out that 'as a community we are familiar with the art of seeking an answer. We question and we don't just do things that we're told. We ask why, we like to argue about everything. Discussing things and being frank are very Jewish traits'.[4]

It is not only in Britain that Jewish agony aunts have reigned. Two of America's most popular and long running advice columns were written by the two Jewish identical twin sisters Esther Pauline ('Eppie') and Pauline Esther ('Popo') Friedman who wrote under the pen names of Ann Landers and Abigail van Buren respectively. 'Ask Ann Landers' was a daily advice column that ran for half a century in the *Chicago Sun-Times* and was syndicated to 1,200 US newspapers read by 90 million people. 'Dear Abby', which first appeared in the *San Francisco Chronicle*, was even more popular, reaching 110 million readers worldwide in over 1,400 newspapers. There was also sex therapist Ruth Westheimer, known as Dr Ruth, who turned the airwaves blue in the 1980s with her fast-talking, frank advice on sexual matters.[5]

Irma Kurtz considered that such a calling was a Jewish gift and that during the heyday of agony columns, a significant number of aunts in print were heiresses of the ghetto, where women practised pragmatic common sense as their brothers practised the fiddle: two portable instruments that could be carried to the next place of safety. Traditionally Jewish women ran the kitchen court, planning marriages, taking care of the emotional concerns of their large and extended families, engaging in what is now dismissed as gossip, but is actually really valuable. Their wisdom was what kept families together, especially on the road.[6] 'You might be thrown out of wherever you live, you might lose all your possessions, but your wisdom and knowledge and experience can never be taken away, so it's something we keep and pass down'.[7]

On the preponderance of Jewish agony aunt columnists and whether it was a coincidence that many came from a Jewish background, Claire Rayner said that 'It may spring from an urgent desire to meddle, to stick your nose into other people's business' which she believed was a very Jewish thing.[8] In Britain, two Jewish matriarchs, Marjorie Proops and Claire Rayner 'became not only the guardians of the nation's morals but household names'.[9]

Marjorie Proops (1925-1996)

Marjorie Proops was an agony aunt, writer, campaigning journalist and a social commentator. She was the nation's confidante. Millions of letters came into her office for over 30 years: cries for help, the need for encouragement, from men as well as women, in the certain knowledge that they were writing not to a stranger but to a friend, to 'Dear Marje'. Behind the witty by-line, the funny drawings, the glamorous photographs, was a woman of extraordinary perception, tolerance and hardheaded wisdom.[10]

She was born Rebecca Marjorie Israel in 1911, the elder daughter of Alfred and Martha Israel. Her father bought pubs and the family would live above them. They lived variously in Dalston, Clissold Park, Hampstead and Stoke Newington.[11] Her younger sister was seen as 'the pretty one' when they were children and her mother would introduce Marjorie as 'the clever one'. She possessed two obvious talents – drawing and singing. Her deep distinctive voice helped her win an England contralto contest when she was 13 but her mother would not let her take up a place with an opera company because she did not want her to travel far from home.[12] She studied at Hackney Technical College and then worked as an illustrator in a studio in Smithfield, London. Her mentor there was Rose May, whom Proops sought to emulate in every way, from her heavy make-up and extravagant hats to her habit of heavy smoking. Her first published work was a drawing of a baby for a knitwear catalogue. Encouraged by this and other minor successes, and in the spirit of enterprise that was to distinguish her entire life, she rented her own studio and went freelance. Within months she was taking commissions from several women's magazines as well as the *Daily Mirror* and *Daily Express*.[13] She was also a fashion illustrator and columnist with the *Jewish Chronicle* from 1935-36.[14]

Whilst Proops was concentrating on establishing her career, her mother was more concerned about her marital prospects. Proops was aware that

5. Marjorie Proops OBE (Photographed by Allan Warren via Wikimedia Commons)

she was failing her in this respect when she set out to find a partner at a tennis club on Christmas morning in 1934 and met Sidney Proops, a Jewish engineer of Dutch descent, whose parents owned a haberdashery shop. He bought her a hot lemonade, revealed his admiration for Jesus of Nazareth, whom he considered the first socialist, and won her heart. Three days later they were engaged but on the strict understanding that she could continue with her career.[15] She was fortunate to marry a man, rare at that time, who recognised her need to work outside the home and supported her wishes when the current social mores demanded that middle class girls stayed home and became housewives and mothers.[16] She and Proopsie (her nickname for him), were married in Shacklewell Synagogue, Dalston, in November 1935. The marriage was not entirely happy but resulted in the birth of a son Robert in 1941. Proopsie, whatever his shortcomings in private as a husband, remained outwardly at least, a loyal and supportive consort to his wife. They both shared a strong socialist ideology. They fostered a small boy from a children's home and befriended and then gave a home to Made Okubadeju from Nigeria, who became a successful pathologist, and whom she always regarded as a second son. However, her relationship with Sidney became headline news when she revealed in her biography that the 53-year-old marriage had been a sham and that she had conducted a 30 year affair with the *Daily Mirror's* company lawyer Philip Levy.

Editor Hugh Cudlipp hired Proops in 1939 to draw hats and represent the *Daily Mirror* at Ascot under the byline 'Sylvaine'. She was kept on a retainer during the war time years. She wrote her first article during the war for *Good Taste* magazine and entered the field where she was to become best known by writing a government information booklet on venereal disease. In 1945 she went to the *Daily Herald* as Fashion Editor and became Women's Editor in 1950. She never learnt to type or do shorthand and wrote all her copy in longhand, developing the effortless, classless style that she never changed. It was during her time at the *Daily Herald* that she had a glimpse of her future. The paper's advice columnist had taken ill and Proops was worried about the letters piling up, taking it upon herself to open and answer them. What she found in those letters in terms of human misery appalled her; she contacted a psychologist and asked if she could come and see him and went through the more difficult letters with him.

Cudlipp hired her as a columnist on the *Daily Mirror* in 1954; he described her later as 'the first British journalist to attain instant recognition status previously enjoyed by film stars'. It was her ability to get along with the subjects of her column that made her so original. They all genuinely liked her: she became Dame Edith Sitwell's 'little friend', Cary Grant's frequent lunch companion, the then Duke of Bedford's partner in a midnight sandwich at Woburn. Sophia Loren talked to her wistfully about her longing for children. She enticed Barbara Castle on to a donkey and listened to Mary Wilson's poetry hot from the pen. She knew many politicians and attended political conferences of both the Labour and Conservative parties. 'Immediately Marje arrived people would stop looking at the prime minister, whoever it was, and rush over to talk to her', recalled Geoffrey Goodman, political commentator and colleague at the *Daily Mirror*. 'She was a true star'. [17]

The nature of her page changed towards the end of the 1960s. She began to write about more serious subjects, reflecting the letters of her readers, about the birth rate of illegitimate children, the Pill, drug addiction, the abortion law. Cudlipp observed the success of her 'Dear Marje' advice column, which ran from 1971 onwards in the weekly magazine *Women's Mirror,* and suggested she do the same for the *Daily Mirror.* She drew on a team of experts, developed connections with the police, doctors and the Church. Only the more lighthearted ones appeared in print; the darker, more complex ones she answered personally, even taking telephone calls from desperate cases, referring them on to whoever she felt best to help.

Proops had compassion for those she felt less fortunate from a young age. She always maintained that her staunch support for the Labour Party stemmed from her childhood observations of the class differences between the saloon and public bar patrons in her father's premises.

> This had an enormous influence on me. From the age or about five or six I became very puzzled indeed, walking through the bar, as to why there were two worlds around me, one for the rich and one for the poor. The world for the rich was the saloon bar where customers wore ties and hats and looked very respectable and drank either gin and tonic or whisky and soda out of little sherry glasses. Then there were the men in the public bar who wore flat hats and mufflers and drank beer out of glasses that were not polished. I used to pester my parents to tell me what the difference was, until my father got so tired of the questions that he admitted that the people in the saloon bar could afford more than those in the pub. From that moment I became a socialist'.[18]

This was not following in her family's footsteps. Her parents and sister were Tories to the bone.[19] She was a staunch member of the National Union of Journalists and became head of a Chapel (workplace structure where the Union is organised). The other members of the Chapel were very sexist in those days; women were a rarity on Fleet Street and they called her 'mummy'.[20]

Proops became a campaigning journalist, changing people's perceptions to an extent now hard to imagine, so thoroughly did she break new moral ground. She was a huge champion of women's causes and spoke out in favour of pre-marital sex, of contraception, of open sex education and a more tolerant attitude towards homosexuality. By the 1970s she became an establishment figure and served on two government committees: One-Parent Families and the Gambling Commission. She was quoted in newspapers, granted an exclusive interview with Princess Anne and involved in Jewish MP Leo Abse's[21] campaign for a change in the laws on homosexuality and children's rights.[22] Proops fought for rape suites in police stations where victims could be interviewed in comfort.[23] She became Assistant Editor of the *Daily Mirror* in 1978 and was appointed OBE in 1968, Woman of the Year in 1984 and given a place in Madame Tussauds in 1977.

When asked if there was any significance in the fact that there were a preponderance of Jewish agony columnists in popular British magazines or whether it was merely a coincidence that a high proportion of problem page writers come from a Jewish background, Proops maintained that a Jew is conditioned at an early age to accept that life is full of problems. She cited an incident from her own childhood when she ran home from school after being bullied due to her first name Rebecca. She was taunted in the playground and called 'Becky the Jew girl'. She then changed her forenames around and used Marjorie as this was safer. Proops was disturbed by what she saw as a fragmentation of the family unit throughout society believing this to be a major cause of an enormous number of problems. 'People need support, love and emotional secure to avoid being lonely'. Taking the Jewish family as an example she argued that 'it might be stifling but I think it's better to be stifled by love than starved of it'.[24] Proops herself had a very protective upbringing. Her mother was very nervous and Proops was not allowed to learn to swim as her mother was afraid she would drown. Her mother later became an agoraphobic and when Proops had to deal with people suffering from this condition she was able to relate to them because of her experience with her mother.[25]

Proops was a regular speaker at Jewish communal events and fundraisers and in relation to her Jewish background, she noted that she was 'non-orthodox but a Jew and I never forget it. I thank God I was in a position to help my parents and ensure that they never lacked the warmth of human companionship'.[26] When guest speaker at a fundraiser for the Jewish Welfare Board, she told those present that 'I am not a devout Jewess and I have been described as an agnostic Jew. But I am a Jewish wife and mother'.[27] When Proops died in 1996 she was buried in Hoop Lane Jewish cemetery, London.

Proops had a profound effect on people.

> In the 20 years or so since I started handing out advice in newspaper and magazine columns, I estimate that close to a million people have written to me. Add to that the immense number of those who have written to other columnists doing similar work and one reaches the conclusion that we fill a vast need which neither the religious bodies,

nor the social services, the doctors or psychiatrists, the welfare workers or the voluntary help organisations can, it seems, adequately answer.

She recalls Dr Ramsey, Archbishop of Canterbury discussing with her where the church appeared to have failed people so that they need to seek help from people like herself. She quoted a lawyer who referred to her sneeringly as 'Queen of the Agony Aunties' and asked her what right she thought she had to set herself up as an oracle.

> I know how useful we are. For the fact is that very few of the thousands and thousands of people who write to us would seek help at all if we didn't exist. Many people with personal problems are afraid to face doctors, scared of anyone who might seem to be authoritarian. They fear the pointing moralising finger of blame. Or they are too inarticulate to express themselves verbally.[28]

Had they championed their causes – justice for rape victims, protection from violent relationships, a women's right to sexual pleasure – in Parliament, more people would have recognised agony aunts as the pioneers they were. As they operated quietly from the back pages of women's magazines, it was easy to underestimate how they shaped so many people's lives. What the agony aunts recognised was that by bringing ordinary women's secrets into the open they could transform the lives of many more people than just the original letter writer. Once one broke the silence, many thousands of readers might realise they were not suffering alone. And when the aunts began taking 'women's troubles' seriously it became far harder for professionals – from doctors to the police – to pretend they did not exist or did not matter.[29]

Proops was the champion agony aunt of them all. Jean Rook of the *Daily Express* said 'she was the one that liberated us all to show what women could do in journalism'.[30] She did, however, have a rival in Claire Rayner who became an agony aunt just a few years later. She was another East End Jewish girl who had the same gift of great communication and compassion to help those in need.

Claire Rayner (1931-2010)

Claire Rayner was a nurse, journalist, novelist and broadcaster who for decades offered reassurance and frank advice to millions of people through

6. Claire Rayner OBE (Contributor PA Images/Alamy Stock Photo, Photographer PA, 21 June 1985)

her columns, health books and broadcasts. In the 1960s and 70s she was one of the first journalists to tackle subjects such as contraception, abortion, homosexuality and divorce, with an openness and humanity that made her a household name. She held opinions on everything from sex to taxation without fear or favour. She was a prolific figure in the sexual revolution of the mid-twentieth century and was at the forefront of the development of sex education in the UK. Indeed, the anti-pornography campaigner Mary Whitehouse once dubbed her the 'antichrist' for promoting explicit sex education in schools.[31] In later years she was a campaigner on social and health issues.

Born Claire Berenice Bekovitch in Stepney in 1931, she was the first of three girls and a boy. Her mother Betty Dion was an orphan, only nineteen when she gave birth to Claire and furious at the world for the poor hand that she had been dealt with. Both her parents had died by the time she was two years old. She was sent first to an orphanage and then to foster parents whom she claimed were hateful to her. She never forgave her much older brothers and sisters for not taking her in. Rayner's father was Percy Berk, a tailor's cutter, whose father had a women's clothing factory in Farringdon Road. Percy, who later changed his name to Peter, was a scoundrel with a wonderful personality but the black sheep of the family. He was always in trouble, always scamming, often on the run. Betty, who worked in a shoe shop, met Percy at a dance hall in the East End. He told her his parents were rich. They married in a registry office and not a synagogue as Betty refused to have a religious wedding. This upset his family, but they found the newlyweds a flat over a fruit shop in Homerton and supported them financially. The family never liked her.[32]

It was a childhood short on love, lived in cluttered flats and cramped digs all over Britain, usually because Peter was on the run from bailiffs, the police and business partners. On one occasion the children were instructed to assume a new surname – Brandon – to help evade being found. The family first left London in a hurry when Rayner was five, moving from place to place until they ended up in Dublin before returning to London when the Second World War broke out.

During the war they moved to Cirencester and Rayner won a scholarship to City of London School for Girls which had been evacuated to Yorkshire. She boarded there, relieved to be away from her unhappy home. Once in Cirencester they changed their name by deed poll to the Anglo-Saxon name Chetwynd[33], a name of the local Gloucestershire nobility. Rayner considered this change of name an example of her mother's endless social climbing. Betty was a terrible snob, and whilst out shopping would claim to strangers that she was from Kensington and put on a 'refined' accent to disguise her London twang, much to Rayner's intense embarrassment. She pretended to read the *Times* newspaper when in reality she read the *Daily Mirror*. Changing their name to Chetwynd helped the family hide away and made the fantasy a little more real. She hated her mother for her pretence and for her cruelty to her in particular, as she did not treat her siblings in the same way. Rayner wondered whether it was because she was the eldest and the one she expected most from, or whether it was because she physically resembled her mother-in-law whom Betty hated.[34]

There were endless beatings from her mother that left Claire battered and bruised and a lot of casual cruelty. Birthdays were never remembered, compliments and encouragement never given, and Rayner felt that she was despised. Her parents were feckless. When she was seven they simply went out for the night leaving her in charge of two small girls until concerned neighbours called the police. At fourteen she escaped her parents for the first time by lying about her age to begin nursing. Unfortunately, her cover was blown when her parents disappeared for a week's holiday leaving her terrified sister in charge of the others and Rayner had to return home.[35]

Her second attempt at escape, when she again lied about her age to return to nursing, ended when her parents threatened to sue the hospital for enticing a minor away from her legal guardians. The family had moved to Canada in 1945 and insisted that Rayner followed. She travelled by ship to Toronto but, ground down by her parents, soon ran away to the States where she worked as a waitress in a diner in New York. It came to an end when she developed Graves' disease, a condition of the thyroid, and had no choice but to return to Toronto. There a doctor took pity on her, but her parents were unconcerned and refused to accompany her to the emergency appointment because they probably felt there were bills to be paid. The doctor said she needed a great deal of rest and suggested that she should go to the Toronto Psychiatric Hospital as no other hospital beds were available. She remained there for 15 months during which time her parents never visited. She also began to display flamboyant psychotic behaviour, copied from other patients, to get the nurses' attention. She was force fed, strapped down on a trolley for refusing food; shoved into a tub of warm water, covered by a tarpaulin with only a hole for the head, a treatment used to placate the manic; bound up in cold, wet sheets to make her immobile. Eventually another doctor recognised that what she really needed was not containment but surgery on the thyroid which could be paid for in Canada, or she would have to return to Britain for treatment on the NHS. Her parents refused to pay for either the surgery or the passage home. She was deported from Canada in 1951 (the shipping line had to take anyone home free of charge that they had brought over if they were deported). Her passport was stamped 'insane, appeal denied'. She never saw her parents again.[36] On her twenty-first birthday she received a telegram from her father in Acapulco, Mexico. Three days later she had a visit from two men from Interpol asking her if she knew his whereabouts.[37]

In 1951 she became a student nurse at the Royal Northern Hospital, London. She was looking for a career that was dramatic and secure and she found it in nursing.[38] She was concerned from an early age that poor people could not afford a doctor.[39] During her six years there she won the hospital gold medal for outstanding achievement and studied midwifery. She was accepted to study to become a doctor at the Northern Polytechnic, but she had married Des Rayner and it was not possible in the 1950s to be a married woman and a medical student. She had met Des, who was originally from Hackney, at the Maccabi Jewish Youth Club. She finally achieved her aim of becoming a doctor when Oxford Brookes University gave her an honorary doctorate in 2000, as did Middlesex in 2002 and Surrey in 2007. Once married she continued nursing, becoming a paediatrics sister at the Whittington Hospital in north London. Her first child was born in 1960 and she left nursing to take care of her.[40]

With time on her hands Claire turned to writing. She wrote for the *Nursing Times, Nursing Mirror* and the *Lancet* and her first book *Mothers and Midwives* was published in 1962. She became a vigorous defender of many causes. One of them concerned children in hospital and she wrote a guide book *What Happens in Hospital* (1963) addressed to children which aimed to eliminate their fear by describing in the form of a story what happens from the ambulance ride to the wards and operation theatre.[41] Books on a vast array of subjects included a *Calendar of Childhood* (1964) which gave advice on monthly concerns including April allergies, holiday planning in May, health and advice on sunburn in July; *The Shy Person's Book* (1973) gave shy young women advice on how to overcome the handicaps of shyness including advice on how to cope with sexual shyness; *Baby and Young Child Care* (1981) and cassettes for expectant mothers entitled *Now You Are Pregnant and Birth Day and After.*

In the early 1960s she branched out into fiction, writing hospital romances under a pseudonym. She wrote close to one hundred novels and self-help books which were read by millions. Although she was not part of any smart literary set, and the books were often dismissed as pulp fiction, she had great storytelling abilities. Her best-known series was the twelve-volume *The Performers* (1973-1986), each set in different areas of London and *The Poppy Chronicles*, mammoth sagas about 'warm family life I never had as a child'.[42]

It was in 1962, when she wrote an article on mothercraft for *Hers* magazine, in the form of five letters with her answers, that she embarked on a new path. She received a flurry of letters from women desperate for information, reassurance and support. She convinced the editor that an advice column using genuine letters would be worthwhile. By the end of the first year she had received more than 20,000 letters. She was not the first agony aunt, but she was the first that brought professional knowledge to the role. 'I treated it the way I would have treated an outpatient session. I never rewrote the letters but let people use their own language – it was the real voice of the reader.' The letters showed up great chasms of ignorance and fear and a desperate need for information. Rayner insisted that every letter should receive an answer. At the height of this activity, working for TV-am, Sky and the *Sunday Mirror,* Rayner had six secretaries, a research assistant and a post clerk for 1,000 letters a week.[43] She also wrote advice columns for *Woman's Own*, one of the most popular women's magazines. The job was given to her by Daphne Claff, another pioneering and empathetic Jewish agony aunt.[44]

She was often the subject of controversy, such as the advice that she gave in *Petticoat*, a magazine for the early teens. In 1972 she was accused of 'encouraging masturbation and promiscuity in prepubescent girls'. Rayner admitted that she had covered the subjects: 'It does happen lovey; the youngsters do get so worried about it, bless them'.[45] Rayner's name become synonymous with the title 'agony aunt' a fact confirmed when she joined BBC's *Pebble Mill at One* in 1972 and the *Sun* newspaper in 1973. It was not just the larger audiences but the personal qualities that she brought to the job. She thought fast, talked fast and believed that people could solve their own problems if they were given respect. She was the first advice columnist in popular journalism to accept that men could have problems too and convinced the editors on the *Sun* that she should be allowed to deal with their problems. When she tackled the hitherto taboo subject of premature ejaculation, 18,000 letters arrived in a week. Rayner was always prepared to take on causes that no one else was prepared to touch. Her appearance in a television advertisement for sanitary towels – *the wings ad* in 1991 – brought her derision from some quarters but was a milestone that changed attitudes towards showing sanitary products on television. Similarly, she was at the forefront of the 1987 safe sex promotions of the early HIV/AIDS campaigns, 'waving condoms over the cornflakes on breakfast television'.[46]

Always a campaigner, she was an early advocate for women going back to work after giving birth. She spoke of the loneliness of the suburban housewife and the complacent censure on working mothers. 'I think all mothers who have the urge to take up their careers again should be encouraged to do so'.[47] She was adamant that 'active minded women isolated in suburbs must work at something constructive to keep their morale up'.[48]

She retired from her last newspaper agony column in *Today* in 1971 which gave her more time to devote to causes that she cared about and to do what she herself did best, 'biting the arses of those in power'. She was an anti-royalist, an atheist and president of the British Humanist Association (1999-2004). She agonised over whether to accept an OBE in 1996 (for her work as an associate non-executive director of the Royal Hospital's NHS Trust and as a member of the Royal Commission on long-term care for the elderly) but decided she could use it as a platform from which to shout louder. She was patron of more than 100 charities and organisations and a member of committees as various as the health advisory board at Holloway Prison and the Royal College of Nursing committee on ethics. She was president of the National Association of Bereavement Counsellors, Gingerbread (charity for single parent families) and the Patients' Association and devoted much of her time to campaigning for improved care for the elderly. She was passionate about universal healthcare for all and in 2009 was a member of the Prime Minister's commission on the future of nursing and midwifery.[49]

Her incredible empathy to those in distress and the ability that she had to advise and help thousands of people could derive from surviving the terrible abuse from her childhood. In a similar vein to Proops, she was more than prepared to discuss the dark corners of other people's lives but not willing to discuss her own. It was only in later years that she revealed an early life of parental abuse that included being beaten by her mother with belts and saucepans. She remembered one time that her mother cut her head with a saucepan and her father had to take her to the chemist for help as they were unable to afford a doctor.[50]

The truth only emerged when she was invited in 1988 to appear on the BBC4 radio programme *In the Psychiatrists Chair* with Professor Anthony Clare. She said that it was an invitation that she could not refuse as she had spent so long asking other people about their emotional lives. Clare pushed her so hard for the facts of her childhood that she burst into tears on air.[51] He commented that her parents were always poorly described. Rayner told him: 'That box is closed. There is no point in digging up past misery if you can't do anything about it'. It was revealed that although Rayner had found a method of coping, the agony had not diffused. 'I was dumped in a hospital by my parents at sixteen but because I was under twenty-one they were financially responsible for me and because they were financially feckless they didn't want to know'. She felt helpless and it left her with a great deal of concern for people who were not well.[52]

Rayner never saw her parents again after she left Canada. She did write to them in 1956 when she became engaged. She did so as she wanted to show them that she had managed without their help. They immediately wrote back to her but when she told them that he was an impoverished actor she never heard another word. Rayner did keep in touch with her siblings who remained in North America and saw them occasionally over the years. Her father's brother Max and wife Muriel became her surrogate parents in England.

When she received a telephone call in 1982 from her parents' neighbour (by this time they were back in England) telling her that they had died she felt intense relief. They are buried in a Church of England cemetery near Cirencester, a curious last resting place for a couple of East End Jews. When questioned whether she thought it was strange that her parents should have ended up buried in a church graveyard, Rayner was not surprised as she said her mother had felt an outsider all of her life – the wrong religion and gender. 'She was a snob and the Church of England was the religion of the upper classes. She would have seen it as being smarter than just another bloody Jew'. There is however a clue on the grave: an English translation of a line from the *Kaddish*, the Jewish prayer for the dead, put there by someone who had paid for the grave.[53] Yet they apparently did not forget their roots. Not long before their deaths, they placed an advertisement in the *Jewish Chronicle* announcing their golden wedding in which they mentioned their children, including Rayner.[54]

Rayner's relationship with Judaism was complex. Unlike Proops, who although not orthodox had no problem with acknowledging her Judaism, being Jewish in any religious sense was not for her. As noted, she was president of the British Humanist Association and a supporter of the National Secular Society and was not interested in any religion. Yet there was a connection to her Jewish background when she was younger. She did meet her husband at the Maccabi Jewish youth club in Hampstead and they married in Willesden synagogue in 1957.[55] She wrote a weekly column for the *Jewish Chronicle* in the 1960s which included articles on sex education for teenagers and men treating their wives as equal partners in matters regarding finance.[56] One of her articles in 1958 advised women that they would still be able to find Jewish husbands if they became nurses. 'Her hours of freedom can be spent among her own Jewish friends. I, for instance, never meet any Jewish people in the course of my work but despite that I have as many Jewish friends as the next girl and I have married a perfectly delightful Jewish man'.[57]

They lived in Harrow and belonged to Middlesex New Synagogue (now known as Mosaic Reform Synagogue). Her son, writer and food critic Jay Rayner comments that she was a devout atheist and had a lifelong suspicion of organised religion. 'She may have seemed like the ultimate Jewish mother, but she fought shy of the community'.[58] He said she had an unusual relationship with her Jewishness. Despite her uneasiness she was completely cognisant of the Jewish cooking tradition and before their Christmas lunch of turkey they always had chopped liver on matzah.[59]

Despite her negativity towards organised religion she did write *Running Years*, a saga of Jewish dispersion through the centuries. The novel starts off in 70AD with the fall of the Second Temple of Jerusalem and concludes in England in 1890. It takes a detailed look at two Jewish families, one Ashkenazi and one Sephardi. She went to Israel for the first time to carry out the research. It traces the Jewish ancestry of Hannah Lazar and tells her story of how, born poor in the East End of London, she rose to be a society dressmaker, married to a man who entertained King Edward VII and had descendants who went their different ways, the last of them returning to Jerusalem.[60] Rayner explained that the subject matter was something that she knew about and that it was to do with ethnicity not religion. She was fascinated by the issue of survival and concluded that the families survived because the women were strong and that the Jews bred for brains. In the *shtetl* the brilliant religious student got the daughter of the richest man. 'I suspect that in rejecting belief in a divine being but enjoying the ethnic part of Judaism, I walk hand in hand with the majority of Jews in this country because we are, by and large, more likely to be educated, more likely to be thoughtful, more likely to have political nous....'[61] Although she regarded herself as primarily English as she had been brought up for part of her childhood in an English country village far removed from any kind of Jewish environment, she nevertheless had a feeling of identity with Jews all over the world.[62]

Rayner never had an attachment to Israel. 'People say Jews have a historic right to live on the land. How can they? You could also say that Sephardic Jews have a right to Spain'. She was never a Zionist and was opposed to any form of nationalism. 'I have great difficulty accepting the way in which Israelis treated the indigenous population when they established a state in a substantially populated area'. Her view concerning suicide bombers was that if you treat a group of people the way the Palestinians have been treated, they will use the only weapon they have which is their individual lives.[63]

With regard to her politics Rayner, as did Proops, supported the Labour Party. On the eve of the 1992 general election, she declared that she would definitely vote Labour.

> Thirteen weeks of Thatcherism would have been too much, let alone thirteen years. I can't stand the greed of it all. The Conservatives don't

care. Look at all the homeless on the streets, the poor one parent families, the nibbling away at the health service. I hope the Labour Party win so I can be proud of this country once more. At present I feel humiliated every time I walk down the Strand.[64][65]

She switched allegiance to the Liberal Democrats in 2001 after supporting Labour for 50 years complaining that 'Labour is no longer the Party I fell in love with'. She considered that New Labour had left behind the principles that old Labour stood for – real equality for everyone. She was particularly concerned with its policy concerning care for the elderly. Appointed by the government in 1998 to a Royal Commission considering long term care, she was bitterly disappointed when its recommendations for free nursing care were not implemented.[66]

A survivor of breast cancer, she never recovered from emergency intestinal surgery she received in May 2010 and died later that year. She told her relatives she wanted her last words to be: 'Tell David Cameron if he screws up my beloved NHS I'll come back and bloody haunt him'. She was outspoken, no nonsense, sympathetic and generous with her time and patronage, both to organisations and individuals. She was respected above all for showing that she both needed and took the sort of advice she offered. Both she and her husband struggled with depression throughout their lives and she approached it as she did with everything – with honesty and frankness. She helped untold thousands of men, women and families over the years who looked upon her as an epitome of what a friend, mother, aunt or grandmother should be – wise, witty and unconditional in her support and approval. She was an exceptionally talented woman. She had a no-nonsense approach to problems and a deep-felt view that past suffering should not be wallowed in but rather used as fuel for an interesting and productive present life.[67]

When asked why she thought she had been so successful, she reflected that it was down to her nursing background as well as her use of direct language. Whilst she was at *Woman's Own* she pushed back the boundaries of what was 'suitable for nice women' as hard as she could , much preferring to offer them things that really mattered, such as giving away free condoms as part of the effort to help women protect themselves against HIV and cervical cancer. She also arranged that the covers of a whole issue (a million copies) had test strips for diabetes in an attempt to track down undiagnosed cases. She produced the first articles about the importance of fibre in the diet as a controller of weight as well as a preventer of a range of diseases including colonic cancer. She considered that this approach contributed to the huge social change in Britain as much as the influence of flower power children. This was evident from the thousands of letters that poured in and that together with other magazines and programmes such as BBC Radio 4's *Woman's Hour*, 'did a great demystifying job for women in Britain, taking them from the unfulfilling dark and dirty minded years to more honest open ones'.[68]

Conclusion

While the British agony aunts who offered up advice and wisdom during the turbulent years of the mid-twentieth century were very often Jewish, their guidance appealed to men and women across all levels of society and was not explicitly derived from a Jewish perspective. This was certainly true for Marjorie Proops and Claire Rayner, but certain cultural aspects of Judaism – an emphasis on matriarchal wisdom, argumentation and discourse, forthrightness and interest in others' business – may well have informed the way in which these women were drawn to and approached the task of listening to and advising people who wrote in with their problems. More directly, it was the hardships of their childhoods and the lessons they learned about poverty, prejudice, family, class, and deprivation that they drew upon in their careers as advice columnists. Also consistent with their Jewish heritage was being drawn to caring professions and championing the underdog. Though they had many similarities in their backgrounds and political leanings, Proops and Rayner had very different attitudes to religion and Judaism and their careers as agony aunts, while paralleling one another, had different trajectories and emphases.

Marjorie Proops' early experiences with prejudice and insecurity and Claire Rayner's truly harrowing childhood were foundational to their later careers as carers and advice givers and to their socialist and Labour political leanings. Proops was unattractive with spectacles and crooked teeth and was consistently compared unfavourably to her sister. Her mother was overly protective and suffered with mental illness, and Proops herself experienced great difficulties in an unsatisfying sexless marriage. The professional involvement developed from a personal need. 'She became a caring mother. The Yiddish momma'.[69] After being subjected to antisemitism, she changed her name from the more Jewish Rebecca to Marjorie, commenting later that she always fought for minority groups as she belonged to one herself and learned early on what abuse felt like.[70] She also recognised class inequalities very early on leading her to becoming a strong supporter of the Labour Party despite coming from a family of

Tories. 'She was wheeled in at TUC and Labour Party conferences and hailed as royalty by members'.[71] Claire Rayner's childhood deprivation of love, caring and security led her to first pursue a career as a nurse. She described herself as an East End kid who had made it into nursing from a very inauspicious beginning.[72] Jay Rayner said his mother's experience of being a neglected child ignited in her a burning indignation at both injustice and the shaming of others which she channelled into words for the newspapers.[73] She, too, become a staunch supporter of Labour and became the patron of more than 100 charities that helped the poor and less fortunate.

These two women, from such similar beginnings did differ in respect to their Judaism and in the focus of their careers. Proops described herself as British first and Jewish second and had a Jewish burial. Despite changing her name as a child to avoid being stereotyped as Jewish, she never tried to hide or downplay her origins and while non-practising, was active in Jewish causes later in her life. Rayner in contrast, was an outspoken atheist who requested a humanist burial service.[74] In Rayner's autobiography there is practically no reference to her Jewish background apart from mentioning that her grandmother came from the Pale of Settlement and her paternal grandparents were moderately religious. She mentioned that she met Des at a drama group in Hampstead, but did not identify it as a Jewish one and noted that she did get married in a synagogue, although she would have preferred a registry office as this is what her husband's family wanted.[75] Career-wise, Proops became an advice columnist only after several decades of journalism on a variety of women's topics, after having first been hired as an illustrator. Rayner only took up the pen after leaving nursing, and her career included authoring novels, appearing on television and radio, as well as writing numerous columns and championing a variety of causes. Nevertheless, both women managed to draw on their difficult experiences to help untold thousands of people in Britain. They were, despite their different identities and personae, known to be Jewish in a very public sphere and vocation in which to be a Jewish woman was not only acceptable but also almost expected.

3

Politicians

Women's involvement in political activity from the early nineteenth-century to the outbreak of the Second World War was extensive and varied. Although it was not until the twentieth century that they became full members of all political parties, before they engaged in political and social reform campaigns, as well as taking part in movements that focused on their own oppression as a sex and sought to challenge inequalities in all areas of their lives. In the early nineteenth-century they took part in a range of political and social reform movements, including franchise reform unions, the Anti-Corn Law League and anti-slavery societies. Working-class women were also involved in a variety of political campaigns. They joined men of their class in the Owenite socialist movement, in industrial disputes, in franchise reform unions and protest over food prices and the imposition of the New Poor Law. They also played an extensive role in Chartism, which was the first instance of a political movement initiated and sustained by working people relying on their own resources alone.[1]

Although they were denied access to parliamentary franchise, women did have the opportunity to take part in political life at a local level through their election to a variety of public bodies. From the 1870s onwards, women increasingly put themselves forward as candidates for school boards, boards of guardians, parish councils and later county councils. The relaxation of property qualifications for candidates to boards of guardians in the 1890s, coupled with the development of socialist groups, encouraged working class women to become involved. Their participation in local elected bodies enabled women from all social classes to 'claim public space' and to exert some influence over the delivery of state welfare policies.[2]

Women first entered the House of Commons as MPs after the Parliament Act of 1918 that granted the vote to women over the age of 30 who met a property qualification. In November 1919 Nancy Astor won her place in history as the first woman to enter the House of Commons, representing the Unionist (now Conservative Party) seat in Plymouth Sutton. For nearly two years Astor was the only woman in Parliament. Many male MPs refused to acknowledge or speak to her, apart from shouting at her when she asked questions from the floor of the Commons. In a 1956 interview for BBC Radio's *Women's Hour*, Astor recalled Winston Churchill telling her that her arrival in Parliament made him feel like a woman had entered his bathroom and he had nothing to protect himself with except a sponge. Astor, who was married to newspaper and proprietor Waldorf Astor, recalls that her personal wealth, social status and connections were an important tool for her as the first female MP, as they allowed her to employ excellent staff and allowed her to draw press and public attention to causes she championed.[3]

Astor's position was in stark contrast to the Jewish women who were becoming involved in politics during this period as they were making their mark in radical politics. When considering Jewish women's high political profile, journalist Tobe Alexander points out that politics attracts Jewish women in a ratio that far exceeds their proportion in the population and questions whether there is anything in their common heritage that predisposes them to become political animals and whether the qualities they possess are fundamentally Jewish or essentially female. 'Politics is about life', said Conservative MP Doreen Miller. 'Anyone who says they are not interested in politics is either a liar or isn't interested in life itself. Politics means getting involved in the community and taking responsibility for decisions which will affect society. The sense of community and the desire to play a part within it is a very Jewish trait.' Dr Leah Hertz, co-chairman of the 300 group, which battled to get more women into Parliament and who stood as a Conservative candidate for Walsall in 1987, was brought up with stories of her grandmother's good deeds, of how she fed the poor and married off the orphans. 'It's a great *mitzvah* (good deed) to take on political responsibility'.[4] This would indeed seem to be the case.

Political responsibility and Jewish involvement in radical movements had its roots in the Pale of Settlement. Russian Jewish intellectuals were confined to that area and excluded from academic posts. After the pogroms in the 1880s, large numbers of the Jewish intelligentsia became involved in political movements opposed to the Tsarist regime. The poverty and dire economic conditions that they lived in, the impact of the pogroms and antisemitism convinced many that the regime should be overthrown for a society based on socialist principles. Socialism attracted Jews of both sexes and a Jewish socialist movement, known as the Bund, became a considerable force for radicalising artisans and workers across the Pale of Settlement.[5] The Bund was founded in 1897 and aimed to unite all Jewish workers in the Russian Empire into a united socialist Jewish party. It was the most progressive regarding gender equality with women making up more than one-third of all members.[6] Many first-generation migrants had been members of the Bund and brought their ideas with them.

With many new immigrants finding themselves destitute or suffering in such harsh conditions in the sweatshops, it is not surprising that a group of anarchists had influence in the immigrant community. In Britain they were led by a non-Jewish German Rudolf Rocker, editor of the Yiddish newspaper *Arbeiter Fraint* (Workers' Friend) who lived with his Jewish partner Milly Witkop. Milly, from an Orthodox Jewish family, came to London from the Ukraine in 1894 and worked in tailoring workshops where the harsh conditions she endured led her to become involved in the anarchist movement. The anarchists met on Friday evenings at the Sugar Loaf pub in the East End. Rocker recorded that 'there were a good many women at the meetings'[7] and that Milly took 'a conspicuous part in the struggle and constructive endeavours of the Jewish workers in England'.[8] The Jewish anarchists played a role in a number of strikes, such as the 1912 Tailors Strike over poverty wages and long hours. During the 1912 Dockers' Strike, Milly helped the children from families involved to be placed temporarily in Jewish homes even though these families had very little resources to feed their own families. 'Milly personally collected children from the docks, most of whom were reduced to a terribly undernourished state, barefoot and in rags'.[9] The anarchist movement started to decline after 1914 but this did not signal the end of political activity in the East End as the trade unions were to play an important part.

Attempts to include women in trade unions had begun in 1874 when the Women's Trade Union League (WTUL) was founded. The WTUL represented dressmakers, upholsterers, bookbinders, artificial flower makers, feather dressers, jam and pickle workers, shop assistants and typists. Members of the WTUL were mainly upper-class men and women interested in social reform who wanted to educate women in trade unionism and fund the establishment of trade unions. Concerned over the plight of the sweat shop workers, the WTUL sought to attract middle class Anglo-Jewish membership and support, as well as East European male union leaders and female garment workers whom it attempted to unionise. Jewish women garment workers helped the WTUL organise the East End Jewish Tailoresses' Union, the Society of Tailors and Tailoresses' in Leeds and the Cigarette Makers' Union.[10]

Although little was written about women individually, one charismatic character was Sarah Wesker (1901-1971) who grew up in the Rothschild Buildings in the East End and who gained a formidable reputation as a trade union organiser in the London garment industry. In 1926 the all-female workforce at Goodman's factory walked out, led by Sarah. She took a leading part in the strike at Polikoffs in 1929 and in the following year led the strike at the Simpson factory in Hackney. She was one of the founders of the United Clothing Workers' Union, its only female member on the executive committee. Mike Mindel, a union activist recalls that at the time there was real resistance to women playing proper roles in the unions as they were neglected by predominantly male leadership but that Wesker set an example.[11] Wesker was the aunt of playwright Arnold Wesker. A thinly disguised theatrical version of her appears in the play *Chicken Soup with Barley*.[12]

With the East End as a centre for left-wing political activity, it is not surprising that two female politicians who came from the area, Minnie Lansbury and Miriam Moses, fought for social justice and campaigned for women and their rights. Minnie Lansbury (1889-1922) was a teacher, union activist and suffragette. She was born in Stepney in 1889 to Polish immigrants Isaac and Annie Glassman. Her father was originally a boot finisher but later became a coal merchant and in 1913 paid the £5 fee to become a British citizen. Minnie married Edgar Lansbury, son of local MP George Lansbury and was a teacher in a local London County Council school. A member of the National Union of Teachers, she became involved in union activism, calling for equal pay for women. She also joined the central committee of the East London Federation of the Suffragettes and played a key role in their campaigns and community actions and was chair of the War Pensions Committee, fighting for the rights of widows, orphans and wounded from First World War.

Lansbury was elected alderman on Poplar's first Labour Council in 1919. In 1921 she was one of five women on Poplar Council who, along with their male colleagues, served six weeks imprisonment for refusing to levy full rates in the poverty-stricken area.[13] She remarked 'I wish the government joy in its efforts to get money from the people of Poplar. Poplar will pay its share of London rates when Westminster, Kensington and the City do the same'. Journalist Hester Abrahams of the *Jewish Chronicle* commented, 'She was a pioneer militant who got stuck in. She organised milk for babies, campaigned for workers' rights and tackled unscrupulous landlords'.[14] As a result of her imprisonment she developed pneumonia and died on 1 January 1922, aged just 32. Her death was announced at a thousand-strong meeting at Bow Baths Hall. 'The audience for a moment was stricken silent... then out of the silence came a woman's cry of grief, followed by the weeping of many women'. The meeting was abandoned.[15] She was buried in East Ham Jewish cemetery and there is a memorial clock in her name on Electric House in Bow Road, Tower Hamlets.

The love and respect that Minnie earnt was also bestowed on another remarkable woman, Miriam Moses OBE (1886-1965), who dedicated her life to social welfare work, was the first woman mayor of the London borough of Stepney and known as the 'angel of the East End'. Unlike Minnie, who had married a non-Jew and was not active in Jewish communal affairs, a great deal of Miriam's time was spent helping the local Jewish community.

Born in the East End to Mark Moses and Hannah (Annie) Ehrenberg, her father had come to England from Torun, Germany as a child. Her life of public service began when, as a young woman in Stepney she became increasingly interested in her father's activities. He was a magistrate, a borough councillor, treasurer of the Federation synagogues, a United Synagogue warden and London County Council Schools' representative. It was in the schools that Miriam started her own activity by distributing soup and bread among pupils and becoming one of the managers of the Hanbury Street School and then their chairman. On her father's death in 1921 she succeeded him on the Stepney Borough Council. A year later she became the first female Justice of the Peace in Whitechapel.[16] She was active in politics throughout her life standing for election as local councillor with both the Progressive Party and as an independent candidate in the 1920s. In 1931 she was elected as the first female Mayor of Stepney and was the first female Jewish mayor in the country. Key aspects of her campaigning were support of women's rights, such as provision of contraception and condemning anti-immigrant housing policies.[17] During the Second World War she was chief air raid officer for the area, establishing a hostel for young women made homeless by bombing. She was awarded an OBE in 1945 for this work.

Her work with the Jewish community was extensive. In 1925 she co-founded the Brady Girls Club as a parallel to the already established Brady Boys Club which provided educational and leisure opportunities for Jewish young people. She helped to run Jewish children's holiday homes, was a member of the United Synagogue's welfare and visitation committee, chairman of the Ladies Guild at the New Synagogue, Stamford Hill and a representative at the Board of Deputies of British Jews, the first woman chosen to represent a constituent of the United Synagogue. Always concerned about the rights for women, she had been a member of the Jewish League for Women Suffrage, a founder member of the League of Jewish Women and for many years she waged a campaign for the right of women seat holders to vote in synagogue elections. This right was eventually granted in 1954.[18]

The poverty and desperate conditions of the East End shaped the politics of the aforementioned women, as they would for Bertha Sokoloff, an active member of the Communist Party elected to the Stepney Borough Council in 1945. Tireless care and campaigning for the London poor led Henrietta Adler (1868-1950), known as 'Nettie', to become one of the first two women on the London County Council (LCC), the body that governed London from 1889-1965. She was one of the first women to take up new political roles once Britain gave women the vote in 1918. The granddaughter of Chief Rabbi Nathan Marcus Adler and daughter of Chief Rabbi Hermann Adler, she developed her social conscience when she was very young and would go with her mother to visit Jewish immigrant families in the East End. She put her energies into philanthropy, supporting training and clubs for young people. When she became vice-president of the Union of Jewish Women in 1902, the *Jewish Chronicle* called her 'one of the most earnest and unostentatious of Jewish communal workers'.

Adler was one of two women who took up seats on the LCC after an election in 1910, the first that officially allowed women candidates and represented Hackney Central for the Progressive Party. She was one of three Jewish women to be appointed when women became magistrates in England for the first time in 1920 and was made a Commander of the British Empire (CBE) in 1934 for her work in London government. Other Jewish women who were involved with the LCC were Lady Eleanor Nathan (1892-1972) and Leah L'Estrange Malone (1886-1951). Nathan was a well-known communal worker and expert in housing and juvenile delinquency. She was first elected to the LCC for the Liberal Party (1928-34) and for the Labour Party (1937-48), serving for the last year as the Council's chair. Malone studied modern history at Oxford University before becoming an inspector with the Ministry of Health. She was active in Labour politics and, as a member of the Executive Committee, she helped to ensure that birth control for working class women was adopted as party policy. She sat as a Labour Party member of the LCC from 1934-39.

In the post-war era, other issues animated Jewish women to enter politics such as Lady Shirley Porter, Conservative leader of Westminster Council, who came from a wealthy background and who, like many middle-class Jewish housewives at the time, was mainly concerned with voluntary work and charitable organisations but who used her experience to become involved in politics. Other women with similar backgrounds in charitable and communal affairs, like Conservative MP Edwina Currie, banded together to campaign nationally and, like Porter, used eye catching techniques in their demonstrations. Their political stance is in contrast to a group of Jewish Labour politicians – Margaret Hodge, Louise Ellman, Luciana Berger and Ruth Smeeth – who have had to fight antisemitism within their Party. In short, this chapter covers a rich variety of Jewish women from different backgrounds and politics from extreme left to right wing, and positions between, who have made significant impacts in both local and national politics over the past eighty to ninety years.

Bertha Sokoloff (1920 - 2018)

Bertha Sokoloff grew up in a Jewish family in London's East End where poverty shaped her radical spirit. Born in Brady Street Dwellings, Whitechapel to immigrants Rachel and Jacob Markovitch, she was the third of their four children. Her father left the family after entering a relationship with a nurse who looked after him following an injury during an army training exercise in the First World War and her mother struggled financially to bring up the family on her own. Sokoloff attended the Robert Montefiore Primary School before gaining a scholarship to the Central Foundation Girls' School. She left at 16 and became a secretary at the Royal Institute of International Affairs and then worked for Victor Gollancz Ltd. To have obtained such a position from a poor East End immigrant background reflects Sokoloff's capabilities.

Sokoloff was a branch secretary of Stepney Borough Council before marrying fellow Communist Stan Sokoloff in 1940. In 1943 she took up work in a factory where the management noticed she was clumsy on machines but good at maths and at inspiring others, and made her productivity officer. A prominent figure within the Stepney Communist Party and its General Secretary in 1940 and 1941, she succeeded at a time when it was a very male environment, and she played a key role in preparing for the 1945 general and municipal elections. She was the agent for Communist Member of Parliament Phil Piratin in 1945 who became elected as councillor that year and a leading organiser in the Stepney Tenants Defence League (a front of the Stepney Communists) which organised rent strikes in the 1930s. She left the Communist Party in 1957 over the response of the Soviet Union to the 1956 Hungarian Revolution but remained politically active all her life.[19]

Sokoloff's parents had come from Rumania in the early years of the twentieth century and married in England. After her father left the family, her mother's life had become an anxious regular trek to and from Old Street Police Court and to the relieving office in the East End's Fulbourne Street. Often the maintenance she was due under the separation order that her husband had to pay after he left did not arrive, and if it was not received she had to report there.[20] An official investigator would call to check on the situation (the tales of saucepan lids lifted and any little luxury sniffed out were true) but Sokoloff cannot remember that her mother was ever reprimanded. Furnishings in the flat were very simple and did not transgress the Poor Law simplicity demanded. Occasionally her mother would go to the Yiddish theatre and she passed on the songs which Sokoloff remembered with joy. In the bedroom were two large beds for all the family. In later years a put-u-up replaced the sofa in the living room for her brother. There were very few possessions, yet they were fortunate not to share water or toilet facilities with another family. 'Somehow my mother managed. She was probably borrowing from Peter to pay Paul'. The children usually had something new to wear for Passover and the New Year even if the item of clothing was minimal. When her brother was born, a fourth child, and her mother was already on her own, people tried to persuade her to put him a Jewish orphanage, but she resisted.

The stigma of not having a father and receiving financial aid was a lasting memory for Sokoloff. She started school at three years old which was probably due to her home situation. School dinners at the time were for the very needy and she was eligible. Visitors would come to the school with boxes of clothes and she remembers with shame how she was called out to the front of the class, in view of all the children, to be 'measured' by having a dress held up against her, a sack like garment in dull colours. She was mortified as only the children whose parents were very poor were called up and therefore she was labelled before the whole class. She was ashamed of her situation. To be fatherless and orphaned was sad; to be deserted was much worse. When she started senior school she invented a story that her father was so badly wounded that he spent most of his time in hospitals.[21]

Suffering such economic hardships, it was not surprising that Sokoloff was drawn towards the Communist Party that had great appeal to the Jewish community living in the East End. To Sokoloff those on the extreme left were doing the most to help. Marxism as a way of overcoming the Depression and reaching a more equal society had enormous appeal. There were many meetings in the streets and community halls. They would discuss matters all the way back home from the Whitechapel Library, where the young who had homework to do would congregate. After supper they would be out again selling *The Challenge* (a magazine periodical produced by the Young Communist League, the youth wing of the Communist Party of Great Britain).[22]

Another threat at the time was fascism. The fascists had their headquarters in Duckett Street, Stepney. Sir Oswald Mosley, leader of the British Union of Fascists, would come and speak to those queuing at the unemployed centres and tell them that their situation was due to the Jews. For the Jews, the very words Duckett Street made them fearful and the news from Germany emphasised the need to resist. The only Jewish family that lived in Duckett Street were afraid to go home at night until they could creep in unnoticed. There were real ways to fight the danger. Sokoloff was drawn, willingly and eagerly, into the fight the Communists were making against fascism. No one fought Mosley harder than they did and Sokoloff remained convinced that if it were not for the Communists, Mosley's defeat in the Battle of Cable Street in 1936 would not have happened. The Communist Party were also taking care of people's needs. Trade unionism was slowly recovering from the failure of 1926 and the Depression, and the Communists were in the forefront, organising the tailors and shop assistants.[23]

Women were politicised during the rent strikes in Stepney that occurred there in the 1930s and 1940s, a period of economic depression and social strife. Jewish women, particularly immigrants, were especially willing to band together in order to champion their rights. Victims not only of sexism but also antisemitism, nativism and cultural bigotry, they lived in slums and worked mostly in the dangerous and dirty sweatshops then prevalent in the garment industry, suffering from the effects of cultural dislocation, material poverty, sexual harassment and even physical danger. They formed a transitional generation, moving between the cultures of their old and new worlds These women emerged from a culture with a well-developed ethic of social justice and as such played an important role in the social and political life of their communities. Socialism was for them more than an economic or sociological doctrine; steeped in the Jewish ethical tradition these women perceived socialism as a system dedicated to building a totally new society, one which would transcend the limitations imposed on them in the capitalist system by gender, ethnicity, religion and rigid class barriers.

Jews in East London were active in the Communist Party in higher numbers relative to their overall distributing in Britain's population than were Britons in general and young Jewish women played an important role. The rent strikes were organised by the Communist-front Stepney Defence League (STDL) and the strikes highlighted the organised political activity of Jewish women at the neighbourhood level. Women chaired most of the tenants' committees formed in specific tenement blocks, organised opposition to eviction attempts, were in the forefront of demonstrations and even picketed shoppers in the West End of London to draw attention to the plight of East London slum dwellers at the mercy of 'slumlords'.[24]

Significant rent battles had broken out across Britain and most dramatically in Clydeside in 1915-16. A group of women formed the Glasgow Women's Housing Association to resist rent rises and threatened evictions. The population in Glasgow had increased as recruits were needed to meet the demand for work in the shipyards and engineering factories that were producing weapons and machines for the First World War. Rent increased by as much as 23% and landlords were taking advantage of women whilst their men were away fighting. Landlords began to issue court orders and threatened protestors with eviction, fines or prison. In response the women made it impossible for the authorities to evict them by blocking access to the tenements. The strikes spread to other cities and grew to an extent that they threatened wartime production. As a result, the Government passed the Rent Restriction Act that froze rents at 1914 levels and gave tenants security of tenure. The Rent Act was prolonged in 1919, but not for new houses, and in 1923 the government allowed rent control to lapse whenever a tenancy became vacant. The rents for decontrolled flats were soon significantly higher than for their controlled neighbours.[25]

The vast majority of households were tenants of private landlords and about 4.5 million were in households which were in theory 'controlled' so that the tenants had the legal right to security of tenure. Rents could not be increased and they were entitled to withhold 40% of the rent if a sanitary inspector certified that repairs had not been done. However, houses vacated between the years 1923-33 were 'decontrolled' which meant the landlord could put up the rent and evict the tenant at will. In practice a high proportion of tenants of 'controlled' housing were not enjoying their rights. Many landlords were overcharging and had registered their tenants as 'decontrolled' when they were not.[26] Rent strikes, reminiscent of those in Glasgow, swept the East End during the 1930s, especially in the borough of Stepney which was home to the majority of London's working-class Jewish community. The strikes were organised by the Communist-front Stepney Tenants Defence League (STDL).

There were sporadic rent strikes in 1935-37. The tenants managed to hold off the bailiff and police and the movement grew rapidly. The STDL taught tenants how to deal with problems of rent and arrears as well as how to organise, determine their legal rights and fight landlords in a collective disciplined way. Historian Henry Srebrnik points out the STDL came into its own by the end of 1938, stimulated by decontrol of much of the area's housing and by the consequent attempts of landlords either to raise rents by as much as 40% or to neglect their responsibilities. The STDL had a grassroots structure: members would pay a penny a week and would be organised in local tenants' committees, usually representing a block of flats or a street. Women chaired most of the tenants' committees, organised opposition to eviction attempts, were in the forefront of demonstrations and even picketed shoppers in the West End of London to draw attention to the plight of East London slum dwellers at the mercy of 'slumlords'.[27] All the different committees together made up the STDL. Decisions were made by the Tenants' Council that met every two weeks and which comprised of representatives from the committees, the STDL executive, several borough councillors and lawyers. Srebrnik explains that although the strikes were a gender-integrated mass movement of social protest, they nonetheless exemplified the organised political activity of Jewish women at the neighbourhood level.

In 1939 rent strikes took place in street after street in rapid succession and many landlords succumbed and signed agreements with their tenants. By 18 June many rent strikes had been settled and membership in the STDL had grown to 7500.[28] The immediate benefits for the tenants were 'five hundred pounds a year more for the kiddies, and better flats to live in, with £2,000 to be spent on repairs.' Tenants had hung out their banners saying, "mansion to let – two rooms and a kitchen, rats included, 22s. 6d a week" and "flat to let; icy cold in winter, burning in summer." The agreement resulted in rent reductions from 1s to 6s a week for tenants and a £500 rent rebate payment, less deductions for any arrears of rent, to be made to the tenants within 14 days. The landlord agreed that the STDL would be the negotiating body on all future disputes.[29]

Such a victory encouraged others. Another joint strike, which lasted 21 weeks was begun on 13 February 1939 by the mainly 340 Jewish tenants of Brady Street Mansions, where Sokoloff lived, and Langdale Mansions against their common landlords, Craps and Gold, who were clothing manufacturers. The tenants' committee were all women. Barricades and barbed wire were set up around the building to prevent the bailiffs from entering and guards patrolled the entrance. The women embarrassed the landlords by demonstrating outside their business premises in London's West End and outside Mr Gold's home.[30] The strikes proved the determination of women who bore the brunt of these struggles and sometimes found themselves picketing through weeks of winter cold. Max Levitas, convenor of the strikes, recalled the Brady women throwing down hot water, hot potatoes and hot coals on police and bailiffs attempting to storm their barricades over the roof of a neighbouring garage.[31]

The STDL, after six months of existence, had effected rent reductions totally over £18,000 per annum and won back for the tenants excess rents amounting to nearly £10,000. It forced landlords to carry out repairs through agreements and certificates of repair under the Rent Acts. One landlord had to increase his staff of workmen from six to 57.[32] Communist Member of Parliament Phil Piratin in his memoir *Our Flag Stays Red,* credits the women's participation in the rent strikes as outstanding: 'Every feminist claim was proved. There was nothing that the men could do that could not be equalled by women and, in fact, they were mostly more enthusiastic and hence more reliable.'[33]

The rent strikes had a great impact on Sokoloff. She was inspired by the Communist Party's fight for people's needs and the strike where she lived 'was an education for me in terms of the value of solidarity, of people standing together'.[34] For most of the Jewish housewives who had manned the barricades the rent strikes gave them their first experience of participating in a political action and the strikes had a big impact on winning the Party further popular support in the Jewish East End.[35] Sokoloff was elected branch secretary of Stepney CP in 1940 and again in 1944 and helped prepare for the 1945 general and municipal elections. Phil Piratin was nominated as the Communist candidate for Stepney in the 1945 general elections and the campaign propaganda called him the 'tenants' champion' and promised affordable housing and control of rents. The Communist slogans for the election included 'premises not promises'. The success of the strikes, in which women played such a prominent role, helped Piratin to win his seat on 5 July 1945.

At an East London area conference held at Holborn Hall on 15 April 1945, Sokoloff explained to the assembled delegates that the Communist Party's aim by the end of June was to have 7,500 listed supporters. 'If we mean business and are going to win the election, this is the minimum we can do'.[36] A few months later voters elected borough councillors. Sokoloff stood in Mile End West.[37] In November 1945 all ten Communist candidates won their seats; three women were elected to the Stepney Borough Council. Writing in the Communist periodical *Jewish Clarion*, Sarah Wesker attributed the victory of women such as Sokoloff and Fannie Goldberg (Mile End North) to the 'tremendous work' they had done during the rent strikes years earlier.[38]

The Communist Party victory was due to the widespread feeling that change was needed. One of the main issues was housing due to the devastation of the area after the Blitz and Sokoloff was involved in the Housing Committee. She tried to specify that people were rehoused in the same area. For Stepney, which had taken some of the worst continual bombing there were just too many people that desperately needed somewhere to live and often had to be rehoused outside the area. In 1949 Sokoloff moved from a condemned East End flat with her husband and two daughters and was rehoused on a London County Council estate in South London. She subsequently resigned from the Council in 1950.[39]

Sokoloff's experience of growing up in poverty in the East End was always remembered together with her experience of being part of the Jewish community. She recalled happy memories: the way the streets would fill on the evening of Kol Nidre (the start of the Day of Atonement) with people going to synagogue; so many that cinemas and other large auditoria became synagogues for the Holy Days, the excitement of Passover and the preparations and going to a tiny synagogue that was little more than a shed behind the shops and being given an apple, orange, bag of sweets and a small paper flag to wave to celebrate the festival of Simchat Torah (the giving of the law). She received religious education at school – Old Testament stories, psalms and English hymns that mentioned God not Christ. She had never heard of many of the hymns and carols until her own children went to school and she later taught in an infant school. At some point she did go to Hebrew lessons after school as she knew the Hebrew alphabet and could read a simple prayer.[40] For Sokoloff growing up as Jewish was as much a cultural as religious phenomenon. Different foods eaten, the shops frequented, the forbidding and frightening territory of the Christians that began a couple of hundred yards from where she lived. There was an invisible line that marked the end of Jewish Whitechapel and Christian Bethnal Green.[41] She never forgot her Jewish roots. An atheist but culturally Jewish she contributed in later years to the social life of Bromley Reform Synagogue.[42]

Sokoloff left the Communist Party in 1957 over the Soviet Union's invasion of Hungary. After teaching in infant schools, Sokoloff graduated in sociology in 1971 at the same London University ceremony as her younger daughter. She loved teaching mature students at Woolwich College in the 1970s. Whether she was running a nursery at Woolwich College, volunteering as a housing adviser in Bromley or protesting in 2013 against the closure of Pocklington House, a home for the blind in Northwood where she lived, Sokoloff was an effective and respected activist all her life.[43]

In total contrast to Sokoloff was Shirley Porter. Born with a silver spoon in her mouth, she used her influence and expertise from her involvement in Jewish voluntary work to further her political career, always maintaining a strong commitment to her Jewish background.

Shirley Porter (1930 -)

During the 1980s, Shirley Porter was Britain's second most famous female politician after Margaret Thatcher. She ruled as the Conservative leader of Westminster City Council for eight years and thrived at a time when the leaders of trade unions and councils were household names, and she was lauded as the Thatcherite antidote to the left-wing municipal 'enemies within'. Porter revelled in her reputation as the mini-Mrs Thatcher as she fought the left, privatised council services, sold cemeteries in her drive to establish Westminster City, the most prestigious local authority in the country as a Tory flagship borough. She had significant inherited wealth behind her and a network of connections.[44]

Porter was born in London on 29 November 1930, the younger daughter of Sarah 'Cissie' Fox and Jack Cohen, who laid the foundations of the supermarket chain Tesco. The family lived in Gunton Road, Hackney. Jack had bought the house from Hackney Council in 1927, one of a very small number to do so, as in the 1920s the sale of council housing to private buyers was virtually unknown. Her father was a defining influence in her life and the growth of Tesco was a powerful determining factor in shaping its course. She gained both her wealth and attitudes from those who built the business, and her political career was largely a reaction against being

7. Shirley Porter (Liam White/Alamy Stock Photo)

seen as just the daughter of Jack Cohen and she used her Tesco connections and wealth to further her career.[45]

Jack (named Jacob but known as Jack from childhood) was born in Whitechapel on 29 October 1898 to Sime Zamrembra and Avroam Kohen. Avroam came from Poland in the mid-1880s and set himself up as a tailor, working as a subcontractor for various textile manufacturers. Jack left school at fourteen and worked for his father as an apprentice tailor. He enlisted in the Royal Flying Corps during the First World War and after demobilisation in 1919 he used part of his pay-off to buy a small stock of foodstuffs which he sold in a Hackney street market, quickly developing the selling strategy – low prices and fast turnover. The first Tesco shop opened in 1929 in Burnt Oak, north London and by 1939 Tesco had more than 100 small stores in London and surrounding counties.[46]

Jack married Sarah Fox in 1924 in the Hackney synagogue. She was the daughter of Annie and Benjamin Fox (anglicised from Fuchs), a master tailor who made suits for Aquascutum from a small factory in Archer Street, off Shaftesbury Avenue. Benjamin, who came from Russia in 1917, had been a solider, often on guard at the Tsar's palace. The family home was in Westbourne Park where they 'lived quietly and rather graciously'.[47] Porter recalled that her mother's family was considerably further up the immigrant Jewish social scale than her father's and that they were very patriotic. 'They felt Britain had welcomed them in and given them freedom. They were British Jews'.[48]

Porter and her family moved to Chessington Road, Finchley when she was four years old. The house was in the latest Art Deco style and filled with every luxury. There were beautiful dolls and teddy bears for the girls who were brought up emulating the little princesses Elizabeth and Margaret Rose. Porter and her sister Irene were brought up to be 'perfect little English ladies'. Porter admits that they were probably very precious, cosseted, spoiled little girls. Yet she loathed the English, upper middle class boarding school, The Warren in Sussex, that she attended during the war years to escape the bombing in London and said that it turned her from a happy child into a rebel. Jack finally allowed her to leave after he argued with the headmistress. He took the view that his daughter had been denied the head girl's post and her name in gilt on wooden panels because of her surname. Porter commented that trade was looked down upon. 'It wasn't quite nice to be a shopkeeper'.[49] After finishing school in Lausanne, Switzerland she spent a year at St Godric's Secretarial and Language School in Hampstead.

In 1949, at the age of 18, she married Leslie Porter at the New West End Synagogue, Bayswater and their 1,000-guest reception was held at the

Dorchester Hotel. They lived in Hampstead Garden Suburb and for the next two decades her life revolved around her husband, who subsequently became chairman of Tesco, and their two children Linda and John. She played golf and was captain of three golf clubs; in the early 1960s she played five times for the Hertfordshire Women second team.[50] She was involved in a great deal of voluntary work and charity organisations. 'My parents were hardworking. They were always involved with helping the community and others less fortunate than themselves'. She became active on the executive of the Women's International Zionist Organisation (WIZO).[51] She later joined the Conservative Party and when asked why she did not join the board of Tesco, she explained: 'In those days it was not considered right and proper for a young woman to be involved in business'.[52]

Porter was a dutiful, almost stereotypical Jewish wife and mother for more than twenty years until her children left home. She realised that she wanted to do more with her life. As she had been an active member of WIZO since 1955, she considered this to be a useful preparation for her career.[53] Porter was very close to her parents but resembled her restless and ambitious father. Jack Cohen was born 30 years before women were given equal voting rights and it seemed he expected little more of his daughters other than they fulfil their roles as wives and mothers. Never wanted to be known just as Jack Cohen's daughter; she wanted to justify herself. Porter was thirsting for some kind of role in life and in 1972 she became a magistrate.[54]

Looking back at that time in her life she remembered her great lack of confidence. 'I came in there and for the first time I wasn't somebody's daughter, somebody's wife, somebody's mother'.[55] She was of the opinion that there came a point in everyone's life when one had to take stock and that Jewish women often lacked confidence which was unjustified as they had a natural talent for organisation. 'Bringing up children and looking after a husband are achievements that should not be underestimated. Their talents should be channelled outside the home so that society can benefit'.[56] She considered that 'if you can run a home, that's administration; public life is just the same nonsense but bigger'.[57] Local politics was about to get their first taste of the fiercely energetic Tesco heiress. Anyone honed on the rough and tumble of Jewish community life was bound to ruffle feathers – the question 'why not' was forever on her lips. 'Jewish women spend an extraordinary amount of time in committee meetings. They know all about organisation, speaking and negotiating. What is more, they are highly intuitive which is crucial in politics'.[58] When she became Lord Mayor of Westminster (1991-92) she called on Jewish women to follow in her footsteps by taking up leading roles in society. 'It is time they came out of their chrysalis. Maybe it is because so much importance is given to men in the Jewish religion that women feel intimidated. But some of them have amazing talent'.[59]

Porter claimed that she got involved in local politics because she had moved to an apartment in Gloucester Square, overlooking Hyde Park, and was disgusted by the litter and dirt in central London. A friend challenged her to do something about it.[60] Andrew Hosken considers that her break into politics seems to have been also dependent on her wealth as her local Conservative Association were strapped for funds and she was asked to make a contribution. Gradually she became involved in her local party and decided to enter local politics and was elected as a councillor for the Hyde Park ward. Porter was not considered a good orator in the council chamber and she decided to make her way up the ranks by focusing her attention on the Highway and Works Committee whose remit included rubbish collection, street cleaning and road works and cemetery maintenance. Her enthusiasm also aided her election as vice chairman of Highways and Works in 1977. Her anti-litter campaign continued and she mobilised schoolchildren. She was no political ideologue but her campaign against litter gave a focus for advancement at City Hall. She joined the Clean Up London campaign and in 1978 became chairman of Highways and Works.[61] She was the first woman to have been elected to the post. Women traditionally only had jobs in the so called 'caring committees'.[62]

Highways and Works had always been considered a fairly safe non-political committee compared to those of finance and housing, but it would prove to be Porter's springboard to greater things. Over the next four years she would use the unglamorous area of street cleaning to demonstrate her flair for action and publicity and began to attract the attention of the media. She knew all about eye catching stunts. She was the daughter of Tesco 'pile it high, sell it cheap' Cohen. Along with privatising rubbish collection in Westminster, she led camels in Downing Street against the 'last straw' rate increase of Ken Livingstone's Greater London Council and dressed up as a squaw to promote an anti-litter campaign.[63]

In 1979 a period of strikes known as the 'winter of discontent' began in earnest with trade unions demanding greater pay rises. Rubbish was left uncollected across the country. As the rubbish piled high across the city, Porter made her first impacts on the national consciousness. She opened 33 emergency rubbish dumps across the borough. Her successive litter campaigns included the Cleaner London Campaign and Cleaner City Initiative in 1980. There were additional street cleaners and increased rubbish collection and local businesses were persuaded to sponsor litter bins.[64] In 1983 she was elected as leader of the council and her initiatives and policies included the Say No to Drugs Campaign and the Plain English Campaign, ensuring council documents were easily understood. In the late 1970s Soho residents were troubled by the growing sex industry. Between 1965 and 1982 the number of sex shops had risen from 31 to 65. Porter became chairman of the General Purposes Committee in 1982 and as a local government act stipulated that Westminster could shut down anyone without a licence, it was decided that the number of sex shops would be limited to 20. By 1983 just 13 sex shops remained in Soho.[65] She was considered the 'iron lady' of the town halls and a Thatcherite star. Until the 'Homes for Votes' scandal broke her most notorious act was to sell off Westminster's public cemeteries for 15p to a Panamanian registered company that were later sold for £1.2 million. It was the sort of audacious move that enraged the left and pleased her mentor Margaret Thatcher in equal measure.[66]

The Conservatives were narrowly re-elected in Westminster in the 1986 local council elections. Fearing they would eventually lose control in the social composition of the borough, Porter instituted an internal policy known as 'Building Stable Communities', later described as the 'Homes for Votes' scandal. It was a disastrous course of action which resulted in what has often been described as the greatest act of corruption in the history of British local government. Edward Heath claimed it was the heaviest blow to hit the Tory Party in living memory.[67]

Porter and her successor David Weeks selected eight wards as 'key wards'. In public it was claimed that these wards were subject to particular 'stress factors' leading to a decline of the population of Westminster. In reality these wards had been the most marginal in the elections; three had been narrowly won by Labour and three had been narrowly lost by them. An important part of this policy was the designation of much of Westminster's council housing for commercial sale rather than a re-letting when the properties became vacant. The designated housing was concentrated in those wards most likely to change hands to Labour in the election. Other council services were subverted to ensure the re-election of the majority party in the elections. In services such as street cleaning, pavement repair and environmental improvements, marginal wards were given priority instead of parts of the city which were safely Labour or Conservative. Another part of the 'Building Stables Communities' was the removal of homeless voters and others who lived in hostels and were perceived less likely to vote Conservative, such as students and nurses.

Other Councils in London soon became aware of the homeless from Westminster, many with mental health and addiction problems, being relocated to their area. If the City Council found it difficult to move the homeless outside Westminster, they were placed in safe Labour wards, such as tower blocks in Harrow Road which were in a poor state of repair and were earmarked for demolition.

The ploy worked and the Tories were returned with an increased majority in the 1990s elections. She was appointed Dame Commander of the Order of the British Empire by Prime Minister John Major for her role in the victory. However, electors went to court and secured a full-scale investigation by the district auditor John Magill and a ten-year battle began. The report from Magill was damning. Porter, Weeks and eight other councillors and officials were found guilty of 'disgraceful gerrymandering'.[68] In May 1996 after legal investigation work the District Auditor finally concluded that the Building Stable Communities Policy had been illegal and ordered Porter and five others to pay £31.6 million. The judgement was upheld by the High Court in 1997 with liability reduced solely to Porter and her deputy leader David Weeks. The Court of Appeal overturned the judgement in 1999 but the House of Lords reinstated it on 13 December 2001, and she was found guilty of political corruption. Porter had transferred substantial parts of her wealth to other members of her family and trusts and subsequently claimed assets of only £300,000. After negotiations and legal proceedings in which the Council sought to show her fortune had not, as she claimed, shrunk to £300,000 she agreed to pay a £12.3 million settlement to Westminster Council.

Aggrieved Westminster residents shouted that she should 'go back to Israel' as she attempted to defend herself from the charges of gerrymandering.[69] She was not treated kindly in the press. Gregory Evans wrote 'Dame Shirley seemed to me Macbeth with shoulder pads. Richard III in a pink velour suit'.[70] John Ware believed she experienced quite a lot of subliminal posh antisemitism. 'When a Tory said, "she's just ghastly" you knew what they meant'. He said the result was that she interpreted all opposition as unjustified and unfair.[71]

Porter had experienced antisemitism at school. She was of the opinion that her Jewishness prevented her from becoming head girl. 'There was a board in the hall with the "head girls" names printed on it and I knew that she (the headmistress) didn't want Cohen to appear on that board. I wonder if that experience made me think that one day I'd just show them'.[72] She helped to expose golf clubs across London for holding antisemitic criteria. The usual excuse given was 'no vacancies' with the ladies' section often becoming mysteriously filled as soon as the committee members became aware of their religion. Her application for membership was turned down by the Mill Hill, Highgate, Finchley, South Herts, Hendon, Moor Park, Porters Park, Hampstead, North Middlesex and Old Fold Manor golf clubs.[73] Once the evidence was revealed, the local Council told the golf clubs that their licences would not be renewed if they continued their discrimination.[74]

Her Judaism was an important part of her life. She came from a traditionally orthodox family that upheld Zionism.[75] When interviewed on *Desert Island Discs*, she chose a recording of Kol Nidre[76] sung by Reverend Simon Hass of Central Synagogue, London as one of her records. Explaining her choice, it said it reminded her of the countless times that she went to synagogue with her family. 'The Day of Atonement is a time of reflection, of looking back and also looking forward. Everything in the Jewish religion has great optimism'. She admitted that although she was not an orthodox Jew she had great depths of feeling about the traditions of Judaism, the way in which one leads one's life and what it means to be a Jew.[77] She was concerned about students who were in danger of losing their Jewish heritage through rejection of religion or because of a crisis of identity. 'Jewish heritage is too precious to be thrown away through ignorance and intermarriage. Young Jews need to learn about their roots'.[78] She was a supporter of the 35s, the women's campaign for Soviet Jewry and of many Jewish charities, both in England and Israel, including WIZO, the Joint Israel Appeal, an old age home in Herzilya, Israel founded by her family, the Council for a Beautiful Israel and was a governor of Tel Aviv University. She was a past chairperson of the Board of Governors of the Oxford Centre for Postgraduate Hebrew Studies. She went to live in Herzliya Pituah, Israel in 1994 when she retreated from public life as a result of the publication of the auditor's first provisional report.[79] She helped establish the Porter Centre for Environmental Studies at Tel Aviv University which opened in 2004.

Throughout her political career she showed the toughness of her father. During her reign at Westminster, Porter probably wielded more political power than any other woman in Britain after Margaret Thatcher. She was a strong and controversial personality who aroused violent pro- and anti-emotions in people. Porter said 'if you make waves, you make enemies but you can not really have an effect upon events and have everyone love you. It's not pleasant but it's one of the decisions you have to take'.[80] She recalls her feelings during the 'Homes for Votes' scandal. 'I stood in the council chamber being heckled and jeered and thought what am I doing this for?

Then I thought of my father, working in the markets where they used to blow a whistle and people had to run to get their pitch. It was the survival of the fittest. You crumble or stay and fight. Like him I stood and fought'.[81]

Showing the same toughness and the ability to elicit the same strong positive and negative reactions from her audience was Edwina Currie. Although a member of the same Party, she came from a northern working-class background and unlike Porter, who had the confidence and conviction to remain strong to her Jewish identity, Currie drew on her Jewish background when it suited her and discarded it when she considered that it would hamper her political ambitions.

Edwina Currie (1946 -)

Edwina Currie is a former politician who served as a Conservative Member of Parliament from 1983-1997. During her political career she blossomed into the most controversial and media-mentioned female politician of the late Eighties. For a while her newsworthiness was to eclipse even that of the Prime Minister.[82] After losing her seat as an MP she began a new career as a novelist and broadcaster and in September 2002, the publication of *Currie's Diaries 1987-1992*[83] caused a sensation as they revealed a four-year long affair with colleague (and later Prime Minister) John Major between 1984-88. Frequently outspoken, she was described as 'a virtually permanent fixture on the nation's TV screen saying something outrageous about just about anything' and 'the most outspoken and sexually interested woman of her political generation'.[84]

Currie was born Edwina Cohen in Liverpool on 13 October 1946 to an Orthodox Jewish family and grew up in the Toxteth neighbourhood which had a large Jewish population and was home to the Princes Road synagogue. She won a scholarship to Liverpool Institute High School for Girls where she was deputy head. Her headmistress encouraged her to go Oxford, although her parents wanted her to go to Liverpool University or Manchester where she could stay with relatives. Her parents were uneasy at the idea of their daughter leaving a community atmosphere for the non-Jewish culture of Oxford. 'They were afflicted with the fears shared with many other Jewish families in post Holocaust Europe. In their eyes it wasn't kosher down there at Oxford'. Yet even as a schoolgirl she knew she wanted to get up and out of Liverpool and she studied Philosophy, Politics and Economics at St Anne's College, Oxford and gained an MA in economic history from the London School of Economics.[85]

A woman who provoked strong reactions, she sprang to prominence

8. Edwina Currie visits the Cliffs Pavilion, Westcliff-on-Sea, Essex as part of Southend Libraries Book Festival (Rob Welham)

when, as a Birmingham City councillor (1975-1986) she brandished a pair of handcuffs at the Conservative Party Conference, Blackpool in 1981. This is an example of performance that was also used by Shirley Porter during her anti-litter campaign. Currie was demanding a tougher policy on law and order from Willie Whitelaw, the Home Secretary.[86] In 1983 she was elected Tory MP for South Derbyshire and her rise in the Conservative Party was meteoric. She served in the Department of Health, campaigning for healthier lifestyle choices and AIDs awareness. Currie resigned in 1988 after issuing a warning that eggs contained salmonella. This sparked an outcry from farmers as egg sales in the country declined rapidly by 60 percent and the loss of revenue led to the slaughter of four million hens. In 1990 she established the National Egg Awareness campaign to improve buyer confidence, gaining the nickname 'Eggwina'.[87] In 1991 Currie became the first Conservative MP to appear on the BBC topical panel show *Have I Got News for You*. She appeared again, two years later, in a special episode commemorating the release of Margaret Thatcher's memoirs, opposite Liverpudlian Derek Hatton. In February 1994 she tabled an amendment to the Criminal Justice and Public Order Bill to lower the age of consent for homosexual acts to 16. The amendment was defeated by 307 votes to 280, although a subsequent amendment resulted in the reduction of the homosexual age of consent from 21 to 18.

Currie was always ambitious. Regarding her childhood years in Liverpool, she recalls that she 'was brought up in an atmosphere of achievement and always felt people like us could do anything. We were an immigrant community yet we had high hopes for the future and were determined to make our contribution to the society around us'. Her cousin Jennifer Henley remembers how after Currie's first term at Oxford she announced that she had joined the Young Conservatives. Henley was shocked as her mother was a Labour councillor and her aunt had stood as a Labour parliamentary candidate. She just did not know any Tories. When she asked Currie why she had joined the Conservatives, Currie replied 'because I'll get on'.[88] Currie says that she was interested in politics for as long as she could remember. Her determination was formidable. She freely admits that from age 19 onwards every move she made was designed to advance her one goal of getting into the House of Commons.[89]

Currie was born into an immigrant family. Her father Simon Cohen's family had emigrated from the Baltic region and while all his siblings moved on to their ultimate destination, America, he chose to settle in Liverpool where he worked as a tailor, eventually setting up his modest business. He had an uneasy relationship with his intensely academic and hard-working daughter. 'Much of his approach to life was negative and fearful, wary and rather hostile. He was the only member of his whole family left behind and he was left behind because he was too scared to go to America. He lived most of his life in a self-protective shell'.[90] Currie explains that before the war, like many Jewish people of that period, he was a socialist but changed his views by the time she was born after he became an employer himself.

He was disabled so he did not have to fight during the war and worked in a factory. After the war was over he set up in business. He was then in a position of being an employer with staff, having to deal with wage councils and trade unions and became very hostile to all kinds of authority. He became a classic small businessman.[91]

He and Edwina often argued about politics but his refusal to vote infuriated her. She tried to persuade him that if he got involved and joined in, he would have some influence. But to no avail.

> Eventually I became convinced that I'd have to go into politics myself. If people like him wouldn't then somebody like me had to. I believe very deeply that people have an obligation to society and to the community in which they live. That's a traditionally Jewish commitment. But growing up in Britain and being exposed to a far greater range of stimuli and seeing what the attitude of 'don't get involved' had done to the Jewish community, I couldn't accept his notion of standing back and just looking after our own. Now *that's* a source of conflict.[92]

The rift between father and daughter was complete when Currie married a non-Jewish accountant. Her father refused to attend the wedding, sat *shiva* (week long mourning period) for her and died four years later without seeing her again or his first grandchild. Currie speaks of her father as a difficult man, a strict Orthodox Jew who disapproved of almost everything. 'The person he hurt most was himself'.[93] She never thought that he would cut her off completely. 'Wicked man, wicked religion'.[94]

Although Currie claims to be neither distressed nor embittered, 'there's no point in having a problem if you haven't got a solution'[95], her father's refusal to ever see her again after her marriage has resulted in a rather mixed and conflicting attitude towards her Jewish background. She rejected her Judaism when she married although she says she never identified as a Christian. 'I got married in a church because there were two young people who were in love and wanted to get married and one family said never darken our doors again and the other said welcome'. Both of her daughters were baptised.[96] She is pleased that her daughters have rejected Judaism. 'For my children are slaves no longer, not to history or culture or tradition. Instead, they are emphatically part of multicultural Britain and totally free of hang ups about it.' Her portrayal of Orthodox Judaism is of rank disdain. Currie – on account of the intransigence of her all-or-nothing Orthodox parents – fled the faith altogether.[97]

She knew from the time she was about 15 or 16 that she was not going to live as part of an orthodox Jewish community.[98] 'My parents were orthodox. I always thought they were a bit stupid. I wanted a more profound philosophy than one that said you can't have butter on your bread if you're having a meat dinner'. She said she got the best A-levels in her school, adding that the only reason she was not made head girl – merely deputy head – was because she was Jewish.[99] As she often spoke about how she was glad to see 'the back of Liverpool' and would denigrate both her Jewish faith and her father, the Liverpool Jewish club for senior citizens cancelled a talk entitled 'My famous daughter' that was due to be given by Currie's mother Pessie Cohen.[100] Although Pessie was to speak of the pride she had in regard to her daughter, Currie did not have a close relationship with her mother until she was in her 50s and her mother in her 80s. 'Early on she was a negative influence. I didn't want to be a homemaker.'[101]

In her quest to climb the political ladder, it would appear that Currie ignored her Jewish background and then made reference to it at times when it was more opportune, such as when she was promoting her novel, *She's Leaving Home,*[102] a semi-autobiographical account of how a bright Jewish teenager leaves Liverpool. It also reveals her sense of local belonging, with the title referring to a Beatles song. In 1963 Helen Majinsky is doing science A levels at an inner-city Liverpool grammar school from which she enjoys sneaking off to the Cavern Club to see her idols, the Beatles. Gifted with an eager, inquiring mind, she is burning to get to Cambridge but she has three obstacles. She's Jewish, she's working class and she is a girl. At home she lacks support both emotionally and intellectually. Her father is a tailor's cutter whose own intellectual potential has remained undeveloped. Her mother is joyless and disappointed. Both her parents want her to stay in their world. Helen is beset by conflicts which intensify when she falls in love with a non-Jewish American. Helen's attitude to her Jewish background is fraught with contradictions. Keeping kosher for her is irksome and unjustified; on the other hand, she is uplifted by the atmosphere of the eve of the Sabbath. Although she considers that she learned basic moral awareness from her family and the kindly Reverend Siegel, she cannot help but regard their unconditional rejection of intermarriage as 'racialist'. She resents being pressured into observance, regardless of whether or not she believes and yet she cannot bring herself to break away completely. No one can point her in the direction of Jewish intellectual life or even suggest that university might offer her opportunities of developing her Jewish identity in ways in tune with her personality. Ultimately the reader is left with the impression that 'Jewish' equals 'narrow'.[103]

The book's publication was at the time when she was leaving her husband and she gave her first interview with the *Jewish Chronicle*. She spoke about her alarm over the rising tide of assimilation. She said she never converted to Christianity, despite having married in a church. She repeatedly paid tribute to her Orthodox upbringing and to Reverend Shalom Segal of Childwall Synagogue. 'I was not damaged by my childhood. I was created by it. I am who I am because of how I was brought up. I am proud of that. Occasionally it has taken a bit of guts and courage to say wait a minute. I'm Jewish, don't say those things'. Her apparent return to the Jewish fold was all the more dramatic given her virtual lack of contact with the organised Jewish community after entering Parliament in 1983. She did not appear on the list of Jewish MPs and was widely assumed by the news media to have converted.

She said that the catalyst for her novel had been Chief Rabbi Dr Jonathan Sacks' book *Will We Have Jewish Grandchildren?* She said that she was appalled at the statistics that said that half of this generation 'is marrying out and is lost' and that there was the prospect that the community was in danger of disappearing altogether in a couple of generations. She had begun to reply to the Chief Rabbi in a personal letter to explain why she had left the fold but decided that it was better if she put her viewpoint in a book. Describing herself and her brother (who although his first wife was Jewish the marriage only lasted eight years and now had a non-Jewish partner) as part of Rabbi Sacks' lost generation, she declared that she cared enough about assimilation to 'stick her neck out and risk the criticism'. '

> A strict religion has an enormous attraction. Religion is about how we treat each other. It's about belief, explanations of God, the Devil, the universe, eternity. The moment religion weakens its rules it weakens itself. But if it doesn't weaken its rules, people are not going to like what they see as restrictions and they will find an easier way. So you have a serious dilemma. If Judaism softens its attitude towards intermarriage there may be few problems with those that intermarry. If you tighten up you move more towards the ultra-orthodox. And if you don't shift, half of each generation marries out and quietly fades away.

She said she would like to debate such issues with Rabbi Sacks.[104]

Writer Chaim Bermant comments that Currie clearly felt that her failure to convert suggested a residual loyalty to Judaism, but he questions whether that is so. She appears to have given considerable thought to the content of her marriage service and asked for reading from the *Book of Ruth*. 'Whither thou goest, I will go'. She says if it was good enough for Ruth and Boaz it was good enough for her. Bermant points out that she appears to have forgotten or perhaps she never knew that the passage in full reads 'for whither thou goest I will go, and where thou lodgest, I will lodge; thy people shall be my people and thy God my God'. He comments that 'as enunciated by Ruth on the way to Judea it represented an affirmation of Judaism. As enunciated by Edwina Cohen in a church could only have meant an affirmation of Christianity unless perhaps she kept her fingers crossed when she was saying it. But whether she converted to Christianity or not, the fact remains that once Mrs Currie was elected an MP and became a health minister in Mrs Thatcher's administration, she seemingly preferred to be thought of as non-Jewish'. He adds that she never mentioned her maiden name in *Who's Who* and does not even mention her parents which is about as far as one can go in denying one's past and now claims to be appalled at the thought of the community being in danger of disappearing. Bermant considers that coming from someone who has done her best to get lost in her own generation she is not short of effrontery. He does point out that there is no such thing as an ex-Jew in Jewish law and even if she had become Mother Superior in a Carmelite convent she would still have been thought of as a loud, pushy and assertive Jew. He adds that she began to discover her Jewish roots only when her political career was over and once her marriage had broken down. 'One might have welcomed the return of the prodigal daughter had it not coincided with a new phase in her career. Where she was once a struggling politician, she is now a struggling scribe. And scribes depend on publicity even more than politicians. She chose her book launch as the occasion to announce the end of her marriage and one can be forgiven for suspecting that the rediscovery of her Jewishness and her aversion to intermarriage may be linked to the same event.'[105]

It has been commented that her high profile did not arrive by accident. She set about it professionally and worked hard for it. Journalist Edward Pearce commented 'An ego certainly but a buzzing worker, a good technician'. *Elle* magazine wrote 'take two parts of Joan Collins and three of Mrs Thatcher and you have Edwina Currie. Behind her she left a trail of people who admired or loathed her'.[106]

During her political career, despite not making reference to her Jewish background, it was suggested that her Jewish background contributed to the jealousy that she encountered. An unnamed Cabinet quoted in the *Sunday Times* that 'Edwina is a woman, she's Jewish and she's able... there had been a lot of jealousy on the back benches. Her Jewish origins seemed to reawaken vestiges of antisemitism in the Tory Party, last apparent when Leon Brittan was forced to resign'.[107] A Channel Four 'Dispatch' programme alleged that Conservative party antisemitism fuelled the row that led to the downfall of Currie as junior health minister. This is despite the fact that she has renounced her religion and describes herself as Church of England after her marriage. The same rumours and whispers can be heard in the Members Tea Room of the House of Commons about the recent resignation of Sir Leon Brittan[108] during the Westland affair and the departure of Lord Young[109] from the Cabinet. MP Grenville Janner said that it only proved that one could not escape and that if you have Jewish ancestry you might as well accept it. Government affairs consultant Anna McCurley, former MP for Renfrew and Inverclyde said 'it may be a mixture of the fact that she's a Jew that brought out the antagonism in some people in the House. I hate to say it but I think there is a degree of antisemitism around'. McCurley said that she had heard Currie described as a 'pushy Jewess'. Melinda Libby, a political researcher who at the time of Currie's departure was political adviser to the then Social Services Secretary John Moore, said that a lot of Tory backbenchers were riddled with prejudices of every kind and anti-women and anti-Jewish happened to be the two that fitted Edwina.[110] When asked about antisemitism during her Commons career, Currie responded that she had encountered prejudice most of her life but it was far more about being a woman than being Jewish.[111]

Since leaving politics, she has tended to dwell on her Jewish background. *The Jewish Chronicle* referred to this as the 'Edwina paradox'.[112] She considers herself Jewish culturally and genetically but not in a religious sense.[113] She says she never really left her Jewish roots despite the dramatic falling out with her family. Being Jewish matters enough for her to say 'I was not damaged by my childhood. I am who I am because of how I was brought up and I'm proud of it'. Among her heroes are the medieval Jewish philosopher Maimonides, whose grave she visited when she was in Israel and Yitzhak Rabin whom she also met.[114] She likens herself to the Jewish people. When after losing her parliamentary seat and there was a period she was without employment she became pragmatic about what she was going to do. 'I'm the way Jewish people have been throughout the centuries: you don't drop out. You continue with your work, your studies, you get your degree. You don't get pissed or get stoned. You keep going. And after a while you look up and the trouble and pain are behind you'.[115] In 1999 she set up a book club at Nightingale House, a Jewish home for the aged, and thanks to her efforts authors such as P D James and Fay Weldon have visited. At one Chanukah tea she recited the blessings.[116]

Currie took part in a BBC programme *Pilgrimage: The Road to Istanbul* that traced an ancient walking route to Istanbul via Serbia and Bulgaria and included two Muslims, two Christians and two atheists.

When asked why she was on the pilgrimage as the sole representative of the Jewish community, she said the itinerary took in countries that she had never visited before and liked the idea of a group from different backgrounds walking and learning from one another. She said she felt 'very comfortable' as the token Jew in the group but also felt curious. As her family were from Ukraine on one side and Poland on the other, she was not familiar with this part of the world where there had been sizeable Jewish communities. Part of her motivation for taking part was hoping to focus on the extraordinary range of the history of European Jewry. In a section of the film she ventured into a disused synagogue in Samokov, Bulgaria. There is almost nothing left of the synagogue now but high on the wall is a painted panel of Hebrew and Currie begins to sing Oseh Shalom, 'he who makes peace in high places'. This is plainly something that she learnt from childhood and had stayed with her. She considered that representing Judaism to her six fellow pilgrims was 'quite a responsibility'. She came back from the trip strengthened in her Jewish identity, more aware of the complexities of Jewish history and its outcomes.[117]

She does not have a particular affiliation for Israel. On a visit there in 1990 her impressions were mixed and not favourable. 'It didn't make me want to go again and it didn't make me regret any of my own history'. She was glad she had a Jewish background but felt no obligation to the place. She felt sadness that the country was in such a mess and a delight that she was British. 'It was good to get home'.[118] She upset people at a WIZO lunch where she was a guest speaker. She stirred controversy when she put forward a case in support of Palestinians, telling those present that those living in Jericho deserved more rights and lived in poor conditions. One guest was so angered that she walked up to Currie and made her point forcefully. This was too much for Currie and she walked out.[119]

Currie relishes in being outspoken and attracting publicity. 'All publicity is good publicity even when it is some piece of gossip in a newspaper column'.[120] She upset people by comments such as good Christian people do not get AIDS[121] and that old people who could not afford their heating bills should wrap up warm in winter and that northerners die of 'ignorance and chips'.[122] During the 1992 general election campaign, Currie poured a glass of orange juice over Labour's Peter Snape shortly after an edition of the Midlands based television debate show *Central Weekend* had finished airing. Speaking about the incident later, Currie said 'I just looked at my orange juice and looked at this man from which the stream of abuse was emanating, and I thought I know how to shut you up'. There was shock when she published details of her four-year affair with John Major (1984-88) which she does not regret. 'Contrary to popular thought I've never regretted spilling the beans in 2002. He was being portrayed as a saint and a martyr at the time, yet his indecisiveness and lack of leadership contributed to the downfall of the Tory party. And besides, if you know something that is historically important, you have a duty to share it'. She likes to make provocative statements. She admitted that she would like to die making love to George Clooney. 'I was once asked where I'd like to die and the answer is under George Clooney. I'm a huge fan. He's more than an actor. He's an activist and he puts his money where his mouth is and I like that'.[123] This brashness could be due to the fact that she was an 'outsider' as a working class Northern Jewish woman.

Since leaving the Commons she has remained in the public eye through her appearances on radio and television. She earnt large sums as a novelist which she invested in property and pension.[124] Her books are referred to as 'bonkbusters' – sex and shopping novels with a hefty dose of House of Commons realism. *A Woman's Place*[125] featured a fictional heroine Elaine Stalker, loosely based on Currie's time in the Palace of Westminster. Currie, true to her reputation, pulled no punches over the treatment of women in the Commons.[126] In May 2004 she won the Celebrity Mastermind contest, her topic being the life of Marie Curie. She was the first dancer to leave *Strictly Come Dancing* in 2011 and came fourth place in *I'm A Celebrity* in 2014 for which she was paid close to £100,000. She is a popular speaker on cruise ships. She is tireless, taking up whatever opportunity comes her way.

While many consider Currie to be an opportunist who did not draw attention to her Jewish background during her political career, the careers of Labour Party MPs – Margaret Hodge, Louise Ellman, Luciana Berger and Ruth Smeeth – have been largely dominated by their fight against Jeremy Corbyn and antisemitism in the Labour Party. These four women were abused, bullied and at the receiving end of death threats due to their allegations about antisemitism within the Party. Yet they did not waver in their stance and showed incredible bravery. Prior to taking on antisemitism under Jeremy Corbyn, Margaret Hodge, who came to Britain as a child, fought against racism, misogyny and anti-immigrant sentiment by

9. Official Portrait of Dame Margaret Hodge DBE (via Wikimedia Commons)

challenging the BNP and its leader Nick Griffin in her constituency of Barking.

Margaret Hodge (1944 –)

Dame Margaret Hodge (nee Oppenheimer) is a British Labour Party politician who has been a member of parliament for Barking since 1994. She previously led Islington Borough Council, has held a number of ministerial roles and served as chairman of the public accounts committee.

Hodge was born in Egypt to Jewish refugee parents Hans Oppenheimer and Lisbeth Hollitscher. Hans Oppenheimer left Stuttgart, Germany during the 1930s to join his uncle's metal business based in Cairo and Alexandria where he met fellow émigré Austrian born Lisbeth Hollitscher. They married in 1936 and had five children, four girls and a boy. At the outset of the Second World War, the couple and their eldest daughter were rendered stateless, effectively stranded in Egypt for the duration of the war. They decided to leave Egypt in 1948, concerned that antisemitism had increased in the Middle East during the 1948 Arab-Israeli war. Determined to assimilate, her father settled in the family in Bromley, southeast London, far from the traditional Jewish areas.[127] He started the steel trading corporation Stemcor that became one of the world's largest privately held steel companies and was run by Hodge's brother Ralph until September 2013. Hodge recalls that the welcome wasn't all warm. 'I remember an inspector coming to test me, aged 10, on my "Britishness". My father made sure we ate cucumber sandwiches and fruit cake and told us to pretend that this was our typical tea.'[128]

Hodge's mother died on Christmas Day when she was 10 and she recalls that her father was unable to give emotional support. Hodge rebelled, fought her housekeepers and was ultimately sent to a boarding school which she hated and later studied at the London School of Economics. Political rebellion followed. While her father and brother built up Stemcor, to which she comments 'only the boys worked there; isn't that terrible?', her political passions ultimately came together in Islington where Hodge moved in the 1970s. Islington, now a fashionable inner London area, was just beginning its gentrification and many future Labour ministers started their careers in its local politics. Hodge got a job at Unilever but was angered that women were given more menial positions than similarly qualified men. When she had her children she gave up work, which was customary at that time, and became active in politics.[129]

She spent ten years rising through the council ranks, becoming head of Islington's housing committee and taking over as council leader in 1982. She enjoyed a fearsome reputation during her municipal career and was described as 'commissar of the socialist republic of Islington'.[130] She was also nicknamed Enver Hodge, a reference to Albanian despot Enver Hoxha. It was considered a 'loony left' council that raised the red flag and had a bust of Lenin in the town hall.[131] Yet she gradually became more mainstream as she started to give her support to Tony Blair. She lived on the same street as Blair and her lawyer husband Henry Hodge employed Blair's wife Cherie Booth. Her political transformation, condemned by some left wingers, was cemented when as the new MP for Barking she co-nominated Blair for party leader in 1994.[132] She commented that she shared his values and supported the direction that he wanted to take the Party; that he was a moderniser, but his policies were based on traditional Labour values.[133]

She has been Labour MP for Barking since the by-election on 9 June 1994 following the death of Labour MP Jo Richardson. The former Labour local council boss whose radical chic reputation and feisty espousal of left wing policies made her a prime target for the tabloid press in the 1980s became the 21st Jewish MP in that present parliament when she almost doubled Labour's majority in the election.[134] From 1998-2001 she held junior ministerial posts in the Blair government and was then Minister of

State at the Department of Education from 2001-2003, responsible for higher education. In 2003-2005 she was Minister of State at the Department of Education, responsible for children's affairs, a controversial position in which she attracted some criticism. From 2005-2010 she was Minister of State at the Department of Works and Pensions. She was awarded a DBE in 2015 for political and public service.

The end of Hodge's service on Islington Council, prior to her entering Parliament, was marred by the emergence of serious child abuse allegations concerning council-run children's homes in Islington. She apologised several times since the emergence of the scandal that directly linked her council tenure with what she admitted in 2014 was 'shameful naivety' in ignoring the complaints of paedophile victims. The scandal broke in October 1992. The *Evening Standard* had exposed a catalogue of abuse at children's homes but Hodge, displaying a characteristic defensiveness with the press, or her critics argue a characteristic arrogance, denounced the report as a 'sensationalist piece of gutter journalism'. Some of the allegations proved true. Hodge argued that she was misinformed by officials and supporters, including Industry Secretary Patricia Hewitt, and stressed that the allegations arose at a time when children were not as readily believed as they are today.

Liz Davies, the senior social worker who went to the *Evening Standard* with the story insisted that while some of the abuse started before Hodge was leader, by 1990 councils were aware of the problems and that she told Hodge of the allegations of a paedophile ring in April 1990 and that Hodge was psychologically incapable of taking on board the details of extreme abuse. In 1985 Demetrious Panton complained that he suffered abuse while in the care of Islington Council in the 1970s and 1980s and claimed that Hodge, as council leader, had ultimate responsibility. She paid heavily for calling him an 'extremely disturbed person'. There was a formal apology in the High Court and a £30,000 payment was made. There was within a few hours heated exchange in the Commons as to whether she should still hold her post. Tony Blair defended her and pointed to her record in boosting investment in childcare, citing support from professionals and insisted that she was the best person for the job.

The clash illustrated the extremes of feeling that Hodge engendered as was the case for Shirley Porter and Edwina Currie. To her critics she was ruthlessly ambitious and a privileged individual who as leader of Islington Council closed her ears to allegations of child abuse out of political expediency, high handedness, or because she was unable to countenance them. To her many friends she was passionate and determined and credited with ramping childcare up the political agenda, was frank and engaging but whose lack of caution led to occasional errors of judgement.[135] Although Blair stood by her and Hodge kept her ministerial role, she has said the Prime Minister thought her 'too outspoken' to be elevated to the cabinet.[136]

She continued to cause controversy when in 2005 she told the *Sunday Telegraph* that eight out of 10 voters in her Barking constituency might be tempted to vote for the British National Party (BNP) because no one else was listening to them. She was accused of giving ammunition to the far right after she argued that 'indigenous' families from Britain had more right to social housing than new immigrants. She said that people in her constituency, where BNP had 12 seats on the local council, often linked new faces and new languages to housing shortages and that there was a need to look at policies where 'the legitimate sense of entitlement to social housing felt by the indigenous family overrides the legitimate need demonstrated by new migrants'. Entitlement to social housing should be based on length of residence, citizenship and National Insurance contributions and that most new immigrant families were economic migrants who choose to come and work here and she questioned whether they should presume the right to access social housing.[137] The BNP praised her comments and a letter in *The Observer* signed by 98 lawyers called for her to resign or be sacked. When the BNP did well in subsequent elections, some Labour activists blamed her and called for her de-selection.[138]

Hodge held on to her seat and went on to contest the 2010 election against BNP leader Nick Griffin. The battle for Barking was one of the highest profile campaigns of the 2010 election, and Hodge doubled her majority as she defeated Griffin in the face of fears that he could win. 'Get out and stay out', she told the far-right party on election night. She considered that at the time this was the most important achievement of her political life. On Griffin's reason for fighting the seat, Hodge commented that 'he hates women, he hates Jews and he hates immigrants and I am all of them'. She faced abuse – one BNP activist told her on Election Day to 'go back to Germany with the rest of the thieving MPs'.[139] She accused BNP canvassers of using her Jewish origins to turn voters against her. 'They have painted me as a rich Jewish immigrant and have repeatedly asked people if they knew what her maiden name was'. She worked alongside Hope Not Hate, an advocacy group that campaigns against fascism and racism who were actively working in Barking, and won the election, pushing the BNP into third place.[140] 'I have spent my life fighting racism and that is a result of experiencing antisemitism as a child as a first-generation immigrant and the daughter of Jewish refugees'. She had spent three years exposing the true nature of the BNP councillors and was determined to expel them, but she called on the community to help as the BNP would be pouring resources into Barking. She wanted to turn this threat into an opportunity to destroy their credibility not just in her constituency but nationally.[141]

Her success against Nick Griffin and the crushing defeat of the BNP earned Hodge the affectionate moniker 'battling granny'. Taking on the BNP leader at the 2010 election was perhaps her biggest challenge and triumph. She had returned to grassroots activism to convince her constituents not to turn to the far right.

> I needed support. I worked really hard for four years and put a lot of effort in. We started in 2006 when Griffin announced he would stand. I shall never forget the Jewish community on that. They really rose to the occasion and supported me. It was right across the political spectrum, not just Labour Jews. We won it because we had spent four years really working to reconnect with the local people.

Hodge's demolition of Griffin precipitated a BNP collapse across the constituency. Two years later the BNP lost all 12 of its council seats in Barking and Dagenham.[142]

More controversy followed Hodge when she became the first woman elected chair of the Public Accounts Committee (2010-2015). She considered that her new role represented the culmination of years rising through the political ranks and that through her 40 years' experience of public service she had touched almost every bit of the public sector. Lord Patten and leading BBC officials were interviewed as well as the Duchy of Cornwall, concerning their tax arrangements. Hodge acknowledged that her committee's approach was grabbing the public attention who were outraged by wealthy individuals and global companies thinking they could avoid paying their taxes and that it was a moral duty for them to pay their fair share.[143] She publicly humiliated the head of the Inland Revenue when her committee discovered that it had done a deal with Goldman Sachs that let them off millions of pounds of tax and she was investigating foreign companies who appeared to make large profits in the UK but paid less corporation tax than some high street businesses.[144] There were attempts to destabilise her in her job. The *Telegraph* published an article on 9 November 2012 maintaining that Stemcor, whose chief executive was Hodge's brother Ralph Oppenheimer, and of which Hodge is a shareholder, paid just 0.01 per cent tax on the £2.1 billion they generated in the UK in the previous year. Hodge replied that the company always promised that they would do absolutely nothing to avoid tax and that she would be very mad if she found out differently.[145] *The Telegraph* subsequently published an apology that there was no inconsistency or hypocrisy in Hodge criticising other companies for tax avoidance.[146]

Hodge was part of growing rebellion against the Labour Party's controversial new code of conduct on antisemitism and part of a group to support a move to force the party's National Executive Committee to reconsider adopting the new code. The full International Holocaust Remembrance Alliance (IHRA) definition included 11 illustrative examples of how antisemitism might manifest itself. The Labour code accepted that seven of these 'are likely to be antisemitic' but had dropped or rewritten the other four. In the Labour code it was no longer likely to be antisemitic to accuse Jewish citizens of being more loyal to Israel or to the alleged priorities of Jews worldwide, than to the interests of their own nation. Similarly, the IHRA definition said it was antisemitic to compare Israel to Nazi Germany but Labour's code says this was only the case if there was 'evidence of antisemitic intent'. Nor did Labour's code agree with IHRA that it is antisemitic to argue that the very idea of a state for the Jewish people is a 'racist endeavour'. The leadership failed to explain why it was unable to use the IHRA definition and in taking this position had gone back on the previous decision of Labour's Equalities Committee in 2016 to adopt the full IHRA definition with all its examples.[147] Labour has altered the IHRA definition, accepted in full by the government and more than 130 local councils, deleting and amending four key examples of antisemitism related to Israel. Under its adapted guidelines, a Labour Party member was free to claim Israel's existence was a racist endeavour and compare Israeli policies to Nazi Germany, unless 'intent' can be proved. In doing so Labour made a distinction between racial antisemitism targeting Jews (unacceptable) and political antisemitism targeting Israel (acceptable).[148]

Hodge confronted Labour leader Jeremy Corbyn in a corridor in the House of Commons and called him an antisemite and racist. Ever since Corbyn was elected the Labour Party's leader in 2015 he faced accusations about his antisemitism but evidence goes back prior to this time. In the aftermath of the Islamic attack in New York on September 11, 2001, he organised with fellow activists the Stop the War Coalition (SWC). It was ostensibly to protest against the American invasion of Afghanistan and Iraq. His partner in SWC was the Muslim Association of Great Britain attached to the Muslim Brotherhood and he argued that the alliance was forged by a mutual opposition to Zionism. Thereafter during protest marches through London, banners against the war would be given equal billing to the Muslim

Association placards urging the destruction of Israel. The Muslim organisers said the two were linked as Zionists were planning the imminent invasion of Iraq and Corbyn agreed. Corbyn frequently associated with Muslim extremists and appeared to share their refusal to distinguish between anti-Zionism and antisemitism.[149]

After Hodge's public denunciation of Corbyn, in a move driven by Seamus Milne, Corbyn's right hand man, Hodge was told she faced formal disciplinary proceedings. As an outspoken critic of Corbyn's failure to tackle anti-Jewish abuse in the Labour party, Hodge told Corbyn 'you have proved you don't want people like me in the Party'. The clash took place only hours after Labour's governing NEC approved, without a vote being taken, the controversial new code on antisemitism. This was later withdrawn when it was met with an angry backlash.[150] The charge against her was dropped. Although a Labour source said Hodge had written to Chief Whip Nick Brown expressing regrets for the manner in which she raised her views, in a tweet Hodge said there had been no apologies on either side and that after 55 years of Labour Party membership, going after her instead of addressing the issue was wrong.[151] She said that facing the investigation for confronting Corbyn over antisemitism made her think about what it felt like to be a Jew in Germany in the 1930s.[152]

Hodge addressed a rally in Manchester, together with the Chief Rabbi, other communal members and MPs against antisemitism. She said that she never dreamt that her identity as a Jew and her work as a public servant of the Labour Party would lead her to a rally protesting against antisemitism in her party. After she defeated leader of the BNP in the 2010 election she expected to receive a lot of antisemitic abuse but what she had received in the last year was greater in number and more horrid in content than what she was subjected to by Griffin and the BNP.[153]

Her prominent position as critic of the Labour Party and its handling of the antisemitism crisis, was the way that she identified with her Jewish background publicly. There was talk of her running for Mayor of London in 2016. When asked about her relationship with the Jewish community and whether she could breach former mayor Ken Livingstone's fractious relationship with London's Jewish community she said that some of the Jewish community are 'a little wary of me and my commitment' which she attributed to the fact that she was not religious and that both of her marriages were to non-Jews. It also stemmed from her stance on Israel. 'I think you can support the Israeli state and you can support their desire for security. But you can equally say that their reaction has been disproportionate'. She says her views on Israel attract hostility from Jewish audiences and appealed for greater tolerance within the community for views such as hers. 'It isn't an attack on Israel, it isn't an attack on the Jewish community if some of us feel that the direction of travel of the current administration in Israel is not supporting a long-term peaceful settlement'. Hodge, who spent time on a kibbutz in the 1960s, insisted her views on Israel are not 'a denial of my race and identity and neither are they an attack on my people'. She repeats that she is 'Jewish to the core' and the way that she leads her life is 'completely informed by Jewish values around family'.[154]

Hodge's strong commitment to her heritage also has to do with her family's experience of the Holocaust. Her family let Germany in the 1930s. Her aunt's husband died in Auschwitz and the discovery of a letter from her grandmother, who was shot outside a concentration camp, plays on her mind. Her grandmother had refused to leave because she was in Vienna and thought that no one would attack her as she was too old. She wrote the letter when she knew she was going to be rounded up and probably realised she was going to die. The letter was full of 'don't forget me, don't forget me'. When Hodge saw the letter it intensified her identity with a downtrodden race.[155] She speaks movingly of the moment when on a visit to Auschwitz she was confronted by a battered brown suitcase with her uncle's initials on it. 'That moment was utterly chilling. All of that is my heritage. It is what I am today'.[156]

It has been commented that 'she wears her Jewishness lightly but with a great deal of affection'.[157] Yet Hodge has acknowledged and supported Jewish initiatives. When 'The Joy of Jewish life', a Lubavitch[158] initiative that promoted family values and helped Jewish parents deal with their children more effectively, received government funding and was launched at the Commons, Hodge who was at the time Children's Minister, praised the scheme and said the government would take elements from it in evolving new programmes to help parents. She considered the scheme was particularly important because it was the first government-funded parenting initiative in the Jewish community. 'Lubavitcher works especially with teenage children and we know little about that area. We want to learn from what you do'. She said the scheme fitted in with the government's shift from protection to prevention with regard problem children and its dedication to support good parenting in the home.[159] She was guest speaker at Norwood's annual dinner where she praised the charity for their work with socially disadvantaged children and their families.[160]

What particularly resonates with her are initiatives that are connected with the Holocaust and the immigrant experience. When she was Culture Minister she marked Holocaust Memorial Day by awarding £100,000 grants to London's Jewish Museum and the Wiener Holocaust Library. She noted that the recipients played a vital part in ensuring that people were aware of what the Jewish community has given to this country and the world and that one must never forget the terrible wrongs suffered during the Nazi era.[161] She spoke at the reopening of the Jewish Museum, London about her own Jewish immigrant roots and of the resonance the exhibits had for all immigrant communities.[162]

Speaking at the 2018 Spectator awards after receiving the best speech award for her words during a House of Commons debate on antisemitism within the Labour Party, she spoke about how her children were the first generation in her family who did not have to leave a country because of discrimination and racism. She said that fighting for her children and bringing the personal together with the political may be really difficult but was probably the most important thing that she had done in her political life. She confessed that she never expected her Jewish identity would become 'central' to her politics. 'My dad tried to make me Jewish and failed, the local rabbi tried to make me Jewish and failed, my Jewish friends tried to make me Jewish and failed. It took the leader of the Labour Party to do that'.[163]

Hodge still retains her seat in Barking, although she announced in December 2021 that she would not be standing at the next general election. 'After nearly three decades I have made the tough decision not to stand again at the next election. Serving as an MP has been the honour of my life and an absolute joy'. Labour Leader Sir Keir Starmer hailed her 'dedication to our Party' which he said was exemplary.[164]

Hodge's fighting spirit and campaign against Corbyn was shared by her contemporary Louise Ellman. Ellman, who came from a working-class Manchester background fought her entire life against inequality and racism and was known for her support for Israel and her strong Jewish identity.

Louise Ellman (1945 -)

Louise Joyce Ellman served as a Member of Parliament for Liverpool Riverside from 1997-2019 and was a stalwart of Jewish leadership and campaigning and could always be called upon to defend Israel on the green benches. She was a target of antisemitic abuse, also within her own constituency, partly as a result of her long-standing support for Israel and her open confrontation with Labour leader Jeremy Corbyn over antisemitism within the Party. She was one of the most influential voices in Parliament through her long-time chairmanship of the Transport Select

10. Dame Louise Ellman DBE Official Portrait of Dame Louise Ellman DBE (Chris McAndrew, via Wikimedia Commons)

Committee of the Commons and was made a Dame Commander of the British Empire in 2018 for parliamentary services.

Born Louise Rosenberg in Manchester to an observant Jewish family, she was awarded a scholarship to study at Manchester High School for Girls but never felt comfortable there. The majority of the girls were from middle class, affluent professional homes. Those who were there on scholarships tended to stick together and this was the case even when there were school reunions. She lived in Salford and was from a working-class background. He parents did not have a lot of money and they encouraged her to study for a scholarship so that she could get the best education. 'I always felt that in some ways I was an outsider'.[165] Ellman's unease in that period may reflect the fact that Jews had rapidly suburbanised in the interwar period and viewed her school and its male equivalent, Manchester Grammar School, which were attended by many Jewish students, as a vehicle by which the children of working-class Jews could progress.

Ellman's Jewish background had an impact on her life and the path she took in life. Friday night dinners were a chance for lively debates. 'I think, because of this, you become very socially aware, very conscious about what is going on in the world'. She had thought that her father was an armchair socialist but subsequently found out that he had given a lengthy interview to Manchester Jewish Museum about his father's Lithuanian background and that he used to go to Labour Party meetings. As a teenager she was interested in socialist ideas. 'I thought inequality was very wrong. I also hated racism. It was all a bit vague but I felt these things from when I was young. I wanted to change society but didn't really have any understanding how to do so'. She became involved with the Labour Zionist movement Habonim as a teenager alongside future playwright Mike Leigh. 'We had wonderful discussions about socialism and society. Everything centred on the kibbutz'.[166]

She studied at the University of Hull, where she belonged to the Jewish Society, and received a BA in Sociology and History in 1967 and then studied Social Administration at the University of York where she was awarded a MPhil in 1972. She was hardly involved in student politics but was very politically involved off campus. She was a member of the Labour Party and worked for Harold Wilson's winning election campaign. She had always been interested in politics and this was the reason that she studied sociology as she was fascinated by the way power was distributed in society.[167]

She met her husband Geoffrey Ellman at university and the couple spent a year in Israel from 1967-68. They were at an *ulpan* (school for the intensive study of Hebrew) in Beersheva, then left just after the Six Day War so that Geoffrey, a pharmacist, could work at a hospital in Tiberias. She agrees that until then most on the left saw Zionism and Labour as completely compatible but the situation after 1967 changed when people on the left who had been supportive of Israel saying they had lost respect for Israel because they had attacked first. After 1967 with Israel in charge of the West Bank, sympathies changed. Ellman's support for Israel never faltered.

Returning to England she was a lecturer for the Open University (1970-76) and elected as a councillor on the Lancashire County Council in 1970 representing Skelmersdale. She was 24 and the Council's youngest ever member. She recalls that many traditional Labour supporters told her that she should have stayed at home and one sent her a note suggesting that she did not speak at all during her first term of office. She persevered, fighting for local services, and by 1974 had become leader of the Council's small Labour group, just 11 seats out of 96. By 1981 she was in power with a small majority. She pioneered partnerships between the Council, business and unions at a time when many in her own party were looking to slash the power of the Councils.[168] Under her leadership the Council saw some of the biggest changes in its history. She increased nursery education and expanded home help services. She was described and dynamic and vivacious.[169] When she was leader of Lancashire County Council in the 1980s it was at the same time that Margaret Hodge was leader of Islington Council. It was unusual to have a woman as a Council leader.[170] Ellman was the first woman leader of a County Council.[171]

In 1997 Ellman became a Member of Parliament, elected to the Liverpool Riverside constituency. She explains that it was a time when the militant types were being removed and people wanted something different.[172] In the months after the election she built a reputation as a hardworking backbencher who led from the front in vital Liverpool issues such as campaigning to save the Liverpool Blood Centre and keep post office jobs in the city.[173]

Once in Parliament she reconnected with her early loyalty to Israel. 'I'd hear people saying things that I thought were awful about Israel', explaining her decision to join both the Labour Friends of Israel and the Jewish Labour Movement.[174] 'It was Labour people and I thought I can't just sit here. But I found that once I stood up and said something I was labelled "that Jewish MP" or "that Zionist". Once I realised I was labelled I thought I'm going to carry on'. She adds that 'It's not that Israel does everything right – no country does - but there are people who think that it's 100 per cent Israel's fault and I have to speak out against that'.[175] In the early months of her parliamentary career she took part in a Labour Friends of Israel trip for MPs, most of whom were not Jewish. The trip followed a parliamentary debate in which MPs belonging to the Labour Middle East Council voiced sharp criticism of Israeli policies. Ellman found their remarks damaging and felt it was important that MPs visit Israel to see another side of the picture.[176] Although her own constituency had few Jewish inhabitants she felt that as a Jew she should speak out on issues such as Israel and antisemitism.[177] The *Times of Israel* said she was as tough as nails and an unabashed friend of Israel. 'Ignore her gentle, soft-spoken manner, she is made of sterner stuff'. She made it clear that she would not be silenced on issues that she cared about. 'It's not in my character to be intimidated. These are issues I feel strongly about and I'm going to keep fighting my corner'.[178]

From her early days in Parliament, Ellman defended Israel and drew attention to acts of terrorism and antisemitism. In 2000 she took part in an acrimonious commons debate between pro-Palestinian and pro-Israel MPs. The debate was launched by Labour's Neil Gerrard who accused Israel of using disproportionate force in dealing with Palestinian demonstrators. This prompted Ellman to counter that younger Palestinians without guns were placed in the front line while protesters carrying weapons took positions behind them.[179] Ellman was one of the pro-Israel MPS hailed as heroes after defying jeers and catcalls to express support during a six-hour Commons debate on the Middle East crisis. She has highlighted the difficulties facing pro-Israel politicians 'in general the feeling in Parliament is that Israel is the aggressor. Many people forget that it was the Palestinians that broke off the peace process'.[180] There was a Parliamentary motion signed in 2009 by more than 40 MPs condemning attacks on the Jewish community as a result of the war in Gaza. Ellman said that criticism of MPs who supported Israel had reached unprecedented levels. 'There are few people willing to listen to us or hear what we have to say. The atmosphere in the House is deeply hostile'.[181] More MPs were pro-Arab than backed Israel and this had made her more determined to be heard in speaking on behalf of Israel. She said she supported a Palestinian state and a return to negotiations.[182]

When President Assad of Syria visited London for talks with Tony Blair, Ellman questioned him at a small private meeting in the House of Commons about his policies on terrorism and Middle East peace. She read to him his statement on Damascus Radio when he described a suicide bombing at Rishon le Zion as 'wonderful and unique'. He told her if she did not like such bombings she should go to Israel to change its policies.[183] She petitioned for a complete arms embargo against Syria and demanded that ministers give full details of all the equipment they have given to Syria.[184] She was the target of fierce criticism by the Muslim Public Affairs Committee who pointed to her activities as a leading light in the Jewish Labour Movement (she was chair from 2006-16) and vice chair of Labour Friends of Israel and questioned her loyalty to Britain.[185] She was never afraid to speak her mind and she took Foreign Secretary Jack Straw to task over references to a Jewish lobby in a Foreign Office memorandum. A leaked internal document warned of repercussions if the Home Office banned radical Islamic clerk Yusuf al-Qaradawi from a return visit to the UK and spoke of the influence of the Jewish lobby.[186] During a Parliamentary debate in October 2006 she challenged Andrew Turner, Tory spokesman on charities, when he quoted a Human Rights report claiming that Israeli aircraft had strafed fleeing Lebanese civilians from the air and that these were tactics of the Nazis during the 1939-40 period. Ellman considered the comment offensive.[187]

One of her last speeches in Parliament concerning the Middle East was in 2019 when she spoke about the scandal of British taxpayers' money being used to fund a Palestinian school curriculum which incites the murder of Israelis and circulates antisemitic material. She spoke as she introduced her International Development Assistance (Values Promoted in Palestinian National Authority Schools) Bill to the Commons. Her bill called for teaching programmes in Palestinian Authority Schools financed by the UK to promote values such as peace, freedom and non-discrimination and which required UK government ministers to publish an annual review to ensure funds are spent in line with UNESCO derived standards of peace and tolerance in education. Britain is to donate £125 million to the Palestinian Authority by 2021. There was an announcement a few months later that the Department for International Development would be reviewing the curriculum.[188]

Ellman's support for Israel came at a personal price. In 2012 MPs who spoke in support of Israel had to limit the information they made available to constituents and take other security measures after being sent death threats and abusive messages by post, phone or online. Ellman had been dealing with such death threats for a decade and commented that 'you are vulnerable as an MP. People approach. You are in public places'.[189] She was targeted by social media. Images were put out of her with 'Juden' and 'disgusting' written on them. Two racist leaflets were distributed in Liverpool against Ellman and Luciana Berger of the Liverpool Wavertree constituency in which they were attacked for their support and contacts with Israel. One was headed 'don't vote for Friends of Israel' in reference to Berger as director of Labour Friends of Israel and the other attacked Ellman for allegedly not listening to her constituents' views over Israel's action in Gaza. Berger is referred to as Ellman's 'protegee' in one and Ellman as her 'mentor' in another.[190] She was repeatedly targeted by Tony Greenstein, a Jewish anti-Zionist activist. He wrote a series of blogs in which he referred to Ellman as 'a supporter of Israeli child abuse' and claimed she had made excuses for Israeli torture and beatings.[191]

With Corbyn's election as Labour leader in 2015 there was a surge of new membership within Ellman's constituency. Many of the newcomers were simply youthful enthusiasts, energised by Corbyn's outside status and populist message. A small minority were hard left activists who found Ellman – a vocal supporter of Israel and prominent member of the Jewish

Labour Movement – an irresistible target. A local council member suggested that the assault came from a 'tiny but vocal group' who seemed 'hell bent on attacking our MP in an orchestrated, horrible personal way'. Another non-Jewish member described the atmosphere as 'terrifying'. Ellman herself said there was 'an almost obsessive focus' on her views on Israel. Antisemitic remarks were alleged to have been made on at least three occasions while leaked emails suggested that members of the pro-Corbyn Momentum group were plotting to oust Ellman.[192] Momentum called her a 'foot soldier' for the Israeli government 'trying to take our democracy away from us'.[193] During one meeting, at which Ellman was present, activists discussed Hamas tunnels being dug from Gaza into Israel and one member was said to have compared the tunnels to those created by Jews trying to escape Nazi persecution in the Warsaw ghetto.[194] The bullying was constant. Former Liverpool mayor Malcolm Kennedy praised her dignity. 'She stands there, as if in the dock, as the Chair allows members to take the microphone during her report and condemned her as if in a Soviet show trial'. She was physically threatened, called a Jewish Labour movement bitch and made to endure obsessive interrogations about Israel-Palestine at every meeting.[195] 'In politics you have to fight and never give up', she declared. 'I want to have social and economic justice for the whole community and that, with my opposition to racism and antisemitism, is what fires me'.[196]

Ellman was at the centre of a fight in Parliament over the Labour Party's failure to tackle the antisemitism crisis that escalated under Jeremy Corbyn. She said it was a fallacy to believe that people who profess to be anti-racist cannot be antisemitic and that antisemitism is confined to the right wing of politics. 'The notion of conspiratorial powerful Jews or Zionists controlling international capital and manipulating the media for their own ends is to be found on the left as well. It is all too evident in the Labour Party's current problem with antisemitism'.[197]

A former aide to Corbyn told the *Mail on Sunday* that Corbyn described Ellman as 'the honourable member of Tel Aviv'. Another senior Labour source said this term was commonly used by his staff whenever her name cropped up or she appeared on the office television and that they could not stand her.[198] Accusing Jews of loyalty to Israel over their own country is an example of contemporary antisemitism according to IHRA definition but not under Labour's definition. Ellman said that if the allegation was correct she was appalled that a potential Prime Minister would use language of this sort against one of his MPs. 'To refer to me as an MP for Tel Aviv is a challenge to my loyalty to this country. A key part of the internationally accepted code on antisemitism that the Labour Party wants to dilute specifically states it is antisemitic to accuse Jews of being more loyal to Israel than their own country'.[199] In 2016 she backed a motion of no confidence in Corbyn by rebel Labour MPs.

Ellman resigned from her post as MP for Liverpool Riverside in October 2019 over concerns of antisemitism in the Party and after facing an increasingly hostile climate in her local constituency. She had been concerned about the situation for some years but wanted to fight it from within. When Jews were starting to feel that Labour was not their Party anymore her message was to stay and fight what was going on. 'Together we can make a difference'.[200] Her view changed when she realised that it was possible that Corbyn could be prime minister. As she believed he was a danger to the country and to the Jewish community, she felt unable to stand as a Labour MP asking people to vote for such a person.[201] She recalled how she went to the Party conference and spoke at a fringe meeting where she gave her view that Corbyn was not fit to be prime minister. When she went to the next constituency meeting in Liverpool, the faces in the room were even more thunderous than usual and she was challenged about her remarks. One member said he'd rather talk about inequality and poverty than antisemitism and everyone cheered. 'I looked round the room at the faces filled with loathing and thought this is the Labour Party at rock bottom'. She realised that she could not stand the situation anymore. Within a day a resolution had been put forward calling for a vote of no confidence in her. The date for the vote was Yom Kippur, the holiest day in the Jewish calendar. A week went by and the date remained unchanged until someone from Corbyn's office called, begging them to withdraw the vote. By this time Ellman had decided to leave the Party.[202] Under Corbyn the Party had become a very extreme and uncomfortable place with no room for dissent. She found the situation extremely distressing and traumatic.[203] Her decision had been 'truly agonising' but she had to carry it out in order to take a stand against the leadership.[204]

Her departure from Parliament will be missed by those concerned about a strong Jewish voice in the Commons. She has been the most dependable voice for the community, defending religious practices, including circumcision and religious slaughtering. Her support has been extensive. In addition to her role within Labour Friends of Israel and the Jewish Labour Movement, she was Vice President of the Jewish Leadership Council and a trustee of Holocaust Memorial Day. Her experience as a Jew had inspired her to work with other minorities. There was no division between being 'a proud Jew and a proud citizen'.[205] Just before her resignation in 2019 the *Jerusalem Post* ranked her as the 23rd most influential Jew worldwide. She was the sole Briton in their 50 strong list.

Ellman re-joined the Party in September 2021 as she considered that there had been changes in the Party and that Party leader Sir Keir Starmer had shown a willingness to confront both the anti-Jewish racists and the toxic culture that had allowed antisemitism to flourish. She will serve on the Recruitment Committee that will decide the panels for the Independent Review Board and the Independent Complaints Board. Their purpose is to ensure complaints are heard by experts from outside the Party and to restore trust and confidence, especially within the Jewish community, in the way that grievances are handled. Labour leader Sir Keir Starmer said that 'Louise Ellman re-joining our party is a poignant moment. Her courage and dignity in standing up against appalling abuse is testament to her Labour values'.[206]

The next generation of Jewish women MPs includes Luciana Berger, who also represented Liverpool, and was subjected to a vicious campaign of antisemitism and chose to leave the Labour Party due to its failure to protect and support her or take a stand against such treatment.

Luciana Berger (1981 –   )

Luciana Berger was MP for Liverpool Wavertree from 2010 to 2019. As an MP Berger joined the shadow cabinet under Ed Milliband's leadership. She was a young high flyer and within four months of the 2010 election she became Shadow Minister for Climate Change, part of a young and reinvigorated frontbench team. An extraordinary rise to a senior opposition frontbench position it showed that she had already earned a high level of esteem and trust from senior colleagues within the Party.[207] She campaigned against dangerous dogs and their owners as well as food poverty and raised the issue of loopholes allowing companies to avoid their health and safety responsibilities. She was re-elected in the 2015 and 2017 general elections. As a former member of the opposition Shadow cabinet, she was the first Shadow Cabinet Minister for Mental Health under Jeremy Corbyn from 2015-2016 and the most senior Jewish figure in Corbyn's shadow cabinet. Berger was critical of Jeremy Corbyn who was elected leader in 2015 and she resigned from the shadow cabinet in 2016. In February 2019 members of her local party briefly proposed motions of no confidence in her for 'continually' criticising Corbyn. Later that month she resigned from the Labour Party and co-founded the Independent Group. She later joined the Liberal Democrats and stood unsuccessfully for Finchley and Golders Green in the 2019 December election. In February 2023 she rejoined the

11. Official Portrait of Luciana Berger (Chris McAndrew, via Wikimedia Commons)

Labour Party after Sir Keir Starmer apologised for the antisemitism and death threats she endured under Jeremy Corbyn and praised her principled and brave decision to leave.

Berger grew up in 'a small house in Wembley'. She affirms that her parents were not particularly political though her ancestry was not without political blood. Her great uncle was Labour MP Manny (Lord) Shinwell, first elected in 1922, who served as a minister in Ramsey McDonald and Clement Atlee's governments, reaching the cabinet as secretary of state for war in the latter. Berger describes how her family would watch the news and discuss the issues of the day but not in a party-political way. Her mother's side of the family ran a small retail business, carpets, curtains, fabrics and interior furnishings, for over 80 years. Berger's father joined the business after studying law at university and spending time practising as a solicitor. At weekends Berger would tour the markets of Northamptonshire with her grandfather, selling women's coats and dresses and remembers being good at market trading.[208]

Her education gave her a strong base from which to develop personal skills. She attended the private Haberdasher's Aske in Elstree even though the family were not well off as it was important to her parents that she had a private school education; her father worked in the family upholstery business six days a week to pay for it. Her mother was a counsellor in a palliative care unit. As a teenager she worked in London's Disney flagship store and made sandwiches in Pret a Manger.[209] She was involved in a varied number of activities including the Duke of Edinburgh award, organised visits to old people's homes and volunteered for Norwood. She became involved in politics when she went to Birmingham University to study Spanish and business and was active in the Student Union. She subsequently joined the Labour Party as it was the Party that her values were most in tune with.[210]

Berger believes her passion for community work comes from her Jewish heritage. She regularly attended the New Middlesex Synagogue (now Mosaic Reform). The family were more culturally Jewish than religious although she adheres to the main Jewish festivals.[211] 'I was part of a strong community'. One of its values Tikun Olam, which literally means 'repairing the world', instilled strong values in her at a young age. She developed a strong sense of social justice and wanted to make a difference.[212] She is very proud of her heritage although she is determined that it does not define her politics, despite her having been a former director of the Labour Friends of Israel. 'People were quick to define me as a Jew. I was different because I celebrated different festivals'. She displayed a certain amount of bravery in taking on the Islamic organisation Hizb ut-Tahrir whilst working as a National Union of Students (NUS) official. She was harassed and spat on. 'They didn't like the fact that I was speaking out against them, a banned organisation on campus. I was ensuring that they were not allowed to hand out materials. They chased me around campus'.[213] She was co-organizer of the NUS's anti-racism and anti-facism campaign and she accused the NUS leadership of having failed consistently to address a full year of anti-Jewish incidents on campus. 'The NUS has been a bystander to Jew hatred'. She was disgusted by their failure to take action against antisemitic leaflets distributed at the NUS conference, including one that cited the Protocols of the Elders of Zion and compared the Jewish people to the Nazis.[214] She resigned from her position as a NUS national executive committee member because of a continued apathy to Jewish student suffering.[215]

After university Berger worked at the Stock Exchange and the Treasury before moving to the NHS Confederation and then Labour Friends of Israel.

This was her first political role that saw her work to ensure stronger relations between Britain and Israel. This could be seen a career move as after she entered Parliament she largely avoided association with contentious Middle East issues, quietly supporting Israel but rarely joining the band of Labour MPs who really defended it in divisive Common debates. She kept her focus squarely on domestic politics and her Liverpool constituency.[216]

Berger applied to become an MP for Liverpool Wavertree and was just 28 years old when she was chosen to stand in the seat vacated by Jane Kennedy who had been the constituency MP for 18 years. She was seen as one of Labour's rising stars but both her strong support for Israel and that she had been 'parachuted in' from London sparked a row. She won the contest against strong opposition.[217] One leaflet was distributed in the constituency headed 'Don't vote for friends of Israel'.[218]

Berger's career in Parliament has been dominated by antisemitism and she has received antisemitic abuse since entering Parliament in 2010. She said that such abuse was a 'by-product of the job' and that her Jewish faith was simply the method used to attack her.[219] She has been the subject of virulent antisemitism via social media. She admits that many of her colleagues also face abuse. She receives it because she is Jewish; others because of their background or sexuality.[220] At the height of the campaign she was subjected to 2,500 abusive messages in three days. Twitter's response was frustratingly slow and the police response had been hampered by an initial reluctance to cooperate from social media sites.[221]

A website based in the United States, orchestrated by the racist, white nationalist website *Daily Stormer*, was behind the coordinated campaign of antisemitic abuse against Berger. The site provided a user guide to harassing Berger and created offensive images to be shared by internet trolls and sent to her via social media sites. It encouraged people to call her 'a Jew, Jew communist, a filthy Jew b***h, a hook-nosey y**.'Tell her we don't want her in the UK; we do not want her or any other Jew anywhere in Europe. Tell her to go to Israel and call for her deportation to said Jew state'.[222] Garron Helm received a four-week prison sentence for sending an obscene tweet. The tweet showed a photograph of Berger with a Holocaust yellow star superimposed on her forehead and the wording 'you can always count on a Jew to show their true colours eventually'. Berger was said to be truly shocked by the incident.[223]

Six people have been convicted of the racially aggravated harassment of Berger (two of them Labour Party members) and two went to prison. Berger had to initiate tight personal security, vary her route to and from home and her children's nursery and carry a panic button. She received vicious posts, such as comparing her to the mass murderer Rose West, and threats to her life were received weekly. In 2016 almost half of Labour's 99 female MPs, including Berger, signed a letter to Labour party leader Jeremy Corbyn condemning a culture where abuse and harassment of women by some of his supporters was 'actively encouraged and quietly condoned'. In September 2018 Berger discovered the Labour Party had withheld details of a threat made against her and had also failed to pass it on to the police. She blamed Corbyn directly. 'At best he's turning a blind eye. At worst, it's wilfully participating in antisemitism'.[224]

She made her way into the headlines, more often than not, as a frequent critic of the Labour Party's handling of antisemitism and someone who was open about her own experiences. Her first move against Corbyn came in June 2016 when she resigned from her position as Shadow Minister for Mental Health. She was part of the mass resignation staged due to a lack of confidence in Corbyn's leadership after the EU referendum. She has since regularly rallied against antisemitism in the Labour Party and Corbyn's handling of the situation. After Labour suspended rather than expelled former Mayor of London Ken Livingstone despite finding him guilty of three charges of bringing the parity into disrepute for his comments about Hitler, Berger described the verdict as 'appalling' and a 'new low for Labour'.[225] Berger told the Commons in 2018 that 'anti-racism is one of our central values and there was a time not long ago when the Left actively confronted antisemitism. The work done by the previous Labour Government to move the equality goalposts in this country was one of the reasons why I joined the Labour Party in the first place. One antisemitic member of the Labour Party is one member too many'.[226] She addressed a crowd of 1500 British Jews and their supporters in Parliament Square in March 2018. The protest was of Corbyn's 'systematic failure'. Berger told the crowd that antisemitism was very real and alive in the Labour Party.[227]

Her criticism of the Party and its leader led to members of her local Labour Party attempting to deselect her, seeing her criticism of Corbyn as disloyal. Senior members of the Wavertree Labour Party called her 'a disruptive Zionist'. Labour Deputy leader Tom Watson intervened in the controversy and offered his support to Berger in what he called her battle against 'bullying hatred' from members of her local party. An MP of great moral fibre, she considered that 'we have a duty to the next generation. Denial is not an option. Prevarication is not an option. The time for action is now. Enough is really enough'.[228]

After she made a request to Corbyn's office to explain why he posted a comment opposing the removal of an antisemitic mural, showing Jewish bankers getting rich off the backs of the poor and her attendance at a rally showing solidarity with the Jewish community, she received a torrent of abuse. One person, who she was told was a member of the Labour Party, told her to kill herself. Messages included accusations that she had two masters, she was 'Tel Aviv's servant and 'a paid-up Israeli lobby operative' as well as being an MP. They called her 'Judas', a 'venal piece of detritus', 'an absolute parasite'. People told her to resign and made physical threats and one person said 'Momentum[229] will be watching you Luciana'. Berger stood her ground. 'I've never shied away from speaking out about the antisemitic abuse I've been subjected to. I'm able to do so because I have a voice as an MP'. She was flanked by security when she attended the Labour Party conference in 2018 due to the death threats she had received.[230]

John Mann, head of a parliamentary group on combating antisemitism said that she did not get support from senior political colleagues and that was outrageous. Although Ed Miliband had said the abuse was 'utterly appalling', the condemnation had not gone far enough or come soon enough. 'It was a moral failure, a moral and ethical failure of profound implications. There was a fear of tackling antisemistism'.[231] The Labour leadership failed to make any contact with Berger after Cressida Dick, the Metropolitan Police commissioner, confirmed the start of a criminal probe into the threats against Berger that appeared in a dossier of abuse from Labour members. The dossier was compiled by concerned Labour activists with 45 cases of antisemitism by Labour members. This conduct left Berger dismayed. General Secretary Jennie Formby did not make her aware of any specific threats against her.[232] The threats were very real and Berger worried for the safety of her family, friends, her team at work and herself.[233]

She left the Labour Party in February 2019 over antisemitism as she felt that she could not remain in a Party that 'betrays the very values – of equality and anti-racism – that led me to join it in the first place'. Sixteen days after she resigned she gave birth to her second child Zion. Throughout her pregnancy she had been the target for antisemitic abuse as well as rape and death threats on social media, many of them from Labour supporters. The MP for Liverpool Wavertree since 2010 she had increased her majority by 79 percent at the 2017 general election. However, in February she had been threatened with deselection after two motions of no confidence were submitted by local Labour Party members over her constant criticism of the leadership. Her constituency had been taken over by the hard left Momentum group. The hard left coup had links with a Trotskyite organisation run by notorious anti-Zionist Gerry Dowling. They gained nine out of ten local party positions.[234] Berger recalls that 'the last local constituency meeting that I attended was so awful, so toxic, there was no humanity in the room. I went into details of the threats that I had been subjected to – messages handed in to my office saying I was going to get stabbed and raped and have acid thrown on me. I was categorically committed to Labour. I worked seven days a week, true to the values that led me into politics but because I would not commit to Corbyn. I was dead to them'. She realised that she could no longer be a member of the Party.

She subsequently joined the Independent Group for Change (Change UK), a new party that was launched in April 2019. An anti-Brexit Party that supported a People's Vote, to give the public a final say over Brexit and to remain in the UK, did not gain any seats in the European elections in May 2019 and subsequently disbanded. Just as Change UK bombed, the Liberal Democrats, to the surprise of everyone picked up hundreds of seats in the local council elections. It felt clear to Berger that many remainders wanted to give their support to an existing party that was committed to staying in the EU and she joined the Liberal Democrats in September 2019. She felt it was 'coming home' and she stood as a Liberal Democrat candidate for the Finchley and Golders Green constituency in the December 2019 election.[235]

Although her time in the Labour Party was overshadowed by the issue of antisemitism, Berger did make contributions to the Party. She was concerned about mental health issues. Although she stood down as Shadow Minister for Mental Health in 2016 she remained a member of the health select committee and urged the government to tackle mental health issues and flagged up the problem of older men who did not acknowledge depression because of the stigma attached.[236] She also campaigned to secure ring fencing for mental health budgets claiming funding promises made nationally were not reaching frontline services.[237] When canvassing in her constituency one witnesses commented on her ability to connect and listen to the concerns of voters on her patch. Staff at a children's centre in one of the most economically deprived wards in Britain praised her campaign to stop government cuts further impacting them.[238] She worked energetically on local health issues and initiatives as well as campaigns to support local businesses.[239] She also consistently pushed for progressive social policy, gave long term support for gay rights, was a frequent supporter of the EU and consistently voted against the bedroom tax and for a more robust support system for people on benefits. She voted for higher taxes on banks and their staffs' bonuses and supported the mansion tax throughout.[240]

She identified and gave support to Jewish community endeavours. She joined the Board of Deputies, British Jewry's main representative body, in 2012. She felt she had a sense of responsibility to lead the way for more women to enter leadership positions in politics, communal life and business. 'We have an issue that we don't have enough women in positions of leadership. I'm here because other people encouraged me to put myself forward and who have been very supportive. There's no reason that other women cannot do the same thing. Anything I can do to encourage other women I will'. She helped launch a Board of Deputies project that would encourage successful women in the community to join the Board. She also took a leading role in the Jewish community's efforts on the IF global anti-hunger project which was discussed at the G8 conference in Northern Ireland in June 2013. She worked with World Jewish Relief to host a launch event in Parliament.[241] She was amongst parliamentarians that wrote to the Prime Minister urging the country to do more to provide restitution to Holocaust victims whose property was seized during the Second World War[242] and took part in community events that prepared food at Edgware Synagogue for a homeless shelter and packed books at St John's Wood Liberal Synagogue for a local refugee centre.[243] She announced her engagement to music producer Alastair Goldsmith in the *Jewish Chronicle*.

Berger, throughout her life, has been brave and proud. 'Since I was a teenager I have been standing up to antisemitism, racism and discrimination in all its forms. I did what I hope everyone else would do and confronted it. An attack on me is an attack on the values I hold dear and I believe the whole country holds dear'. She has always urged the Jewish community to stand up to the rising tide of extremist activity. 'We are strong as a community and we are strong for the country when we stand together. The Jewish Community Trust, a charity that protects British Jews from antisemitism and related threats, applauded Berger's courage in reporting antisemitic abuse and giving evidence in court.[244] Heroism is a rare word in politics but that word is appropriate for Berger.[245] Labour's Yvette Cooper who spoke in Parliament at the launch of the Sara conference, convened to address the antisemitic abuse of women, praised Berger's incredible strength by speaking out against antisemitic abuse on behalf of all Jewish women 'and in fact all women and all of us'.[246] She was a role model for young Jewish activists, especially women. They regarded Berger as their inspiration.[247]

Berger wept as her career as an MP came to an end in the December 2019 elections. The Liberal Democrats had parachuted her into the Finchley & Golders Green constituency where it was hoped her Jewish background would entice voters. However, she fell 6,000 votes short of the Conservative MP Mike Freer, pushing Labour to third.[248] Berger's strength and commitment to all that she does will no doubt serve her well in her new position as managing director of advocacy and public affairs at communications firm Edelman UK.

Sharing the same passion and commitment in the fight against antisemitism and racism is Berger's contemporary, Ruth Smeeth. Both Berger and Smeeth, who were recipients of death and rape threats, were applauded in the Commons following their speeches during a debate on antisemitism.[249] Though no longer in Parliament, Smeeth has chosen to remain in the Party with which she has identified for her entire political life.

12. Official Portrait of Ruth Smeeth, Baroness Anderson of Stoke-on-Trent (Chris McAndrew,via Wikimedia Commons)

Ruth Smeeth (1979 -)

Ruth Lauren Smeeth (nee Anderson) was a Labour Party Member of Parliament for Stoke-on-Trent North and Kidsgrove from 2015-19. Dedicating her life to the Party since she was a teenager, she comes from a strong political and trade union background. She counts as one of her heroines the American Jewish trade unionist Rose Schneiderman who coined the phrase 'bread and roses' in 1912, forever linking the Labour movement to the rose, demanding more for working class women than the bare necessities and subsistence living.[250]

Born in Edinburgh, Smeeth's mother was Jewish and from the East End of London and her father was a Scottish trade unionist. Her paternal grandfather was a steel worker and a miner. An only child, her father left when she was three and she had no further contact with him. 'My mum is my heroine'. Her maternal family arrived in England from Russia in the 1890s. Her grandfather set up a Jewish trade union branch for carpentry. 'My grandmother was literate and wrote complaint letters for all the old dears on the council estate. It was a version of councillor surgeries. Her favourite story was when Sainsbury's changed the cap colour of semi-skimmed milk and the people were angry. Her grandmother coordinated a joint letter to say that they had bought the wrong milk and it had cost them a fortune'.[251]

Smeeth grew up in Bristol where her mother worked as the deputy general secretary of the Amicus trade union. She had a strong Jewish identity from an early age as she celebrated her bat mitzvah[252] at the city's Progressive Synagogue and taught Hebrew classes there.[253] She attended a local comprehensive school and earnt her pocket money delivering leaflets from a young age for the Labour Party. This political affiliation was ingrained in her. 'It was in my family'. She used to have to submit to her mother an official pay claim for her pocket money from the age of eight and she included leafleting as one of her chores.[254] She was the first person in her family to go to university and acknowledges that she owes every opportunity that she had to the Labour movement.[255]

Graduating with a degree in politics and international relations from the University of Birmingham in 2000, she worked as a policy and research officer for a trade union. Following a secondment at Westminster think tank The New Health Network, she worked in public relations at Sodexo (2004-5) which provides healthcare in the defence and education sectors. She then became director of public affairs and campaigns at the British Israel Communications and Research Centre (BICOM) that was set up in

2000 to counter alleged anti-Israeli messages to the British media and produces research and analysis about Israel and the Middle East to increase understanding of the area and was also employed by the Community Security Trust[256] and the Board of Deputies of British Jews.

Smeeth was selected as a Labour Party candidate for the Burton constituency in the 2010 election. An East Staffordshire Borough Council Labour member said she was the overwhelming choice and people were impressed by her energy, enthusiasm and knowledge. She was elected for Stoke-on-Trent North in 2015.[257] She considered it a great privilege to represent the people there as the area had huge challenges. The major industries that fuelled the city's rise, pits, pots and steel, had shrunk or disappeared altogether, with ceramics remaining the core industry. It is an area afflicted by poverty that sees children coming to school hungry and malnourished. She was intent on tackling child food poverty and secured her first adjournment debate on Holiday Hunger to raise awareness of the plight of children whose families could not afford to feed them during the school holidays and she worked hard to highlight the threats facing the UK ceramics industry. She commented that it was an incredible feeling, as a Jewish woman from a working-class immigrant family, that she was sitting on the same green benches her childhood heroes once sat on and to speak up for the causes that she believed in.[258]

Always concerned about those who were disadvantaged, she spoke in the Commons against big housing developers who were failing in their responsibilities, pointing out the housing crisis and the need for more homes. She brought to attention the quality of finish on new homes on estates in her constituency, built by Taylor Wimpey, where properties and roads were left unfinished and the playgrounds had safety issues. This was an occurrence throughout the country where in the previous year 51% of owners in new homes, which were built quickly and cheaply and whose faults went unchallenged, were experiencing similar concerns. She commented that again there was 'one rule for the rich and one for the rest of us'.[259]

Throughout her political career she has taken up the fight against racism. Since 2015 she has been a board member of Hope Not Hate that campaigns against racism and fascism and in 2016 she attended a commemoration march to mark the 80th anniversary of the Battle of Cable Street that prevented Oswald Mosley's Blackshirts from marching through the streets of London in October 1936. Smeeth spoke about her grandmother, a young child at the time, who had prepared rotten fruit to throw at the Fascists. Her great uncle had gone to the bars and pool halls collecting wood to be turned into weaponry and collecting money to bribe police officers.[260]

Smeeth has a long track record of antisemitism work. She was the anti-racist campaigns coordinator for the Community Security Trust, a charity that protects British Jews from antisemitism and related threats, who launched the 'Your Voice Not Theirs' campaign at the Board of Deputies of British Jews plenary meeting to prevent the British National Party (BNP) from winning seats in the May 2008 local and general elections. In London there were particular fears that they could achieve the 5% threshold to give it its first seat in the London Assembly and the campaign urged people to go to the polls to stop the BNP making gains. The Board worked with different ethnic minority campaigns such as Operation Black Vote, who work towards greater racial justice and equality, to try and increase voting levels in other communities. One BNP seat was won on the London Assembly but they did not make the large scale gains nationally or in the capital that some had feared.[261]

Once in Parliament Smeeth was extremely vocal in her concerns about antisemitism within the Party, as shown in her connection with the Chakrabarti Inquiry. The Chakrabarti Inquiry was an investigation into allegations of antisemitism and other forms of racism in the Labour Party. Chaired by barrister Shami Chakrabarti, the Inquiry was launched following comments made by two high profile Labour figures MP Naz Shah and former Mayor of London Ken Livingstone that some asserted were antisemitic in nature. The Inquiry presented its findings on 30 June 2016 stating that although antisemitism and other forms of racism were not endemic within the Labour Party there was an occasionally toxic atmosphere.[262]

Smeeth's verbal evidence was taken by Chakrabarti and this resulted in an invitation to the Inquiry launch. Smeeth recalls that the atmosphere was strange; at least half the room did not know why they were there, just that it was a 'Jeremy event'. Leaflets were distributed attacking the report as unfounded and unnecessary. Mark Wandsworth, a Momentum activist, began handing out 'press releases' calling for deselection of certain MPs, including Smeeth. She asked for a copy but he refused. Someone said it was a Jewish event, she was a Jewish MP and that he should give her a copy. He asked her name and she replied 'Darlin, my name's Ruth Smeeth'. He wrote it down and three journalists offered her their copies. She took the one closest to her from Kate McCann of the *Daily Telegraph*. McCann then tweeted that Labour MPs were getting abuse from Momentum. In a Q and A during the proceedings, Wandsworth was allowed to speak and he said that Smeeth was working hand in hand with the right-wing media to attack Corbyn and the audience started to shout at her. Corbyn said nothing and Smeeth walked out in distress, fleeing in tears. She waited for a call from Corbyn or his office but none came. She issued a statement saying Labour was no longer a safe space for British Jews. Corbyn's office manager called to say that he would be in touch that evening but there was no word until 10 days later and then only 45 minutes before giving evidence to the Home Affairs Select Committee. When Corbyn's office eventually arranged a meeting he failed to attend.[263]

As a critic of Corbyn's response to antisemitism that had engulfed Labour, Smeeth subsequently received 25,000 pieces of abuse, much of it racial, including 20,000 in the 12-hour period after the Chakrabarti Inquiry incident and the police strengthened her security after she received a death threat. Panic buttons and CCTV cameras were fitted at her home.[264] One person from the Far Left penned a 1,000-word essay on how he would kill her. She was repeatedly referred to as a 'Yid' in an abusive message which claimed that the gallows would be a fine and fitting place for her to swing from.[265] In April 2018 Smeeth was accompanied by around 40 Labour MPs and peers to a Labour hearing into Wandsworth's conduct. Wandsworth was expelled for bringing the Party into disrepute.

Smeeth commented that she had never seen antisemitism in Labour on this scale and had raised the issue with Corbyn 'privately' on numerous occasions from December 2015. Each time she received the same answer 'I am anti-racist therefore it is not a problem'. She added that 'it was not even acknowledged. He ignored it'.[266] In June 2016 she resigned 'with a heavy heart' her post as Parliamentary Private Secretary to the shadow Northern Ireland and Scotland teams, alongside others, in protest at Corbyn's leadership. She supported Owen Smith in the failed attempt to replace him in the 2016 Labour Party leadership election.[267] In 2019 there was an expose by the *Sunday Times* into Labour's failure to properly process complaints against hundreds of activists accused of antisemitism. The report was based on internal documents leaked to the newspaper in which Labour members posted online abusive comments. Smeeth sent a WhatsApp message to Corbyn following publication of the report but he did not respond. Within the report one of the offensive emails was about Smeeth and she said she would have thought that just from a duty of care someone would have contacted her.[268] Smeeth considers that she was the subject of racial abuse. Since she had not spoken on Middle Eastern matters, her crime was not 'Zionism' it was being Jewish. 'My biggest issue is that he knows it's happening'. She concluded that Labour 'was no longer a safe space for

British Jews'.[269]

Despite the negative experiences that she had encountered, Smeeth still felt her place was in the Labour Party. 'The last few years have been quite tough to be Jewish and be involved in the Labour Party. But we are members of this Party because of the values that we share and those are Jewish values. The idea that we hand over and walk away from our Party and the values we believe in, that would be nonsense. We stay and fight and make sure the Labour Party represents us'.[270] Always true to her beliefs, she was of the opinion that it did not matter what people thought of you. 'Just be confident and believe in what you are doing. I'm still fighting. No one is going to tell me to be quiet'.[271] In 2019 she seconded a Parliamentary Labour Party motion questioning the Party's general secretary Jennie Formby in regard to methods that she had used to intervene and protect members accused of antisemitism that were due to go before a disciplinary panel. The motion questioned how many times Formby had used delegated powers to take no further action. After the meeting Smeeth said 'this is not over yet. No one is going to force me out of the Party to stop me carrying on this fight'.[272] Speaking at the exit poll of the December 2019 election, she blamed Corbyn for the disastrous result for the Labour Party and how he should have left many months previously. 'His actions on antisemitism have made us a racist party'.[273] She lost her seat in the election to Conservative Jonathan Gullis.

Smeeth, an exuberant and lively character, never hid her Jewish origins. In April 2019 she was elected Parliamentary Chair of the Jewish Labour Movement. She wore a gold Star of David under the neckline of her dress but shied away from talking about Israel or Palestine. She points out clearly that the abuse she received was not about anything she said in regard to Middle East politics. 'I don't participate'. She considers herself culturally Jewish and was married to an Irish Catholic. 'I don't want to be known as "the Jewish MP". I am an MP who happens to be Jewish. One of the things that makes me most angry about this whole thing is that I've ended up as the Jewish MP. Worse: a victim and a target. I should be the MP for Stoke-on-Trent North, a hardworking, lifelong member of the Labour Party'. She described herself as 'a Labour, socialist, Jewish, woman' in that order. She then corrected herself: 'Actually: British first: British, Labour, socialist, Jewish, woman'.[274]

Smeeth is currently chief executive of Index on Censorship, an organisation campaigning for freedom of expression and which produces a quarterly magazine of the same name. A previous chief executive was Ursula Owen, also of Jewish origin. The organisation was founded in 1972 and in its first decades provided lifelines to dissidents as they endured harassment in Soviet regimes. Smeeth commented that she was excited to join the organisation at a time when its work to promote free speech was more important than ever. She explained that as governments and citizens seek to navigate complex and intimidating global issues, from Covid-19 to systemic racism, it was easy to see how easily one's fundamental right to freedom of expression was threatened. 'From the arrests of journalists covering Black Lives Matter protests in America to the silencing of medics in China who sought to inform the world about the effects of Covid-19, it's clear that the fight to enshrine and protect the right to free speech across the world has not yet been won'. Trevor Phillips, chair of the organisation, praised not only her expertise but her courage and that her independence of mind and non-partisan approach to freedom of expression was what was needed at a time when voices from all backgrounds and minorities needed to be heard. She was praised as a campaigner against fascism and racism, unwavering in her principles. 'Freedom of expression needs tough defenders and in Ruth we have one'.[275]

Since November 2022 she has been a member of the House of Lords. She was nominated by Labour leader Sir Keith Starmer and has the title Baroness Anderson of Stoke-on-Trent. Smeeth describes taking her seat as a surreal experience and thought about how, as a working-class Jewish woman whose great grandparents had fled the pogroms, now be a Baroness. She thought of her Nana and Papa, a cook and a kosher butcher who had settled in the East End, throughout that special day. She doubted whether they had ever visited the Houses of Parliament or imagined that their only great-granddaughter would one day become an MP and then a Baroness. 'So although I suffered not a little imposter syndrome, it was absolutely dwarfed by the utter pride I felt at joining Parliament's second chamber; proud that Kier nominated me, proud to serve him, my party and our country on the red benches. Immigrant families like mine want to give back to a country that gave them refuge'. [276]

Conclusion

Though not united by background, political convictions, or when, how and why they entered politics, the seven women featured in this chapter are connected by gender and Jewishness. As women, they have fought for their place in a male-dominated arena and in one way or another, their Jewish heritage has played a major role in the course of their political careers. While most of these women identify as cultural or non-practising Jews, despite many having been raised in orthodox or observant families, all but

Edwina Currie embraced their Jewish identity as politicians and they experienced varying levels of antisemitism both before and during their political lives. For the cohort of Labour MPs—Margaret Hodge, Louise Ellman, Luciana Berger and Ruth Smeeth—who were politically active during the years Jeremy Corbyn led the party, the fight against antisemitism came to define their political careers.

The backgrounds of these female politicians ranged from abject poverty to enormous wealth, from immigrant to well-established families, and they hailed from London's East End to the northern industrial cities, but they shared in common a desire for the best possible education and a passion for effecting change in their communities and beyond. For Shirley Porter and Margaret Hodge, who came from wealth, attending private boarding school was a given, but Bertha Sokoloff, Edwina Currie and Louise Ellman, who came from working class roots secured their high school educations by earning scholarships and middle-class Luciana Berger's family had to work long hours in order to afford a private school for her. Perhaps not surprisingly, the two women born in the interwar period did not go on to university, but all those born after the Second World War did obtain university degrees, though Ruth Smeeth, who like Bertha Sokoloff was raised by a single mother, was the first person in her family to do so.

Their family backgrounds, educational experiences and issues in their communities were formative to their political activism and the course of their careers. At school, Shirley Porter and Edwina Currie were denied head girl positions because of antisemitism and Bertha Sokoloff and Louise Ellman felt the sting of class prejudice and the stigma of being the recipients of state aid and scholarships, which ignited in Ellman a lifelong hatred of racism and inequality. Even Shirley Porter was subjected to snobbery at her exclusive school because her father was 'a shopkeeper'. Bertha Sokoloff, surrounded by poverty and want, became a Communist and was activated by housing conditions in London's East End to stand for her borough council. Porter, though coming from a diametrically opposed socio-economic background and political perspective, was also galvanised to become politically involved in her city's government over her anger at the trash and filth in her upscale London neighbourhood, though unlike the others, she came to politics relatively late in life, after many years of voluntary and charity work. Likewise, Margaret Hodge, rejecting her privileged background, was influenced by the radical left politics of Islington where she moved as a young wife and mother and also began her political career by rising through the ranks of the local council. Luciana Berger became politically active at university while for Ruth Smeeth, affiliation with the Labour Party came from her mother, who worked for a trade union. Though most of the working-class women were attracted to left wing causes as a result of their backgrounds, Edwina Currie took a different turn and joined the Conservative Party while at Oxford, eager to shed her working class roots and orthodox Jewish heritage.

In the male dominated world of politics, many of these talented, ambitious and determined women were subjected to overt and subtle misogyny, often entwined with antisemitism, during their careers. The very qualities that enabled them to rise through the ranks of local and national politics were often framed negatively, especially in Parliament. Because they were women, both Shirley Porter and Margaret Hodge were excluded from their families' successful business empires, which contributed to their turning to politics as an outlet for their energies and convictions. They gained reputations for toughness and outspokenness, though these qualities were not always appraised positively. Hodge, whose fearsome reputation as a local councillor earned her the nickname 'commissar', was characterised as arrogant and ruthlessly ambitious as a Labour MP, and despite her obvious political talents, her forthrightness denied her a cabinet post. Party was no bar to this kind of misogyny, and Edwina Currie, whose outspokenness was often derided, felt that the prejudice she encountered from her Tory colleagues was due far more to her gender than her religion. More insidious was the online abuse received by women MPs including Luciana Berger that prompted a letter to Jeremy Corbyn condemning the culture of harassment by his supporters that they believed was both encouraged and condoned.

Whether or not they identified themselves with Jewish causes, and despite the fact that most were non-practising, the political lives of all seven of these women were defined in some way by their Jewish heritage and identity. For Bertha Sokoloff, who grew up in a largely closed Jewish East End environment, her Jewish identity posed no challenges and was secondary to her radical politics and the fight for better conditions for the local population, the majority of whom were Jewish like her. In contrast, Shirley Porter, who embraced a strong Jewish identity, dealt with antisemitism her entire life, enduring boarding school snubs, fighting golf club anti-Jewish policies and subjected to 'posh antisemitism' in the Conservative Party after the 'homes for votes' scandal ended her political career. Unlike Porter, Edwina Currie actively downplayed and minimised her Jewish identity in her parliamentary career and personal life, marrying a non-Jew and reclaiming her Jewish roots as a novelist and broadcaster only after her marriage and political career were over.

For the cohort of women who entered Parliament in the 1990s and 2000s, all as members of the Labour Party, antisemitism and racism were forces that proved to be the defining factor in their political careers. Margaret Hodge, who married twice to non-Jews and did not have a strong Jewish identity or dedication to Israel or Jewish causes when she entered Parliament, credits her own party for making her Jewishness central to her politics after she was compelled to take a stand against Labour's and Jeremy Corbyn's antisemitism. Suffering more antisemitism from her own party than she had from her fight with the BNP awoke in her a strong sense of her Jewish heritage and family's Holocaust history, making her feel 'Jewish to the core.' In contrast, her contemporary Louise Ellman embraced her longstanding Zionism and dedication to Jewish causes as an MP and faced such relentless antisemitic abuse and bullying from her own party under Jeremy Corbyn, including questions about her loyalty to Britain, that she resigned in protest. Ellman's younger colleagues, Luciana Berger and Ruth Smeeth, who despite avoiding association with Middle East political issues when they entered Parliament, were nevertheless subjected to similar abuse from their Labour colleagues, exacerbated by viciously antisemitic social media campaigns against them, in response to which their party offered no support. Both had entered Parliament as rising stars, but antisemitism drove them out of politics in 2019 – Berger, by resignation, and Smeeth by electoral defeat.

The seven Jewish women politicians featured in this chapter span almost a century of political activism in local and national arenas and represent a range of ideologies from communism to right wing conservatism. In the course of their careers, they achieved much for their communities and constituents, from improvements in housing, to public works and social policies. Some of their work was marred by controversies, including Shirley Porter's 'homes for votes' corruption charge, Edwina Currie's egg and salmonella debacle, and Margaret Hodge's child abuse scandal, though they were not career ending for the latter two. They proved to be effective, dedicated politicians, even when fighting the headwinds of misogyny and antisemitism, while being open about their Jewish identity in their careers as councillors and MPs.

4

Media

From the rise of the mass circulation press in the nineteenth century to the advent of radio and television broadcasting in the twentieth century, women have had to fight for representation in British media. Men have dominated in both print and broadcast journalism and throughout the twentieth century, women who managed to secure positions in media were often relegated to reporting on 'softer' subjects and the traditionally female realms of home and fashion. It was not until the late 1960s that women began to fill editorial and production roles and to appear as newsreaders and political commentators. Throughout this period, Jewish women journalists have been trailblazers in expanding the representation of women in newspapers, radio and television.

British journalism underwent a dramatic series of changes during the nineteenth century that led to the creation of a mass circulation press. The shift from a traditional form of journalism with a limited circulation to a daily and Sunday press encompassing millions of readers is one of the significant events of the century. It solidified the integration of newspapers into the social and cultural life of Britain.[1]

The abolition of the newspaper tax in 1855 began a period of unprecedented growth in the British newspaper industry. By 1900 titles had multiplied, readership had expanded and the industry was on the verge of a revolution from which would emerge the mass market newspaper industry of today. A growing appetite for newspapers among an increasing literate public and the growing ambitions of a new generation of press barons was to propel British newspapers into an era of unprecedented wealth and influence. Leading this revolution was the *Daily Mail* (1896), the first British newspaper to achieve sales of one million, followed by the *Daily Express* (1900) and *Daily Mirror* (1903), which really established the importance of photojournalism in the British press. The heart of this revolution was London's Fleet Street.[2]

Fleet Street has always been seen as the domain of men, whether they be newspaper magnates, editors, publishers, journalists, photographers or newsboys. Despite this, there have been independent strong minded women who achieved much in this 'man's world', paving the way for future generations of women in Fleet Street.[3]

The few women who managed to have a career in journalism often provoked antagonism and their assertiveness was seen as a threat. They were often restricted to the so-called 'women's sphere', reporting on the latest frocks and society gossip. Politics were considered out of bounds for them and they were not welcome in the press gallery of the House of Commons.[4]

It continued to be an uphill struggle for women journalists in the twentieth century. Women employed by newspapers worked mainly in secretarial roles. Those who did make it into the editorial departments were usually expected to cover domestic issues, celebrity gossip and fashion. The press gallery at the House of Commons remained closed to women and they were barred from all men's clubs.[5]

When the first female sub editor was employed at the *Daily Mail*'s Manchester office in 1968, one veteran complained that a woman's presence would spoil the culture of the newsroom because they would not be able to swear. A newspaper office was four-fifths men. Meanwhile, newspaper editors realised they had to create women friendly features in order to boost readership numbers.[6]

Julie Welch recalls the late 1960s and early 1970s when young women thought that was the best time in history to be their age with the advent of the pill, their own magazines and exciting clothes. 'We might have believed that the world was at our feet at last. But in Fleet Street women were a separate species, pigeonholed as agony aunts, bitchy columnists or experts on childcare and domestic life. Half the human race and its thoughts and insights were cordoned off in an area called The Women's Pages. Anything 'serious' was written by men: politics, business, finance, sports news. Because this 'women's sphere' was not considered important, neither were the vast majority of women journalists. Any female who did manage to break the mould had to battle with the popular assumption that she had not got her job through hard work and talent'.[7]

The situation was not dissimilar in radio and television. In 1922 the BBC transmitted its first radio programme marking the beginning of official state broadcasting and a new era for listeners at home. John Reith became the first director general and under his influence the BBC set out its mission to 'inform, educate and entertain'. Reith's vision of the public service broadcaster was entirely masculine in its emphasis. Women were not permitted to read the news as it was judged that their voices did not have the necessary authority or resonance. This view persisted until the late

1960s.[8]

On 30 September 1929, a handful of amateur wireless enthusiasts were treated to their very first experience of television. Watching on mainly home built sets they viewed and listened to speeches; the first actual broadcast of television to a public watching in their own homes. Regular television broadcasts started in 1936.The world would never be the same again.

If it was not easy for women to break down the barriers in Fleet Street, it was also not always plain sailing for women in broadcasting. It took a long time for women to be regarded as suitable for all types of television news presenting, a hangover from the patriarchal attitudes which had spread from radio into television. It was only in 1975 that Angela Rippon became the first permanent newsreader on the BBC. The slow pace of change to a position in which women were considered acceptable in news and current affairs was partly due to a general male domination of public affairs.[9]

The women highlighted in this chapter managed to overcome these strongly ingrained patriarchal, misogynist attitudes to succeed and because of the power of this sexism, their achievements are all the more remarkable. As ever, Jewish women in Britain were at the forefront of breaking down barriers, if often at great personal cost.

Rachel Beer (Sassoon) was editor of the *Observer* and *Sunday Times* in the 1890s, the first and only woman to edit two national newspapers. In the late nineteenth century, at a time when women were denied the vote and were not given equal access to education, it was exceptional that Beer held such a position. When one considers that many of her women contemporaries hardly had access to a newspaper, her accomplishments are all the more remarkable. Beer adamantly refused to limit herself to 'feminine' topics. She fearlessly raised her voice on foreign and domestic matters throughout her time at both newspapers.[10]

Beer had incredible wealth and connections that enabled her to make her mark. For Olga Franklin, who came from a working class family with financial difficulties, it was a tough struggle to even become a reporter in the 1940s. She eventually became one of the *Daily Mail's* best-known columnists but as a woman was unable to secure an editorial position that was reserved for men at that time. Eve Pollard was more fortunate as by the 1980s attitudes were starting to change and she became the second newspaper editor in Britain in modern times.

Despite the same prejudices existing for women in radio and television, Esther Rantzen became a trailblazer for women in broadcasting. After completing her Oxford University education she started her career in the

1960s and rose from a clerical position within the BBC to launch her programme *That's Life!* in the 1970s. It attracted millions of viewers and ran for over 20 years. Yet sexism within the industry was rife. Nicola Shindler who produced the 2021 BBC series *Ridley Road*[11] remarks that horrible sexism still existed in the industry in the 1990s and when she arrived at the BBC the women were script editors and the men producers.[12] Nonetheless Kay Mellor fought her way through and succeeded as a popular television writer in the 1980s, spurred on by tough life experiences that gave her the determination to fight her way through.

The great contribution that Jewish women have made to broadcasting has culminated in Emily Maitlis becoming the lead anchor of BBC's current affairs programme *Newsnight* and Emma Barnett the youngest presenter of BBC Radio 4's *Woman's Hour* which since it was first aired in 1946 has charted a social and political revolution in women's lives, covering everything from backstreet abortion and the introduction of the pill to the fight for the Equal Pay Act. Like all their gender, the women featured in this chapter had a fight to achieve prominence in the media, even the trailblazer Rachel Beer, whose family and connections enabled her to break into that male-dominated realm a generation earlier than the rest.

Rachel Beer (Sassoon) (1858-1927)

Rachel Beer was born in Bombay (Mumbai) into the immensely wealthy Iraqi Sassoon dynasty. The family fortune came from opium and cotton and her father David was known as the 'Rothschild of the East'. He was sent to England in 1858 to develop the cotton side of the business that became the main supplier of cotton to the British spinning mills and the British market. The family had a country estate in Walton-on-Thames and a mansion in Regent's Park London. Her mother Fahra (Flora) Reuben, also from Mumbai, was her husband's cousin and the daughter of a scholarly merchant from Baghdad. One of Rachel's nephews was the war poet Siegfried Sassoon.[13]

She was a precociously intelligent, highly verbal child and a gifted pianist. Her father died when she was nine, leaving her a fund of £10,000 'for her sole and separate and unalienable use and benefit from the control of or engagement of any husband'. She grew up to be a strong independent woman, creative and erudite, who refused to settle for the conventional life of a wealthy Victorian wife. She escaped from the confines of home by first working as a nurse (and as a journalist she campaigned on issues of public health including the status of nurses).[14]

She resisted her orthodox Jewish family's attempts to arrange a marriage.[15] She defied them by marrying Frederick Beer whose family came from Frankfurt. His father Julius came to London and made his fortune through investing in the emerging technologies of the time – railroads and submarine telegraphy. Julius, who converted to Anglicanism, bought the *Observer* in 1870. When Rachel and Frederick married they united the wealth and histories of their grand families.[16] They were a very modern couple who espoused equality in the relationship. They were well suited. Both were born with proverbial silver spoons in their mouths. They were almost thirty, free from paternal scrutiny. Regarding herself as a pioneer woman, she felt as if she was on an equal footing with Frederick and expected to have a free hand in the relationship, to be the queen of her own world. They had a passionate interest in both the visual and performing arts and were very much in love.[17]

The day before the wedding Rachel was baptised an Anglican and her family never forgave her for marrying a non-Jew and ostracised her.[18]

Beer was both a rich Victorian society lady and a social progressive. She was a significant figure in Victorian London, using the two newspapers to promote her progressive views and entertaining the Prince of Wales and the elite at her Mayfair home. Although she was able to acquire a position of such prominence due to the wealth of her husband's family, her biographers Eilat Negev and Yehuda Karen point out that this should not take away from her achievements. She had wanted to do something with her life. She married into a capitalist family but her views were practically socialist. She wanted equality for women, she was an advocate of trade unionism, suffrage for women and a universal state pension.[19]

With no training she began contributing articles and in 1891 became editor of the *Observer*, then two years later of the *Sunday Times*. As editor she wrote strident editorials on foreign policy and women's rights and in 1898 her scoop was the exclusive story of the forgery behind the Dreyfus Affair.[20] She wrested a paid confession from French anti-Semite Charles Esterhazy of having, under order, forged a document to frame the Jewish captain Alfred Dreyfus of being a traitor and a spy.

Her involvement with the Dreyfus affair required her to stand firm on many of the issues she cared about passionately, including justice, an end to persecution and the fair treatment of minorities.[21] This was a brave stand as many people considered that Dreyfus was guilty.

Unfortunately, she was also a victim of her own time. Her career which blossomed in the late 1890s came to a halt in 1902 when Frederick died of tuberculosis at the age of forty three. Although she soldiered on as an editor for several months after his death, her grief made it difficult for her to continue. Such was her desolation that her relatives were worried that she would fall victim to a fortune hunter or give her money to the many charities that she patronised. Scared that they would lose their inheritance (she had no children) they called in a doctor to declare her 'of unsound mind' which meant she no longer had free access to her own funds and was not allowed to write her own will. She lived out her declining years in Tunbridge Wells, Kent and when she died in 1927 was buried locally in unconsecrated ground.[22] A fortune beyond most people's wildest dreams had empowered her to fulfil her dreams but that same wealth was instrumental in her incarceration at the hands of the patriarchy at a time when women were chattels.

Beer was certainly ahead of her time. It was not until 1987 (eight years after Britain's first female prime minister) when Wendy Henry took over the *News of the World* that Fleet Street got its first woman editor since Beer. There had been a long bias against women journalists: Arnold Bennett wrote in *Journalism for Women: A Practical Guide* (1898): 'Of all the dwellers in Fleet Street, there are, not two sexes, but two species — journalists and women-journalists – and the one is as far removed from the other as a dog from a cat. Female journalists were unreliable, they ignored deadlines and their faults included inattention to detail and a slapdash approach to spelling and grammar'.[23]

Rachel Beer defied these stereotypes and for a decade competed on equal footing with her male counterparts in the press. But it was to be at least a generation before another Jewish female journalist, Olga Franklin, made a name for herself in this male-dominated world. Franklin, who had none of the inherent advantages that made Rachel Beer's career possible, was a fearless reporter for the *Daily Sketch* and *Daily Mail* and throughout the 1960s was one of the *Daily Mail's* most feted columnists. A determined woman in a media sphere ruled by men, she scooped her rivals time and again.[24]

Olga Rose Franklin (1911-1985)

Olga Rose Franklin was born in Birmingham and came from a totally different background than Beer. Her grandfather. Lewos Davis (Izvozchik) arrived in Birmingham from Minsk in the 1870s and worked as a glazier; her grandmother, Betsy, took in washing and mending. Olga's father Izzy, one of nine children, had an erratic business career and her mother,

Rebecca Bernstein, was a nurse. Olga went to the prestigious King Edward's School in Birmingham but had to leave school after one of her father's business fiascos in order to earn money. She took a language course and worked as a German interpreter for a number of manufacturing firms in the Birmingham area.

In 1934 she married Norbert Franklin who originated from Poland but the marriage was tragically short as he died in 1937 from lung cancer. Broken hearted, Olga attempted suicide but fortunately had, unlike Rachel Beer, family support and recovered. In 1938 she decided to try her luck in London and found a job with a German firm representing British armament manufacturers that sold heavy guns and tank materials to the Polish government. She was one of the last people out of Warsaw in September 1939 before the war began.[25]

Olga had always wanted to be a journalist. In 1940 she landed a position as a typist with Reuters and then got her first break at the *Newcastle Evening Chronicle* where one of her first assignments was to track down a prince called Philip, a naval officer who was staying on Tyneside while his warship was commissioned. She was the first British journalist to meet the future Duke of Edinburgh. Olga arrived in Fleet Street in 1945 when she joined the *Daily Sketch* as part of the reporting team and was sent on the 1945 Election trail where she trailed after Winston Churchill on his long car drives.[26] There were months that she sat around with nothing to do as 'no one was interested in an Olga'. It was only when they wanted a piece on Warsaw and Olga said she had been there that she was given a chance to write a story.[27] In 1956 Olga became a columnist with the *Daily Mail* where she remained until 1970.

She was the first Russian speaking reporter in the British press and in the 1940s and 1950s travelled frequently to Russia and shadowed Khrushchev across the USA when he went to meet President Eisenhower at Camp David in 1959. She was the newspaper's first stunt girl and she took on roles as an air hostess, bus conductor, washing machine attendant and saxophone player. This is an indication that she had to try much harder than other journalists to make her mark. She also pursued Princess Grace of Monaco, visited ex-King Zig of Albania, dug a hole in the road on the M1 and tried out a 'wonder drug' at an old people's clinic in Rumania.[28] She took it all in her stride and it was commented 'not the least of Miss Franklin's accomplishments is the ability to laugh at herself'.[29]

After she left the Daily Mail she wrote for the *Daily Telegraph*, the *Guardian*, the *Daily Mirror* and the *Spectator* and was a regular on *Woman's Hour*, *World at One* and the BBC World Service. Her Russian background helped her career. She was often mistaken for a Russian and this could be the reason her colleague Bernard Levin called her 'the grand duchess'.[30] As a fluent Russian speaker she was a particular expert on Soviet matters throughout the Cold War. She connected more with her Russian background than her Jewish one. Her family had belonged to the Birmingham Jewish community where, after her father lost all his money and they went from living in a big house to a small cottage, they were known as 'the poor Davises' as they could no longer afford to pay for a seat in the synagogue.[31] Her mother was particular about her going to Hebrew school three times a week although they ate bacon and eggs in the home. She commented that 'our father did not like to be reminded that we were Jews'.[32] He admired the English and wanted very much to pass as one of them.[33] Olga's marriage took place in Birmingham's Singers Row Synagogue but she did not take an active part in communal affairs although she occasionally addressed Jewish gatherings.[34]

Despite not connecting to her Judaism, she was marked out as different. She attributed this to her name Olga. 'Some people think names don't matter but I think they do. It marked me out from the others who all had nice English names'.[35] Colleagues also saw her as 'different'. She recalled that whenever someone arrived at the newsroom and could not speak English, whether it be an Arab, a Portuguese or Congolese, the editor would call out, 'Send Olga. Put Olga on it'. She put this down to her name. 'And because Englishmen still believed that all foreigners spoke the same funny language'.[36]

Although quick to call on Olga for such situations and the fact that she had proved herself as an intrepid reporter, she did not achieve a senior editorial position. 'The trouble with having arrived in Fleet Street there was no place to sit down. There were no editorial chairs in journalism for women, except on a few magazines, which was a different kind of business altogether. Men could become editors, assistant editors or production editors. These were the sitting down Jo's. Me — I was still on the road'.[37]

Although Olga Franklin did not have the material and familial advantages of Rachel Beer, her skill with languages and her willingness to take on a variety of assignments enabled her to break into Fleet Street journalism and forge a long career as a reporter. Despite her success, the top editorial positions eluded her and she was always made to feel like an outsider. It was only in the 1960s, when newspapers wanted to increase their circulation figures and needed to attract a female audience through features that would particularly interest them, that the situation for women journalists began to change. One of the women who was able to break through the barriers of the gentleman's club was the Jewish journalist Eve Pollard, who started at *Honey* magazine before becoming fashion editor of the *Daily Mirror* and editor of the *Sunday Mirror* and *Sunday Express*. She is considered to be among the First Ladies of Fleet Street with a career that has spanned glossy magazines, tabloid journalism, radio, television and novels.

Eve Pollard (1945 —)

Eve Pollard lived in Maida Vale, London with parents Izzo and Martha and younger twin brothers Peter and Ralph. Her mother had left Vienna in 1938 and her Hungarian father arrived with the Free French in 1940 and they met in London.[38] Pollard recalls that 'they were fantastically proud of being British. This country had saved their lives. But they were lost. All my grandparents died in the concentration camps. I know nothing about them; had never seen pictures. My parents could never talk about it. It was taboo'. She grew up with very few family members. Her mother's brother was sent to Dachau and her grandparents secured his release by paying an enormous fine. He managed to get to Britain, where he married and had one daughter. She found it strange that the family was so small. She attended an all girls' Catholic school in south London where she felt different from the rest. When she went on school picnics, everyone had sandwiches with white bread and jam and she had brown bread and salami. She dumped the sandwiches at the earliest opportunity as she did not want to stand out from the others.[39]

Pollard appears to have had a somewhat complicated relationship with her father who was very Victorian in attitude. He was a difficult man who ran the household with an iron rod. 'You could tell by the way that he turned the key in the lock when he came in, what mood he was in. I was very bookish and scholarly and not the sort of daughter he wanted'. Pollard would spend her summer holidays in her father's factory where he invented various strange contraptions such as a tent that came out of the roof rack of a car. There were good and disastrous years. Her mother, who she refers to as 'absolutely fabulous', worked with her husband in the factory and was a real asset as she was 'lovely, charming and warm'.[40]

Her parents had no ambitions for her other than to marry and have children. Pollard considers that her whole career has been a result of putting two fingers up to her father as he did not want her to go to university. Her parents were strict and all boys had to be vetted before she went out with them. 'Like a lot of people who had been through the Holocaust experience

13. Eve Pollard OBE, Editor of Sunday Mirror newspapers attends industrial tribunal 3 June 1991 (Mirror Pix/Alamy Stock photo)

they were overprotective and worried. They didn't want anything else bad to happen to them'. [41] This was the case of many survivor parents who often showed a tendency to be over involved in their children's lives and the feeling that their children existed to replace what had been so traumatically lost.[42] Pollard used to get engaged as hobby and after a couple of failed engagements she met her husband Barry Winkleman, publisher of the *Times Atlas of World History*. They married in 1968 and had one daughter TV presenter Claudia Winkleman. Although they divorced in 1975, they always lived in the same post code and spent every Christmas together until their daughter was 34. Pollard married Sir Nicholas Lloyd, former editor of the *Daily Express*, in 1979 and they had a son Oliver.

Unlike Olga Franklin who was encouraged to work to supplement the family income, Pollard's father did not want her to have a career but fortunately she found one by chance as a result of her working at Simpsons department store, London. Whilst there she encountered girls who were working in fashion journalism and who came in to buy clothes for fashion shoots. She decided that this was what she wanted to do. Her career began as a tea girl, then fashion assistant at *Honey* magazine and she was promoted to fashion editor in 1967. *Honey* was a monthly magazine, launched in 1960, and a pioneer in its time as it recognised a new market for young people who up until then were 'seen and not heard'. In 1985, as editor in chief, she launched *Elle* magazine in the United States and then in 1987 became the second female editor in Britain in modern times when she edited the *Sunday Mirror* (1987-1991) and the *Sunday Express* (1991-1994). The first editor was Wendy Henry, who some months earlier became editor of the *News of the World*. Henry was also Jewish, a product of the St Anne's Jewish community,[43] and the daughter of a Manchester Jewish market trader. Henry had been a member of the International Communist League and was once arrested for attempting to throw a carton of milk at Edward Heath.[44] Her father said that although they were not a religious family, his daughter felt very Jewish and was proud of her heritage. Henry's daughter had a Jewish education as she attended the JFS School in London.[45]

Hadley Freeman considers that these first female editors tended to be of a certain type: namely bold, opinionated and with a good line in quotable lippiness.[46] This is no longer quite the case; the newer generations of editors tend to keep lower profiles, possibly reflecting women's greater confidence in high positions. If these early women editors tended towards the mouthy then that was simply because they occasionally needed to shout over the shocking sexist grumblings. There were men that did not like a woman boss. Pollard recalls that when she became editor one older male journalist went around all the pubs in Fleet Street saying he would not be able to deal with her. She asked him if he would prefer to be contacted by a memo to which he agreed. When she started to hand out trips to New York and Paris she could not be bothered to write memos and therefore the trips went to other journalists. It was then he decided that he could face talking to her.[47]

When Pollard became a newspaper editor she said she would 'pollute' Fleet Street with as many women as she could. She managed to muddy the waters, promoting women to positions of news editor and magazine editor.

She says that she never felt ambitious but 'I always felt that I had to have my own money. I watched my mother. I always knew that if she needed money she had to be charming to him, catch him in the right mood. I've never wanted to do that, be put in the position of supplicant'. The picture painted of Pollard on Fleet Street was that of a female colossus.[48] She was renowned for her thigh high minis and plummeting necklines that revealed her buxom physique. Yet her irrepressible confidence and brash, upfront personality raised her profile to legendary heights and was seen as a strength rather than a weakness.[49] Pollard was independent, strong minded and paved the way for future generations of women on Fleet Street. She had to be tough. When she became editor of *Sunday Mirror*, she signed a contract with no maternity leave and was back at work after six weeks. She says that when she first worked on Fleet Street women were such a rarity that the male reporters did not know what to make of her or anyone with a high flying position. 'You're not their mum, you're not their sister, you're not their wife – so they make you a sort of monster nanny figure'.[50]

Yet for her many readers, Pollard was someone whom they could confide in. She became Agony Aunt for the *Sunday Mirror* in 1997 and the strapline read 'Dear Eve – Eve Pollard the agony aunt you can trust'. She was another Jewish agony aunt in the British press, alongside Claire Rayner and Marjorie Proops. A familiar face on television, Pollard was known to millions of viewers beyond Fleet Street. For 23 years she covered Royal Ascot as the fashion commentator for the BBC and she often appeared in a similar role on other BBC programmes. She became a regular panellist on the popular ITV show *Through the Keyhole* with Sir David Frost, in which a celebrity's house is chosen and the panellists try to guess the homeowner and *Loose Women*, a television chat show comprised of women from the entertainment and journalism worlds. She also covered on television the royal weddings of Princess Anne and Captain Mark Phillips, Prince Charles and Lady Diana, Prince Andrew and the Duchess of York, Prince Edward and Sophie Wessex, Prince William and Kate Middleton and the birth of Prince George. A novelist, Pollard wrote *Jack's Widow* (2007), a fictionalised story about the post-White House life of Jackie Kennedy. She was also one of three co-authors, together with Joyce Hopkirk and Val Corbett, of *Splash* (1995) an expose of Fleet Street which deals with issues of loyalty, intrigue, betrayal and deception, *Best of Enemies* (1997), *Double Trouble* (1997) and *Unfinished Business* (1998).

In 2000 Pollard started the magazine *Aura* which was aimed for the older woman. A vast majority of glossy women magazines were aimed at women in their 20s and 30s. Older women in their 40s and 50s tended to be ignored or left with publications that suggested their only interests were looking after the home. *Aura* was aimed at women between the age of 35 and 50s that were referred to as the most provocative and vibrant generation. They were considered to be the best educated and financially secure and unlike many of their mothers before them they did not want to drop out of the world once they hit middle age. Pollard felt that many of the problems facing older women were simply ignored by most magazines and she was tired of women being encouraged to hide their education. As many people went to university there was no point in hiding this fact.[51]

Pollard was a campaigner, particularly in regard to women's issues. 'In my time I've campaigned for everything from having baby seats on supermarket trolleys to getting rid of the Dalkon Shield'.[52] In 1979 she joined in the Trade Union Congress demonstration against the anti-abortion Bill which sought to amend the 1967 Abortion Act by reducing the time limit for an abortion from 28 to 20 weeks. In her capacity as editor of a major newspaper she continually voiced her concern regarding women's issues and backed the 1980 campaign for the pressure group the Maternity Alliance for better provisions for mothers to be that included greater access and less wait time for ante-natal clinics. The year before 5,000 babies had died just before or soon after birth with another 5,000 surviving with major handicaps.[53]

In 1992 she founded Women in Journalism, a networking, campaigning and training organization providing guidance and support for women working in print, broadcast and online media at every stage of their careers. In 2003 she became the Vice Chairman of Wellbeing of Women, a charity dedicated to improving the health of women and babies in the UK. Her concern regarding improvement in women's health care was also a personal one as her mother died of ovarian cancer at the age of 55. In 2016 she was appointed the first Chair of Reporters Without Borders in the UK. Reporters Without Borders is a leading international non-profit non-governmental organization to promote free and independent journalism and to defend media workers. Pollard, whose appointment reflects her importance as a media person, explains that the main aims are to try and free journalists held in jails all over the world who are not being fairly treated and often without access to lawyers. There were already 13 offices around the world and London was seen as a beacon of light for a fair press. She hoped that with more publicity, further funds for lawyers would be generated and a greater level of support to deal with the safety of journalists.[54] She received an OBE for services to journalism and broadcasting in 2008.

Extremely vocal on campaigns for greater justice for women in all fields, she is somewhat more reticent in respect of her Judaism. 'It is through her children she maintains links, albeit tenuous ones, with her Judaism but it is a subject she does not like to discuss.'[55] This could be a result of her upbringing as a child of survivors where her family history was never discussed. Her father went back once to Budapest and Prague but her mother never returned to Vienna although Pollard was of the belief that in her heart she would have liked to have visited. The subject was only discussed once. Her mother said that as her home was looted after she left she could not bear the possibility of sitting in a café and seeing someone wearing her mother's necklace. She just would not know how to react. She came to Britain at the age of 17 as a domestic and this was a great change in fortune; she had never in her life made her own bed. After the war her personal maid Emma came from Vienna to Britain but the visit did not work out as Pollard's father did not like the closeness of the relationship. 'Emma had all the memories of my mother as a middle-class girl'. Any talk about the family and its history was forbidden. The effect on Pollard was that it made her more family orientated to her two children and grandchildren as she had such a lack of family. She was always a very hands-on mother and derives great joy from her grandchildren. 'When you become a grandparent you realise how much you lost for not having someone in that position.'[56]

Nevertheless, Pollard does not totally shy away from her background and although her campaigning is in other fields she is still willing to put her name to mainstream Jewish charities. She took part in a 1989 Jewish Blind Society 'community call' fundraising campaign[57] and a Jewish Care fundraising lunch in 1990. In 1993 she was presented with Jewish Care's Women of Distinction Award for ongoing achievements within the newspaper industry. The Women of Distinction Award began in 1985 and the first recipient was Dr Deborah Greenspan for her pioneering work on the AIDS virus. For Jewish Care the principle of recognising the achievements of a wide range of British Jewish women was of vital importance.[58] Pollard took part in the Jewish Care Annual Dinner 2001 and was a guest speaker at UJIA dinner in Liverpool 2004 and Leeds UJIA Women's Annual Appeal 2008 where she said that she greatly admired UJIA's work and praised its investment in northern Israel.[59] She addressed the 65th anniversary lunch of the League of Jewish Women where she lauded their diverse welfare work[60], the annual dinner for the Jewish Association for Mental Illness (JAMI) in 2011 and Jewish Care Dinner in Redbridge (2014). She was interested in interfaith dialogue and was a speaker at the first women's interfaith network. She encouraged each participant to befriend someone from another faith. 'We need to step out of our isolation'.[61]

In 2019 she was awarded the prestigious Journalists Laureate prize at the London Press Club Ball for being an inspirational editor and broadcaster and she called on journalists to help cure the 'poison' of antisemitism. 'Jeremy Corbyn's Labour Party – one I do not recognise as the once great party it was – has made antisemitism acceptable and enables it to grow. You are journalists, you hold truth to power. As one of you and as a direct child of the Holocaust and a proud first-generation Brit, I ask you to wield your pens and do everything you can to cure us of this poison.[62]

The award was a fitting tribute to a long and illustrious career. Ray Massey and Robert Johnson, joint chairmen of the London Press Club Ball, said Pollard had been a true trailblazer who has led by example and inspired generations of young journalists, both male and female. 'But she has been a particular force during her illustrious career in working tirelessly to promote women in our trade'. Eleanor Mills, chairman of Women in Journalism and editorial director at the *Sunday Times*, said Pollard was a Fleet Street legend. 'She has not only propelled herself to greatness but made sure she brought other women along the journey with her. Her career has been a beacon to many women within the industry, proof that you can be successful but remain a real person – the true meaning of having it all'.[63]

Eve Pollard may have 'had it all', but her success was hard won, as she battled male dominance her entire career – first in defying her father and later in confronting the barriers to women serving as editors on Fleet Street. And even though she rose to the top of her profession by dint of her own hard work and determination, her journalistic endeavours remained largely focused on women's issues and interests rather than politics, the economy and foreign policy, which remained in the men's domain.

It was also not always plain sailing for women in broadcasting. Like Olga Franklin and Eve Pollard who began their careers as support staff in print media, many women who found employment at the BBC after its formation in 1922 took on domestic roles within the workplace, oiling the wheels of the growing Cooperation, ensuring that the cleaning and tea making was done. The BBC had a number of openings for clerical workers, telephone operators, typists and secretaries. They wanted to be seen as a modern and forward-looking institution. However, in recruitment, mobility and pay, unspoken gender inequalities were clearly identifiable in the early BBC. Even if some individual women were successful, the 'old boys network', Oxbridge and the military enabled mediocre and uninspiring men to have dynamic careers whilst women's career progression was tentative and even when they put in the necessary hard work and long hours, they did not always achieve the most senior posts in the Corporation.[64]

Esther Rantzen, whose broadcasting career began as many did in a clerical role, did manage to rise to the top of her profession as a presenter and producer. Backed by a supportive family and strong sense of her Jewish heritage, she parlayed her Oxford degree and her early work in a Liberal Synagogue youth club into a career as one of the first and most renowned female broadcasters in the history of the BBC.

Esther Rantzen (1940 -)

Esther Rantzen was a trailblazer for female broadcasters. She started her career in the 1960s as a BBC clerk, rising through the ranks to become a presenter of the television series *That's Life!* which was launched in 1973 and ran for 21 years, regularly attracting 20 million viewers. It was an eclectic mix of consumer news and investigative pieces on serious subjects alongside talking dogs and indecently shaped vegetables. She was one of the first women to produce, as well as present, a television programme. 'I was aware that if I didn't do a job well, preferably better than a man would, I would make it harder for next generation of women. And I did know that women were not given this responsibility before and I also knew that a lot of the programmes that fascinated me, often about people's emotional lives, were not considered suitable for broadcast by gentlemen so I was making programmes about post-natal depression and stillbirth and things that affected people's real lives. I was not getting experts to tell me what it was like to lose a baby but was actually listening to people that had that experience. I was aware that I had to do it justice'.[65]

Rantzen was born in Berkhampstead, Hertfordshire in 1940 to Katherine Leverson and Henry Rantzen. She came from a privileged middle-class background and describes her childhood as a very happy one. She remembers her father used to come home at 6.30pm and her mother used to have his slippers and a glass of sherry ready for him and ask him how his day had been. 'I rapidly picked up that he had the interesting life'.[66] Her maternal grandparents, Louis and Emily Leverson, lived in large brick house in Hampstead with an entourage of staff. Her grandfather made a very comfortable living from importing the best cigar tobacco and her grandmother had a beautiful collection of precious jewels. Her mother Katherine and her sisters were brought up by nannies and under-nannies and sent to Cheltenham Ladies College and Roedean. Katherine was pretty with a wicked sense of humour. She was totally different to her husband

14. Dame Esther Rantzen DBE at Nightingale House, Jan 2011 (Brian Minkoff – London Pixels)

Harry who was an intellectual, a scientist with a passion for music. He became head of the BBC's pioneering Lines and Design Department that was responsible for developing television.[67]

Rantzen had great affiliation for her Jewish roots although she came from a non-religious family. 'We were and are a Jewish family'. Her grandparents were among the first Liberal Jews in Britain and were completely anglicised. The synagogue services were almost completely in English and Rantzen never learnt to read Hebrew. Her grandmother celebrated a traditional Victorian Christmas. In her parents' home there was bacon and ham and they only attended synagogue on the high holy days. Candles were never lit to bring in the Sabbath on a Friday night although Rantzen carried out this custom when she married. 'And yet being

Jewish made an enormous difference to my life.'[68] She had her bat mitzvah (Jewish coming of age ceremony) at 16, which was the norm in the Liberal synagogues in the 1950s and her three children also had bar/batmitzvahs and read Hebrew fluently. Her husband Desmond learnt Hebrew when he converted. It was his idea to undergo conversion inspired by a strong affection and respect for Judaism and the Jews that he had known.[69] After her husband had undergone heart surgery, they married again on their 21st wedding anniversary in the St Johns Wood Liberal Synagogue as they had previously married in a registry office. 'It was a spiritual commitment, a public gesture in front of my community of friends and family, in the centre of my Jewish faith'. When her husband lay dying in hospital, she and her family read from their prayer books and recited the Shema, 'the prayer which is the core of Judaism'.

Her connection to the Liberal synagogue goes back many years. In the 1960s she ran a youth club there called Phase 2 for people in their twenties and thirties. They invited a galaxy of guest speakers that included Barry Humphries and Marty Feldman. 'We had controversy with psychic researchers, fascists and communists and marriage brokers. Looking back, without realising it, I was creating the mix for a daily talk show'. She was also involved in the synagogue's club for the disabled, Out and About. She would go round and collect some of the members for meetings and was shocked by how much poverty and isolation could be created by disability. This early insight would contribute greatly to her future work.[70]

She talked about her Judaism when interviewed on *Desert Island Discs*. One of the pieces of music that she chose was the original soundtrack for the film *Shindler's List*. She considered that *Schindler's List* showed that there could be hope at the darkest time and the fact that one man could make a difference — Oskar Shindler, a German businessman who saved more than a thousand mostly Polish-Jewish refugees from the Holocaust by employing them in his factories during World War II. Rantzen considers herself fortunate that she interviewed Nicholas Winton who saved a generation of Czech Jewish children. 'When I hear this music I think of him, of hope and how much I owe my Jewish heritage. It is very important to be part of a minority because it teaches you so much about the importance of tolerance and diversity'.[71]

Her appreciation for her Jewish heritage goes hand in hand with her love for Britain. Rantzen was critical of actor Maureen Lipman's threat to leave the country because of the rise of antisemitism: 'I would never dream of living anywhere else. My identity, my loyalty and above all my gratitude, is to Britain. And I feel that accusing this law abiding, democratic country of antisemitism is to put it bluntly, unfair, insulting and even ungrateful'. She explained how her family had come to escape the pogroms and that her father's family had arrived from Poland with nothing and settled in Spitalfields nearly 200 years ago. 'Britain allowed the Rantzen family to arrive, stay, live and work in a country where they were able to worship, educate their children and plan for a future. I was born and brought up to believe in Britain and to be forever grateful to the British'. During the war her parents fostered a seven-year-old Jewish boy Charlie from Germany and she learnt early on about the atrocities that were happening in Germany. She never felt at a disadvantage for being Jewish. 'There is no conflict between my love for my country and an adherence to a religious heritage. They enrich each other'.[72]

Rantzen described her parents as 'terrific' who never thought that she or her sister should be educated differently from boys. Their aspirations were not typical of the time. Her mother had never had a job but she wanted her daughter to have a career.[73] Rantzen was educated at North London Collegiate School and studied English at Somerville College, Oxford. After training in secretarial skills, Rantzen was recruited by BBC Radio as a trainee studio manager. She began her television career as a clerk in the programme planning department, then obtained her first production job working as a researcher on the BBC1 late night satire programme BBC-3 (1965-66). She moved to the BBC2 documentary series *Man Alive* in the mid-1960s.

In 1973 she became the main presenter of *That's Life!* which became one of the most popular shows on British television. Rantzen was unaware of the challenges she would face. 'I had no idea of the peaks and troughs ahead of me. I had never planned my career strategically. How could I? It would have been absurd to contemplate a career as a television presenter when there were so few women on the screen and even more ridiculous to think of being a producer/presenter. There simply were not any'. *That's Life!* was a unique catalogue of life in Britain– the funny, the tragic, the wicked, the ridiculous. It was a celebration, week by week, of many different aspects of viewers' lives. Health issues, safety issues, what went on in prisons, psychiatric hospitals, local councils and schools. The con men, the altruists, the eccentrics, the 'jobsworth' officials, the sinners and saints. 'We took on the medical profession, the legal profession, the trade unions, even the BBC itself, on behalf of our viewers'.[74]

During that time it expanded the traditional role of the consumer programme from simply exposing faulty washing machines and dodgy salesmen to investigating life and death issues. This included a campaign for more organ donors, which featured Ben Hardwick, a two-year-old dying of liver disease whose only hope was a transplant, and the investigation of a boarding school, the headmaster of which was a paedophile who employed several paedophile teachers. To lighten some of the serious themes and issues, there were some humorous spots, such as reading of amusing misprints sent in by viewers and comic songs. *That's Life!* was influential in many different ways, not least in the introduction of the video link for child witnesses in court procedures. *Desert Island Discs* presenter Lauren Laverne asked Rantzen how this came about. Rantzen explained that if you were lucky enough to work on a programme with 20 million viewers, the people who make the noise have to pay attention because they know that so many of their voters were watching. An additional factor was that the programme was transmitted on Sunday nights, a time when MPs tuned in.[75]

That's Life! was responsible for the launch of *Childline* in 1986, the first national helpline for children in danger or distress. Rantzen had proposed the *Childwatch* programme (BBC, 1986) to BBC1 Controller Michael Grade after the death of a toddler who had starved to death, locked in a bedroom. The aim of the programme was to find better ways of detecting children at risk of abuse. Viewers of *That's Life!* who had themselves experienced cruelty as children were asked to take part in a survey detailing the circumstances of their abuse. Rantzen was sexually abused when she was young by someone known to the family. 'He was not a blood relative but I can still see him now. He used to call me "bright eyes". It was not the most serious of assaults but it was horrible'. When she told her mother she did not believe her. 'My mother cared about the social circles she mixed in and did not want to cause trouble'.[76] After that broadcast Rantzen suggested the BBC should open a helpline for children, in case any young viewers suffering current abuse wished to ring to ask for help. The helpline was open for 48 hours, during which it was swamped with calls, mainly from children suffering from sexual abuse that they had not been able to disclose to anyone else and had been threatened into silence. This gave Rantzen the idea for a specific helpline for children in distress or danger, to be open 24/7 throughout the year, the first of its kind in the world. Funding was obtained from the Department of Health and the Variety Club of Great Britain. There were 50,000 attempted calls on the first night that the helpline was launched. *Childline*, which has counselled five million children and young people, now has 12 bases around the United Kingdom and its formula has now been copied in 150 countries around the world.

In 2013 Rantzen set up the charity *Silver Line*, a free confidential telephone helpline offering information, friendship and advice to older people. Rantzen had written about her loneliness following the death of her husband television producer Desmond Wilcox in 2000 and described loneliness among the elderly as a 'creeping enemy' which 'erodes confidence'. [77] She was invited to a conference addressing the isolation of elderly people held by the Campaign to End Loneliness and the Centre for Social Justice. This led to a meeting with MP Paul Burstow, then a minister in the Department of Health, to discuss the creation of a helpline. The charity, which has 5,000 trained befrienders, took 2.2 million calls in five years.[78] Now in her 80s, she has not stopped working and has produced a podcast with Adrian Mills who was with her on 'That's Life' called 'That's After Life!' that features news, views, comedy and commentary plus guests such as Michael Palin, Barry Humphries and Imelda Staunton gossiping and championing favourite causes.

Esther Rantzen made a career of exploring difficult subjects and investigating the issues affecting those whose voices often remained hidden, including children and the elderly. Her contemporary, Kay Mellor also forged a reputation as someone who could craft the stories and struggles of ordinary citizens into compelling prime time listening. Although from a very different background than the more privileged Esther Rantzen, Mellor shared with her fellow broadcaster a commitment to exposing the hardships faced by people in every walk of life.

Kay Mellor (1951 — 2022)

Kay Mellor (Daniel) was one of British television's most popular and highly regarded television writers. She became known for her superb ear for dialogue and sharp talent for ensemble pieces and spent the last few decades making television shows rich with real life resonance. She is proof of the old cliche of 'write as you know', compelling narratives born out of difficult situations.[79]

Mellor was born in Leeds in 1951 to Irish Catholic George Daniel and Dinah Vates whose Jewish family originated from Lithuania. They were a working class family; her father sold vacuum cleaners, and they lived on a council estate in the north part of the city. Her mother divorced her father due to domestic violence. Mellor was just a small child when she found her mother knocked unconscious on the kitchen floor. She ran to a nearby house to get help. 'It was a terrifying night'.[80] Dinah had been beaten up by her husband and she threw him out of the house. Mellor remembered watching from the window as she saw her father walk away wearing his trilby hat and carrying a suitcase. He never gave the family any financial

15. Kay Mellor, wearing her OBE at Buckingham Palace after investiture ceremony 16 February 2010 (PA Images/Alamy Stock photo)

support but her mother was strong and did not crumble. Mellor and her brother were the only children on the estate from a single parent family. Her mother, who worked as a seamstress, did not care what people thought, and she would not wear a ring or take state benefits. Mellor's father made contact with her when she was 21 but the relationship was soured by images that she had in her head and it broke down quite quickly.[81]

Although it was not an easy time and there was very little money, Mellor recalls that her mother let her daydream and encouraged creativity. She lived in a fantasy world, directing imaginary plays. She loved to entertain as a child and would make up stories and sketches for her classmates during dinner breaks. She could always tell a story and started to write them down. Nevertheless, she did not do well academically as she failed her 11+ and left secondary school without any qualifications.

She met her husband Anthony, who was an apprentice motor mechanic, on a blind date. She fell pregnant and married at 16; her husband was just a year older. They married in Leeds Registry Office with a reception in the Co-op. Her mother said that she did not have to get married and could continue to live in the family house with the baby despite the fact there was such a stigma at the time about being a single mother. Mellor was intent on marrying Anthony. They were impoverished and lived with his mother and slept in his single bed.[82]

When Mellor initially found out about her pregnancy she was fearful of telling her mother as she did not know anyone who had a baby at 16. 'Everyone else was on the pill but I fell pregnant the second time I had sex with my boyfriend. I should have known better but I was not street savvy'.[83] The morning after she broke the news, her mother told her that she had ruined her life. 'I felt terrible as if I had let her down'. At the same time she was boiling her an egg and telling her that she had to eat properly now that she was pregnant. 'She was torn. She wanted the best for me. I promised I would go back into education'.[84]

Mellor was the mother of two girls Gaynor Faye and Yvonne Francas[85] by the time she was 20. It was when she began her own play group and had to study psychology that she discovered her love of learning. She began taking her O and A levels and it was her drama tutor at Park Lane College, Leeds who told her that she should consider going professional. He pushed her to apply for Bretton Hall College, Wakefield and she was their first mature student. After leaving college she formed the Yorkshire Theatre Company and toured with her own plays.[86] She acted on television shows but came to realise that scriptwriting was more to her liking.[87]

As a writer she began working for Granada Television in the 1980s, writing for the soap opera *Coronation Street* and many episodes for the Channel Four soap *Brookside*. She wrote for ITV's children's anthology drama series *Dramarama* and was co-creator of Granada Television's children's drama *Children's Ward* which won Best Children's Drama in the 1997 BAFTA awards. She also created ITV's soap opera *Families* (1990-1993) which followed two families in Cheshire, England and Sydney, Australia.

Another series was Granada Television's *Band of Gold* (1995) which revolved around the lives of a group of sex workers who lived and worked in Bradford's red light district. Her inspiration for *Band of Gold* came when she was driving through the district and saw the prostitutes lining the pavement on Lumb Lane. At the time she was working one day a week for the charity Careline and connected with a girl that worked 'The Lane' who became the inspiration for one of the girls in the series. The project was turned down by the television companies until Granada, which had a reputation for new drama, commissioned the series.[88] Mellor recalls that it was not always easy for women to break through as they 'tended to be pigeonholed and had to fight a lot more to get stuff on'.[89] Mellor's tough life experiences at an early age gave her the confidence to speak her mind. When the producer of *Band of Gold* tried to tell her what her series was about, she disagreed with him and told him 'to get your hat and coat on and go up to Bradford and meet those women like I did. And then you wouldn't tell me what my series is really about. It takes a certain courage to talk to a producer like that. I think my life experience, so different to his, gave me that courage'.[90]

Band of Gold made her one of television's most sought-after writers. Subsequent productions included *Playing the Field* (BBC, 1998) that followed the lives of the Castlefield Blues, a fictitious female football team from South Yorkshire and *Fat Friends* (ITV, 2000-2005) which explored the lives of several slimming club members from Leeds with a focus on the various ways their weight had impacted on them. The BBC drama *The Syndicate*, which was first aired in 2012 and features groups of people whose lives turn upside down after they jointly win the lottery, returned for a fourth series in 2021. Each was based in a different Yorkshire location and included themes of terminal cancer, child abduction and domestic violence.

One of the subjects closest to Mellor's heart was *In the Club* (BBC, 2014) which followed the experiences of a group of heavily pregnant women and their partners in the run up to the births. One storyline concerned a 15-year-old schoolgirl who fell accidentally pregnant and was modelled on Mellor. She found writing about the experience was cathartic as in 1967 attitudes had been so different and knowledge, on her part, had been sorely lacking.[91]

She both wrote and directed the successful stage play *A Passionate Woman* in 1992 about a middle-aged housewife reviewing her life on the day of her son's wedding. Her mother was the inspiration for the play. She produced the feature film *Fanny and Elvis* (1999), a romantic comedy in which two people are forced together when their loved ones elope together and in her parallel career as a television actress appeared in her own adaptation of *Jane Eyre* (1997).

Mellor had an extraordinary talent to turn ordinariness into something that touches anyone and everyone who watches her work.[92] She was awarded the BAFTA award for outstanding writing for television (1997) an honorary doctorate from Leeds Metropolitan University (1988) and the Writers Guild Award for outstanding contribution to writing (2014). She received an OBE for services to drama in 2009 and was made a Fellow of the Royal Television Society (2016).

A doyenne of the television industry, Mellor contributed to the public's understanding of tough subjects such prostitution, rape and domestic violence. Brought up in a harsh housing estate in Leeds was not easy and it shows in her writing: her female characters are smart, gritty and show resilience when the going gets tough. True grit runs in the family as she says her mother was extremely strong and believed women were equal to men long before feminism. Resilience was something that Mellor had to develop in the male dominated world of writing for television. It took eight years to see her series *Band of Gold* reach the screen.[93] She was also not brought up to expect a successful career. 'If you had said to me do you want to be a writer you might as well have been asking do you want to be the queen of England or an astronaut'.[94]

She also had to deal with the feeling of being an outsider. 'I had no father. I was Jewish and felt acutely poor'. She did not know anyone else from a single parent family.[95] Being an outsider is something she believes is common to many writers. Due to her family circumstances she felt an outsider in the Jewish community. 'My mum married out and we didn't live in the right part of Leeds'.[96] They were also very poor. She has no memory of her mother sitting down to eat with her and her brother and that might have been because there was not sufficient food to go around.[97] She gives an example of when her mother was working at Burtons there was the possibility of earning more money if you worked on collars. She did not know how to do the work but applied to do it nevertheless to try and earn extra money for her son's barmitzvah. She was found out and after explaining to her boss the reason, there was more money in her pay packet and no one referred to the incident ever again.[98]

Her mother remarried when she was 10. Her step-father Abe Harris was a Jewish upholsterer, a radical socialist and a vegetarian; these were unknown identities on the estate.[99] They then moved to the more Jewish area of Moortown. 'I learned lots about Jewishness and found it fascinating but I wasn't brought up that way'.[100]

Mellor never gave much thought to the fact that she was born Jewish until she went to a traditional Jewish wedding to research a character for *Fat Friends*. The experience was so powerful it left her questioning many aspects of her life. The identity issues left her sad and restless and yearning for what could have been a very different life if she had been brought up in a Jewish environment. 'I connected with lots of things at the wedding, it was like an electric shock going through me. I thought I would have loved this, this could have been my life, this could have been me'. It made her reassess her life. The only thing she could do was channel it into her work and she rewrote *A Passionate Woman* with her mother as a Jewish woman in her 20s. Her reawakened Jewishness brought into sharp focus a tour of post-war Europe that she made when she was a teenager, which was not the norm at that time, when she was taken to Anne Frank's house, Auschwitz and Dachau. 'It was a very profound experience and I think it contributed to my writing in a big way. I always put forward the idea that you should stand up for what you believe in, say what you think, be active and don't be silent.'[101]

With regard to her Jewish identity, Mellor comments: 'I couldn't describe myself as Jewish, I couldn't describe myself as Christian. I am right in the middle. I am Kay Mellor. I am a writer. I am my own person'. If her Jewish upbringing was somewhat lacking – 'I believe in basic goodness' – she is nevertheless very aware of her heritage. 'I recognise my bloodline and I am very fast to defend the Jewish faith if anyone ever criticises it. There are times in my life I have felt instantly drawn to the Jewishness in me'.[102] Mellor received the Jewish Care Woman of Distinction Award in 2004. It was considered that she earned the award for climbing to the top of the ladder as a screen writer and then adding a few rungs of her own and that her writing was 'spot on the pulse'.[103]

Although Mellor never had a series devoted solely to a group of Jewish characters as she preferred to create a diverse range of people in her stories, Jewish characters do occasionally appear in her work. They are not central but they are not forced into the storyline or neglected. In *Fat Friends*, which centred on the trials and tribulations of a slimming club in Leeds, the Jewish actress Eleanor Bron played Marilyn, a typical Jewish mother. Marilyn's daughter Lauren (played by Mellor's daughter Gaynor Faye) is single and a desperate wannabe actress. Marilyn invited Lauren to a Friday night meal, featuring lokshen soup, chopped liver and roast chicken. Comic touches included Lauren imagining the kind of man she would be introduced to at a wedding, such as an overweight dental surgeon and sighed that all she wanted was to hold hands with someone on a Friday night. She falls for an unsuitable man and wonders what to tell her family.[104] Lauren exasperates her orthodox parents by failing to get a proper job, selling vibrators to make money between acting jobs and seducing the local vicar. There was Jewish dialogue that was not toned down for the prime time audience as they learnt about chopped herring bagels and *shabbes* (Sabbath) dinner.[105]

Love, Lies and Records (2017) follows a registrar as she tries to juggle her personal life with the daily dramas of births, marriages and deaths. In one episode registrar Kate Dickenson turned up for a Jewish wedding but Lindsey turned out to be a man dressed in white rather than the bride she had been expecting. While technically a civil ceremony it came complete with a *chupah*[106] and klezmer music.[107]

Mellor considered that she had been lucky to have had so much success in television as the industry is often criticised for its lack of opportunities for older women, both in front of and behind the camera. 'There was a time when I really had to battle to get my voice through. But there have been certain people along the way who have really trusted me and got my voice.' She comments that she knows that in the industry many older women feel invisible and she is determined to put that right.[108] Her series *Girlfriends* (ITV, 2018) focuses on the lives of three middle aged women, an under-represented group on British television, who have been friends since their teenage years as they negotiate the dramas, disappointments and delights of ageing.

She was passionate about mentoring emerging talent and through her production company Rollem Productions she actively worked with new writers to develop their products. Mellor knew only too well that it was a hard road to navigate before she became one of the most respected television writers of her generation as she was a poverty stricken girl, abandoned by her father and pregnant at 16. Radio and television presenter Kirsty Young commented that it was a rare journey to do so well and questioned how it came about. Mellor explained that it was support from her family and people who had faith in her even though she was 'a working class girl who did not speak the language'.[109]

Mellor, who died in on 15 May 2022, had written some of the most powerful television productions. Her roots were always deep in Yorkshire and she never left Leeds. Her creativity was inspired by the area. Her plays are recognisable for portraying working class characters, the people she grew up with and showing gritty emotional truths. She wrote on difficult subjects that include prostitution, to empower women by her work.[110] Mayor of West Yorkshire Tracy Brabin said that Mellor became a new 'voice of the earth'. She was an avowed socialist but the characters are the centre of her dramas were not there merely to make a political point. They emphasised the compassion and humour of working class life, often in the face of hardship and duress.[111]

Like others who preceded her, Kay Mellor had to battle the headwinds of sexism and classism so prevalent in the post-war media, but her hard work helped pave the way for a new generation of women journalists who have been able to take more straightforward paths into broadcasting and rise to top positions as political reporters and presenters. Interestingly, like Mellor, several of these Jewish media personalities have their roots in the North, including Emily Maitlis, who was raised in Yorkshire and had a successful career as a business and political reporter before being promoted in 2019 as the lead presenter of *Newsnight*, the BBC's flagship news and current affairs programme noted for its in-depth analysis and often robust cross examination of senior politicians.

Emily Maitlis (1970 –)

Emily Maitlis is a journalist, documentary filmmaker and the lead anchor of BBC Two's news and current affairs programme *Newsnight*. Her coverage has included elections for the BBC in UK, US and Europe. As one of BBC's main news presenters, she has gained a reputation for being a formidable interviewer.

16. Reporter Emily Maitlis, recording a segment on the UK's 2010 Leadership Debate for BBC News at One show, on Bristol harbourside, opposite the event venue, the Arnolfini Arts Centre (Gothick, via Wikimedia Commons)

Maitlis was born in Hamilton, Canada to British Jewish parents. Her father Peter Maitlis was born in Berlin two weeks after Hitler came to power in 1933. When he was three, his father Jacob Maitlis[112] secured a university job but was called in by the police who told him that he was unable to take up the position because he was Jewish. The family managed to escape and came to England.[113] A bracelet made from the bangle her grandmother escaped with is Maitlis's most treasured possession.[114] At the time of her birth Peter Maitlis, Professor of Inorganic Chemistry and fellow of the Royal Society, was teaching at McMaster University in Hamilton. He then took a job at the University of Sheffield and moved his family back to England.[115]

Her mother Marion stayed at home with Maitlis and her two older sisters. Marion was a great linguist, studied for an Italian degree, tutored at home and at the age of 60 trained as a psychoanalytic psychotherapist. Maitlis would learn French, Spanish and Italian with her mother and is fluent in these languages. It was a relaxed household and her parents never pushed her in one direction or another.[116]

Maitlis was educated at the local comprehensive school King Edward VII School (when she joined *Newsnight* in 2019 she was the only presenter not to have attended a private school) and then studied English at Queen's College, Cambridge.[117] After graduating in English from Cambridge in 1992 she went to Hong Kong. 'I really didn't know what else to do. But then I realised what an explosive place I was in. it was just ahead of the hand-over to the Chinese and the politics really intrigued me. I wanted to be the one asking the questions.'[118]

She spent six years in Hong Kong with TVB News and NBC Asia, initially as a business reporter creating documentaries and then as a presenter charting the collapse of the tiger economies in 1997 from Cambodia, China and the Philippines and the transfer of sovereignty of Hong Kong with Jon Snow for Channel 4. She then moved to *Sky News* in the UK as a business correspondent before her appointment as one of the channel's main news reporters. It was there that she covered major international stories including the US and Israeli elections, the Concorde crash, the Afghan hostage crisis and the fall of President Slobodan Milosevic in Belgrade.

She joined *BBC London News* when the programme was launched in 2001 and subsequently joined *Newsnight*, the BBC's news and current affairs programme that provides in-depth investigation and analysis of the stories behind the day's headlines. She was a key figure in the BBC's election coverage in the UK and US. She once grabbed Donald Trump's short-lived communications director Anthony Scaramucci on the lawn of the White

House to secure his first UK interview, while her vital grilling of former White House press secretary Sean Spicer earned her a profile in the *New York Times*.

Other presentations have been on the game show *The National Lottery: Come and Have a Go, BBC Breakfast* and *STORYfix* a light-hearted look at the week's news set to up-beat music. She has made documentaries for BBC Two on Donald Trump, Nicolas Sarkozy, Mark Zuckerberg and, for Radio 4, a programme on Madonna and writes regularly for UK newspapers and magazines. In 2019 she became the lead presenter of *Newsnight*, alongside Emma Barnett and Kirsty Wark. Esme Wren, editor of *Newsnight* said that Maitlis's promotion was testament to her journalistic excellence, passion and tenacious interview style.[119]

This was evidenced in November 2019 when Maitlis interviewed the Duke of York, Prince Andrew about his relationship with American sex offender Jeffrey Epstein who died in the August whilst awaiting trial on sex trafficking charges. The interview was broadcast on BBC's *Newsnight*. Due in part to the disastrous fallout from Prince Andrew's performance during this interview, he later resigned from his Royal duties. The interview even provoked the FBI to summon Prince Andrew for questioning in the quest for more information surrounding Jeffrey Epstein.[120]

The interview with Prince Andrew that took place at Buckingham Palace won her the network presenter of the year at the 2020 Royal Television Society Journalism awards. The judges described her interview as 'historic' and considered that 'in a year of political chaos her nose for nonsense led to bruising encounters with politicians and her interview with a member of the Royal family will live on in history.'[121] At the time it was commented that 'she is the best presenter/interviewer now at the BBC for her brilliant demolition of Prince Andrew'.[122] It is a reflection of her position as a top interviewer that she was chosen for the assignment. The Queen had given her permission for the interview.

It has been said that charming though she is, the immediate impression on meeting her is that she is 'not a woman to be messed with'.[123] She certainly needed all her strength to deal with an uncomfortable period when Maitlis herself was a news story. She was stalked by Edward Vines, a former friend from university, until court cases resulted in a restraining order. In 2018 he was jailed for three years after bombarding Maitlis with letters and emails for more than twenty years. He continued harassing her from jail and after his release which resulted in a further sentence. The judge said that the repeated contact amounted to psychological torture. Maitlis has described his behaviour as posing a constant threat to her and her family's life and that it was tantamount to having a chronic illness.[124]

Another issue that she finds difficult to deal with is her Judaism. 'I think it's the thing that I probably beat myself up most about', referring to the fact that she is not bringing up 'practising Jewish boys'. Her two boys did attend Hebrew classes before the lure of Sunday morning football drew them away. 'It's just the tension of growing up where both parents are not on the same page. It's much harder to instil one type of arrangement'. She considers it to be one of the most difficult aspects of her life. 'Not in a tragic way but it's been a hard thing because my husband's Catholic and I'm not very practising. I guess the boys have been raised – and I embrace this – in a family where nothing is indoctrinated particularly, so every thought, every opinion, every exploration, is sort of up for grabs'. Her husband Mark Gwynne is an investment banker who was brought up in a polo playing, hunting, shooting and fishing environment.[125]

The family attend synagogue on Rosh Hashana and Yom Kippur and celebrate Chanukah and the boys know a great deal about modern Jewish history and call themselves Jewish. The family celebrate the Passover seder meal with her older sister and family who belong to the London Sephardi and Portuguese synagogue as her brother-in-law is Sephardi, together with her parents and other relatives. These seders are quite different from the ones she grew up with, marking the occasion with her grandparents in Finchley, north London, where they went on for four hours. Shortcuts were for the fainthearted, whereas the present ones are 'the express version'.[126]

Maitlis enjoyed a strong Jewish upbringing in Sheffield despite the small size of the community and attended Sheffield Jewish Congregation Hebrew School. 'Our family were culturally Jewish. But there were only three Jewish children at school. When I came to London it was bewildering – there were Jews everywhere'.[127] Maitlis was exposed to other influences when she was growing up. Her mother comments that her daughters considered her to be rather wacky and eccentric in those days and she did have them learn transcendental meditation after she and her husband had watched meditation in a Japanese monastery.[128]

Maitlis's most significant Jewish moment was when she married her husband whom she met whilst working in Hong Kong. They had a rabbi and priest doing the service together and she has a photo of them dancing to klezmer music. It was an important moment to have her family there. It showed that they accepted her choice and for that reason it was extremely emotionally profound.[129] They are a close family. Maitlis lives in Kensington and her parents live very close by as does one of her sisters.

Her Judaism is an important part of her life but she does not see herself particularly as a role model. 'I don't think like that. I don't hide my Judaism, I don't shout it. I just sort of get on with it'. She has not been a target of antisemitism. 'I get more misogyny than antisemitism. I know that it exists and people I know who say they get it badly. I get more of the female load'.[130]

It is fortunate that she has not been a target of antisemitism considering that she is so much in the public eye. She does not appear to refer to her Judaism in the non-Jewish press. She rather skims over the fact with saying that she is 'not very practising' but it is noted that she wears a bracelet that was fashioned out of the one that her grandmother had when she escaped Nazi Germany.[131] She appears to steer clear of talking about Jewish matters. She has a lively personality, is extremely glamorous and is at ease with whomever she interviews and used to mixing in a wide range of circles. There was an incident when she was reprimanded by the head of the BBC when she delivered a highly critical monologue about the Dominic Cummings lockdown controversy, and she voiced what a lot of people were feeling. She said that Cummings had broken the rules and made the public look like fools.[132] She received praise on Twitter for her criticism of the Government's Covid language. She lambasted ministers for implying that people who recover from Covid show more resilience and fighting spirit. She said that the disease was not a leveller and how those on the front line were more exposed. It was commented that 'Emily speaks for the nation'.[133]

She is a strong presence at Jewish charity events, in particular World Jewish Relief (WJR). She saw first-hand their work in Moldova and felt privileged to have seen the extraordinary work that they do. She was shocked by the poverty that families were experiencing. 'The things that we saw were genuinely silencing. They stopped me in my tracks and made me rethink a lot of things'. She has also commented that whenever she reflects on the people that WJR help 'I can not but conclude that for the grace of God they could be my grandparents, parents or even me. This really is our extended family and we have to make a difference for them'.[134] She supports other Jewish causes and these include the launch of the PJ library which provides free monthly children's Jewish books on modern non-denominational themes.[135] She has also chaired sessions with Simon Schama at Jewish Book Week, hosted a Holocaust Memorial Day commemoration in central London and annual dinners for Langdon, the Jewish charity for young adults with learning difficulties.

She has a strong social conscience for those less fortunate. Some stories have left a particular mark. 'I was quite shocked the first time I went to Cambodia, seeing five year old kids at dump sites trying to find any bits of food or metal that they could use'.[136] Her charity work includes Action for Children that supports and helps vulnerable children; Debate Mate that uses university students to run after-school debate clubs in areas of high child poverty with the aim to develop confidence and interpersonal skills and Wellchild, the national UK children's charity that helps to get seriously ill children and young people out of hospital and home to their families. She was involved in the launch of Make Poverty History campaign where she joined MP Oona King and actor Colin Salmon at 19 Princelet Street, the site of a former synagogue in London's East End. The event followed a plea from Nelson Mandela for Britons to press world leaders to eradicate man-made poverty.

In 2019 she published a book *Airhead: The Imperfect Art of Making News*, a behind the scenes look at how news is made, in which she chronicles the pains and perils of news television. A compendium of her biggest interviews with politicians, celebrities and thinkers, she shows what happens in front of the camera as well as the chaos behind. It includes the diverse assignments that she has covered: the Bataclan terrorist attack; the report on the umbrella democracy protests in Hong Kong and meetings with Donald Trump and the Dalai Lama. She paints a vivid picture of the intensity and unpredictability that come with her assignments.[137] She was described in the 2019 Cliveden Literary Festival programme as 'our most thrilling political broadcaster' and has received an honorary doctorate from Sheffield Hallam University.

In 2020 Maitlis began presenting the BBC podcast *Americast* alongside the BBC's North America editor Jon Sopel. The podcasts originally focused on the 2020 election and contain analysis as well as an array of interviews across the political scene. The podcast was due to end after the election but continued due to its popularity. In February 2022 Maitlis resigned from the BBC after an exclusive signing with Global to launch a daily podcast and joint radio show with Sopel.

Jeremy Vine, who has co-hosted election night with Maitlis, said that she is 'super smart and very funny and personable. She's got a quality that goes above and beyond'. She has been a regular household presence and this shows that 'there is a clear changing of the guard at the BBC with more female interviewers taking over'.[138] Emily Maitlis is the embodiment of a new generation of women broadcast journalists who have proven that they deserve to take their place alongside the male reporters and presenters who have dominated the airwaves from the earliest years of radio and television. Maitlis's co-host on *Newsnight*, Emma Barnett, also hailing from the north, represents the most recent generation of bright determined female journalists rising to the top of her profession. Known for being a fearless interviewer, Barnett's career trajectory demonstrates how far women have come in the media in the twenty-first century.

Emma Barnett (1985 –)

Emma Barnett is a British broadcaster and journalist who is known for her agenda setting interviews and broadcasting firsts, including the BBC's first joint live radio and television phone-in with Prime Minister Teresa May and Camilla, Duchess of Cornwall's first guest edit, live from Clarence House. In January 2021 she became the youngest presenter of BBC Radio 4's *Woman's Hour*, one of the longest running programmes on British radio.

She was born in Manchester on 5 February 1985. Her father Ian Barnett was a commercial property surveyor and her mother Michelle, who had worked in publishing but gave up her job to look after her daughter, later

17. 2016 (Re:publica Germany, via Wikimedia Commons)

became a special needs assistant at King David, the local Jewish school. Barnett was an only child and attended Manchester High School for Girls. She graduated with a degree in history and politics from the University of Nottingham. She had toyed with the idea of acting but noting the unemployment rates chose journalism instead. She does not deny that there is a performative aspect to her work.[139] She took a postgraduate course in journalism at Cardiff School of Journalism, Media and Cultural Studies.

Following her postgraduate course Emma began her career in journalism at *Media Week* in 2007. She joined the *Daily Telegraph* in 2009, and was the first media editor launching the paper's digital section 'Wonder Women' in 2012. She was then appointed women's editor where she tried to steer content away from lipstick, celebrities and fashion towards more weighty issues. She received her broadcasting break two years later on the commercial phone-in and talk radio station LBC. Starting out on the graveyard shifts at night she soon made her mark and was later voted radio newcomer of the year. In 2016 she was offered a solo slot on the BBC's Radio 5 Live which had been dubbed 'Radio Bloke' because of its heavy emphasis on sport. Barnett's arrival was seen as a way of redressing the balance and covering a wider range of topics. She said she wanted to smash taboos and no subject was off limits; to create a show where people shared strong views and had conversations on air that would normally happen in private. One of the first debates was about endometriosis, a condition causing severe period pains and from which she suffers.[140]

She regularly hit the headlines over the years with her outspoken comments about periods. She said that if men had periods 'menstrual leave would be baked into HR policies'; she claimed women's health issues were ignored and under-funded because there was a gender medicine gap that prioritised men's needs. When talking on Radio 5's *How Do You Cope?*[141] She commented that conditions which only affect women have had little scientific research while those that impact men as well, such as fertility, were well understood. She has criticised the lack of money spent on female only conditions. In March 2019 she published a book *It's About Bloody Time* which covered her experiences of endometriosis. She has revealed that she often goes on air with a hot water bottle because of the pain it can cause and that she was not listened to seriously for years over her condition and this can make people not want to speak about their periods.[142]

Her speciality is the 'take no prisoners' political interviews. She described being in the hot seat when interviewing Jeremy Corbyn in 2017 as 'a dream come true'. She dragged him across the coals for his failure to produce his Party's figures on childcare. Corbyn's dithering and ham fisted attempt to dig them out of his iPad was described as a 'car crash' moment.[143] She had Theresa May confess to shedding a tear when the election exit poll was revealed. She caught Rory Stewart, former Secretary of State for International Development, plucking from the air the percentage of Britons who agreed with him on Brexit and when she interviewed MP Andrew Clarke, newly returned to the back benches, she retorted to a reply 'that's the script, not the answer to my question'.[144] In 2015 her 'tough love' agony column began in the *Sunday Times* and from 2017 she was a co-presenter of BBC One's *Sunday Morning Live*. She won Radio Broadcaster of the Year in 2018.

Barnett admits that starting her career at the *Daily Telegraph* was not easy. She was initially writing about digital media in which no one was particularly interested. Yet it was a toughening experience, as was her father's imprisonment. 'It was about as grubby a crime it is to imagine coming out of a comfortable upbringing in Manchester'.[145]

Her father, who had originally been involved in commercial property, was jailed for three years in 2008 after he admitted keeping brothels in the Greater Manchester area. A judge at Manchester Crown Court branded him 'evil and immoral'. He also pleaded guilty to controlling the prostitution of a woman who was trafficked to Britain from Lithuania by an Albanian crime gang who had promised her a job as a cleaner. Ian Barnett claimed that he got involved in prostitution when he helped to run an escort agency 'as a favour to a friend' around 1999. This led him to purchasing a small hotel in Blackpool whereby he obtained prior consent from the Blackpool CID and Licensing Officer to change from a hotel to a discreet brothel.[146] This was subsequently sold and he then ran four brothels in Altrincham, Cheetham Hill, Levenshulme and Shudehill.[147] His wife was convicted of money laundering and given a suspended sentence.[148] They lived in a six bedroom house in Broughton Park, drove a Rolls Royce and x-type Jaguar and lived a wealthy lifestyle. They had benefitted £5 million from the business.[149]

As a result of the court case Barnett said she grew up overnight by two decades. She refers to her very traditional Jewish upbringing with her father as a local businessman and her housewife mother. It would appear that when she was a young teenager a drastic change in her father's fortunes led to what she sees as a terrible decision on his behalf when he became involved in the running of massage parlours. She claims she had no idea of what had been going on until she arrived home one day from university and found the lock loose on the front door. After much questioning and eye avoidance from her mother she learnt that they had been raided by the police that day. A huge part of the trauma was discovering many things about her father's businesses from the newspapers that she had not known previously.[150]

She stood by her father and visited him in prison despite the anger she felt towards him and the shame caused by the publicity. 'I was angry at him; angry at the world. And while I felt deeply embarrassed and huge shame washed over me as his story hit the newspapers, I made a big decision. I decided to try and thrive. The sins of the father are not the sins of the child'. She considered that this was not her mess and she had a choice: either let it break her into tiny pieces or use the anger to fuel her passion for life, love and her work. She chose the latter. 'I changed irrevocably. For the better. By seeing a side of life very few people get to experience I developed an empathy and humility beyond my years. And I wanted to hear and tell other people's stories more than ever'. Although the load has got lighter over the years she is still traumatised by what happened and admits that she became an old soul before her time.[151] 'Now I had a greater understanding of the human condition, far from the chocolate box existence I had grown up in'.[152] She became a volunteer for Pact, a nationwide charity which provides practical and emotional support to children and families of prisoners. She is also a patron of Smartworks, a charity which helps economically disadvantaged women get into the workforce through interview training and having the right outfit to make the first best impression.

By overcoming the familial shame and channelling her energies and confidence into work, Barnett has achieved success that belies her age. In January 2021 she became the youngest presenter of BBC Radio 4's *Woman's Hour*, a crucial public space that broadcasts to some 3.5 million weekly. On announcing her appointment, Radio 4 controller Mohit Bakaya said that 'Emma brings a terrific combination of intellectual inquiry, robust journalism and curiosity about the human condition and that she was the best person placed to carry on the important job of identifying and exploring the issues that matter most to women'.[153]

Barnett has a long association with *Woman's Hour*. She did work experience there whilst a pupil at Manchester School for Girls. Presenter Jenni Murray had come to the school to speak at a cancer fundraiser for a friend who had died. Seizing the moment Barnett asked her for the programme's email address and applied for a position. Years later, at the age of 26, she was the show's youngest ever stand-in and whilst working at the *Daily Telegraph* she moonlighted as the show's first-reserve presenter when Murray or Jane Garvey, the other regular host, were away.[154]

Woman's Hour was first aired on 7 October 1946. It was given a 2pm slot, a time when morning chores and the lunchtime washing up would be finished.[155]From the early days the programme responded to the concerns of its audience, and so *Woman's Hour* tracked and reflected the tremendous changes in the lives of women since the end of the War. It tackled a diverse range of topics and was always a more radical presence than its image might suggest. Early talks with titles such as 'Putting Your Best Face Forward' and 'How to improve Your Whatnot' were mixed with others on current affairs and on subjects such as childcare and equal pay. Over the years *Woman's Hour* frequently broke new ground in discussing issues such as the menopause, illegitimacy, homosexuality, divorce and prostitution. It remains the longest running radio programme for women in the world.[156]

Barnett presented her first *Woman's Hour* on 4 January 2021. It began with her reading out a message from the Queen who sent her 'best wishes' to mark the show's 75th year and credited the programme with having played a significant part in the evolving role of women. 'During this time you have witnessed and played a significant part in the evolving role of women across society both here and around the world'.[157]

Part of Barnett's incredible success is due to her confidence. Journalist Andrew Billen asked her where this confidence came from: to be able to talk about her periods in public, her fearlessness in questioning politicians, her ambition. She attributed it to the opportunity of attending the private school Manchester School for Girls where the suffragette Emily Pankhurst sent her daughters. 'It was the making of me as a person'. She edited the school newspaper and joined a Jewish theatre group where she played Tevye's wife Golde in *Fiddler on the Roof*.

She also considers being Jewish a contributing factor. 'It is Jewish culture to question, to interrogate, to debate and that happens around the table with children.' She gives as an example the Passover meal. 'The whole thing hinges on four kids at the table asking the adults really hard questions and not relenting until they answer'.[158]

Barnett's relationship with her Judaism is complex and she comments that she does not fit in with either Orthodox or Reform Judaism despite growing up in a traditional Orthodox family. 'That was the form of Judaism showcased to me on infrequent visits to synagogue. She knows how to read Hebrew but no idea what the words means, recognise tunes but has no idea of the order of the service. In Orthodox services she feels like an ill-educated fool. Yet she feels isolated from Reform services as they feel foreign as they lack the familiar rhythms of Orthodox Judaism she grew up with. The result is that she does not feel at home in either branches and consequently less tethered to any community. 'I know that I will never reach the highs demanded in Orthodoxy and I worry Reform Judaism is too different to the Judaism associated with my roots. The result is inertia.'[159]

Due to her appearance she was able to 'operate as a Jew in disguise, undercover. Blonde haired and blue eyes I confused people and continue to do so'. She cites an example when a colleague whispered to her about another co-worker who did not think the same as they did as she was a 'North London Yiddisher girl'. Flouting the visual stereotype has its benefits as being incognito gives her privy to conversations that she would not normally be part of and to confront stereotypes head on.[160]

There are many occasions when she is openly Jewish. Her involvement with Jewish organisations have included participation in Habonim summer camps as a teenager, chair of the UJIA Jewish media network and the UJIA Skirt Network, a networking group of Jewish women. She said the reason for creating the latter group was that after Israel tour and the young UJIA events there was a gap in the organisation before women were at the age of going to ladies lunches.[161] She was a columnist for the *Jewish Chronicle* and supports the Norwood charity. She attended the 2019 Chanukah reception at Buckingham Palace held by the Prince of Wales to celebrate the UK's Jewish community contribution to all areas of British life. She married in an Orthodox synagogue in 2012.[162]

Her religion had not been relevant in the early years of her career as working at the *Telegraph* covering media and technology 'there was no requirement to show my religious hand'. She was also reluctant to do so as for her faith was very personal.[163] All of a sudden she needed to. Her role as a radio host forced her to 'come out'. She explained that 'presenting radio, especially phone-ins is all about putting the real you out there. Listeners won't call if you don't share'. At her first shift on LBC she came out publicly as Jewish for the first time during what became a heated early morning debate on circumcision.[164] Terrorist attacks against Jews around the world had pushed her to speak out against antisemitism.[165] She became experienced at challenging anti-Semites who phoned in to her Radio 5 show.[166] She said that after her interview with Jeremy Corbyn in which he came out so negatively, the anti-Jewish sentiment that she received from his supporters was extraordinary.[167] She was called a 'Zionist shill' on the internet.[168]

She spoke out on BBC Radio 5 about the rapper Wiley's antisemitic views,[169] reading out his words and saying that his words 'burn deeply and play on a very well hidden fear a lot of Jewish people have that some day antisemitism will rise once more'.[170] She recounted her own Jewish heritage, including her grandmother, who escaped the Nazis in Austria and found sanctuary as a housemaid in England. 'Why is a 41 year old bloke from enlightened Britain attacking Jews on a random Friday?' she asked. 'And he's not alone'. She then addressed her comments to Wiley and anyone who supported him. 'Just in case you need something clarifying. Jews don't run the law. Jews don't run the banks. Jews don't run, as you put it, the world. I hate to disappoint you and anyone else who got your antisemitic memo, but it ain't true'. She added that she was not interested in an apology; she was interested in where such views came from and curing society of such racism.[171]

Her determination and openness is already evident in her handling of guests on *Woman's Hour*. During the first week of broadcasting, it was commented that she was a tough interviewer, a total contrast to her predecessors and there could be a possibility that she would end up as a national institution. Her iron confidence was reassuring for the listener; she effortlessly owned the show.[172] It was also commented that she had undertaken a great challenge: to come across as a breath of fresh air while also seeming respectful of the show's 75 year history. 'Barnett navigated that perfectly, just what you want the future of the BBC to sound like. Authoritative and comforting but not fuddy duddy. New but not gratingly iconoclastic either. *Woman's Hour* is in safe hands'.[173]

Emma Barnett took a venerable media institution in Woman's Hour and brought it into the twenty-first century, a period that has been characterised by demands for equal pay, shared parental leave and access to leadership positions despite gender, race, age, ethnicity and socio-economic background. The century has been a turning point for true gender equality, including in the tech sector, and there have been consistent attempts to reduce the gender gap in 'tech' and to attract more women to work in various tech fields. This is reflected in the work and campaigns carried out by Nicola Mendelsohn, an active diversity and inclusion activist and regarded as one of the most influential women in technology.

Nicola Mendelsohn (1971 —)

Nicola Mendelsohn, with her fierce ambition and relaxed charm, describes herself as a 'proper northern lass'.[174] She was born in Manchester to well-known kosher caterers Celia and Barry Clyne. She attended Manchester High School for Girls and then studied English and Theatre Studies at Leeds University. Her incredible organisational skills were already evident during her time at University where she was involved with the National Union of Students anti-racism committee and organised large events that included a national ball for 1,000 people.

18. Nicola Mendelsohn CBE (Courtesy of Nicola Mendelsohn)

She decided against pursuing a career in performing arts, although she did have a place at drama school, because as an observant Jew she would have been unable to keep the Sabbath. She was fortunate that she had a friend who had a job in advertising and on his recommendation decided to explore the advertising world. She joined a graduate training scheme at the British global advertising agency Bartle Bogle Hegarty in 1992 and rose to become business development director before leaving to join Grey London as its deputy chairman in 2004. In 2005 she was named one of the 'Top 35 women under 35' by *Management Today*. Four years later she left to join then independent agency Karmarama, as partner and executive chairman. Karmarama devised campaigns from BT to Nintendo, including the catchy Costa Coffee advert in which dancing heads, buried up to their necks in coffee beans, sang along to *I Was Made For Loving You Baby* by Kiss and another, that Mendelsohn was particularly proud of, in which they gave monkeys coffee-making making equipment to demonstrate that a monkey could not be trained to make a proper cup of coffee.[175]

In 2013 she was headhunted from her twin role at Karmarama and president of the Institute of Practitioners in Advertising, the first woman ever to hold the position, to join the social media company Facebook as vice president for Europe, the Middle East and Africa. She was to be responsible for growing Facebook's advertising revenues and improving relationships with brands across the region. With this move she sealed her position as one of the world's top business women, joining the likes of Facebook Chief Operating Officer Sheryl Sandberg and Easyjet chief executive Carolyn McCall, whom Mendelsohn calls 'one of my rock star heroes' as a role model for all working women. 'We're talking about the importance of a cultural shift that means women can see role models that can get them there'.[176] In the Queen's Birthday Honours 2015, she was made a Commander of the Order of the British Empire for Services to the Creative Industries.

Back in 2013, Facebook founder and CEO Mark Zuckerberg had only recently floated the company on the stock market and bought Instagram for what was then seen as an incredible sum of $1 billion dollars (it made an estimated $47 billion in 2021). Mendelsohn says 'the journey over the past decade has been extraordinary with three and half billion people using the services and now users are now much more closely connected as a result of the platforms'.[177] Although the company has evolved from when she started work there, from a staff of less than 200 in its London office to currently over 4,000, Mendelsohn explains that the culture is still very similar. 'As much as we are a tech company and we like to be able to move fast, it's a very open culture where people can really bring their true authentic selves to the company. At the heart is also the fact that we're giving back to the world and we're creating a positive social impact'.[178]

In October 2021 Facebook changed its name to Meta to reflect its focus on building the metaverse, which will feel like a hybrid of today's online social experiences, sometimes expanded into three dimensions or projected onto the physical world. It will let users share immersive experiences with other people even when they cannot be together and do things together that could not be done in the physical world. It is the next evolution in a long line of social technologies. Some of Mendelsohn's experiences have been a moonwalk with Nasa, a deep sea dive with a group of schoolchildren and weekly meetings with the company's senior management team in which they explore virtual beaches and mountains. Mendelsohn, who has now moved to New York, is now vice president of Meta's global sales group where she oversees the company's advertising business, a massive portfolio that makes her the biggest booster of Facebook, WhatsApp, Instagram and the company's burgeoning metaverse-focused products like Oculus to businesses around the world.

Mendelsohn explains that with tech innovation we are going through a transformative period in history and with that comes challenges and huge opportunities. She is passionate about the role of education in getting more girls to see science and maths as a way into these jobs. 'Encouraging women in tech is a personal thing for me but a company priority too'. The number of women working in Facebook has increased fivefold over the past five years. 'Although many girls and women might not think that software engineering is for them, one must encourage them to consider careers in technology as it makes you future proof'.[179] Meta is currently working towards 50/50 gender equality. 'The data is clear that firms with a higher proportion of women in the company tend to invest more in innovation and tend to be better from a financial perspective'.[180]

A strong advocate of a work-life balance and flexitime for women with families, she herself worked a four-day week for 16 years from the birth of her first child until she joined Facebook. By this time her children were older and did not need her in the same way as when they were younger. She has four children with husband Lord Jonathan Mendelsohn, former adviser to Tony Blair, fundraiser for Gordon Brown and business and international trade spokesman for the Labour Party in the House of Lords. 'It also meant that Jon and I had a conversation about him stopping travel so that one of us would be more based at home so that I could travel'. [181] She believes that working from Monday to Thursday helped boost her professional-personal life balance. She has long campaigned for companies to offer flexible working hours, arguing that it is outdated to insist that the traditional 'nine to five' work structure is the best way of getting the most out of people. She is a firm believer in securing improved roles for women in business and has hosted a series of high-profile events, including Women's Leadership Day. One of the initiatives that she is most proud of at Facebook is She Means Business which she launched in 2016, a partnership that looks to inspire future women business owners and includes training that provides them with skills needed to grow their audience and business. 'We have now trained over 1.5 million women in over 38 countries which I still pinch myself about given where we started'.[182] Mendelsohn comments that empowering women was 'not just the right thing to do but the smart thing to do' as she received Jewish Care's Woman of Distinction Award from Samantha Cameron in 2018. One of the things that she really loves is working with female entrepreneurs and she considers that the tech revolution has been an amazing enabler for women who are able to start a business with just a mobile phone.[183]

The importance of women role models stems from Mendelsohn's personal experience as she was inspired by female family members who always worked. Her grandmother made aprons and boys' trousers to sell on her husband's market stall and her mother Celia used to give cookery lessons at home to groups of women before going on to set up a successful kosher catering company. For Mendelsohn, working women was 'her normal'.[184]

Mendelsohn comes from a loving, supportive home with Judaism at its heart. She attended both the Holy Law and Higher Prestwich synagogues in Manchester and joined the local Bnai Brith Youth Organisation (BBYO). 'It was an incredibly special, informative time in my youth', she recalls. 'The mantra at the time was that it was for the youth, by the youth and we learned so much about leadership. We actually had leadership programming: that's what we gave to each other. You were learning from it and from your peers around you'. She now considers, from a business perspective, the most important thing is who one learns from and that to learn from someone who is just one or two years older but can communicate in a way that is easy to understand is something that is very important. She underwent a big learning curve at the age of 16 when she organised a BBYO weekend in Manchester for hundreds of young people coming from all over the country. It proved to be a big logistical undertaking to organise where people were staying, the catering and the activities. Being part of BBYO was also important from a social values perspective as she would visit elderly people in a care home on Sundays and campaign to get people released from Soviet Russia. 'BBYO was where I honed both my leadership perspective, social values perspective and the importance of organisation'. She calls upon the lessons she learnt at BBYO on a regular basis at Facebook. She points out that the BBYO teachings are part of her DNA. 'Being curious and asking questions are both very much a part of what makes me who I am'.[185]

The ability to challenge and to question helped Mendelsohn deal with a difficult situation at school. She felt her life could have been 'destroyed' by the discrimination she suffered at Manchester High School for Girls. 'I was told that I wasn't very good, that I wasn't very clever, that I wasn't going to pass my exams'. Looking back in hindsight she thinks that there was probably some antisemitism. As she has always been religious and observed the Sabbath, she would leave school early on a Friday afternoon in the winter months. She recalls that there were a couple of teachers who would always insist on starting new topics on a Friday afternoon. When her parents complained, they were told that if they insisted on observing the Sabbath, it was not the school's problem. She had an English teacher who used to mark her down and give her two or three out of ten. 'I was in a good school and these were not my marks. My confidence was smashed by these teachers telling me I wasn't good, I wasn't smart. I didn't think I would do A-levels or go to University at that time'. Despite their negativity, she obtained an A in her English A-level. After receiving her results she returned to the school to confront the teacher and told her how 'she could have destroyed her life'.[186]

Away from her work, Judaism is the key to Mendelsohn's world. She is an observant Jew and before moving to New York, was active in Finchley United Synagogue, London where her husband was a past chairman. She describes herself as having a strong faith which gives her an incredible framework for living. It puts family at the centre, and that creates moments of joy and moments of coming together. She has a strong sense of community and this was something that her close knit family impressed upon her during her childhood when she was playing in the streets and sorting out buttons for her grandparents' fabric stall in the market. 'There's research to say that people who are involved in community life or charities are happier, more fulfilled'.[187]

Faith is what has helped Mendelsohn get through a traumatic time. For the past six years she has lived with follicular lymphoma (FL), an incurable form of blood cancer. In 2016 she found a small lump in her groin that turned out to be malignant. The diagnosis was a complete shock as she did not feel ill. She has described telling her four children 'one of the hardest moments of my life'. She endured six months of chemotherapy and immunotherapy, followed by 18 months of maintenance therapy. She then had to contend with being at high risk during the pandemic. Mendelsohn has been upfront about her condition. She could not imagine carrying on with everything that she was doing and at the same time being secretive about her illness.[188]

She is using her experience and great determination to find new ways to deal with her disease. Sixty percent of people with lymphomas live more than 10 years and that percentage is rising. That might be an acceptable prognosis to give to people in their sixties and seventies but not to Mendelsohn, who was in her forties when diagnosed. She was determined that a cure should be found. Lymphoma is the fifth most common cancer diagnosed in the UK and the most prevalent form of blood cancer. Yet it is not a high profile cancer and does not have the same level of money going into research in comparison with other cancers. Therefore, as well as continuing in her job, she set up the Follicular Lymphoma Foundation in 2019, the first global charity dedicated to finding a cure for the disease and which will contribute £1.75 million into research. Her work with the Foundation is very important to her. She explains that if you are diagnosed with an incurable cancer you will think about it every day. She had treatment and is grateful that it was successful but with this particular cancer, even though she is technically in remission, it is still there on a microscopic level and doctors are unable to tell her when it may or may not come back. She is the co-administrator for a Facebook group called Living with Lymphoma and spends time on the group most days. 'We have just hit 10,000 members which is the highest number of FL patients that have ever been assembled – a real blend of the personal and work coming together'.[189] Her ambition is to find a cure so that her Foundation will not need to exist.[190]

Her philanthropic work extends across the board. She has been on the corporate board of Women's Aid and she and her husband are co-presidents of Norwood, the charity that supports vulnerable children. She is often 'hands on', such as taking part in Mitzvah Day with a Facebook team at a Salvation Army shelter where she helped to repaint the hallways and served up lunch to people who live in the shelter. 'I passionately believe in how people can help each other. It's part of my identity, part of being Jewish. It's one of the key messages my parents instilled in me. It's a fundamental part of being a good human being. Facebook is about connecting people and this embodies similar values'.[191]

Mendelsohn has achieved so much and has been able to become one of the leading lights in her industry due to her incredible talent and the freedom, in contrast to the lives of those featured earlier in this chapter, which has allowed women of her generation to move forward. Yet there are still challenges they have to face in this male dominated industry and Mendelsohn is helping many achieve their goals through the programmes that she has helped set up and support. With her determination and strong Jewish values and identity, she believes that anything is obtainable. 'Women are rubbish about asking for the next thing. If you don't ask you never get. *Chutzpah* is everything'.[192]

Conclusion

For more than one hundred years Jewish women have forged careers in journalism, first in print media and later in radio, television broadcasting and the tech sector. In the early years, the male-dominated media world kept them from the top positions and limited the stories and issues they were allowed to cover, but each successive generation managed to break through barriers to raise women's visibility and representation in the most prestigious and influential media roles. The seven women profiled in this chapter came from diverse backgrounds, had varying levels of family support, took different paths into journalism and often had complicated connections to Judaism, but they all became trailblazers in their fields and many were champions of feminist and social issues while contending variously with sexism, classism, antisemitism and ageism.

In the late nineteenth century, the only way that a woman could break into journalism was to have the kind of wealth and family connections possessed by Rachel Beer, yet by the late twentieth century, a career in journalism was possible even for a woman whose background included poverty and teenaged pregnancy. Some, like Esther Rantzen, Emily Maitlis and Nicola Mendelsohn came from stable middle class backgrounds and enjoyed encouragement and support from their families, but for Olga Franklin, Eve Pollard, Kay Mellor and Emma Barnett financial insecurity, family trauma and varying levels of parental support made their successes in media all the more remarkable.

Rachel Beer was able to parlay her educational, financial and familial advantages into a position as a newspaper editor, but the succeeding generation was forced to enter the field obliquely, first working as clerks, typists and tea girls who were later restricted to reporting almost exclusively on 'women's topics' and lighter news. As the careers of Emily Maitlis and Emma Barnett show, it was not until the twenty-first century that women were able to embark on journalism careers straight from university and to take up positions in the hard-hitting news realms that were once the exclusive purview of men. That it took so long for women to break into the men's clubs of Fleet Street and the BBC is indefensible, but the fact that women like Barnett can now take over venerable programmes at a young age is a testament to the tenacity and drive of the women journalists who preceded her, many of them, like her, Jewish.

Their Jewish heritage impacted these women's lives and careers in various ways, and several had quite complicated relationships with Judaism. Rachel Beer defied her Orthodox family and married into a family that had converted to Christianity, doing her utmost to assimilate into English society. Yet at the same time she made no attempt to hide her Eastern roots and one room in her Mayfair mansion was designed in Moorish style and she would wear shoulder to arm coral and gold bracelets. Likewise, Emily Maitlis, who grew up culturally Jewish married a Catholic and harbours conflicted feelings about not raising her sons as observant Jews. Like Maitlis, Eve Pollard, had parents who escaped the Nazis by emigrating to Britain, and this Holocaust adjacent background has been one prism through which these women have viewed their Jewishness. For Esther Rantzen, who is open and positive about being Jewish, being part of a minority was an asset as it taught her about tolerance and diversity and enabled her to have empathy and reach out to a large audience. Similarly, Nicola Mendelsohn's faith has always been a strong and necessary part of her life, and though she encountered antisemitism and discrimination in school, she has maintained her observant life despite her high-profile career in the tech world. In contrast, Olga Franklin identified more as Russian than Jewish, and Kay Mellor, the child of a Catholic father and Jewish mother, identified as neither Christian nor Jewish, while both always felt like outsiders.

Outsider status was shared by all the women profiled in this chapter, and for many, this spurred them on to champion the underdog and campaign for social justice both within and outside their journalism careers. Whether it was as a woman in a man's world, a Jewish minority in Christian Britain, a working- or middle-class woman trying to make it in a profession dominated by elites, or an older woman in a milieu that valued youth, they all battled headwinds in their quest for careers in media. Rachel Beer may have found success as an editor and political reporter but the prejudice she faced was exemplified by the snide remark of a newspaper proprietor who said that her complexion had 'a suggestion of un-European darkness'.[193] And when her husband died, the career she had forged over a decade was taken away from her, demonstrating the power of the male prerogative over women's lives at the time—even women of immense fortune and privilege. More recently, Esther Rantzen and Eve Pollard were both able to achieve positions at the pinnacle of their fields—Rantzen as a presenter and producer, Pollard as a Fleet Street editor—and used their influence to promote opportunities for other women and campaign for the rights of children, for the elderly and for feminist and women's issues including abortion, child care, and domestic and sexual abuse. Kay Mellor forged her writing career from her own experiences as a teenaged mother, and compassionately portrayed the lives of sex workers, overweight and pregnant women. Similarly, Emma Barnett has been an outspoken advocate for women's health and against antisemitism and active participation in Jewish causes remained a particular interest for Pollard, Maitlis, and Barnett.

The Jewish women whose lives and careers have been explored in this chapter represent a rich tapestry of interests, backgrounds and achievements. Despite the roadblocks they encountered, each successive generation built on the gains of those who preceded them and though they often had to work harder than others, they proved themselves to be tough and determined in pursuit of careers in the media, many gaining positions at the top of their fields.

5

Lawyers

Women in Britain only started practising law in 1919, a year after women won the right to vote. On 23 December 1919 the Sex Disqualification (Removal) Act was passed, allowing women to enter the legal profession in the United Kingdom for the first time. Following its enactment women could become students of the Inns of Court with the express purpose of being called to the Bar and could take examinations to qualify as solicitors. The opening up of the legal profession to women had been a long process. They had been able to study law at university for over forty years but could only work as clerks in legal offices, copying documents or sometimes preparing paperwork. A few weeks after the Act was passed, each of the Inns of Court admitted their first female students.

It continued to be an uphill struggle for women for women if they did not have husbands or fathers who were lawyers and it was often financially impossible for them to get articles for which a yearly premium had to be paid. Although wealthy parents may have been willing to invest in their sons, paying for their daughters was rare.[1] Access to the Bar and obtaining tenancy was difficult for women outside the middle and upper classes. Throughout the 1920s and 1930s women constituted just two to six percent of those called to the Bar.[2] This chapter concentrates on two case studies, Rose Heilbron who rose to prominence in general law and Myrella Cohen who was more Jewish law focused, both of whom faced challenges and were remarkable for their time.

Jews filling top positions in the medical and legal professions in Britain was not achieved without a struggle. Until 1914 the number of Jewish professionals in Britain was small with no more than 90 or 100 doctors practising in London and a slighter smaller number of Jewish barristers. Until the 1950s and 1960s it was uncommon for Jews to reach the higher levels in the judiciary. There were four post-war Jewish high court judges but they were male and came from well-established families belonging to the Anglo-Jewish elite, such as the Mocatta family, who were from Spain and settled in England in the seventeenth century, establishing the banking house of Mocatta and Goldsmid.[3]

Rose Heilbron did not come from a well-connected wealthy family, making her success even more noteworthy. In 1957, a year after Heilbron was appointed Recorder of Burnley only 68 women were nominally at the Bar and out of those only 45 were actually practising. Her climb was determined but not without difficulties; she had to overcome a great deal of prejudice from colleagues and clients at the start of her career.

Rose Heilbron (1914-2005)

Dame Rose Heilbron DBE was a high court judge whose career included many 'firsts' for a woman. She was the first woman to achieve a first class honours degree at the University of Liverpool in 1935, the first to be awarded a Lord Justice Holker Scholarship to Gray's Inn, one of the four Inns of Court in London, one of the first two women to be appointed King's Counsel and the first woman to take the lead in a murder case. She was one of the most successful defence advocates of her day and made legal history when in 1956 she was appointed Recorder of Burnley, the first time a woman had been appointed as a borough judge. In 1972 she became the first woman to sit as a judge in the Old Bailey and in 1974, the year she was made Dame of the British Empire, she became only the second female high court judge. In 1978 she was made presiding judge on the northern circuit – the first woman presiding judge of any circuit. In 1985 she was elected Treasurer of Gray's Inn, the first woman to be treasurer of any of the Inns of Court. She blazed a trail for women in the law and became an icon of her day. She was the most celebrated lawyer of her time.[4] Her legal career was truly remarkable.

Rose Heilbron (originally named Rosie) was born in Liverpool on 19 August 1914 to Max and Nellie (Summers) Heilbron. Her parents had married in 1910 at Princes Road Synagogue and they had an older daughter Annie. Max's father was German and mother American and Nellie's father Polish and her mother German.[5] Max, who had begun his working life as a watchmaker, was in business with his father and one of his brothers. The Heilbrons had various interests: they were cigar merchants and owned several boarding houses and Max had also invented a beauty aid known as Max's Panstick. Their main income came from their hotel in George's Square, where emigrants en route from Europe to a new life in America stayed while they awaited passage.[6] By all accounts the family had done well for themselves. The business was prosperous and for the first years of Rose's life the family was very comfortably off. They had a car and the family could afford holidays in Europe and lived in an affluent suburb of Liverpool.[7]

19. Dame Rose Heilbron DBE (Trinity Mirror/Mirrorpix/Alamy Stock photo)

Max's business was severely hit by the Great Depression and he had to find an alternative means of livelihood. In 1935 they opened a small hotel, The Dorchester. All the family had to help run the business. It was a struggle physically and financially and a marked contrast with the life that they had lived in previous years.[8]

Nellie Heilborn, who died of cancer in 1938, was the driving force of the family, a strong inspirational woman who encouraged her daughter to have a career. This was unusual for the time. Within post war Britain women's main role was seen to be in the home and Jewish women were less likely to be economically active than their non-Jewish counterparts. In a 1950 *Jewish Chronicle* survey which included just under 2000 women, only 11% of Jewish women were economically active compared to 34% in the general population. This domesticity of Jewish women reflected the celebration of the home both within Jewish culture and the general society at the time. Mothers have always been central to the maintenance and reproduction of the Jewish home.[9]

Rose was sent to Belvedere School, then a direct-grant grammar school. Nellie also arranged for her to have elocution lessons. She won several prizes and in 1931 became the youngest person in England to pass the Licentiateship of the Guildhall School of Music in elocution. Her trained voice stood her in good stead in later life as a barrister. It enabled her to modulate the tone of her voice and to project it without raising its pitch. She was able to dispel the frequently used criticism that women's high pitched voices made them unsuitable to be barristers.[10] Her carefully trained voice undoubtedly gave her the confidence her parents longed for her to have but they must have been alarmed when, at seventeen, she left Liverpool for London where she hoped to become an actress. She adopted the stage name Rose Bron, found herself digs and joined the cast of a play called *Hokuspokus*. Six months later she admitted defeat and returned home.[11]

In October 1932 she took up a place at Liverpool University to study for a law degree. She was awarded a first-class degree, the first woman at Liverpool University to achieve such a distinction and only the second in the country. She joined Gray's Inn in November 1935 and in 1937 received her LLM (Master of Laws) after which she began to read for the Bar. As a result, even before she had begun to practise, she found herself a minor local celebrity. The *News Chronicle* reported her degree in the headline 'her ambition – youngest barrister'.[12] Her introduction to Gray's Inn had another important consequence for her. For many years she had used her name Rosie interchangeably with Rose. She was advised to use Rose when she was a barrister.[13] The choice of the name Rosie suggests speedy acculturation on behalf of her parents in such a naming as it was a very popular name at the time.[14]

Heilbron was called to the Bar on 2 May 1939, Britain's youngest woman barrister, and elected to the Northern Circuit on 2 February 1940. The first woman called to the Bar was Ivy Williams in 1922. Enlightened attitudes towards women had not gained any significant foothold at the Bar by the beginning of the Second World War when Heilbron began in practice on the Northern circuit. She was one of 12 female barristers out of approximately 300 barristers on the circuit. Although she had gained a first class honours at Liverpool University and a scholarship at Gray's Inn, she had great difficulty in getting pupillage, a twelve month apprenticeship to be a barrister. One set of chambers explained what others had left unsaid, that it was because 'the other men in these chambers and the clerk would not welcome a woman pupil'. She was frequently warned that women would not succeed at the Bar because of the smallness of their voices and the prejudice of solicitors. In the 1940s social etiquette had not caught up with women barristers. Women were not allowed to enter a courtroom without a hat or to be present when cases with a sexual content were being heard.[15] Jonathan Goldberg QC remembers from his own first days on the Northern Circuit in the early 1970s the jealousy and backbiting which her success provoked. Undoubtedly those were misogynist and sometimes antisemitic.[16] This is an indication that her success was all the more remarkable given the exclusive nature of law practice in its higher echelons.

Her call to the Bar attracted the attention of the national press. She told the *Daily Express* that she was not a blue stocking. 'The general impression of a woman lawyer seems to be a sober old maid. I have not adopted the law as a hobby. I am serious about my career but that does not mean I shall give up dancing, swimming, golf or tennis. Legal problems will not keep me from other jobs I love – housework and gardening'. She talked of how when she would marry, she would continue on her career and that she would not sacrifice her life for her career and encompass both. Talking about a career was not the same as having one and it soon became apparent that securing a pupillage was more difficult than she assumed.[17]

By September 1939 she was taken on by a chambers in Castle Street, Liverpool. The timing was fortuitous as, due to the outbreak of the Second World War, many of her male colleagues across the city were leaving to fight. Solicitors who might otherwise have been wary of her were now seeking her out. Soon after she began practising a favourable article appeared in the *Birkenhead News*. 'Local history has been made this week when for the first time a woman barrister has pleaded in the Birkenhead police court. Only 24 years old, a dark vivacious Jewess, Miss Rose Heilbron, has already attracted a good deal of attention in the legal world'.[18] This comment shows an element of sexualisation and exoticism. Despite the comment that she was 'different', her practice began to thrive and in October 1942 she became the first woman to lead in a murder trial, securing a manslaughter charge for her client Harry Larkin, a dock worker who had cut the throat of his lover with a razor.

In April 1945 she was introduced to Nathaniel (Nat) Burstein, son of

Jewish Polish immigrants and a local GP. Nat had seen Heilbron at the Assizes when visiting with a friend who was involved in the Prison Board. He subsequently engineered an invitation to a party he knew she would be attending. Their courtship was swift and they were married on 9 August 1945 in a small ceremony in Harrogate Synagogue conducted by her cousin Rabbi Samuel Daiches.[19] Nat would play a crucial role in Heilbron's future success. His own work came with manageable hours and did not involve trips away from home. He was easy going and funny and an asset when it came to the social events that they had to attend in respect of her professional life. He had a steady income and Heilbron was able to lease her own premises in the city and became head of her own chambers. She gave birth to her only child Hilary on 2 January 1949. The story goes that she even took her legal papers into hospital with her when she went into labour. Six weeks later she was back in court.[20]

Her meteoric rise after the war proved she was head and shoulders above most of her male colleagues. A Liverpool journalist recalls she succeeded by the clearness of her mind and an acute intelligence.[21] By 1946 she had appeared in 10 murder trials and in 1949, at the age of 34, she was made one of the first two women King's Counsel (KC).[22] In the 1950s Heilbron became something of a household name to the crime loving public and a queen to her home city. In 1950 she became the first female barrister to appear as leading counsel in a murder trial. She defended the gangster George Kelly, accused of shooting dead the manager of the Cameo cinema in Liverpool. George Kelly, the defendant in her famous 1950 murder case, initially wanted a 'fella' because 'whoever heard of a Judy defending anyone?'[23] Kelly had been accused of shooting dead the manager of a Liverpool cinema. She was unable to save Kelly from the gallows (in 2003 the Court of Appeal quashed his conviction as unsafe), her successes in the first half of the 1950s included the defence of four men accused of hanging a boy during a burglary; she was able to show the death had been an accident.

There was also the case of Louis Bloom, a Hartlepool solicitor accused of murdering a former client Patricia Hessler with whom he was having an affair. Bloom had been trying to end the relationship and when she objected, he had grabbed her throat and strangled her. Heilbron dragged into court a two-foot high red and yellow plastic model of a human neck to illustrate medical evidence to the jury. Under cross examination she was able to get the Crown pathologist to concede that there were no outward signs that the victim had died from asphyxia and that death from inhibition of the Vargas nerve (pressure on it causes the heart to stop) is not always the result of violence. She convinced the jury that if a woman was screaming, it was natural to press on her neck and tell her to be quiet and that if a mistake was made and one pressed too hard, the result would be fatal. The jury returned a verdict of manslaughter and Bloom was given a three-year sentence. A fan wrote to her: 'Dear lady. You can't go around persuading juries that men are entitled to strangle their lady friends'.[24]

Other famous successes included the 1951 Bootle Bath Murder in which she defended 27-year-old Anna Neary accused of drowning her neighbour Emma Grace in her bath. Neary was acquitted. In 1952 Mary Standish was charged with murdering her husband with a knife. Rose argued in court that Standish had only meant to frighten her husband who had been drinking and who had hit her earlier in the evening. Standish walked out of court a free woman. Another client, the Knowsley Hall footman, escaped the gallows on the grounds of insanity after shooting two men dead and seriously wounding the Countess of Derby in the smoking room of her stately home. Heilbron's bold decision to call a psychiatrist as the only defence witness was considered a master stroke.[25] She was soon wanted for all big cases. She defended Vicky Clarke, accused in 1956 of setting fire to an Essex houseboat which resulted in the death of her two sons. Heilbron succeeded, in part due to the mores of the time, by persuading the jury that Wright would not have put her hair in curlers knowing that she would meet the fire brigade. A fellow lawyer said of her, 'she defends more than a set of facts. I think it shows that she is a woman and that helps her'. In 1955 she defended the London gang leader Jack 'Spot' Comer, accused of participating in a stabbing in Soho in which another man was injured; he walked free out of the Old Bailey, saying 'she's the greatest lawyer in history'.[26] Her mind was razor sharp. One of her crowning triumphs at the Bar was in 1970 when her successful appeal to the House of Lords resulted in an important ruling on the liability of landlords of premises where cannabis had been smoked.[27]

For most of the 1950s and part of the 1960s Heilbron was the only practising female Silk in England and Wales. Most of her cases, which were fascinating, gripped the public's attention, particularly the murder trials where the gallows loomed and which she had a number of notable successes. The rarity of her position as a successful and young working wife and mother led to her acquiring an extensive public and press following, both nationally and globally. Glowing articles were regularly written about her. Nevertheless, she was never allowed to talk to the press or give an interview which would at the time have been professional misconduct.

Her success and fame belied the slow progress that women were generally making at the Bar. Only two other women took Silk between 1949-1969 and in the mid-1950s there were only 64 women practising at the Self-Employed Bar, increasing to about 100 by the mid-1960s. The first female High Court Judge, Elizabeth Lane, was appointed in 1962 and it was not until 1974 that Heilbron became the second, also assigned to the Family Division, rather than the Queen's Bench Division, despite her vast experience in criminal and civil law. This was probably due to the fact that she was a woman. Women were still excluded from Bar Mess, the twice weekly dinners held during Assizes. It was said that their presence would 'spoil the atmosphere'. Heilbron was also barred from judges' dinners. During her career at the Bar there was no maternity leave, no flexible working hours, no Chambers grievance policies as these developments came much later. The Equal Pay Act only came in 1970, the Sex Discrimination Act in 1975 and it was not until 2008 and 2010 that further anti-discriminatory protections were put in place. Her daughter Hilary Heilbron points out that she managed to juggle home life and work and paved the way for others to follow. She used her position to encourage other women, speaking frequently on women's issues and criticised the prejudice that women met in the professions. Another barrister, Margaret Thatcher, when studying for the Bar and recently married also encouraged women in their careers. In an article in the *Sunday Graphic* in 1952 entitled 'Wake Up Women' she cited Heilbron as a role model. 'Unless Britain, in the new age to come, can produce more Rose Heilbrons, not only in the field of law, we shall have betrayed the tremendous work of those who fought for equal rights against such misguided opposition'.[28]

In 1975, in her role as a high court judge, she made an 11-year-old girl with Sotos syndrome, which made her physically advanced despite having learning difficulties, a ward of court in order to prevent the sterilisation her mother had agreed with the paediatrician and gynaecologist. Heilbron held that it was neither medically necessary nor in the girl's interest to perform an operation that would involve the 'deprivation of a basic human right, namely the right of a woman to reproduce'.[29] That year she was appointed by the Home Secretary to head a committee of inquiry into the rape laws. She said the laws allowed the victim to be put on trial instead of her attacker and it was wrong for a woman's private life to be made public as a way of throwing doubt on her evidence. One of her findings was that names of rape victims should be kept secret. The report called for tougher curbs on the freedom of defence lawyers who might try to destroy the victim's character in the witness box. Another significant ruling was over the right of a woman and her unborn child. In 1987 a 23 year old Oxford student had sought an order on behalf of himself and his unborn child to stop his girlfriend having an abortion. Heilbron gave the abortion the go-ahead. She ruled that in the law the foetus, which was nearly 18 weeks old, had no legal standing to bring an action through the father to keep itself alive. Within 36 hours of the precedent having been made she won the backing of three Appeal Court judges and three law lords.[30]

Rachel Cooke points out that it would be difficult to overstate how well known and admired Heilbron was in her day. Due to the death penalty, murder trials were followed far more avidly as a life was at stake. A decade after the end of the wars there was still widespread unease about what violence people had experienced meant for civil society and whether its long-term effects were on display in the criminal courts. Even among the famous lawyers whose names filled the newspaper columns, Heilbron was in a class of her own. She was beautiful and determined and the papers reported everything she said and did. In the eyes of the press, her brilliance in the courtroom and her hefty earnings – facts that might otherwise have irked then – were softened and made more acceptable by the knowledge that she was also married with a small daughter and kept a delightful house. The *Daily Mail* reported that at home in Liverpool Heilbron leaves behind her wig and gown and the majesty of the law becomes the quiet attractive housewife in a fawn coat who, as the tradesmen say 'wouldn't dream of trying to use her position to jump the queue'. The same article noted that her family's favourite foods included liver sausage, olives, gherkins and salad and that she owned a magnificent collection of classical records and drove a Triumph. Others wrote of the Bechstein piano and the pink geraniums in the porch. Actress Joanne Heal who met her at a reception reported that for all her cleverness she was most anxious to talk about the thrill of owning a new dish washing machine. For the most part the newspapers were reverential. The *Liverpool Post* said that success had not spoiled her and that she was charming, unaffected and liked nothing better in her spare time than doing her own shopping.[31]

The press's love affair with Heilbron had taken a difference stance in respect of women. Until her advent the newspapers had been on the side of those who still regarded the admittance of women to the Bar as an unhappy experiment and columnists often reported on how unnatural it was for a woman to appear in court. They did concede that they made 'splendid solicitors as they were conscientious, excelled at correspondence at dealing with wills and conveyancing'.[32] Those jealous of her career have said she benefited from the fact that for the first six years so many able men were in the armed forces. Given the prejudices of the Bar at the time there is little doubt that without the Second World War she would have faced more limitations, but her spectacular rise once the men were back proved she was head and shoulders above most of her contemporaries.[33] Her dazzling ability, combined with her looks, her earthy Liverpudlian roots and a set of professional rules which dictated that she could not accept the invitations she received to appear on poplar panel shows meant that she was a person to be admired from afar. She became a Liverpool celebrity. Whether she went to America for a Bar conference, took the salute as honorary colonel of the East Lancashire Battalion of the Woman's Royal Army Corps or appeared as the first woman in Liverpool to wear a calf length evening dress, she was news. Her daughter Hilary Heilbron, a barrister and QC, stresses that her mother did not set out to be a pioneer. She enjoyed her career and it was a hobby as well as her work and that fame was something that came with it. 'I think she captured the public's imagination because what she did was rare. She was also very good at what she did'.[34]

In demand as an after-dinner speaker, she told her audiences that prejudice was still rampant and women must not flag in their efforts to overcome it. Nor should they ever forget those who had won for them such rights as the vote. She believed in equal pay for women and was disdainful of laws such as the Income Tax Law of 1918 which said that if a married woman saved money from her housekeeping, such savings still belonged in law to her husband which put them in the same bracket as those that were insane. Her mother had encouraged her to go into law. Speaking at a Jewish women's discussion group in Manchester, she said she did not want housewives' minds to get rusty and felt that women should have outside interests.[35] She considered that it was wasteful to the woman herself but also to the community that a woman should have to relinquish her outside occupation.[36] In 1952 she spoke up on behalf of professional women who, having married and had children, wanted to resume their careers and that a qualified woman should not be lost to her profession on the advent of a family.[37] She was a keen member of Soroptimist International, the worldwide organisation for women in management and professions, working to advance human rights and the status of women.

Heilbron managed to combine a career and home. The press eulogised her prowess, finding it remarkable at the time that she could combine such a demanding career successfully with family life.[38] She grew up in a happy family environment. Her parents were orthodox Jews and she was instilled with Jewish culture. The family went to synagogue regularly and she attended Hebrew classes at Princes Road synagogue, where her mother's family were long standing members, and she later taught Bible classes there. Whilst at Liverpool University she was treasurer of the Jewish Students Society.[39] She had a strong Jewish identity and was active on behalf of many Jewish and Israeli causes. She was a member of the Merseyside Aid Committee of the Jewish Blind Society and often spoke at Jewish fundraising appeals, such as a Jewish Board of Guardians event where she stressed how help was essential and urged people to help their brethren in need and referred to the Board's contribution to solving the housing difficulties of a number of women by the conversion of two large houses into flatlets and that there was a long waiting list of women for such accommodation.[40] Soon after she became a High Court Judge she moved to London where she lived in a flat in 2 Gray's Inn Square and joined the West London synagogue.[41]

She was awarded Dame Commander of the Order of the British Empire in 1979 and retired in 1988. The Lord Chancellor wrote on her retirement: 'My barrister and judge, you have pioneered the way for many women who will follow you'.[42] Cherie Blair QC recalls that when she grew up in her grandmother's house in Liverpool the name that made her grandmother excited was Rose Heilbron. When Heilbron was arguing a case before a jury at Liverpool Assizes her grandmother would follow her cases avidly. Heilbron became a role model for Blair and an example of what a Liverpool girl could achieve in the law. Blair was shocked to later discover that the reason Heilbron was so famous was that she was a rarity in her profession. She broke the mould because she was a brilliant lawyer, a working mother who always found time for her family and a much-loved employer to both her domestic and professional staff. Throughout her public life she spoke up for women's right to achieve what men take for granted – a fulfilling career and a wonderful family life.[43]

Heilbron died on 8 December 2005. She was one of the most celebrated defence barristers of the post-war years; no woman before her had enjoyed anything like her success rate at the criminal Bar.[44] She was the one who first lit the torch which current and future female barristers and judges carry and will carry. She paved the way, not in any strident manner, but by simply getting on with the job and in doing so helping to promote the role of women. Most of the reforms which she advocated in relation to legal and women's issues have, after many years, come to fruition.[45] She was the Margaret Thatcher of the law, a woman who broke through the glass ceiling by sheer force of personality and talent.[46]

Heilbron's career was one of great achievement, no one succeeded at the Bar on sentiment or chivalrous loyalty. Any success in law must be obtained through merit as a lawyer and an advocate, irrespective of sex. She had to prove that she was not only the equal of a man, but a little better.[47] It was a remarkable feat for a young woman to crash both ethnic and gender barriers at that time. Another woman who managed to succeed, if in a more precise and less newsworthy part of the law, in this period was Myrella Cohen. Although she did not achieve the same national limelight as Heilbron, she did much to contribute to alleviate the plight of Jewish women who were unable to obtain a divorce.

Myrella Cohen (1927-2002)

Myrella Cohen QC was one of the first female judges in Great Britain and at the age of 44 the youngest judge in the country at the time with a formidable reputation as a 'no nonsense' judge in criminal cases. She was a firm believer in women's education and careers and although religiously observant castigated the traditional attitude that pushed women into early marriage and tied them to the home. When she retired in 1995, Myrella was the longest serving woman judge and longest serving Jewish judge.[48] Strongly committed to orthodox Judaism, she was proud that she never compromised her observance throughout her career. She was a member of the Chief Rabbi's working party, which produced the prenuptial agreement used in the United Synagogue, and was instrumental in bringing reform to English law by tying civil divorce to agreement on religious divorce.[49]

Myrella was born in Manchester to Sam and Sarah Cohen. Her parents wanted to name her after their mothers Myra and Ella, so they came up with the combination of Myrella. The only child of parents who ran a clothing shop in Manchester and who were themselves children of immigrants and unable to fulfil their educational potential, she was encouraged to go on from Manchester High School and Colwyn Bay Grammar School (following evacuation) to read law at Manchester University with the full blessing of her parents. 'They were typical of their generation. My mother was very intelligent and my father would have loved to be a lawyer.'[50] She acknowledged the fair treatment given to Jews in Britain and that it had been possible, despite the fact that she came from a humble background and the grandchild of Lithuanian immigrants, to make good.[51]

She was called to the Bar at Gray's Inn in 1950. When Myrella started training as a barrister women still found it difficult to obtain a place in chambers and were rarely instructed in high profile civil work which involved acting for big business or insurance companies so they drifted into family and criminal law. Even later in the mid-1960s Jewish circuit judge Dawn Freedman,[52] remembered that many chambers restricted their number of female members, unofficially or otherwise.[53]

During her time at Gray's Inn she met a solicitor from Sunderland, Mordaunt Cohen, when he travelled south to represent a client in court. They married at the Central Synagogue, Manchester in 1953 and she moved to Sunderland for the major part of her career. With her husband she formed the first husband and wife team to hold judicial posts at the same time when he was appointed chairman of industrial tribunals in England and Wales in 1974. She was the first woman barrister in Newcastle in 1953. An early pioneer of the career break, she worked part-time for eight years to look after her two children. Her appointment as Assistant Recorder in Teeside in 1967 made her the first woman in the north-east to hold judicial office. In 1970 she became the second Jewish woman, after Rose Heilbron, to be appointed Queen's Counsel and only the fifth woman overall. That there were two Jewish women out of the five was quite remarkable. On her appointment in 1972 as the north-east Circuit Judge and High Court Family Division Deputy Judge, she was the country's third woman and youngest judge.[54] A member of the Parole Board 1983-86, she was acutely conscious of the problem of family breakdown from repeated sentencing; her most notorious cases included wardship hearings arising out of the 1987 Cleveland abuse scandal.[55] She moved to London in 1989 after her husband retired so she could be nearer to her children and began sitting in the Central Criminal Court at the Old Bailey. Unused to commuting, she preferred to sit instead at Harrow Crown Court that was nearer to her home in Edgware.[56]

Myrella attributed the secret of her success down to tenacity, organisation and a strong belief in family and religious commitment.[57] She regarded family life as the cornerstone of stability. Renowned for her tough sentencing in court, she blamed much of the disturbing rise in crime and violence on the modern day breakdown of the family unit. It did not take long for hardened criminals to quiver in the dock when they heard that Myrella Cohen was to sit in judgement on them.[58] She was not a controversial woman but she had a healthy impatience when confronted with red tape and a firm hand with the out and out villain. 'As a judge she is tougher than most. Described as a stern judge with a well-known reluctance to suffer fools gladly. Her summing-ups can be lengthy and sometimes outspoken and her concern for discipline in the home a recurrent theme when the need arises'.[59] Myrella remarked that she had heard that she was a tough judge and although she did not necessarily agree she admitted that she leaned towards the heavier sentence when crimes of violence were concerned. Sitting in the family court in Newcastle and hearing divorces, battles of custody of children and wardship cases drove her towards setting up the Sunderland and South Tyneside family conciliation service.[60] A court official commented that she was an extremely hard working competent woman who had to overcome strong prejudice 'not only the fact that she was a woman but also that she was a Jewess'.[61] This observation reflects how much she achieved despite the obstacles.

Her move to London, two years before the appointment of the new Chief Rabbi Dr Jonathan Sacks, made her ideally placed to participate in the Chief Rabbi's review of the role of women in the Orthodox community. At the end of a long legal career as a circuit judge in the north-east and in the London courts, Myrella gave her attention to help formulate more sympathetic Jewish divorce laws and was a key figure in a raft of measures to alleviate the plight of women who were refused a religious divorce by their husbands. The problem was of unresolved divorces, where an English civil divorce had been granted but not a Jewish religious divorce. This left the parties free to remarry civilly but not in Jewish law. However, an imbalance resulted because a Jewish husband's second union could be countenanced under the not quite obsolete tradition of polygamy, which meant that his subsequent children were legitimate in Jewish law. A woman, however, was completely debarred from second marriage or cohabitation. Any children of a subsequent union were considered illegitimate.

As it was so crucial for a divorcing wife to avoid being an *agunah* (chained woman), still tied to a man from whom she had a civil but not a religious divorce, the way was wide open for blackmail by a husband contesting the financial settlement or child custody. Without a *get* (Jewish divorce) a woman could not remarry in a synagogue. Myrella put her considerable intellectual and organisational talents to the task of making the civil and religious processes interdependent. Working with Dawn Freedman she produced a document for Rabbi Jonathan Sacks who wanted to start his term of office in 1991 with a fresh look at the somewhat milder Anglo-Jewish equivalent of the suffragette movement.[62]

Myrella considered that better rabbinic training might help clergy find solutions for an *agunah*. 'The emancipated, liberated, educated woman of today may resent some of the disabilities imposed on her by *halachic* law (Jewish law) which her uneducated sisters accepted without complaint. The time has now come to bring our concerns into the open. Where there has been a monologue let there be a dialogue. Where there have been recriminations let there be solutions even if it means rabbinic education should be more widely based so the clergy can understand the concerns of modern society and be able to interpret problems more compassionately'.[63] She criticised some rabbis who encouraged or instigated behaviour contrary to Jewish ethical law, resulting in injustice. She condemned the disgraceful and immoral bargaining and horse-trading over money and the future of children that can precede a *get*. She called on the community to ostracise recalcitrant husbands. 'Don't buy from his shop. Don't invite him into your home. Make him a social leper'.[64]

Myrella gave her full support to the The Agunot Campaign that was started by Sandra Blackman and Gloria Proops in 1995 to put pressure on men who would not give their wives a *get*. Blackman's marriage broke down after their child died aged 21. Her husband walked out in 1987 and there was a civil divorce. In the early 1990s Blackman realised she did not have a *get*. She contacted the Beth Din but they were not sympathetic. 'Douglas never openly refused to give me a get. He just delayed. The Beth Din (rabbinical court) would invite him in but he never turned up'. Sandra eventually received her *get* in the mid 1990s.[65]

Blackman campaigned hard on behalf of others. Press releases were sent and banners made with the words 'Agunot of the World unite. You have nothing to lose but your chains'. One example was Susan Zinkin who had been battling to receive a *get* since her civil divorce in 1962. Vigils were staged outside the home of her husband Errol Elias in Golders Green, London where leaflets were handed out to the public with a tear off letter to Elias urging him to grant the *get*.[66] The Agunot Campaign operated throughout the country and demonstrations were held with well-known personalities such as Maureen Lipman coming to give their support. Blackman gave praise to the role that Myrella played in her endeavours to help changed the law. 'She was very calm, in control of the situation and very mindful. She could balance the English law and *halakha* (Jewish law). She was respectful of the *dayanim* (judges in the Rabbinic Court) and very measured in attitude. She would speak to the *dayanim* and try and see where there was a loophole and room for manoeuvre. [67]

A prenuptial agreement in 1993 was the first stage in dealing with the problem. However, as it was confined to synagogues under the Chief Rabbi's authority, its remit was too narrow and ministers were psychologically averse to discussing divorce on the eve of marriage. It also could not guarantee the essential link with civil marriage. Myrella pursued her quest for an effective solution under the aegis of the Jewish Marriage Council, working with sympathetic MPs and the Lord Chancellor's Office as well as the Emeritus Chief Rabbi, Lord Jakobovits in the House of Lords. She drew up the Jakobovits Amendment which ensured that a civil divorce between Jewish parties took into account the requirement for a religious divorce. The Amendment, although accepted when first introduced as part of the Family Law Act 1996, fell within a section that was dropped from the final version. It was reintroduced with the passing of the Divorce (Religious Marriages) Act 2002.[68]

Eleanor Lind QC, Chairman of the Board of Deputies *Get* group said that Myrella's contribution was of the utmost importance to the debate and the ultimate success of parliamentary legislation.[69] The Act enabled either party to apply to a judge to withhold a civil divorce where the religious divorce has not been completed. It meant that wives whose husbands refuse to give a *get* – or husbands whose wives refuse to accept the *get* – could ask a judge to defer the decree absolute. [70] Rabbi Sacks acknowledged that Myrella was a prime force behind the campaign for this legislation, bringing to it the legal wisdom that made her so exemplary a figure in Jewish life. 'The positive benefits of this law will be a legacy to her and all that she stood for'.[71]

Although one of the first ever female judges in Britain, epitomising what a woman can achieve in the male dominated legal world and fighting hard for the case of women in the Jewish divorce laws, she did not consider herself part of the feminist movement at the time. 'Success is not to be gained for joining that band of women who burn their undergarments'. She shied away from any politics and never attended political functions with her husband, leader of the Conservative group on Sunderland Council, a rule that a Newcastle councillor believed she took to extreme.[72]

She believed in the maxim that hard work brings its own rewards and was insistent that women should be given equal educational and career opportunities.[73] At a talk at Jews' College, London she told the audience that Jewish girls should go out in the world equipped with a good education and not rush into an early marriage and that it was impossible to put back the clock and confine women to the home. Men should appraise their attitude to women and realise that the synagogue was no longer a men's club. In the smaller ageing communities it was the women who kept the community alive and she called for women to hold office on communal and synagogue organisations. She pleaded with rabbis for change and deplored what she described as 'holier than thou' attitudes. As one who was Orthodox, she refused to pray behind a curtain or attend social functions where she was not allowed to sit next to her husband. 'I cannot understand or justify this any more than the thanks given in the daily prayer for being a man rather than a woman. The phrasing of this prayer should be altered'.[74]

Despite these views Myrella never once compromised her religious observance. On winter Fridays she went in to work early and worked through her lunch time in order to leave early to be home to prepare for the Sabbath.[75] She would joke that she and Judge Dawn Freedman were the only judges who put chicken soup on the stove to cook before they sat at Harrow Crown Court on Fridays.[76] During her time in Newcastle there were occasions when she stayed in a local hotel on a Friday night rather than travel to her Sunderland home if she could not get home before the Sabbath began. It was commented that 'although very religious she was never blinkered about life in the raw'.[77]

Affiliated to Jewish organisations from a young age, she had been chairman of the Manchester University Jewish Society and Graduates Society and Salford Jewry Executive Council. She belonged to Emunah and Wizo and was a founder of the north-east branch of the League of Jewish Women and a life member of its council. She was well known as a speaker for the central Jewish lecture committee of the Board of Deputies and a long-standing member of the Jewish Marriage Council's legal group and chairman of the UK branch of the International Association of Jewish Lawyers and Jurists. Both she and her husband were very involved with the local Jewish community. Mordaunt played an active part in Jewish affairs, locally and nationally. He was life president of the Sunderland Hebrew Congregation and was involved with the Sunderland Association of Jewish Ex-Servicemen and a member of the Board of Deputies. Myrella's commitments did extend beyond the Jewish world. A sufferer from cancer, she was vice president of the North of England Cancer Research Campaign, a founder of International Family Mediation Services, honorary member of Sunderland Soroptimist International, patron of the Sunderland Council for the Disabled and the Suzy Lamplugh Trust.

Myrella died in London on 25 October 2002 and was buried in Jerusalem.[78] In his eulogy Chief Rabbi Jonathan Sacks described her as 'one of the most remarkable figures with whom I had the privilege to work. Highly respected as a judge and a proud observant Jew she brought both identities together in her life-long pursuit of justice'. Judge Martin Zeitman QC said she commanded great respect within both Jewish and secular society, synthesising the best of both cultures. As a judge she was renowned for her firm but fair approach. Her pride was that she reached her position without any compromise of her Jewish principles. She defended the prenuptial agreement against its Orthodox rabbinic challenges, refusing to be browbeaten by the establishment. While never considering herself a feminist, she always promoted women's education and careers and thought women had a rightful place on communal and religious bodies.[79]

Conclusion

Both Rose Heilbron and Myrella Cohen achieved top positions in the legal profession at a time that it was not easy for women to do so. Though their rise as QCs and judges and foci of their careers differed in some respects, they shared many similarities. They came from provincial Orthodox backgrounds and their families gave them the utmost support and encouragement to study. Both women maintained a strong Jewish identity throughout their lives, albeit Cohen remained strictly Orthodox while Heilbron did not. Both were able to balance marriage and children with their active legal work and importantly, both were able to forge highly respected careers in the law despite the many impediments placed in their way by an overwhelmingly male-dominated profession.

Unlike many of the Jewish women profiled in these pages, both Rose Heilbron and Myrella Cohen came from British born Jewish parents, though Heilbron's family were more comfortably middle-class during her childhood. Both sets of parents wanted their daughters to attend university and strive for professional careers at a time when most Jewish women centred their lives around home and family. They were not discouraged from studying law despite the barriers they were inevitably bound to encounter in entering the profession in the first few decades after it was finally opened up to women.

Their supportive upbringing in Orthodox homes also led both women to maintain their strong connections to Judaism and Jewish causes. Myrella Cohen remained an observant orthodox Jew, both privately and professionally throughout her life. She kept a kosher home and observed the Sabbath, even if it meant juggling her working hours or avoiding travel on a Friday and she was proud of the fact that she had never compromised her religious observances during her career. Heilbron, on the other hand, did not maintain the orthodox life of her childhood, but nevertheless kept a strong Jewish identity and was active for Jewish causes, joining the West London Synagogue, which is affiliated to Reform Judaism. Myrella was also very active in Jewish organisations in northeast England and her concern for the Jewish way of life extended into her career where for many years she endeavoured to change the law to alleviate the plight of Jewish women.

As one of the pioneering early women barristers, Rose Heilbron faced chauvinism in the legal profession and was subjected to the gender biases of the day in the court of public opinion. By the time Heilbron was ready to read for the bar, on the eve of the Second World War, only a handful of women were practicing barristers in the UK and though eminently qualified, she herself found it difficult to secure the necessary apprenticeship for admission to the Bar. The war proved fortuitous, as many men with whom she might have competed for pupillage and cases joined the forces, though those who were jealous of her wielded this circumstance as a cudgel to denigrate her success. However, Heilbron's meteoric rise in the post-war period proved her worth as she gained fame for her many high-profile criminal cases. But the sexism present in both the legal world and society more broadly continued to have an effect on her career and the way it was reported in the press. Focusing on her appearance, the press, which reported every trial, called Heilbron 'the woman judge pin up girl' and made much of her ability to balance her career with domesticity reporting that she was charming, unaffected and like nothing better in her spare time than doing her own shopping.[80] More significantly, like most women, Heilbron was initially denied the opportunity to represent high profile civil clients and made her specialty criminal law. When she ascended to the High Court, she was assigned to the Family Division, not, despite her considerable experience the Queen's Bench, and for most of her career was excluded from professionally socialising with male colleagues.

Though only thirteen years separated the women in age, Cohen's path to becoming a barrister and eventually a QC and Judge was somewhat easier due in no small part to the pioneering work of Heilbron and a handful of other female barristers who had come up in the 1930s and 40s. Though by 1950, there were not as many barriers to the Bar as previously, Cohen was nevertheless also denied the opportunity to take on prestigious civil cases and made her career in the area of family law, specialising in the subject of Jewish divorce. Her barrier-breaking successes as a barrister and a judge were all accomplished in the northern provinces, rather than in the more visible and high-profile Home Counties. Nevertheless, Cohen finished her career in London and her contributions to family law have been considerable. Like Heilbron, Myrella Cohen balanced career and family, setting an example by working part time when her children were young. She championed women's education and equality, even within the Jewish orthodox faith.

Despite fighting for their places in the man's world of the law, neither Rose Heilbron nor Myrella Cohen saw themselves as radical campaigners for women's rights. Though they both strived for equal opportunities for women, Myrella never considered herself a feminist[81] and Heilbron's daughter Hilary commented that her mother 'paved the way, not in any strident feminist manner, but simply by getting on with the job and in doing so helping to promote the role of women'.[82] They were both ground-breaking in their own time and their own fields, and serve as inspirations and role models for future generations of female barristers and judges.

6

Doctors

Women's role in medicine and healing is evident throughout history, from the ancient world to the present day. Women were not, however, allowed entry into British medical schools until the late nineteenth century. In the preceding years they faced a long struggle to become doctors. Arguments against women practising medicine were based on beliefs about women's physical, mental and emotional natures and the idea that medicine was not an appropriate career path.

Midwifery was the only clinical profession in which women were allowed to practice, partly because its lower status did not attract men and it was traditionally considered a woman's role. The 1858 Medical Registration Act did not exclude women explicitly but the Royal Colleges, universities and medical institutions did so by either prohibiting women from studying medicine or from the academic examinations that would allow them to practise. In 1874 a group of women established the first medical school in Britain to allow women to graduate and practise medicine: the London School of Medicine for Women (now the Royal Free Hospital School of Medicine).[1]

The establishment of the first medical schools for women led to an increase in the number of women practising medicine in the early twentieth century. In 1881 there were still only 25 women doctors in England and Wales, rising to 495 by 1911. There were still restrictions on where women could study medicine as they were admitted to only a small number of medical schools. The First World War allowed women to take up posts in hospital that would ordinarily have been occupied by men. From 1915, some London hospitals began to train women, including Kings College Hospital and University College Hospital. But despite their competence, female physicians still faced major career obstacles in the interwar period, including discrimination on the basis of their marital status. Marital bans, restricting employment once they married or became pregnant, were adopted by many employers, particularly in professions, even in post-war Britain.

Various bars on women studying medicine continued until 1944 when as a result of sustained public pressure, a government committee decided that public funds would only be made available to those schools that allowed a 'reasonable proportion of women, say one-fifth'. While this was a positive step to improving women's participation, these recommendations became the basis for quotas that restricted all but the strongest of women candidates from entering the medical profession.[2]

The difficulty of finding medical posts was further compounded for Jewish women. It was only in the mid-eighteenth century, and in Scotland in particular, that Jewish doctors began to graduate as previously Jews had difficulties in gaining admission to universities and the developing Royal Colleges, and also in obtaining apprenticeships. The early nineteenth century saw the opening of University College, London where Jews, among other non-Anglicans, could graduate.[3]

With its strong employment prospects and prestige in both Jewish and wider society, medicine was often the aim of both the ambitious child and parent. The interwar period saw a growth of Jewish interest in medicine, especially among the second-generation immigrants whose move into the profession began in the First World War when many medical school places were freed up by conscription. During the 1920s and 1930s grants and scholarships became available for students of restricted means. The route into medicine was not an easy one even with the assistance of financial aid. Antisemitism often blighted their time in training and employment. At times, formal Jewish quotas in medical schools, such as the University of Leeds during the Second World War, limited the number of places for would-be Jewish doctors.[4]

During the 1920s and 1930s many newly qualified Jewish doctors anglicised their surnames, and sometimes their first names, in order to conceal their Jewish origins and help their career advancement. In Leeds, for example, Israel Liberman changed his name to John Morrison Lever and Jacob Rosenscwige became Jack Rose. On 21 June 1930, an advertisement appeared in the *British Medical Journal*: 'Wanted, Midlands, Assistant (doctor), male… No Jews or men of colour'. In the late 1940s and throughout the 1950s it was almost impossible for Jews to secure senior surgical posts in any field in the central London teaching hospitals and in Manchester and Leeds.[5] Anthony Radcliffe, an eminent ear nose and throat surgeon, saw an advertisement in 1938 for a position at the Royal National ENT Hospital, London and obtained the post after changing his name from Rakoff to Radcliffe on the suggestion of a non-Jewish governor of the hospital. Jewish doctor Ian Gordon of the London Jewish Hospital commented that there was a certain amount of resistance to appointing

Jews to senior appointments. 'They wanted someone who was a peer rather than someone who is of a different species'. Jews were regarded by many as a different species. [6]

Class was another barrier and not only for Jewish candidates. Certain hospitals were known for the public school and Oxbridge backgrounds of their resident staff and consultants. Jewish doctors particularly suffered from this since a much higher proportion of Jewish medical students came from a working-class background than was the case generally. [7]

Given this blatant gender and racial bias, it is remarkable that the first two women profiled in this chapter, Muriel Elsie Landau and her contemporary Hannah Billig, both rose through the ranks of the medical profession just as women were beginning to be qualified as doctors. Though pioneers as female physicians, they practised largely within the Jewish community, both making their careers in London's East End. A generation later, though gender bias remained a challenge, Miriam Stoppard was much freer than her predecessors to forge a widely varied career that included practicing medicine and dispensing medical knowledge and advice as a television presenter and columnist. During her career, Stoppard has seen the barriers to women's participation in all aspects of medicine fall, but when Landau began the medical studies that would lead to a career as a renowned surgeon, there were fewer than half a dozen female surgeons in England.

Muriel Elsie Landau (1895-1972)

Muriel Elsie Landau was born in London on 21 January 1895 and was one of the first female surgeons in England. It was an incredible feat. The first woman surgeon was in 1911 and by 1919 there were only four women Fellows of the Royal College of Surgeons of England.[8] Muriel was the first Jewish woman to be elected and made her reputation over a span of fifty years as an eminent surgeon in the specialist field of gynaecology.

Muriel was born into a strictly Orthodox family. Her mother was Chaya Klara Kohn from Nordlingen, Germany, the daughter of Rabbi Marx Mordechai Michael Kohn. Her father Marcus Israel Landau, a shoemaker, was from Belarus. He was born in 1837 with the name Mordechai Fredkin. He managed to avoid being conscripted into the Cossack army and fled Russia at the age of sixteen using a passport of a dead man named Landau. As Marcus Landau he made his way to Paris and then Frankfurt where he married and in 1855 the couple moved to England.[9]

Marcus Landau was drawn to the spiritual and the physical. He was by profession a boot and shoe manufacturer, a *shochet* (kosher slaughterer) and later a grocer. He was also a Hebrew scholar, a mystic, an amateur mathematician and an inventor. He published a newspaper *The Jewish Standard* (subtitled The English Organ of Orthodoxy) in his basement from 1888-1891. He was interested in the new science of aeronautics and corresponded with the Wright brothers who paid him a visit when they came to London in the early 1900s. He had a passion for intricate arithmetical calculations which he would do in his head, and was drawn to the invention of lamps – safety lamps for mines, carriage lamps, street lamps – and he patented some in these in the 1870s. A polymath and autodidact himself, he was passionately keen on education for all his children. Seven of his sons were eventually drawn to mathematics and the physical sciences as he was. His daughters, by contrast, were by and large drawn to the human sciences, to biology, medicine, education and sociology.[10] Muriel was fortunate that her father was ahead of his time in respect of his daughters receiving further education that enabled them to enter professions.

Landau was educated at Dame Alice Owens School, Islington, where she gained an entrance scholarship to the London School of Medicine for Women. She qualified in 1918 and after house appointments at the Royal Free and at Queen Charlotte's Hospital was enrolled as a registrar to the Hospital for Women, Soho Square. In 1921 she took her MD in obstetrics and gynaecology and at the early age of 28 was appointed to the staff of the Elizabeth Garrett Hospital in Euston Road, London. Her interests were mainly obstetrics and gynaecology, but she also practised general surgery and eventually became the senior consulting surgeon, giving her services to the hospital from 1921-61, the year of her retirement. During the Second World War when the hospital was evacuated to the countryside she continued her work there, travelling to London often in the black-out. She also built up a large private practice, which she continued after her retirement, and was on the staff of the Marie Curie Hospital for Women, Hampstead and the London Jewish Hospital.[11]

The London Jewish Hospital in Stepney Green (1919-1979) was established to serve the needs of the Jewish East End. Nearly all of the staff were Jewish, most of whom could speak Yiddish, and the facilities were kosher.[12] Landau was also resident surgeon at the Jewish Maternity Hospital, known as Mother Levy's (after a long serving superintendent) in Underwood Road, where she was called to assist in difficult labour or complicated obstetrics cases. Her son Oliver Sacks commented that there was nothing she loved more than a challenging delivery – an arm presentation, a breech – brought off successfully.[13] It was reported in the

East London Observer, a local newspaper that was sympathetic to Jews, that 'it is noteworthy that while deaths in childbirth are said to be on the increase, of the 350 Jewish women delivered during 1927 there was not a single death which speaks volumes for its medical staff'.[14]

Lara Marks explains that religion and ethnicity played a vital role in shaping the form of health care afforded to Jewish mothers in East London. These issues were critically important at a time when comprehensive medical care and maternity services were minimal. Jewish patients had special needs that were not always catered by the outside community. Their special needs spurred the Jewish community to establish an innovative form of aid for mothers through its home help schemes. Evidence strongly suggested that the Jewish poor had much lower rates of infant mortality than their neighbours. One contributory factor could have been the access Jewish mothers and their infants had to Jewish communal support such as the Jewish Board of Guardians, the Sick Room Helps Society (SRHS), and the Home Helps Scheme established in 1895 which was ahead of its time. Alice Model (1856-1943) was instrumental in setting up the SRHS. In 1897 she established the Jewish Day Nursery in Spitalfields which initially prioritised the children of widows so they could work. The nursery provided children with regular meals, and places to wash and disinfect their clothes. Daily visits from doctors also prevented illnesses. Model grew up in a middle-class family in Hampstead. Like others in her position she expanded the acceptable horizons for women through her involvement in charitable activities.

The SRHS undertook to supply nurses to those who were sick and poor and midwives to those in confinement. The provision of home helps filled in the gaps between nurses' visits and carried out domestic chores that mothers normally did. Other nursing associations who were striving to distinguish between what they saw as domestic work and what they saw as 'professional nursing' did not embrace the idea of home helps as fully as the SRHS and it was not until nineteen years after the creation of the SRHS that the Central Committee on Women's Employment, inspired by the SRHS model, created its own home help scheme for east and west London.[15] The SRHS led to the opening of Mother Levy's, complete with midwife training school, at 24 Underwood Road in 1911. This was Britain's only Jewish maternity hospital. It was extended in the 1920s to provide an infant welfare centre and an antenatal clinic. Facilities for the children included medical checks, fumigating the children's clothes to prevent the spread of disease, subsidised meals and a fund for mothers' dinners enabling them to eat with their children.[16]

Mother Levy's was the birthplace of thousands of East Enders, including singer Alma Cogan, composer Lionel Bart and playwright Arnold Wesker. It had a reputation for being a homely and cosy place, in contrast to the nearby enormous London hospital, and patients felt comfortable being attended by a nursing staff who were sympathetic to Jewish rituals. The mothers were surrounded by familiar Jewish faces from their neighbourhood who understood their cultural and religious background.[17] Candles were lit by the nurses in every ward on Friday nights, challah bread was served, and services were held in the synagogue. Landau invariably brought a home-made cheesecake to every session she attended. There were many patients who only spoke Yiddish and many of the signs were in Yiddish. Many older patients felt more comfortable confiding personal matters to a Jewish doctor to whom they would relate more easily.[18]

Landau's involvement with Mother Levy's and the London Jewish Hospital reflected her close connection with her Jewish heritage. She passed an exam for teachers of Hebrew and religion at Jews College with distinction.[19] She first met her husband Samuel Sacks, who was born in Lithuania in 1895, when they were both medical students and members of the London University Zionist society and they married at Dalston Synagogue in 1922. Dr Sacks went on to become a family doctor spending some twenty years tending to the immigrant Jews of Whitechapel. He started his practice in New Road, Whitechapel in 1918.[20]

The couple were a rumbustious, cultivated, polymathic Jewish family.[21] They lived in a large rambling Edwardian house in Brondesbury, northwest London with lounge, drawing room and library. Landau had consulting rooms there. There was a whole staff of helpers and servants.[22] The house became a meeting place for Jewish cultural activities. Together they stimulated interest in modern Hebrew studies and in Jewish scholarship and many meetings of the Brit Ivrit Olamit (the World Association for Hebrew Language and Culture which fostered the study of Hebrew) were held at the house.[23] They had four sons; three became doctors including the leading neurologist and writer Oliver Sacks. From 1965-66 she was elected President of the Medical Women's Federation of Great Britain. She also found time to help Zionist aspirations and for over 15 years was chairman of the Doctors and Dentists Group for the Joint Palestine Appeal.[24] Despite communal affiliations, Oliver Sacks reflected that she was a shy woman who did not enjoy social occasions. There was, however, another side to her character where she could be expansive, exuberant and a performer when she was at ease with her students. She loved to tell medical stories and had total absorption in her work.[25]

Landau was a staunch traditionalist and went every Saturday to Walm Lane Synagogue.[26] She was deeply religious and reacted badly when she found out that her son Oliver was homosexual. She told him that he was an abomination and she wished he had never been born. She did not speak to him for a few days and when she did speak there was no reference to what she had said. 'My mother so open and supportive in some ways, was harsh and inflexible in this area. She was a Bible reader and loved the Psalms and Song of Solomon'. He commented that she was haunted by the verses in Leviticus 'thou shall not lie with mankind, as with womankind it is an abomination'. He had to keep reminding himself that his mother was a creature of her Orthodox upbringing and times, in which England treated homosexual behaviour not only as a perversion but as a criminal offence. To his surprise, however, her son discovered another, more compassionate side to his mother when he went to have a consultation with Dr Margaret Seiden, a neurologist at Columbia University Hospital who told him that she had been his mother's student. She was very poor at the time and his mother had paid her medical school fees. Sacks also met at his mother's funeral a number of her former pupils who she had also helped financially. He had been totally unaware of her efforts to help these impoverished students. He had always thought of her as frugal, even parsimonious, and never realised how generous she was.[27]

Landau died in 1972 while on holiday in Israel. Her memorial service was attended by more than 500 people including the emeritus Chief Rabbi Sir Israel Brodie and representatives of many Jewish communal organisations.[28] She was an exceptional person for her time when viewed in the context of difficulties faced by women, and particularly those of Jewish origin, to enter the medical profession.

Although the First World War had allowed women to take up posts that would ordinarily have been occupied by men, female physicians still faced major career obstacles in the interwar period.[29] It was during this period that Muriel Landau's contemporary Hannah Billig also obtained her medical training and qualifications. Like Landau, she remained in London's East End, setting up a general practice and focusing her efforts on providing care for the poor. Her heroic responses during the bombing of the East End during the Second World War earned her the sobriquet the 'Angel of Cable Street'.

Hannah Billig (1901-1987)

Hannah Billig was a dedicated physician who for some 40 years cared for the sick of Stepney with selfless dedication. She was much loved by the people who regarded her as a latter-day Florence Nightingale. Her exceptional medical work during the Second World War earned her honours and awards and she devoted her life to healing the sick in England and in later years in Israel.

Billig was born in the East End on 4 October 1901. Her parents Barnet and Millie Billig came from Russia at the end of the nineteenth century. They were an Orthodox family and lived above a newsagent in Hanbury Street. Barnet worked initially as a newsagent and then a cigar and cigarette maker. Many books were bought for the family and the living space resembled a library. The children were not allowed to play out in the street with the other children of the area but encouraged to read. Of their six children, four of them qualified to become doctors, one an Arabist scholar and another a nurse.[30] Billig, like Landau, was encouraged by her family to take up a career which was unusual for women at that time.

A bright student, Billig won a scholarship to Myrdle Street Central School, Whitechapel and a subsequent scholarship to read medicine at London University. She trained at the Royal Free Hospital and the Royal London Hospital and qualified as a doctor in 1925. After working for two years at the Jewish Maternity Hospital (Mother Levy's) she opened a small surgery at Watney Street, Shadwell which was a poor area on the edge of Docklands. Women doctors were uncommon in those days but she built up a thriving practice and her patients trusted her completely because she was kind, considerate, a good communicator and showed great compassion.[31] She was also a medical officer at the Jewish Day Nursery founded by Alice Model.

Billig moved to a bigger surgery at 198 Cable Street, Shadwell in 1935 and was often on call as a Police Doctor. During the Second World War she was the medical offer in charge of several air raid shelters. She was called out to tend to the injured at a blast at Orient Wharf in Wapping on 13 March 1941. As she was working another blast blew her off the steps of the shelter. Her ankle was badly injured, but unperturbed she bandaged it and carried on tending to those who had been hurt. She carried on for four hours until all the injured were taken to hospital and a further bomb landed only twenty yards from her. For her bravery she was awarded the George Medal (Victoria Cross) by King George VI. She was a local heroine and referred to as the 'The Angel of Cable Street'.[32]

In 1942 she joined the Indian Army Medical Corps with the rank of Captain. She spent the early part of her time in Assam treating soldiers who had retreated following the Japanese Army's advances in Burma, often presenting with malaria and typhus, as well as local victims and refugees fleeing the conflict. Billig was awarded the MBE in the 1945 honours list for her work in Calcutta at the time of the famine (1944-45).

In 1946 she returned to her practice where she helped with the infant welfare services and was an active member of the local division of the British Medical Association. She was a long serving member of the Stepney group hospital management committee and of the Medical Women's Federation. In 1962 she was elected president of the London Jewish Hospital Medical Society.[33] The Medical Society had been established in 1928 to enhance the prestige of the Jewish Hospital, spread information about the good work carried out there and attract wider professional and financial help for its development.[34]

She retired to Israel in 1964 where her brother was living and settled in Caesarea. Billig came from a Zionist family. Her brother Levi, a graduate of Cambridge University, was a professor of oriental studies at the Hebrew University, Jerusalem and was assassinated in 1936 by an Arab terrorist whilst in his study. She had been elected to the Medical Section of the Friends of the Hebrew University in 1931. She continued her medical work after emigration, working in Arab villages and Jewish settlements near to her home.

At her retirement party in London she was presented with an original oil painting by Lady Rose Henriques depicting an East End scene.[35] She said Dr Billig had brought great light and comfort into the neighbourhood and St. George's in the East would be the poorer for her leaving. She was described by a former medical officer of health for Stepney as kind, courageous and adventurous and a borough councillor said she was Stepney's Florence Nightingale.[36]

Billig, who never married, dedicated her life to the medical needs of the poor of the East End. She epitomised the old-fashioned family doctor, riding around on a bicycle with her black bag strapped to the carrier. This was later replaced by a Morris Cowley and she would take children for a ride whilst visiting the sick. Often when she visited people at home she would drive herself to the chemist to buy the medicines that they needed. She considered the locals wonderful and 'the salt of the earth'.[37] She was very unassuming. When she was awarded her MBE in 1945 she did not go to Buckingham Palace to receive it. She said she was 'too busy' tending to the sick and wrote to the Palace asking them to post it to her instead. She achieved much respect and admiration at a time when women doctors were

The Distinguished
Physician
Dr Hannah Billig G.M, M.B.E
1901 - 1987

Known locally as
"The Angel of Cable Street."
Honoured for her Bravery in
World War II and
Famine Relief Work in India

Lived and worked here
1935 - 1964

20. Blue plaque at 198 Cable Street, Stepney, London E1 0BL

not the norm. It was only in 1948 that educational reforms that came with the inauguration of the National Health Service required 'that a reasonable proportion of medical students were women'.[38]

The post-war generation benefitted from the significant changes in the 1960s-1970s that encouraged female participation in the labour market more generally as well as in medicine. Amidst wider social pressure to provide equal rights to women and new legislation such as the Sex Discrimination Act in 1975,[39] medical workforce planners also recognised the need to increase members of British trained doctors and reduce reliance on an overseas medical workforce. This need was predominantly met by an increasing number of female doctors from 1960s onwards.[40] The social, cultural and professional changes that occurred in this period enabled women, including female physicians to make their voices heard in a variety of mediums, including newspapers and television and one of the most notable of this new generation was Miriam Stoppard, who took her medical training out of the surgery to reach millions of British people through her work as a television presenter and newspaper columnist.

Miriam Stoppard (1937 -)

Medical doctor, television presenter and advice columnist, Miriam Stoppard has been at the forefront of the revolution in health information since she began her writing and broadcasting career in the early 1970s. After practising medicine and specialising in dermatology, she entered the pharmaceutical industry and then developed a career in television where she became a media medical star well known as a leading authority on parenting, childcare, women and family health. She was appointed Officer of the Order of the British Empire (OBE) in 2010 for services to healthcare and charity.

Stoppard was born on 12 May 1937 in Newcastle upon Tyne. Her father Sidney Stern, whose family had arrived in Newcastle around 1908 from Hungary, was a nurse, which was an unusual occupation for a man at that

21. Dr Miriam Stoppard OBE (Courtesy of the office of Dr Miriam Stoppard)

time. Her mother Jenny, a half Irish, half Scottish working-class Catholic Geordie who undertook an Orthodox Jewish conversion to marry, worked for the Newcastle school dinners' service.[41] Stoppard grew up on a council estate and attended the Central Newcastle High School on a scholarship. 'My education there was the foundation for the rest of my life.'[42] She trained as a nurse at Newcastle General Hospital and went on to study medicine at King's College, Durham. After qualifying as a doctor she worked at Newcastle's Royal Victoria Infirmary and specialised in dermatology as a senior registrar at Bristol Royal Infirmary.

Her father wanted his first born to be a doctor.[43] Stoppard became a medical student at his insistence. 'It was nothing to do with me, he pushed me.'[44] For her parents, education meant freedom. She was brought up to believe that anything was possible. When on her first day at medical school her professor turned to her and said 'we never give girls good jobs, girls just get what is left over', she vowed to herself that she would prove him wrong. 'I decided I would arm myself with postgraduate qualifications to give myself the edge over men, there was no way I would take second best.'[45] She recalls that when she was newly qualified as a doctor in the early 1960s she soon realised that being a woman in medicine was going to be a very hard road ahead. 'That was like a challenge to me. My mother was a great trier and she had no truck with people who didn't give things a go. She imbued me with that quality so my reaction to be told I should know my place was to set my sights on becoming a consultant.'[46] This was the same attitude she took when she moved into research in a pharmaceutical company 'in a fit of pique because an inferior man got the job I wanted' and she had become exasperated with the old boy's network in medicine. This led to her becoming the managing director of Syntex.[47]

Stoppard's career began at the Royal Free Hospital, London where she was involved in clinical research and contributed to a radio programme about the contraceptive pill. She became BBC Radio London's doctor and was subsequently invited to take part in a television show *Don't Ask Me*, a popular programme that attempted to answer science-based questions.[48] During the third series in 1972 she was doing a piece about knees and lifted up her skirt to show how they differed from those of men. The viewing figures shot up. Stoppard commented that it was unusual in those days for a doctor to be risqué. Shortly afterward a medical colleague suggested she write a baby book that resulted in *Book of Babycare* (1977). Since that time she has published more than 80 books on conception, pregnancy and birth, childcare and development, women and family health.[49] Her appeal was that there was something about her that inspired confidence. Her double viewpoint as a doctor and a mother meant that anything that she wrote tended to be knowledgeable, informative, practical and down to earth.[50]

Her popularity increased in the 1980s. This was an era of rapid change for women. There were suddenly more opportunities to get ahead, whatever one's gender or background. Two-thirds of women now had a bank account compared with one in three in 1974. Women could finally get mortgages too.[51] Programmes designed for women increased and Stoppard launched *The Health and Beauty Show* (1988) on ITV focusing on the care and comfort of women's bodies that included diet, make up, physical exercise, stress, self-image and appearance. It attempted to appeal to people who would not normally bother with the luxuries of health and beauty.[52]

Stoppard was one of the first commentators in the field of rearing children but then started to include the more emotional elements of family life when she honed her talents as an agony aunt. She succeeded Marjorie Proops, who was a good friend, as agony aunt columnist on the *Daily Mirror*, having previously answered readers' letters for the *TV Times* magazine. Her column was headed: 'Dr Miriam Stoppard, the advice columnist you can trust'.

In *Where There's Life*, a light-hearted down to earth medical magazine programme, Stoppard was not afraid to be controversial. Subjects included baby snatching, the problems of toxic shock, the eating of placenta and the subject of surrogate mothers. In one episode she kissed an AIDS victim to allay fears about how the illness was transmitted. Working in a similar vein was agony aunt Claire Rayner who was at the forefront of the early AIDS campaigns 'waving condoms over the cornflakes on breakfast television'.[53] The programme also gave viewers the opportunity to see natural childbirth techniques which attracted nationwide interest and attention. Stoppard considered that medicine was at a crossroads and people were beginning to question the traditional role and attitudes of doctors and that was having a profound effect on how medicine was practised.[54]

Throughout her career, Stoppard showed great determination and this was also reflected in how she overcame the obstacles of her very strict and restrictive Orthodox upbringing. 'My parents were more kosher than a bagel'.[55] She and her younger sister Hazel walked three miles to *cheder* (Hebrew classes) and then three miles back every day after regular school. She suffered antisemitism at school and was stoned by some children and called Jesus killer; she can still see the corner of the brick coming towards her. Sexually, almost everything was taboo. When she went to a Jewish youth club at the age of 15 wearing lipstick, her father put her face under the tap and scrubbed it off with soap that her mother used to wash the floor and called her a harlot. Her parents were not affectionate. She knew that her father was proud of her but that was not the same as knowing he loved her. She worked hard to encourage that pride.[56]

Her life amongst the Newcastle Jewish community appears not to have been easy. Her niece, Baroness Oona King,[57] daughter of her sister Hazel, talks about her mother and aunt growing up on the wrong side of the social tracks, as daughters of a convert. She describes them as 'the outcasts of the outcasts' in Newcastle's Jewish community. 'Despite embracing Judaism in a typically convert way and separating meat from milk tea towels, they were looked down on'.[58]

Both daughters rebelled. Hazel married African-American Preston King, an academic and civil rights activist. Stoppard married her first husband, a Quaker, when she was in her 20s. 'My father covered all my pictures up and boarded up my bedroom. I was dead to him. They didn't think they were doing anything wrong. They were doing something that, in the eyes of God, would be seen as a righteous act.'[59] Stoppard explains that for them there was only one way to react. 'Marrying out was as great a betrayal as you can have. My Dad cut me off, said I didn't exist, that I'd died.'[60] Stoppard did try and mend the rift and would ring her parents every Friday night for three years; every time they put the phone down on her. The rift was never fully healed although some kind of reconciliation was achieved when her first marriage failed and in 1972 she married Czech born British playwright and screenwriter Tom Stoppard who was Jewish, after which her parents spoke to her again.[61] They divorced in 1992 and in 1997 she married industrialist Sir Christopher Hogg.

Stoppard has no regrets about rebelling against her orthodox Newcastle background. 'I went to medical school in London to get away from the claustrophobic Jewish life in Newcastle. I didn't think it then, but I now look on my Jewish upbringing as highly oppressive'. Despite these feelings she has remained proud of her Jewish heritage. 'It's part of me and while I don't practise Judaism it is an intimate part of my self-image'.[62] 'My Jewishness runs through me like Brighton rock'.[63] She made sure that the two sons she had with Tom Stoppard knew about their religious background. They were not circumcised and she did not bring them up to be religious as she did not want to force Judaism on them. 'I planted a seed and let it grow and because of that they are now open about the religion and proud to be Jewish'.[64]

Stoppard connected with her Jewish roots whilst on a trip to India to film the BBC1 series *The Real Marigold Hotel*.[65] She says that her father sitting *shiva*[66] for her when she married a non-Jew was the most painful betrayal a parent could heap on a child. She finally forgave him whilst visiting the twelfth century synagogue in Jew Town, Cochin. Although her parents' attitude softened with the passing of time, she considers it was never a really loving relationship because it had been so damaged. The visit to the synagogue had a huge emotional impact.

As she had been brought up within an Orthodox community, she had never walked in the lower part of a synagogue. The caretaker asked her if she wanted to go up on the *bimah*[67] and the ark. 'I was awestricken'. When he asked if she wanted to touch the Torah scrolls she recalls 'raising my shaking hands to the silver ornaments' before holding one and 'seeing the whole of my life flash before my eyes'. She explained that she became very emotional and connected with the Judaism she had known, and which had been such an integral part of her childhood but which she had not connected to since. She was ready to give forgiveness.[68]

Now at a stage when she is reflecting back on her life, she considers that 'of all the things I have done in my life work has been the source of more controllable happiness than anything else'. There was a time when you could not switch on the television without seeing Dr Stoppard or open a magazine without seeing her in one of her guises as wife, author and mother. One was always reminded of her superwoman lifestyle as mother, chatelaine of a Palladian mansion, tireless campaigner on health issues, television presenter, author, company chairperson and glamorous wife.[69]

Conclusion

Muriel Landau, Hannah Billig and Miriam Stoppard all possessed tremendous drive and determination that enabled them to overcome formidable gender and ethnic biases and forge careers of great achievement and renown. Landau and Billig came into medicine in the interwar period and their careers share many similarities. While Stoppard enjoyed a much wider range of opportunities in the post-war years of social and cultural change, all three women shared commonalities in their religious and family backgrounds and the circumstances and focus of their rising medical careers.

All three women were raised in orthodox Jewish homes, though religion was a much more central to Landau and Billig's lives and careers. These two women had both grown up in London among large Jewish communities and their medical practices included work in Jewish hospitals and in Jewish neighbourhoods. Landau lived more affluently and worked within more middle-class Jewish circles and would appear, as evidenced by her reaction to her son's homosexuality, more conservative. Billig kept within her East End working class community and it would appear was accepting to all. She chose to work in poverty-stricken Cable Street because she felt that she was needed there and saw patients whether or not they could pay. 'It was my duty'.[70] They both, however, were kind to those in need, as Landau's financial aid to her impoverished students demonstrated. They were also ardent Zionists, Billig retiring in Israel, and Landau dying there while on holiday. Stoppard, in contrast, grew up in Newcastle and had a difficult relationship with its Jewish community due to her mother's conversion. Stoppard rebelled against her orthodox background in both her marriage and her career choices, which ranged far from her Jewish roots. Nevertheless, Judaism profoundly influenced all three women lives and careers.

The strongest common denominator for these three women was the support and encouragement they received from their families to excel and push through barriers when it was not the norm. All three grew up in families that valued learning with parents who pushed their offspring to aspire to professional careers, despite not being professionals themselves. With the exception of Miriam Stoppard's non-Jewish mother, all their parents were first generation Jewish immigrants who were intensely ambitious for their British born children – ambitions that were largely fulfilled when their children qualified as doctors, scholars and scientists. Landau achieved great success as one of the first women surgeons, a formidable achievement; Billig built up a medical practice at a time when it was rare for a woman to do so, and Stoppard became a household name in the media for her medical advice.

Finally, all three women's careers were strongly influenced by the circumstances of their times, and they were able to take advantage of the social, educational, cultural and economic changes that occurred in Britain after the First and Second World Wars. For Landau and Billig, the period immediately following the First World War saw the emergence of substantial new rights for women and these advances coincided with the years in which they undertook higher education, allowing them to qualify among the first wave of female physicians. Significantly, however, their times also circumscribed to some extent the areas of medicine that were open to Jewish women, and they thus concentrated their work on the medical needs of women, fellow Jews and the poor. Stoppard benefitted from the changes that occurred in the wake of the Second World War, enabling her to branch out and share her medical knowledge with millions through the media. However, she too was affected by gender biases both in her training and early career, and like her predecessors, concentrated many of her efforts in medical education and advice on the health concerns of women and families. In spite of the constraints that these pioneer doctors experienced, Muriel Landau, Hannah Billig and Miriam Stoppard broke barriers and forged outstanding medical careers of substance and significance.

7

Scientists

In the late nineteenth and early twentieth century science as a field was increasing in importance and expanding as a profession. Nevertheless, women did not find it easy to take part. Women have always taken a backseat to their male counterparts in math and science careers. Despite the steady rise of women entering the field since the nineteenth century women have had to work tirelessly to prove that they are cut out to share the scientific world with men. Their position as science students were even more tenuous than that of other women and they had difficulty in taking physical sciences at university. In the public mind physics and chemistry were too difficult or unsuitable for girls.[1]

At the heart of this issue is the very nature of women as compared with that of men. The dominant view which persisted well into the twentieth century was that women were incapable of rigorous intellectual activity because of their 'weak' nature which involved the biological function of reproduction. This meant that the systematic pursuit of knowledge involved in science was barred to them. Related to this particular view of woman's inferior nature was also the question of education and to what extent they should be educated.[2]

Given the gender barriers, it is not surprising that the few female high achievers were often from the upper or middle ranks of society as their social standing provided them with a chance to gain access to scientific activity. However, opportunities also lay open to those who were able to take advantage of family circumstances, contacts or the rare scholarship and award. Of the four women profiled in this chapter, only Rosalind Franklin, who came from a wealthy, well-connected family and Nina Wedderburn, whose parents were both scientists, could have expected to attain the advanced education necessary to pursue a career in science. Yet the other two, Hertha Ayrton and Susan Greenfield, who both came from economically struggling families, were both able to pursue careers in science thanks to the help of their extended families, financial aid and encouragement from mentor figures.

The other factor that could help a woman in the sciences was a supportive husband, especially before the emancipation of women in the early twentieth century. Dame Kathleen Lonsdale[3] commented that for a woman, especially a married woman with children, to become a scientist she must first of all choose or have chosen the right husband. Among the four women discussed here, only Rosalind Franklin did not marry, and though she was unencumbered by having to care for a family, she encountered greater gender discrimination than the others when her male colleagues took credit for her most significant scientific discovery. The other three all married and had children, but the female Jewish scientist who arguably benefitted most from having a supportive husband with whom she worked collaboratively was Hertha Ayrton, though she owed her Cambridge education to the personal support of her mentor Barbara Bodichon.[4]

Hertha Ayrton (1854-1923)

Hertha Ayrton, mathematician, physicist and suffragist was born Phoebe Sarah Marks on 28 April 1854 in Portsea, Hampshire. In the late nineteenth and twentieth century when few women had access to opportunities in science, technology, engineering and mathematics, Hertha held all these roles. Following her work on ripples in sand and water, she developed the Ayrton fan, an anti-gas fan that was used in the trenches during the First World War. She was described at the time as Britain's foremost woman inventor and the most distinguished woman scientist in Great Britain.[5] She was the first woman nominated to become a fellow of the Royal Society but her candidature was refused on the grounds of her ineligibility for the fellowship. As a married woman she had no legal existence in British law. In 1906 she was awarded the Hughes Medal of the Royal Society for original discovery in the physical sciences, the first woman to receive it for work exclusively her own.

Her father Levi Marks was the son of a Polish innkeeper and her mother Alice Teresa Moss, one of twelve children, was the daughter of Joseph and Amelia Moss. Joseph Moss originated from Poland and was a glass merchant of Portsea, Hampshire. Alice's great grandfather was one of the founders of the Portsmouth Jewish community established in 1747 and her grandmother Sara Davids was the first Jewish child born there. Hertha's parents married in Portsmouth Synagogue in 1851. Portsmouth was one of the oldest and biggest provincial Jewish communities after the readmission of the Jews to Britain in 1656. Levi Marks was a watchmaker by trade; his gift of mechanics was afterwards a marked characteristic of his daughter.

In 1860 he was granted a 'licence for a hawker trading on foot' which indicated that his business was not doing well, and he had to resort to hawking his stock of clocks and watches around the countryside. He died in 1861, leaving many debts. His widow, who was pregnant with their eighth child, supported the entire family by her needlework.[6]

At the age of nine Hertha went to live and study with her maternal aunt Marion Hartog (nee Moss) at 300 Camden Road, London. It would appear that Marion and her siblings had been exposed to secular works during their childhood as their father read romantic poetry to them while they sewed, that included Byron's *Childe Harold* and Scott's *Lady of the Lake*. Marion and her sister Celia took up the cause of female education. They moved to London and became teachers and soon published their collections of historical romances, *The Romance of Jewish History* (1840) and *Tales of Jewish History* (1843). Marion wrote *The Jewish Sabbath Journal* (1854-55), the first Jewish women's periodical in modern history, intended to provide mothers with material with which to further their children's Jewish education.[7] The two women shone brightly in the intellectual firmament of Anglo-Jewry in the second half of the nineteenth century.[8]

Marion had married Alphonse Hartog, a professor of French at Jew's College and they ran a school in London, where their children and Hertha attended. Hertha studied French and music, the usual subjects of a governess, but she also learned mathematics and Latin from her male cousins. Her cousins included Numa, later the first Jewish Senior Wrangler (top mathematics undergraduate at Cambridge University); Marcus, Professor of Natural History at Queen's College, Cork; Sir Philip Hartog, a chemist and industrialist who undertook this role in England and India and was associated with the founding of the School of Oriental and African Studies, London; Helena Arsene Darmester, a successful portrait painter who exhibited at the Royal Academy and musician Cecile Hartog. At sixteen Hertha began work as a live-in governess in London, taking in needlework to earn extra money to support her mother. In the course of her upward struggle she made embroidery for the designer and social activist William Morris.[9]

It was at this time that Hertha was befriended by the family of Karl Blind, Jewish-German emigres. Karl's daughter Ottilie nicknamed Sarah 'Hertha' after the heroine of a novel by the feminist writer Frederika Bremer.[10] Ottilie encouraged Hertha to study for Cambridge University Local Examinations for secondary schools. Hertha passed the examinations in 1874, taking honours in English and mathematics. Ottilie took Hertha to a suffrage meeting where she met the most significant mentor in her career Barbara Leigh Smith Bodichon (1827-1891), the leader of the Langham Place Circle, a feminist activist organisation formed in the late 1850s to advocate changes regarding women's access to employment and educational opportunities. In 1869 Bodichon and suffragist Emily Davies had co-founded Girton College, Cambridge, the first university college for women. Bodichon organised and paid for Hertha's advanced mathematics lessons and arranged a loan so she could attend Girton where she read mathematics and started the Mathematical Society. Hertha became a protégée of Bodichon and her friend the writer George Eliot. As George Eliot described Mira, heroine of *Daniel Deronda*, she thought of Hertha's singing of Hebrew hymns. When she returned to London after Cambridge she taught mathematics, ran a working girls' club and held a singing class for laundry girls.[11]

Hertha came to science through invention. As a student she invented a sphygmomanometer, a device for measuring blood pressure. Soon after leaving Girton in 1880 she patented her first significant invention, a line-divider, consisting of a series of parallelograms, designed for the purpose of dividing a line into any number of equal parts; while its primary use was likely to be for artists for enlarging and diminishing, it was also useful for architects and engineers. Bodichon and Lady Louisa Goldsmid,[12] also of the suffrage movement and a major benefactor of Girton, together advanced her enough money to take out patents. This invention was shown at the Exhibition of Women's Industries and received much press attention.[13]

In 1884 Hertha started to attend evening classes in electricity at Finsbury Technical College given by Professor William Edward Ayrton, a pioneer in electrical engineering and physics education and a fellow of the Royal Society. Hertha married Ayrton, a widower, on 6 May 1885, taking on the role of step-mother to his four year old daughter Edith. Edith, who married Israel Zangwill[14] wrote a novel *The Call* (1924) which was a fictionalised version of the suffragette campaigns, with a woman scientist as heroine. Hertha's own daughter was born in 1886, named Barbara Bodichon in honour of Hertha's mentor.[15]

Hertha came midway between two great periods and had the intellectual qualities and the originality of mind to absorb and reflect some of the meaning of both. As a brilliant young girl, she moved in the circles of the later Victorians such as George Eliot and William Morris and then as an early Girton student with educational pioneers where she experienced the beginnings of the modern woman's movement. The next period of her life brought her into the scientific world where, as the acknowledged

22. Blue plaque erected in 2007 by English Heritage at 41 Norfolk Square, Paddington, London W2 1RX, City of Westminster

authority on the electric arc and the discoverer of startling new phenomena in wave motion, she became widely known in scientific circles.[16]

In 1893 Will Ayrton's research papers on the electric arc were used by a servant to light a fire. While helping him to replicate his experiments Hertha made a significant discovery. Electric arcs were used to produce bright light, the carbon electrodes and the gas between them being heated white-hot by the high-voltage discharge. Hertha developed the theory connecting the length of the arc with pressure and voltage and traced the hissing noise to oxidation rather than evaporation of the electrode material. This work was published in *The Electrician* in 1895. The Institution of Electrical Engineers invited her to read a paper in 1899, the first ever read by a woman. She was the first woman elected to membership in that year; the second was not admitted until 1958. At the International Congress of Women, held in London in 1899, Hertha presided over the physical science section, and she spoke at the International Electrical Congress in Paris in 1900. Her success there led the British Association for the Advancement of Science to allow women to serve on general and sectional committees.[17]

In 1902 she published her pioneering text *The Electric Arc*. As a result she was nominated as a candidate for fellowship of the Royal Society, the first woman that had ever been proposed. The Royal Society lawyers pronounced that a married woman was not a 'person' eligible for this fellowship under the charter. Such arguments were quashed by the Sex Disqualification Removal Act (1919) but nevertheless no woman was proposed again until 1944. Remarkably, for a medal is worth more than a fellowship, the Royal Society awarded her its Hughes Medal in 1906 for her work on the electric arc and sand ripples.[18] Although this medal was awarded annually 'for original discovery in the physical sciences' it took another 102 years before a woman won that medal again.[19] It may have been these experiences that prompted her to write to *The Times* asserting the right of her friend, physicist and chemist Marie Curie, to be the sole discoverer of radium as the newspaper had awarded the credit to her husband. She conducted a vigorous campaign commenting that 'errors are notoriously hard to kill but an error that ascribes to a man what was actually the work of a woman has more lives than a cat'.[20] She was considered the nearest English parallel to Madame Curie.[21]

Ayrton was on holiday in Margate when she became interested in the sand ripples on the beach. 'Sand ripples may seem a small thing, but any explanation of their formation involves all the principles underlying the motion of waters and of all the bodies oscillating in the water. It will be of great use in dealing with coast erosion and quicksands'. Her first experiments were conducted in her lodgings where her only apparatus was a zinc bath containing sand and water.[22] From 1905 to 1910 Hertha worked for the War Office and the Admiralty on standardising the types and sizes of carbons for searchlights and filed patents in this area, as well as for arc lights.

During the First World War gas was a new and deadly weapon first used in 1915 at Ypres. Chlorine, phosgene and mustard gas were all used; mustard gas was the worst as it caused hideous blisters on the skin and slowly ate away at the victim's lungs. Hertha applied the knowledge she had discovered about currents and vortices in water to the movement of air and designed a fan or flapper to push the gases out the trenches. Her anti-gas fan consisted of a sheet of waterproof canvas supported by braces of cane down the middle. It had two transverse hinges and a hickory handle. The War Office dismissed her invention and acrimonious exchanges followed in the press until the War Office finally issued 104,000 'Ayrton' fans to soldiers on the western front.[23] Officers declared that countless lives were saved by the fan.[24] Hertha spent the rest of her career in research related to clearing noxious miasma from mines and sewers.

Hertha was a noted supporter of women's rights and the suffragettes in particular. In chairing the physical science section of the International Congress of Women in London in 1899 she encouraged women to take up applied science and was involved with the International Federation of University Women when it was set up in 1919. She supported the militant suffragists, marching in all their processions. In 1872 she joined the Central Society for Women's Suffrage and in 1907 the Women's Social and Political Union (WSPU), which was the militant wing of the women's suffrage movement, helping to finance the organisation and was a founder member of the Jewish League for Women Suffrage set up in 1912. She was part of the Black Friday deputation to Parliament in 1910, which was met with alleged police brutality. In 1914 she gave £100 left to her by Bodichon to help form the United Suffragists, after deciding that the WSPU's tactics had become ineffective. Hertha was 'very proud' when her daughter Barbara[25] went to Holloway prison in 1912 for smashing windows.[26] Hertha's most significant role came during the operation of the notorious Cat and Mouse Act of 1913 under which suffragette prisoners on hunger strike were released, only to be incarcerated again when they had sufficiently recovered. Some of the hunger strikers, including Emmeline Pankhurst, were cared for at her home in 41 Norfolk Square, Paddington.[27]

Hertha was considered one of the ablest women of science, a champion of freedom and progress.[28] She considered herself a free thinker. Although she had grown up in an observant Jewish household and had at a young age been devoutly religious, she began to question her beliefs during her adolescence. She was always an intellectual rebel and her scientific mind took nothing for granted so no one convinced her as to the reason or soundness of any religious dogma. When she decided to marry out of the faith, she wrote to her mother: 'You know how much I love you, dear mother, and I would do anything I could to make you happy but the one thing I could not do would be to give him up.'[29]

Nevertheless, she did not renounce her Judaism when its religious observances ceased to have any meaning for her. She never lost an opportunity of expressing pride in her Jewish background 'and it may have been an instinctive desire to testify openly to this pride of race, as well as devotion to her mother that made her continue to go home year after year to help with Passover'. After she moved to London she was reminded by one of her younger siblings to light a *yahrzeit* (memorial) candle on the anniversary of her father's death. 'Mother says you are to light up for poor father - peace to his soul'.[30]

Hertha died of septicaemia on 26 August 1923. She had directed that her remains were to be cremated and the ashes scattered to the winds.[31] During her lifetime she had registered 26 patents, five on mathematical dividers, 13 on arc lamps and electrodes and the rest on the propulsion of air.[32] She was clearly a woman of courage, energy and scientific ability. She was not religious but through her Jewish family and fellow suffragists she had access to intellectual life in London and with Will Ayrton's help was able to ignore significant social barriers of class, religion and gender in Victorian and Edwardian society. [33]

Although Hertha was fortunate to have had sponsorship and connections in order to pursue a scientific career at a time when it was unobtainable for so many, Lisa Yount considers that the discrimination and discouragement that most women scientists faced did them a favour. Great scientists, like great achievers in other fields, need to be supremely self-confident and determined. They frequently propose ideas that are the opposite of what other scientists think, and if experimental evidence supports their views, they must be willing to stick with those ideas in the face of criticism.

These women scientists could not have succeeded without these attributes and this was especially true for women who grew up in the nineteenth century. From adolescence onwards these women had to fight prevailing opinion, starting with that of their parents. The first task was to gain permission to seek a higher education. Even after they overcame the opposition of parents and obtained their degrees, women scientists had to continue fighting in order to advance their careers.

Fighting family, cultural expectations and institutional discrimination may have helped a few women develop the confidence, determination and flexibility that served them well as scientists. But for every woman who succeeded in overcoming these obstacles there were hundreds more who dropped out of science careers because of the formidable opposition they knew they would face.[34]

In the generation of women that followed, Hertha Ayrton and Rosalind Franklin stood out as fiercely determined to succeed in the face of all obstacles. Franklin, who had known since the age of 15 that she wanted to be a scientist, came from a family with the means to support her though university, but she ran into parental opposition when she wanted to attend college as her father thought higher education made women unhappy. He suggested that instead she focus on the volunteer philanthropic work for which the family was renowned, and which he believed would bring her more satisfaction. Franklin responded as she would always do when someone tried to block her – with passionate opposition – and faced with such determination her father gave in.[35] Franklin went on to become one of the most innovative and promising scientists of her generation before her early death cut her brilliant career tragically short.

Rosalind Franklin (1920-1958)

Rosalind Elise Franklin was a British chemist and crystallographer who is best known for her discovery of the structure of DNA. A picture she took, an x-ray made of evenly spaced blobs, did not look very exciting. But to those who understood it, it offered the key to one of life's most imposing secrets: how living things pass on traits to their offspring. She made it by shining the beam of X rays through DNA (deoxyribonucleic acid), the chief chemical that carries inherited information. The pattern made by the reflected X rays suggested how the complex DNA molecule is constructed. This was just one of her achievements. Her discoveries about the molecules of carbon led directly to the creation of strong, lightweight materials used in experimental cars and planes and she carried out pioneering work on the structure of viruses which can cause devastating diseases.[36]

Franklin was born in Notting Hill, London on 25 July 1920 to Ellis Franklin and Muriel Waley. She came from a different background to that of Hertha. Hertha came from an intellectually rich background but not a wealthy one. Franklin's family were part of what writer Chaim Bermant called 'the cousinhood', the Anglo-Jewish aristocracy of the eighteenth and

23. Rosalind Elsie Franklin, English chemist and X-ray crystallographer (Author CSHL, via Wikimedia Commons)

nineteenth centuries.[37] The first Franklin (the original name was Fraenkel and was anglicised) to come to England was Abraham, son of the Rabbi of Breslau, who settled in London in 1763. He lived in the City of London in Cook Court, Jewry Street. A rabbi and a teacher, he married Sarah, the daughter of Lazarus Joseph, who emigrated from Hamburg around 1760. Their two sons went to Portsmouth for apprenticeships in watchmaking and shopkeeping and became successful businessmen. From 1868 the Franklin's financial base lay in the City of London in A. Keyser and Co, a private merchant bank, a source of employment for the Franklin sons for the next century. Among the City's so-called 'Jewish banks', Keyser's was the only one to observe all the Jewish holidays. From 1902 Franklins were publishers as well as bankers. Keyser's bought the publishing house of George Routledge in 1902 and then Kegan Paul in 1911. In 1862 Ellis Franklin, the grandson of the original immigrant, left the City of London to live in Porchester Terrace, Bayswater in an affluent part of London and which remained in the family possession until it was bombed in the Second World War. He was one of the founders of the New West End Synagogue on St Petersburgh Place and his seven children, all of whom married within the faith, were all known for their philanthropy. In succeeding generations there was scarcely a Jewish organisation, hospital or old people's home without a Franklin on the board and many secular charities benefitted from them as well.[38]

Muriel Waley's family had arrived in Portsmouth in 1740. The Waleys and Franklins had been acquainted for more than a hundred and fifty years since the time when Waley children had been sent to learn Hebrew with Abraham Franklin. The families were united by marriage as well, so that Muriel and Ellis had cousins in common. Jacob Waley, Rosalind's great grandfather, was the son of an East India Company merchant. He went to University College London at the age of thirteen, holding a scholarship in mathematics. He became a very successful barrister and held a professorship in political economy at University College, London, the first Jewish professor in an English university and was one of the founders of the Jewish Board of Guardians. He married Julia Salaman, a niece of Sir Moses Montefiore and sister of Sir David Salaman, the first Jewish Lord Mayor of London and the first Jew to take his seat in Parliament.[39]

In class-stratified Edwardian England, eighteenth century origin placed the Franklins in the upper middle class, high above the new wave of Jews crowding into London's East End in flight from the pogroms in Russia and Eastern Europe. These families were secure, able, influential and socially conscious. Its members dressed for dinner, were presented at Royal Court and had their portraits painted by Singer Sargent. Many kept both Christmas and Passover, ate kosher and played cricket. What was the stronger loyalty – to country or to faith? Franklin's father said 'the whole idea is that Judaism is a religion not a race… the English Jews are as much English as other English'. As far as heritage was concerned an alliance between Waley and Franklin was plainly as equal, a prime example of 'the cousinhood' in action.[40]

As Orthodox Jews the Franklins were committed to philanthropy and had two centuries of unbroken service to Anglo-Jewish community welfare. These ranged from working class housing schemes to the organization of schools of religious education for the children of poor Jewish parents, and from baby care institutes in the slums to the causes of women's suffrage and socialism. The intensity of personal involvement was often very significant, and the Franklin women worked beside the men when they were not running projects and causes of their own. They all possessed great determination.

> Rosalind's grandmother Caroline Franklin was an educationalist who managed schools in the East End slums under the London School Board, founded and supervised a Jewish Lads Club and a welfare centre for mothers and children in East London.[41] Rosalind's father devoted a lifetime of voluntary work to the Working Men's College, founded in 1853, aimed at bringing together men of the working class and men from universities with the common aim of teaching and learning. He began as a teacher and later became vice-principal.[42] Her mother was heavily involved with the work of the Jewish Welfare Board.[43]

By the time she was born in 1920, the Franklin family were held in high esteem in British public life. Just before her birth her great uncle Herbert Samuel became the first High Commissioner of Palestine. Her position as an English gentlewoman and a Jew shaped her life.[44] The family lived at 5 Pembridge Place, Notting Hill and Ellis Franklin worked at Keyser's Bank where his father was a senior partner.

Her childhood was spent in a settled world of nursery, school, park, pets, pantomimes, birthday parties, holidays, sports days and country weekends at her grandparents' estate at Chartridge, Buckinghamshire with its tennis courts, croquet lawn, a farm producing its own milk, chicken and turkeys and a resident *shochet* for kosher slaughtering.[45] As a child she was strong willed, purposeful and extremely efficient. Even as a small girl she had no use for dolls; she preferred to build Meccano. At school she entered into all projects with great seriousness and won scholarships.[46]

Franklin derived from her parents a capacity for deep commitment that could operate in any chosen direction. She chose science. Her education was excellent. She was sent to St Paul's Girls School where standards were very high. Much was expected of its pupils and a considerable number went on to notable careers although she was under no obligation to earn a living. In the 1930s few women pursued professional careers in science and they had not made much of a visible mark. It was only in 1944 that the first women were elected Fellows of the Royal Society. Rosalind's father, although he recognised her intellectual powers, was uncertain about whether she should embrace a working career in science and suggested some sort of voluntary social work that needed devoted and intelligent recruits and which gave deep satisfaction to women of his daughter's background. She resisted strongly.[47]

At just six years old Rosalind was according to her aunt 'alarmingly clever'. She was fortunate that a Jewish woman of that era was able to capitalise on her intelligence in a world where her chosen university Cambridge did not yet award degrees to women, where women were not expected to combine family and career and where 'women scientists' were a contradiction in terms.[48] Cambridge had admitted women since 1869 but it refused to accept them as 'members of the university'. Female students were not considered undergraduates, merely students of Girton and Newnham Colleges, the only two colleges they could attend. They were unable to graduate as full members of the university until 1948. They could sit examinations but were only given titular degrees mailed to them in the post and their names did not appear on the degree ceremony list.[49] Cambridge changed Franklin's life. It gave her a profession and enabled her to distance herself from her parents and become a mature adult with a sharp political and social conscience.[50]

Rosalind enrolled at Newnham College in 1938 where she studied chemistry. Upon completion of her degree she worked as an assistant research officer at the British Coal Utilisation Research Association. In 1947, with a PhD in physical chemistry specialising in the structure of coal, she joined the Paris laboratory of Jacques Mering, a Russian-born Jewish scientist. He taught her X-ray diffraction, which would play an important role in her research that led to the discovery of 'the secret of life' – the structure of DNA. In addition Franklin pioneered the use of X-rays to create images of crystallized solids in analysing complex, unorganised matter, not just single crystals.[51]

In 1951 Franklin began working as a research associate in the biophysics unit, King's College London where director John Randall used her expertise and X-ray diffraction techniques on DNA fibres. Franklin and her student Raymond Gosling made an amazing discovery. They took pictures of DNA and discovered there were two forms of it, a dry 'A' form and a wet 'B' form. One of their X-ray diffraction pictures of the 'B' form of DNA, known as Photograph 51, became famous as critical evidence in identifying the structure of DNA. The photograph was acquired through 100 hours of X-ray exposure from a machine that Franklin had herself defined. Despite her cautious and diligent work ethic, Franklin had a personality conflict with colleague Maurice Wilkins. In January 1953 Wilkins disclosed without Franklin's permission or knowledge her Photo 51 to competing scientist James Watson who was working on his own DNA model with Francis Crick at Cambridge.[52] Franklin loathed Wilkins and Watson and Crick mostly learnt about her findings through Wilkins. During social weekends in Cambridge they pumped Wilkins for her latest results.[53] Their theoretical work lacked visual evidence and they used what they saw in Photo 51 as the basis for their famous model of DNA.[54] While Franklin manifested a rather British caution about her work, the American Watson had no doubts about the significance of what he saw. In April 1953 the world was presented with the dramatic breakthrough in the uncovering of the secret alphabet of life in *Nature* magazine and for which Watson and Crick received a Nobel Prize in 1962.[55]

Franklin's sister Jenifer Glynn is convinced that her sister died unaware of the extent of her contribution to the discovery. 'She never knew how much they relied on her work. If she had there would have been an almighty explosion. She had a very strong sense of justice and if she'd known that they'd taken her data without her knowledge she would have been furious'. Although the pair acknowledged Franklin's work in their seminal 1953 paper on the structure of the DNA, she was not made a co-author, the implication being that her crystallography images merely served as confirmation rather than actively helping them to deduce the structure. Crick later wrote that 'the data which really helped us to obtain the structure was mainly obtained by Rosalind Franklin'. But Glynn believes the acknowledgments came too late. 'She obviously did realise the huge importance of DNA but at the time she was more focused on the science than on her legacy'. Glynn said she was disappointed that Watson did not reflect the extent of her sister's contribution in his book *The Double Helix* which was first published in 1968. The book is generally seen as unsympathetic to Franklin's scientific competence including lines such as 'clearly Rosy had to go or be put in her place'. However, Glynn said in retrospect it was only the reaction to Watson's book that brought Franklin's achievements to the fore.[56] Her research data was crucial to their discovery, the final boost to the summit. From evidence of her notebooks it is clear that she would have got there by herself.[57]

In 1950s England, as Franklin worked in the world of science research, she was a lone figure in a man's world. Glynn said her sister probably would not approve of her portrayal as a woman struggling in a man's world although she had complained about overt sexism, such as the rule forbidding women from entering the main dining room of King's College, London. The poky female common room contrasted poorly with the spacious accommodation for men. In the 1950s women engaged in scientific research were still a rarity. Of all the sciences, physics was the most male dominated.[58] Yet Franklin because of her privileged background and education had confidence and intellectual snobbishness. When she arrived at King's she commented that none of her colleagues had a first class or good brain amongst them.[59] A member of staff commented that she was typically upper class and that she stood out from those around her who were from ordinary backgrounds. 'She looked like an aristocrat and acted like one.'[60]

Franklin's male colleagues at that time held her in a mixture of awe, respect and irritation. In *The Double Helix* Watson depicts her as dowdy and spinsterish. 'Though her features were strong, she was not unattractive and might have been quite stunning if she had taken an interest in clothes. This she did not. There was never lipstick to contrast with her straight black hair, while at the age of 31 her dresses showed all the imagination of English blue stocking adolescents'. When John Maynard Smith reviewed *The Double Helix* in the *Listener* he said it was the most unattractive and unsympathetic account ever given by one scientist to another. The outstanding work of preparing and taking X-ray photographs of DNA that Franklin undertook at Kings College, London and the hypothetical research into the structure of DNA by Watson and Crick at Cambridge were complementary. But because of the professional lack of trust and private lack of understanding shown by all sides it was an unhappy time for Franklin.[61]

Francis Crick said that Franklin had a good, hard analytical mind but that she lacked intuition. Her difficulties were mainly of her own making. Underneath her brisk manner she was oversensitive and too determined to be scientifically sound and to avoid shortcuts. She was rather too stubborn to accept advice easily from others. She mistrusted intuition with a wariness for which her Jewishness is as relevant as her gender. Chaim Bermant wrote in *The Cousinhood: The Anglo-Jewish Gentry* that 'a Jew often feels compelled to try that much harder than his colleagues; a woman in a man's world has a similar compulsion. Rosalind perhaps tried too hard on both scores and approached her work with a jealous determination which some of her colleagues found alarming'. Franklin felt as a Jewish woman that King's was inherently biased against her.[62] She told her sister 'I was always consciously a Jew'. Watson as he ages utters opinions that are deemed to be racist and sexist, such as Africans are of lower intelligence than Europeans and women are less effective at maths. In a 2007 *Esquire* interview he said that 'some antisemitism is justified'.[63]

With respect to her Jewishness, in contrast with the rest of the family who played an active part in Jewish life, Franklin cared little for 'good works' or for attending synagogue. She turned up at family Seder nights all her life because her affection and sense of family seem to have overcome her impatience with what appeared to her as meaningless ritual.[64] There was a certain amount of class expectation and pride of heritage in being part of the Franklin family. Although not ultra-Orthodox in religious observance Franklin's grandfather made a Will specifying that if any of his descendants married non-Jews they would be 'cut off without a penny'. The family had a strong sense of duty to engage in communal work. There was the belief that good works and charity were the ideal destiny for a girl of her background.[65] Her brothers were involved in communal affairs. Roland was the chair of the Jewish Welfare Board, David the treasurer of the New London Synagogue and Colin the honorary secretary of the Jewish Historical Society. She had worked as a schoolgirl volunteer at the centre set up in Woburn House, London to aid in the rescue of Jews from Nazi Germany where her father worked tirelessly, and the family had taken in two *kindertransport*[66] children during the war.[67] She had an intense interest in the plight of Jews driven out of Europe. Yet she did not always go along with what her family wanted. The family had long lent their support to the Working Men's College and at the annual dinner the women of the family were required to serve the men. Franklin said 'why should we serve the men when they don't even admit women to the college?'.[68]

She was strikingly uninterested in conventional goals for women.[69] For Franklin science was a full-time job. Jennifer Glynn said that she would not like to say that her sister chose not to get married. It just did not come her way.[70] An attempt to match her with an unattached Jewish Marxist Ralph Milliband aborted on their first date.[71] The strong sense of duty that moved the rest of the family to engage in communal work seems to have stirred Franklin to live out her life as rationally as possible, according to her own strong principles. She had high standards herself and demanded the same from friends and colleagues. She liked to stand by her word, to get things done, to see a situation clearly defined and this concentration of purpose sometimes made life difficult for her in her work. She was a convinced Socialist and stubbornly refused to touch the income that she had inherited. When she went to America on a grant she confounded the government department responsible by bringing back money she had not used.[72]

Franklin was agnostic and placed her faith in reason and in scientific fact and she found it hard to understand and to forgive those who did not. Yet she was undogmatic, constantly questioning her own attitudes and putting them to the test. When she visited Israel In 1953 she read the whole Bible from cover to cover 'just to see if I found it as much nonsense as I thought it was'.[73] Franklin was not a Zionist. She did spend time in Israel with her cousins, one of whom, Herbert Samuel's grandson, worked at the Weizmann Institute. Attracted by its compactness and idealism she was tempted to join the faculty but decided against it on learning that women scientists had the right to take time off after childbirth, a concession that struck her as profoundly unserious. She was further deterred by extreme Orthodox Jews and their way of life and by the brash attitudes that she found in Tel Aviv. In a letter to her family she commented that Tel Aviv would make anyone antisemitic.[74] Yet it would appear that all her life she was more comfortable whilst amongst Jewish people. She worked with the Italian Jewish crystallographer Vittorio Luzzatti with whom she got on well. By no means were all her close women friends Jewish but most of her men friends were. While it is hardly rare for any scientist to have Jews as colleagues, it is a fact that throughout her career, Franklin's most productive research was done with male scientists of Jewish background.[75]

Franklin left King's College in March 1953 and relocated to Birkbeck College where she studied the structure of the tobacco mosaic virus and the structure of RNA (a nucleic acid present in all living cells). As Randall let Franklin leave on the condition that she would not work on DNA, she turned her attention back to the studies of coal. Between 1953 and 1958 she published 17 papers on viruses and her group laid the foundations for structural virology. In 1956 she discovered that she had ovarian cancer and died in 1958. The year that she died *The Times Scientific Review* commented that a great future seemed certain. In an obituary in *Nature* Professor Bernal of Birkbeck College wrote that as a scientist Franklin was distinguished by extreme clarity and perfection in everything she undertook. He considered that her photographs were among the most beautiful X-ray photographs of any substance ever taken. She inspired those who worked with her and her early death was a great loss to science. In 1965 he commented that 'Miss Franklin would certainly have had a claim to share the Nobel Prize had she lived'.[76] She died tragically young with much work left undone.

Franklin was buried in the family plot at Willesden Jewish cemetery. On the gravestone is written: 'Scientist: her work on viruses was of lasting benefit to mankind'. Her work was her life, the core of her identity. During her life she was overlooked partly due to antisemitism and partly through sexism.[77] As her posthumous reputation grew she was accorded a highly sympathetic portrayal in the 1987 BBC Horizon programme's *Life Story* with her role played by Juliet Stevenson. Her portrait was hung in the National Gallery in 1998. In 1992 English Heritage decided to put up a coveted blue plaque outside her former London home in Donovan Court, Drayton Gardens, Fulham maintaining that she never received adequate recognition. Her name was also immortalised by the naming of the King's College Franklin-Wilkins Building in 2000, which belatedly acknowledged her achievements and the Royal Society Rosalind Franklin award, established in 2003, is awarded annually to a woman for an outstanding work in any field of science, technology, engineering and mathematics. Her grave was listed by Historic England to mark International Women's Day in 2017 to celebrate the contributions of female scientists. In 2021 a bronze tondo portrait was erected at Hampstead Manor, Hampstead which is attached to the old Westfield College, founded by women for the education of women, and where Franklin was a research associate. She had the rare accolade of having her name given to the European Space Agency's Mars rover which is due to land on Mars in 2028 where it will travel across the Martian surface for signs of life.

Hailed as a feminist icon in recent years,[78] she achieved an international reputation in three different fields of scientific research while at the same time maintained a passion for travel (she was a keen mountaineer), and a strong political conscience. She never flagged in her duties to the distinguished Anglo-Jewish family of which she was a loyal, if combative, member. From childhood she strove to reconcile her privileges with her goals. She did not find life easy – as a woman, as a Jew and as a scientist. Many of those close to her did not find her easy either. The measure of her success is the strength of her friendships, the devotion of her colleagues and a legacy of discovery that would do credit to a scientific career twice its length.[79]

Rosalind Franklin's close contemporary, Nina Wedderburn, a fellow Newnham graduate, shared with Franklin the advantage of coming from an established and illustrious Anglo-Jewish family who could support her academic studies. Additionally, Wedderburn's parents and grandfather were scientists themselves, and provided her with a rich, stimulating and encouraging childhood, giving her solid support for her own scientific ambitions. An early marriage and family threatened to derail her research career in biochemistry, but as a single parent in her late thirties, she resumed her studies and went on to build an important career as an educator and researcher in immunology and virology.

Nina Wedderburn (1928 – 2020)

Nina Wedderburn was s a leading researcher at the Royal College of Surgeons and an authority on how viruses affect the immune system. She was born in London in 1928, the eldest of four children, to Dr Myer Salaman and Esther (Polianowsky). Myer Salaman (1902-1994), a pathologist and cancer scientist, was educated at Clifton College and contemplated entering the rabbinate. He won a scholarship in Hebrew for Trinity College, Cambridge but switched his interests to science and a medical career. From 1948 he was director of cancer research at the London Hospital Medical School. After his retirement he worked in collaboration with Nina.[80]

Nina's mother was Esther Polianowsky (1900-1995),who had been a research physicist at the Cambridge Cavendish Laboratory. Originally from Zhitomir, Ukraine, Esther escaped from Russia in 1917 and joined a group of pioneer settlers in Palestine. She later left for Berlin where she gained admission to the Physics Faculty of Berlin University and was a pupil of Einstein. Due to the political situation, Einstein advised her to leave Germany after graduating and she came to Cambridge in 1925 armed with his recommendation to Sir Ernest Rutherford. She was helped to take up a research studentship at the Cavendish Laboratory by Redcliffe Salaman and it was through him that she met his son Myer. When they married she gave up her studentship, not wishing to make a career in sciences but to devote herself to literature. Her books included *The Fertile Plain*, a reminiscence of her childhood in a Ukrainian Jewish timber merchant family.[81]

Nina was the first grandchild to physician and scientist Redcliffe Nathan Salaman (1874-1955), and Nina Davis (1877-1925). Redcliffe was born in Kensington, London in 1874 to a prosperous London merchant who traded in ostrich feathers at the height of the plume trade and invested in London real estate. The family migrated to Britain from either Holland or the Rhineland area in the early eighteenth century.[82] Educated at St. Paul's School and then at Cambridge, he trained in medicine and worked at the London Hospital where he was director of the Pathological Institute. When he developed pulmonary tuberculosis he retired to the country to live with his family at Homestall, Barley, close to Cambridge. It was there, on the advice of his gardener, that he became interested in the potato and worked between the laboratory and the field. His later scientific investigations were devoted to the genetics and diseases of the potato and one of his major achievements was the initiation of stocks of virus-free seed potatoes. He was vitally concerned with many aspects of the life of the Jewish people and there was no concealment of his Jewishness. As a scientist he made a number of valuable contributions to the study of genetics as they affected Jews and was involved with the Jewish Health Organisation and the provision of homes for the Jewish aged. He was a life-long member of the council of Jews' College, a governor of the Hebrew University of Jerusalem and president of the Jewish Historical Society (1920-22).[83]

Nina bore the name of her paternal grandmother Nina Davis Salaman, the renowned Hebrew poet, translator and Jewish scholar whose father Arthur Davis was a precision instrument manufacturer. Arthur Davis taught himself Hebrew and became a highly proficient scholar and observant Jew. He passed on his knowledge to his children and Nina would have an hour's lesson in Hebrew before breakfast.[84] Nina translated and published medieval poetry in the Anglo-Jewish press whilst she was still in her teens. She published *Songs of Exile by Hebrew Poets* in 1901 and many of her poems are used in festival prayer books still used today. She was an active member of the Jewish League for Woman Suffrage, campaigning not only to win the vote but to improve the status of women in the Jewish community and to allow women seat holders to vote in synagogue elections. She encouraged Jewish women to educate their children. On 5 December 1919, Salaman became the first woman to preach in an Orthodox synagogue when she spoke on the weekly portion to the Cambridge Hebrew Congregation and the event caused a stir even outside the Jewish community.[85] She was engaged in many causes both general and Jewish with particular disposition for the Federation of Women Zionists and the Tottenham Talmud Torah for Girls.[86] Both she and her husband were members of New West End Synagogue, London.

With such a family background it is not surprising that Nina excelled in her chosen career. Education was a high priority and she received a great deal of intellectual input and scientific influence whilst growing up from her parents and family friends such as the Cornfelds.[87] From 1940 she and her family shared a large home in Cambridge with Frances and Francis Cornfield and their children. Frances, whose grandfather was Charles Darwin, was a noted poet and Francis was a classical scholar and translator known for his influential work on ancient philosophy. Her daughter Lucy

Wedderburn comments that 'she followed her father Myer in her own intellectually curious sphere of medicine and science'.[88]

Nina attended Channing School in London and then Perse in Cambridge before going to Bedales, a coeducational boarding school near Petersfield where her father and aunts had also been pupils. Bedales was founded by John Haden Badley in 1893 to be a humane alternative to the authoritarian regimes typical of late Victorian public schools. Badley took a non-denominational approach to religion and the school has never had a chapel. Its relatively secular teaching made it attractive in the early days to non-conformists, agnostics, Quakers, Unitarians and liberal Jews who formed a significant element of its early intake. Nina loved the school's philosophy and the freedom it allowed, as well as the science lessons. Lucy Wedderburn considers that Bedales would have been very supportive of women wanting to study science.[89]

Nina gained a place to study natural sciences at Newnham College, Cambridge in 1947.[90] She gained her degree in biochemistry in 1950 and went on to start a PhD at Kings College, London in 1951. Her marriage to Kenneth William Wedderburn (Bill), later Lord Wedderburn of Charlton, a lawyer and fellow student at Cambridge, led her to decide to stop her PhD and move back to Cambridge with her husband when he was offered a teaching position at Clare College. Bill Wedderburn, who was not Jewish, was a direct descendant of radical leader and anti-slavery advocate Robert Wedderburn, became a politician and member of the House of Lords, affiliated with the Labour Party. Nina was a life-long member of the Labour Party.

Soon after the birth of her third child, her marriage ran into difficulties and she divorced Bill in 1961. She moved back to London with her children and in 1965 returned to science, working part-time when the children were small. She studied as a PhD student at the London Hospital and started to develop her interest in viruses and how they affect the immune system. This was a new field since the workings of the immune system were little understood. It was a challenging time for her as a single parent but she successfully completed her PhD in 1969 and moved her work to the Royal College of Surgeons (RCS) where she rapidly developed her own group.[91] Scientists came from all over the world to train with her, especially as her group became well known for its work on malaria and how it affects the immune system and the Epstein Barr Virus.

Her early work focused on how malaria alters the immune system's ability to control cancer. She then developed a model to understand how viruses can suppress immunity and in particular the Epstein-Barr Virus

(EBV) linked to a childhood cancer in Africa. This virus causes a specific form of cancer called Burkitt's Lymphoma in children in Africa, yet it causes glandular fever in countries where there is a higher standard of living. Burkitt's Lymphoma is most commonly seen in areas where children get malaria many times before their fifth birthday so the link between malaria and childhood cancer began to become clear. The roles of different parts of the immune system (T cells, B cells, antibodies) in their response to different viruses were not yet evident in the 1970s but Nina developed collaborations with experts in the emerging field of immunology to understand this better. To fully understand the interaction between malaria and EBV she had to develop a model in a system that allowed close scrutiny of all arms of the immune system. Her work on EBV, which led to many publications, contributed to an emerging field to understand problems caused by EBV in patients who have a bone marrow transplant since during this time their immune system is depressed by the drugs and the EBV virus can reappear, causing major problems. She subsequently became a senior lecturer at the RCS, Dean of the Hunterian Institute and Fellow of the RSC (Dental Faculty).[92]

Lucy Wedderburn points out that her mother's work was multidisciplinary. During her scientific career she worked with biochemists, immunologists, virologists, vets, pathologists and cancer doctors. 'She exemplified the golden advice which is still given to students today: follow the route you need and develop the methods or models to answer the question, do not stay in one box or discipline, move outside your comfort zone'. She is remembered for her patient mentorship, support and encouragement of students and fellows. Many of her PhD students went on to establish successful careers all over the world.[93] She provided the same kind of support for her daughter. Lucy Wedderburn is a Professor in Paediatric Rheumatology at the Institute of Child Health and a consultant at Great Ormond Street Hospital.

Nina's intellectual interests were reflected in her relationship to Judaism in her later years. Although she did not have an orthodox or religious childhood her parents clearly identified as being Jewish and she was brought up with a strong sense of Jewish identity. Her parents believed you could have this identity and not be religious. Nina remembered large Seder services and events at her grandparents' country house in Barley.[94] For many years she did not belong to a synagogue until she joined London's Liberal Jewish synagogue (LJS) in her later years. Lucy Wedderburn remembers that when she was growing up, despite it being a non-religious household, they did celebrate Passover and Chanukah.[95] Although Nina was not religious her Jewish identity was at the core of her being and she developed an interest in philosophy and Jewish texts, Jewish history and the Talmud. She applied herself to this study as she had done to science: with patient careful reading.[96] Rabbi Alexandra Wright of the LJS reflected that Nina came to her Judaism and her Jewish learning quite late in life. 'I think intellectually she enjoyed the challenge of Jewish learning and was stimulated by it.'[97] She added that she was much loved by her friends at LJS where she was a member of the Keep in Touch group, visiting frail and household members in their homes and kept in touch by telephone with those who were lonely. 'She was a good and loyal friend and had a strong sense of duty and morality'.[98]

Although Nina's achievements were extremely noteworthy, Lucy Wedderburn commented that it was typical of many women during this period that she did not push to be put forward to become a professor, and this was very common for women scientists at this time.[99] Gendered perceptions persisted even after the Second World War, affecting the next generation of women scientists, including Susan Greenfield, Professor of Pharmacology at the University of Oxford, first female director of the Royal Institution and famous as a populariser of science. Despite her high profile and many accomplishments, she has never been elected to the Royal Society and professional jealousy and animosity has led at least two anonymous fellows to threaten to resign if she was elected, exemplifying the sexism that still pervades science.[100]

Susan Greenfield (1950 -)

Baroness Susan Greenfield is a scientist, writer, broadcaster and member of the House of Lords. Her research has focused on the treatment of Parkinson's disease and Alzheimer's disease. She is popular on the lecture circuit, delivering rapid-fire commentary on the neurochemistry of the human brain, taking people through the mysteries of memory, cognition and perception. Her aim is to open science to sectors of society that previously thought it was not for them: to bring mainstream science to people so that there is a scientifically literate society.[101]

Greenfield, who was born in Hammersmith, London in 1950 overcame poverty and prejudice to succeed. Her father Reginald Myer Greenfield was an electrician, the son of a first-generation Yiddish speaking Jewish immigrant and grew up in the East End. His father came from Poland and settled in Bow where he started a chocolate factory, S. Greenfield Chocolate Works. He lost all his money and overnight the family went from riches to

24. Official Portrait of Baroness Greenfield CBE (Roger Harris, via Wikimedia Commons)

rags. He died before Greenfield was born and by that time the family had moved first to Shepherd's Bush and then Chiswick.

Greenfield's mother Doris (Thorp) was not Jewish. She had been a dancer and a chorus girl. Her parents met at a time when there was a lot of antisemitism, and her maternal grandmother was very wary of anything alien. 'She apparently told my mother that if she went ahead with the marriage she would put her head in the gas oven. My mother called her bluff and offered her a cushion and a shilling for the meter'.[102]

Both families violently disapproved of the marriage. The Jewish side of her family were horrified, due to the fact that not only was she not Jewish but she was also a dancer. Her grandmother had remarried Lewis Shoot, choirmaster at the Great Synagogue in Duke's Place. It was a very orthodox household and the family had a Shabbos goy.[103] Greenfield remembers visiting her grandparents on a Friday night and her parents, both smokers, being unable to smoke.[104]

Greenfield's family were very poor but had a respect for education. Although she secured a place at the prestigious independent girls' school Godolphin and Latymer she never saw herself as particularly academic. Her parents, although bright, were not educated and could not help with homework which she used to do on the bus. 'Because I have got a native wit I kind of just winged it. I got by'. When it came to studying a third language at school, there was the opportunity to study Greek. When she informed her teachers that she was interested, they told her that it was a difficult subject and they were not sure whether she would manage. This made her determined to succeed and in the first-year exams she received top marks. She started to apply herself in the same way to her other subjects and she went into the Oxbridge stream. She read experimental psychology at St Hilda's College, Oxford and was the first person of her immediate family to go to university. She went to Oxford at a time when there was a 8:1 ratio, men to women. 'Oxford was the making of me. You were encouraged to be the individual that you were'.[105]

Since her Oxford days Greenfield has proved to be force in British science, has been showered with honours and is Britain's best known female neuroscientist. Her many positions have included research fellowships in the Department of Physiology, Oxford, the College de France, Paris and NYU Medical Center, New York and she served as Chancellor of Heriot Watt University, Edinburgh (2005-2012). She was director of the Royal Institution of Great Britain (1998-2010). Her books include *Journey to the Centres of the Mind* (1995) in which she articulates the theory of consciousness, *The Human Brain: A Guided Tour* (1997) and *The Private Life of the Brain* (2000) and *Tomorrow's People: How 21ˢᵗ Technology is Changing the Way We Think and Feel* (2003) which explored human nature and its potential vulnerability in an age of technology. In 2000 Greenfield was named Woman of the Year by the *Observer* and awarded a CBE for her contribution to the understanding of science. In 2013 she co-founded the biotech company Neuro-bio Ltd to develop a disruptive approach to Alzheimer's disease based on her research exploring novel brain mechanisms linked to neurodegeneration.[106] She presented the BBC series *Brain Story* as well as many other television and radio programmes, has received 30 honorary degrees, honorary fellowship of The Royal College of Physicians (2000), as well as the Ordre National de la Legion d'Honneur

(2003). In 2014 she was included in Debretts 'Top 500' of the most influential people in Britain today.

Greenfield is a member of the House of Lords, one of the 'people's peers' appointed by Tony Blair in 2001 'to put oomph into the upper chamber'.[107] She sits in the House of Lords as a crossbencher, Baroness Greenfield of Otmoor, having no formal affiliation. She has spoken on a variety of topics including education, drugs and economic empowerment for women and consistently voted against raising university fees. She is a patron of Alzheimer's Research UK and Dignity in Dying and a founder and trustee of the charity Science for Humanity, a network of scientists, researchers and technologists that collaborates with not-for-profit organisations to create practical solutions to the everyday problems of developing communities.

People have a mixed reaction to Greenfield. Some have dismissed her scientific qualifications whereas others have praised her ability to communicate science to the public.[108] She was the first woman director of the Royal Institution of Great Britain (1998-2010) and became known publicly after giving their Christmas lectures in 1994, entitled 'Journey to the Centre of the Brain', the first woman to do so since they were founded in 1825.[109] The Royal Institution (RI) was founded in 1799 and has long worked to promote science to the public. Its Christmas lectures are a British tradition.

Her time at the RI illustrates the controversy that she can create. When she first came there, *Nature* magazine ran an editorial showing her in a miniskirt with the headline 'highbrow club gains the common touch'. She felt proud as her father had been an electrician, her mother a dancer and she was proud that one could democratise science and bring in a sense of irreverence and fun.[110]

After running the RI for more than a decade, a period in which she spearheaded a controversial and costly physical renovation of the science body's historic London headquarters, Greenfield found her director position eliminated. The RI struggled with a financial crisis following a £22 million development programme masterminded by Greenfield. The project ended £3 million in debt and the institution had to sell off some of its property assets.[111]

The trustees said it was a cost saving move and that the requirements for the role of Director had ceased to exist. Greenfield considered legal challenges to her dismissal that may have included sexual discrimination charges.[112] A prolonged struggle ended with Greenfield settling out of court. One insider said 'the trustees were looking for someone to blame for this and the finger pointed at Susan'. Some say 'old boy culture' led to the move as she was the only female appointed to the iconic post throughout the RI's history.[113]

Greenfield does appear to ruffle feathers. Her success, coupled with her television work and best-selling books popularising such weighty matters of the meaning of consciousness seems to have stirred almost as much envy as respect among academics.[114] She dresses in designer clothes, is popular in the media and appeared in magazines such as *Vogue* and *Hello*. This could have contributed to the fact that she was proposed to be a member of the Royal Society but not elected. The Royal Society, originating in 1660, is the oldest scientific society in the world and the leading national organisation for the promotion of scientific research in Britain. There are approximately 1,700 Fellows and Foreign Members. Each year up to 52 Fellows and 10 Foreign Members are elected from a group of around 800 candidates.[115] As of 2018 female fellowship of the Royal Society was 124, or 8.5%.[116] Notwithstanding the low ratio, it is surprising that someone of Greenfield's calibre has not been admitted to the Royal Society.

She is portrayed in the media as the rebel woman scientist who dresses in a sexy manner with long blonde hair. 'This just tells you how science is perceived. The implicit prejudice is that a scientist is normally a white middle-aged man with a tie. The fact that you are not is noteworthy'.[117] Greenfield defends her position. 'I think in life you just have to be yourself and the most important person you have to square up to every morning is yourself. For me the most important thing is personal integrity. I wear what I wear. It is predicated on a curious assumption about scientists. If I was an advertising executive, would that be an issue?' Some see her as symbolising the struggle between traditionalists and modernists.[118]

There has been a bias against women in science. In 2002 Greenfield completed a report for Patricia Hewitt at the Department of Trade and Industry on women in science and for physical sciences the gender ratio was 90:10 towards males.[119] It was reported in 2019 that the number of women climbing the career ladder in science is 'disappointingly low'. Women make up half of students in the life sciences according to data from 500 scientific institutions worldwide. It found women had fewer chances to serve on committees or speak at scientific meetings. The data published in Cell Stem Cell back the view of many people in science that more must be done to address the problem of the 'leaky pipeline' where women leave the profession due to problems such as harassment and issues around promotion and pay.[120] When Greenfield was asked whether there is sexism in science, she confirmed that it existed. 'The best way of combating it is to show you can do a bloody good job and act as a role model to others'.

Successful female scientists are, by definition, resilient. They have overcome well documented barriers throughout their lives: discouragement by teachers, family and society to pursue careers in STEM (science, technology, engineering and mathematics) fields; a lack of role models, hostile and sometimes abusive work environments and biases against them in favour of men in every aspect of their professional lives.[121]

Greenfield has exemplified this resilience throughout her life. She encountered prejudice at an early age within her own family. Her two grandmothers never spoke to each other and would not even be together in the same room. 'The only merit was that the prejudice was equally vociferous on both sides. That is why I am particularly sensitive to racism and sexism and ageism and all the other isms'.[122] She was aware that she had a Christian and Jewish side, without knowing what that meant as her parents were totally non-religious. 'I knew that Jewish people and Christian people didn't get together and that I was half and half'. She remembers asking her mother which half of her was Jewish. At the time it was popular for girls to wear crosses and she wanted one. Her mother who was always very sensitive to the cultural tectonic plate said that she could wear one as long as she wore a Star of David as well and she went to school with both round her neck.[123]

In her gap year before going to Oxford University she went on a scholarship to Israel in 1970 for six months and stayed on Kibbutz Gesher Haziv on the northern border. By that time she was aware of her culture and heritage. Despite not being an orthodox Jew 'I felt I was coming home in an eerie way'.[124] Whilst she did not do 'expressively Jewish things' during her time at Oxford, she admires what she perceives as Jewish values and culture. She considers that Jewish families are much closer than Gentile ones.[125] She recalls regular visits with the Jewish side of her family. Her grandmother would hold court and pass around everyone's school reports. 'What I remember is a lovely feeling of an extended family'. When she received her place at Godolphin and Latymer there was a long list of school items to be purchased. As her father was a poor electrician, her uncle paid for everything that was required.[126] She says there was a Jewish emphasis on education within her family.[127]

The aspects that Greenfield respects in Jewish culture are a sense of people looking after each other, the respect for older people and for education. 'I think I am lured by the notion that there are things more than just money, more than just impressing people and status and that it is important to develop a sense of community'. She says that people tell her that she does not seem English and that she has a certain energy level, curiosity and enthusiasm that is found in Jewish groups.[128]

It was in 1998 when she was appointed director of the Royal Institution that her embrace of the Jewish community properly began. Among the events that she inherited were the annual Weizmann Institute Friends lectures and in 2001 she was appointed to the Weizmann Institute Council in Israel. She was also on the Israel British Business Council and on the Board of Britech, a government organisation which fosters collaboration on spin-out companies in Israel and Britain. She was awarded an honorary degree from the Hebrew University and Haifa University and has spoken at many Jewish charity events in Britain. In 1998 she received the Jewish Care Woman of Distinction Award for contribution to science and in 2012 was included in the Jewish Chronicle Power 50 that celebrated influential women across arts, science, religion and politics that are shaping society.

She became known in the Jewish community for her passionate antipathy to the proposed academic boycott of Israel in 2002. Some of her colleagues were signatories and she was asked to sign. She responded in the *Times* with an attack on the idea of a boycott and pointed out that there were echoes of book burning that took place in 1930s Nazi Germany. She tried to put together a delegation of British scientists to see the work being done in Israeli universities and their expertise in technology transfer. Unfortunately, it was then the time of the Iraq war and plans could not go ahead.[129]

Greenfield is never afraid to speak her mind and is no stranger to controversy. She is a committed feminist. 'I run my lab in a less confrontational way than men'. She upset a number of women colleagues when she said that she did not think being a mother was compatible with making it to the top in science. She decided not to have children.[130] She was married to academic Peter Atkins (1991-2005) but they divorced. She is also not afraid to cause alarm. She coined the phrase 'mind change', an umbrella term comparable to 'climate change' to describe the effects of internet use on the brain. According to her findings children's attention spans are being shortened and we are all becoming self-centred and addicted to instant gratification because of Facebook and Twitter.[131]

Despite having always been a polarizing figure in the academic world, Greenfield nevertheless belongs to a rare breed. She is able to communicate easily highly specialised knowledge to a general audience. Perhaps the public have taken to her because they recognise that she is, by her own account, something of a maverick. She comes from a working class background, was the first member of her family to go to university and unusually for an Oxford Professor of Physiology she does not have a chemistry O-level. It has been commented that If Greenfield is an ubiquitous media figure it is because not only does she talk about the brain so clearly but she also passes on some of the excitement of working with scientific ideas. She talks about the brain the way other people talk about fine art or football –it is a thing of endless beauty and fascination.

Conclusion

Like other Jewish women whose lives are profiled in this book, these four scientists encountered formidable obstacles in the pursuit of careers in their chosen fields. Like those who challenged the male domains of law and medicine, their gender imposed far more barriers than their Jewishness. Although these women scientists came from different eras and varied backgrounds, connected to their Jewish identity in diverse ways and differed in their paths to scientific careers, they all came from families that valued education and overcame numerous hurdles to establish themselves as scientists in their own right.

Whether they were raised in privilege or relative poverty, Hertha Aryton, Rosalind Franklin, Nina Wedderburn and Susan Greenfield all received critical encouragement and support from their immediate or extended families as they pursued their passion for education and science. Franklin and Wedderburn came from lives of relative privilege and were provided excellent private schooling, while Aryton and Greenfield had to rely on extended family, mentor figures and loans and grants in order to achieve their academic goals. Both Aryton and Wedderburn experienced breaks in their educational and career paths, the former out of financial need and the latter due to family commitments, but all four women managed to complete university courses—three at Cambridge and one at Oxford.

That they all managed to attain such educations and succeed as scientists is all the more remarkable in the face of the misogyny that they encountered across the span of their combined careers, from the 1870s right through to the twenty-first century. Denied equal educational opportunities, snubbed by professional organisations, treated dismissively by their male colleagues and subjected to judgments about their appearance, these women encountered gender bias at every stage of their scientific careers. Aryton and Franklin entered Cambridge before women were accepted as full members of the university and were denied the status of their male peers. Aryton, a brilliant inventor, succeeded in large part because of her marriage to a fellow scientist, with whom she collaborated.

However, marriage also disqualified her from acceptance into the Royal Society. More than a century later, Susan Greenfield faced similar exclusion—not as a married woman but as a non-traditional, popular scientist that ruffled establishment feathers.

The most damaging prejudice levelled at women scientists denied them full credit for their innovative research and ground-breaking discoveries and inventions. Nina Wedderburn who, despite doing important work on viruses and immunology, never attained a professorship or gained admission to the prestigious scientific societies. Aryton successfully patented a number of important inventions and was awarded the Royal Society's Hughes Medal, but her Aryton fan, which saved thousands of lives in the First World War, was initially dismissed by the War Office. Perhaps the most tragic example is Rosalind Franklin, who was never given appropriate recognition for her discovery of the structure of DNA, while her male peers Watson and Crick took all the fame and credit, later gratuitously insulting her appearance, demeanour and scientific mind for good measure.

Though all shared a common Jewish heritage, religion played only a small part in their professional lives. Raised in orthodox environments, both Aryton and Franklin were non-observant in later life and though Franklin never married, Aryton married a non-Jew. Both acknowledged their heritage and remained connected to Judaism through their families though Franklin had a very conflicted relationship to her Jewishness, especially after visiting Israel. Although being Jewish did not seem to overtly affect their careers, it may have contributed to the way in which they pushed themselves to excel, in the same way that being a female in the male dominated field of science did. Notably, Franklin felt more comfortable when working with male Jewish colleagues, pointing to the more subtle prejudices that may have been in play in her work environment. Wedderburn and Greenfield, who was only half-Jewish were raised in non-religious households and had developed connections to Judaism as adults. Wedderburn approached her religious heritage intellectually in later life and Greenfield connected to her Jewish side on a gap year in Israel. Like their predecessors, neither appeared to have experienced any overt antisemitism professionally. While religion did not present these women with significant obstacles in their careers, they faced considerable other hurdles in establishing themselves as scientists and gaining recognition for their accomplishments. Nevertheless, all four succeeded on their own merits as innovative thinkers and scientists, contributing important and ground-breaking work that has benefitted both man and womankind.

8

Rabbis and Religious Leaders

For nearly 2000 years, the position of rabbi was limited to men. By the time the Mishnah, the first major written collection of Jewish oral traditions and the Talmud, the primary source of Jewish law and theology, were circulated, women were less educated, and less important in the structure of society than they had been in the Biblical period partly due to the Hellenistic influence on Jewish society. It is from precisely this period that much of Jewish law dates and the real problem that emerges from this attitude to women is that their legal status was lower than that of men. They were never chattels but many fundamental rights were denied to them. A wife could not divorce her husband while a man could divorce a woman relatively easily. They could not give evidence, act as Judges, form part of the necessary number for a full service at a synagogue (ten men), and were excused from any positive commandment – mitzvah – for which there is a fixed time. They were exempt apparently because of their duties with home and children but that meant they were not obliged to take part in synagogue services or in the religious activities of the community. They were not obliged to do any of these things yet at no stage was it suggested that they were not allowed to do them. It was over the course of time that exemption became exclusion, putting women at a real disadvantage. It limited the religious life of the woman to the home and dietary laws. In traditional Judaism she was not a religious equal to her husband.

Texts that date from the eleventh to twelfth centuries discuss whether women should be called to the reading of the scrolls of the Law in the synagogue or to blow the *shofar* (ram's horn) on the Jewish New Year and although this could be permissible, it was discouraged out of respect for the men in the congregation. Another restriction was the introduction in the early medieval period of the *mehitzah*, the division between men and women in the synagogue. This was probably originally just a division in seating but it led to women sitting up in a gallery or behind a curtain. As a result of the exemptions and lack of religious involvement such as the study and teaching of Torah, women received less and less education. They were unable to take an active part in the public life of the community.[1]

It was not until the late nineteenth century that the long-standing Jewish patriarchal hegemony was challenged by women who aspired to become rabbis. The idea of women becoming rabbis was first presented to American Judaism when Ray (Rachel) Frank began attending classes at Hebrew Union College in 1893 but she did not compete the programme. Ten years later Henrietta Szold was admitted to the Jewish Theological Seminary with the clear understanding that she would not pursue a course of studies that would lead to ordination. It was only in the twentieth century that the situation began to change in communities linked to the Progressive forms of Judaism, such as the reform movement in Germany, UK and USA. In 1935, Regina Jonas (1902-1944) was ordained in a private ceremony in Germany. Jonas had longed to be a rabbi for most of her life but struggled with the restrictions against women in higher education and rabbinical studies. When Jonas matriculated at the prestigious Berlin Academy for the Science of Judaism, her 1930 thesis argued that there was no law forbidding women to become rabbis but despite praise for her academic work, she was only granted a teaching degree. She continued to lobby for ordination, which she achieved in 1935. She worked as a pastoral counsellor at the Jewish Hospital in Berlin and was invited to serve several congregations in Berlin as the deportations of male rabbis under the Nazi regime began.[2] Jonas herself was eventually deported and perished at Auschwitz in 1944 and the details of her life were only discovered in the archives after the fall of the Berlin Wall in 1989.

After Jonas, there was a long pause before women's ordination became possible again. Influenced by societal changes wrought by the Women's Liberation Movement of the mid-twentieth century, the first American woman rabbi, Sally J. Priesand, was ordained in 1972 and Jackie Tabick became the first woman rabbi in the UK in 1975. When asked what led her to become a rabbi, she explained that it was probably due to the fact that her father died when she was eight, and that as a child she blamed herself and looked to religion to sort herself out. When she was ten, the family joined a reform synagogue in Ilford where there was an inspirational rabbi. 'It was a real eye opener'. They had conversations about being a rabbi and it made an instant impression on her. He told her to take a group of children and talk about prayer and this led her to realise how little she knew. She went to synagogue regularly, was the youngest member of the choir and joined the World Jewish Progressive Synagogue youth section. She became entranced by Jewish learning.[3] Tabick started her career as an assistant rabbi at West London Synagogue before leading her own community at North West Surrey Synagogue in 1998. She is the convenor of the Movement for

Reform Judaism's Beit Din (rabbinical court), the first woman in the role, and has played a leading role in interfaith initiatives.

The rise and integration of women into the rabbinate over the past five decades has transformed many aspects of Jewish life. An estimated 1,500 women have become rabbis across most Jewish denominations. Along with female academics, female rabbis have expanded the canon of Jewish study and stretched the parameters of Jewish practice to include women and their perspectives. By dint of their presence as religious authorities, female rabbis are toppling the traditional gender-orientated differentiation of roles between Jewish men and women.[4] Women rabbis are now role models in the progressive Jewish world while just making slow ripples within the mainstream Orthodox communities.

The lives and careers of four ground-breaking religious leaders are examined in this chapter, including Lily Montagu, Britain's first female Jewish minister, Julia Neuberger, the second ordained woman rabbi in the UK, and the first to have her own synagogue congregation, Elizabeth Tikva Sarah, one of the first representatives of the LGBT community to become a rabbi and Lindsey Taylor-Guthartz, who took an unusual path to the rabbinate from a non-observant and assimilated family that had all but renounced its Jewish heritage.

Lily Montagu (1873-1963)

When the Liberal Jewish Movement in Britain, initially known as the Jewish Religious Union (JRU), was founded in 1902, a woman leading a service or having a major role in a British Jewish movement was unheard of. It was through Lily Montagu, one of the three founders alongside Claude Montefiore and Israel Muttack, that the situation changed. Lily Montagu was a social worker, a magistrate in the London juvenile courts, a suffragist, a religious organiser and a spiritual leader who helped establish Liberal Jewish Synagogues across Great Britain.

She played a key role in making Liberal Judaism more than a fringe movement in Great Britain. Raised in an orthodox home, Montagu questioned the aspects of Orthodoxy that were, for women especially, contradictory, expecting her to foster a close relationship with God without providing the necessary tools, such as membership in a congregation or Hebrew education. Seeking a different religious community that accepted and encouraged women's participation, from its very foundations, liberal Judaism has championed gender equality. Montagu led services and men and women were allowed to sit together.

25. Lillian Helen Montagu CBE (National Library of Israel, Schwadron Collection)

Montagu was born in 1873, the sixth of ten children born to Ellen Cohen and Samuel Montagu. A self-made millionaire by the age of thirty, Samuel was a banker and bullion broker, member of the House of Commons and later the House of Lords. He was also an observant Jew who worked tirelessly to strengthen the organised, institutional life of the late nineteenth and early twentieth century Anglo-Jewish community. Ellen was the daughter of Louis Cohen, a successful banker and stockbroker and a member of one of the oldest and most prominent Jewish families in England. Although Ellen was observant, Lily remembered that her sense of religiosity was 'elastic'. She was willing to answer all of her children's religious questions, however radical, incorporated English prayers into home worship and, unlike her husband, believed that one could not expect young people to want the pattern of their lives to be the same as previous generations.[5]

Lily was influenced considerably by her parent's religious beliefs. Although she later rejected many of her father's religious followings, the sincerity with which they were held made a lasting impression on her. It gave her the resolve to make Judaism a central part of her life. Yet by the age of fifteen she became convinced that Orthodoxy offered her, and other women, little room for religious self-expression. As she had received limited religious education, she questioned how she could pray in a language that she did not understand, or be part of a congregation that did not count her as a member. She found in the works of Claude Montefiore, a Jewish scholar and advocate of Liberal Judaism, a vision of Judaism that mirrored her own understanding of true religion as personal in nature, universal in outlook and best revealed through daily conduct.

Montagu was driven by inner piety and faith to reform English Judaism. In establishing the JRU, Montagu revealed her own understanding of society and the concept of human obligation. She believed that it was not enough to possess religious faith; one needed to share that faith with others. She had a deep spirituality and her determination to revitalise Anglo-Jewry's religious life was also rooted in the conviction that God had called her. She maintained that it was her duty, not just as an individual but of the Jewish 'brotherhood' to testify to God's reality and to bring others to God.[6] For Montagu, the orthodoxy in which she was raised was external, neither beautiful nor meaningful: a hindrance to the development of true religious faith. Her goal was to be fully Jewish and fully spiritual without being an Orthodox Jew: to identify being Jewish with the spirit of the modern age.[7] She wanted to make Judaism relevant to Jews in England.

In 1899 she published in the *Jewish Quarterly Review* 'The Spiritual Possibilities of Judaism Today', in which she asked all religiously committed Jews to help her form an association aimed at strengthening the religious life of the Anglo-Jewish community through the propagation of Liberal Jewish teachings and this resulted in the establishment of the JRU. She was concerned with the drift away from Judaism by an increasingly assimilated Jewish community. She regarded the Orthodox Judaism of her father as a major cause of this drift and believed that a new and progressive style of Judaism accessible and understandable by all was the only answer to this problem.

Montagu was committed to access for women in Judaism and

concerned with the welfare of underprivileged working-class girls. To help make a difference to the harshness of their lives she and her sister Marion founded the West Central Club in 1893 where girls were given the opportunity to worship and socialise. She enabled so many young working women who had to serve on Saturday mornings to have a synagogue experience when she created and led the afternoon services.

The services were in English and featured topics that were of interest to the girls and retained only those traditional prayers which she thought 'had meaning for modern Jews and Jewesses in the actual circumstances of their lives'.[8]

Montagu became a lay minister of the West Central Liberal Synagogue in 1928, a position in which she was formally inducted in 1944. Following Montefiore's death in 1938 she assumed the presidency of the JRU, later renamed the Union of Liberal and Progressive Synagogues and helped found and eventually become president of the World Union of Progressive Judaism.[9] Montagu was brave and fought the cause for others.[10] She was an exceptional woman to have achieved what she did in her time and it took three decades before other Jewish women succeeded to the rabbinate: first Jackie Tabick in 1975 followed by Baroness Julia Neuberger, who became Britain's second female rabbi in 1977 and the first to have her own synagogue.

Julia Neuberger (1950 -)

Baroness Neuberger holds the unusual double distinction as both a rabbi and a member of the House of Lords. She is an avid human rights crusader who is outspoken on the need for equal rights and treatment for all.

She was born on 27 February 1950 to Liesel (Alice) Rosenthal and Walter Schwab. Her father was from a German Jewish Orthodox family who had come to England before World War One. Educated at Trinity College, Cambridge, he intended to take up medicine but never completed his studies. Against his parents' wishes he went to Palestine to work on a kibbutz and for a time was employed as a bus driver. Soon after Hitler assumed power in Germany, his mother, who was chairperson of the welfare committee for refugees in London, persuaded him to return to Britain and enlisted his support in helping young refugees adjust to their changed circumstances. After serving in the Second World War, he joined the civil service and was assistant secretary in the Department of Housing and Local Government. He was deeply involved in Anglo-Jewish affairs and edited many of the Jewish Historical Society publications.[11]

26. Official Portrait of Baroness Julia Neuberger DBE (via Wikimedia Commons, Roger Harris)

Neuberger's mother was born in Heilbronn, Germany, where her parents were wine merchants. She came on her own as a refugee to England at the age of 22 in 1937 and initially worked as a domestic servant. Her parents and brother later managed to join her but most of her family were not so fortunate and died in the camps. She was a collector of German and British prints of the 1920s and 1930s and throughout her life collected art, befriended and supported artists and was closely involved with both the Association of Jewish Refugees and the Ben Uri Art Gallery where she organised exhibitions and played a leading role in the creation of the 'Permanent Collection of Works from Jewish Artists'.[12] The Schwab Trust, which supports and educates young refugees and asylum seekers, was later set up in her parent's name. Neuberger grew up in a house filled with rare Hebrew books and describes her father as a 'passionate and observant Reform Jew'.[13]

She attended South Hampstead High School and Newnham College, Cambridge where she first studied Assyriology. After she was refused entry to Turkey because she was British and then to Iraq because she was Jewish, she changed subject and studied Hebrew full-time. Her lecturer at Cambridge, Nicholas de Lange, also a reform rabbi, suggested that she should become a rabbi. She obtained her rabbinic diploma at Leo Baeck College, London. It was not what she had expected to do. 'I was not very religious, also female, and not sure that being a rabbi was sufficiently academically rigorous for me'. Her parents were amazed at her decision. Her mother had been a communist in her youth and had little time for religion.[14]

After ordination Neuberger took on a post at South London Liberal Synagogue (1977-1989) and a professorship at Leo Baeck College. In 2011 she became senior rabbi of the West London Synagogue from which she retired in 2020. She was Chancellor of the University of Ulster and served as chief executive of the King's Fund, a think tank that organises conferences and funds charities focused on health issues. In 2003 she was made a Dame of the British Empire and was elevated to Baroness the following year. She has been active on Parliament's Science and Technology Committee where she helped draft the bill regulating the use of human tissue and embryos in 2008. She became chair of University College London NHS Foundation Trust in 2019 and Chair of Whittington Health NHS Trust in 2020 and is chair of the charity Independent Age which advises older people. She has made significant contributions to public and political life in Britain through her social commentary, writing and activism. She is married to Anthony Neuberger, Professor of Finance at Cass Business School

As well as religion, much of Neuberger's life has been given over to refugee advocacy, philanthropic and volunteering work and her prolific writings include *Not Dead Yet – A Manifesto for Old Age* (2008), *Is That All There Is? Reflections on Life, Mortality and Leaving a Legacy* (2011) and

Antisemitism – What it is. What It Isn't. Why It Matters (2019). In *The Moral State We're In* (2005), her manifesto for the twenty-first century, she set out a range of practical measures that needed to be taken including free care for the elderly after those who are able have paid their way for two years, legislation of voluntary euthanasia, and a new more open regime in children's homes. She hoped that the combination of rabbi and campaigner would bring her the sort of attention declined to others speaking out on the same issues. 'I come out of that broad Jewish social-justice tradition which teaches us that we do have an obligation as human beings to open things up'.[15] She also had a real Jewish passion for seeing her religion through the eyes of the prophets and rabbis who saw Judaism as having a role in putting right the wrongs of the world. 'It's not that other things are not important, but that this -nourished by Jewish learning and spirituality – gives us a sense of purpose and a sense of continuity with our ancestors, and we hope with our great grandchildren and beyond that reaches right back into the biblical period'.[16]

She grew up in a family surrounded by different forms of activism. She also felt that doing only what was absolutely necessary was not enough. From her grandmother's work with refugees from Nazi Germany and the Stepney Jewish Girls' Club to her parents' work with the Ben Uri Art Gallery, she grew up thinking it was a standard part of life. 'It was both about being Jewish and being a decent citizen. You gave money and time. If you did not have to be at your paid work, there was something useful you could do for someone else'.[17]

Whilst still at school she volunteered for an organisation that worked with isolated elderly people and became very involved in issues about poverty and hunger. At the end of her time at university, then during her rabbinical training, she started spending time with people who were suffering and dying. She learnt that almost everyone who was dying had regrets about what they had not done and it taught her that one needed to fill one's life with as much as possible. She found a road map through religion; a form of Judaism that is very much about social conscience and social action and what one does in this world. 'What I get from religion is Jewish teaching and the sense of community acting together'.[18] During her time at South London Liberal Synagogue she spoke of the need for synagogue members to be trained in bereavement counselling to help widows who often felt excluded from a community that revolved around couples.[19] She was appointed the Government's Champion of Volunteering (2007-2009).

Throughout her career she has made an extensive contribution to healthcare policy and management. She chaired the review for the Liverpool Care Pathway (LCP) in 2013. The Pathway was developed in the 1990s to give health and care practitioners' guidance on providing an excellent service for people close to death. Despite regular updating there was increasing criticism about the lack of proper professional leadership and poor consultation with service users and carers. In 2013, the Minister of Care commissioned a review of the LCP carried out by Neuberger. As a result of the findings, the LCP was to be replaced by an individual approach to end-of-life care for each patient with a personalised end of life care plan.

Neuberger was a long-time member of the Labour Party, as were her parents, before leaving to help form the centrist Social Democratic Party. After running as a parliamentary candidate for Tooting in the 1983 general election, she was appointed to the House of Lords where she sat for the SDP's successor party, the Liberal Democrats. She resigned from the Party and became a crossbencher in 2011 when she took up her post at the West London synagogue.[20]

She describes her feelings at Labour's descent under Jeremy Corbyn as 'quite a big sense of betrayal'. She publicly rebuked Corbyn and the Labour Party for their handling of antisemitism within its ranks. She was part of a group of prominent Jewish writers and thinkers who wrote to the Party in 2019 to express their 'bewilderment and disgust' with the Party's handling of the antisemitism crisis. Her anger and frustration had been building for a number of years in proportion to the rise of left-wing antisemitism. She backs the right for people to speak out against the actions of Israel but according to one of her theses, anti-Zionism 'morphs into antisemitism… when their tone in their criticism of Israel is such that they would not use it about other countries'.[21]

Neuberger has had a great impact on British society, both within the Jewish and non-Jewish communities, yet she sees herself as an outsider and believes that she will always remain a second-generation refugee. This has given her an advantage in what she does. 'I've realised that you have to play it both ways if you are really going to change things. You have to be sufficiently trusted by the insiders that they don't think you are a complete nutcase, and you have to be enough of an outside to get the bigger picture'.[22] She considers being a rabbi in the House of Lords has been helpful. 'You have a particular authority talking on some issues, such as assisted dying, as a rabbi. People will listen to me differently as a result of my pastoral experience'.[23]

In recent years she has re-examined her feelings about her German heritage. 'My parents' homeland has dealt with its Nazi past. After the Brexit vote, I want to embrace my continental European origins'. As a child she had German au pairs, and her mother spoke German to her parents, as their English was not fluent. She was aware that Germany was not a country the family visited and that terrible things had happened to the Jews there. She was 10 when she learnt the full extent and subsequently realised that her grandfather's mental health had been permanently affected as a result.

Most of her mother's family, from Heilbronn in southern Germany, perished as did some of her father's family. Neuberger's feelings about Germany were quite negative for most of her life. She was unhappy on a trip as a teenager to stay with her mother's friends and deeply uncomfortable when she went to Germany to make a BBC film on Wagner. Her feelings changed when her synagogue took a group to Berlin, where the emphasis was on remembering, marking where Jewish families had lived with *Stolpersteine* commemorative plaques, recording the history and celebrating the contribution Jews had made to German culture. Her mother's hometown published a biography about her and in 2016 the city gave a huge welcome to the 150 people who came to the book launch. It was the first time that Neuberger felt comfortable in Germany.

She also felt great admiration for Chancellor Angela Merkel, for her open arms to refugees from Syria and elsewhere. Her change in attitude resulted in her deciding to apply for a German passport when Britain voted for Brexit. 'I am a European as well as a proud Briton. I think it is perfectly possible to be a proud Briton – and a grateful one – and to hold a German passport too'.[24]

She is articulate on every social, ethical and political problem that is thrown at her. Completely fearless about being controversial inside and outside her faith, as adept at taking middle England to task over its attitude to women as she is lambasting the Chief Rabbi Immanuel Jakobovits for his suggestion that gays and lesbians could be cured. [25] She constantly thinks about what she can do to change the country. 'In this little bit of life I have left I would like to see what I can do to make the world a better place'.[26]

The lack of fear and great determination can also be attributed to Elizabeth Tikva Sarah who also has a long history of activism both inside and outside the world of Judaism and a steadfast voice against inequality and discrimination.

Elizabeth Tikva Sarah (1955 -)

Rabbi Elizabeth (Elli) Tikva Sarah[27] is a feminist activist and author. She was one of the first women and one of the first openly gay rabbis to be

27. Rabbi Elizabeth Tikva Sarah 7 September 2001, Brighton (Simon Dack/Alamy Stock Photo)

ordained in Britain, the first to lead a mainstream synagogue and a pioneer of lesbian and gay inclusion.

Rabbi Elli had a very strict upbringing in a household in which there was a clash of cultures. 'It was not a happy marriage' she said of her parents, who came from entirely different backgrounds.[28] Her mother Eddie was the youngest of nine and was born and brought up in Highbury, north London where the family belonged to Dalton (Poet's Road) Orthodox synagogue and Yiddish was her first language. Eddie's parents had met in the East End shortly after they both arrived in the country around 1905. Her mother was from Siemiatycze, near to Bialystok, Poland and her father was from Czernowitz, Ukraine.[29]

Rabbi Elli's father, Paul Klempner, came from an affluent Viennese Jewish family whose family had a tie factory. He had his barmitzvah in a progressive synagogue in Vienna and was not interested in religion. He went to live in South Africa in 1936 at the age of 22 and whilst there was able to organise domestic permits for his parents which enabled them to flee to England together with his brother and sister. Apart from two cousins the rest of his extended family were murdered in the Holocaust. As a child, Elli was aware of living in the midst of a clash of Jewish cultures. Her mother was fairly religious and had a love of Yiddish and Hebrew and her father had a love of fine things and the Austrian tenor Richard Tauber.[30] Whenever her mother sang in Yiddish he tended to leave the room.[31] 'The battle between Eastern European and Central European Jewish life, between two "murdered worlds" was fought out in the kitchen and at the dining table in Yiddish and in German.'[32] Her mother was an ardent Socialist Zionist, but her father was not although the family went to donate blood at the local synagogue at the time of the 1967 Six Day War.[33]

Always aware of her Jewish identity, Rabbi Elli experienced antisemitism at summer camp and school and as a young adult in the mid-1970s when she was involved with the anti-apartheid movement. These experiences made her feel different. She was an active member of the International Marxist Group during her time as a first year sociology student at the London School of Economics but when she read one of the far left publications that described Israel as a puppet of Western imperialism she stopped being an IMG activist and decided that first and foremost she was a Jew.[34] Shortly after she graduated in 1977 she discovered feminism, became active in the Women's Liberation Movement and was involved in writing, editing and historical research. She joined the Lesbian Line collective, a helpline service by and for lesbians.

Rabbi Eli came out as a lesbian in 1978. As a child she was a 'tomboy' and had a very definite sense of choosing a male identity. She called herself John and would only wear button-fly jeans. She was one of the first in her class to have a boyfriend but on her fourteenth birthday she decided she was never going to go out with a boy again.[35] Nevertheless, she did marry in 1975, just before her twentieth birthday, but became aware very quickly that the marriage was not right. She cut off her hair and started to wear her husband's jackets. She left the marriage in 1978. It was a big learning curve, and it gave her the opportunity to explore her identity. 'I came out fully to myself in that situation'. She fell in love with a woman who was living in Israel on a kibbutz and she went to be with her. The relationship did not work out and she returned to her parents in London.[36] She had tried to repress her lesbian feelings and her sense of being different for several years. Her engagement with feminism, her increasing awareness that lesbians not only existed but celebrated their lives, helped her come out.[37]

The publication of the Wolfendon Report in 1957 was a watershed movement in LGBT (lesbian, gay, bisexual and transgender) history. It recommended that homosexuality should no longer be a crime, making private homosexual acts between men legal. However, this was not made law until the Sexual Offences Act in 1967. It had a profound effect on LGBT

Jews, paving the way out of the 'Jewish closet' and beginning a conversation among Jews about the possibility of accommodating LGBT identities within the faith.

Prohibited by British as well as biblical law, the situation of gay Jewish men seemed impossible before homosexuality was decriminalised. At the same time, the refusal to acknowledge the existence of lesbianism meant that many Jewish lesbian and bisexual women felt estranged from their religious community and British society as a whole.

On 13 October 1972 the Gay Liberation Front was established at the London School of Economics. The movement campaigned for radical changes in society that would lead to wider acceptance of lesbian and gay people. As the 1970s progressed many LGBT Jews were more confident in being 'out and proud'. Groups such as the Jewish Gay Group (JGG) provided opportunities to meet. A new sense of solidarity and purpose meant that LGBT Jews were an increasingly visible presence in the 1980s and 1990s. Although progressive Judaism in the UK accepted LGBT people into their communities, more traditional strands struggled with those who led alternative lifestyles. Being Jewish and LGBT made one doubly 'different'. LGBT Jews often had to come to terms with the social and religious effects of living with both a LGBT and Jewish identity. In a course of a single lifetime LGBT Jewish identity has been transformed from something not even named to something celebrated. Fifty years ago being Jewish and LGBT meant you were invisible and unwanted.[38]

The Women's Liberation Movement in the 1970s challenged the way society saw gender by uniting in the fight for equality. While many Jews joined radical feminist groups, some felt that being Jewish and feminist was difficult. Rabbi Elli explains that 'the whole sisterhood thing was fine as long as you were white, Anglo-Saxon Protestant. As long as you weren't different then you could be part of something which was the sisterhood of similarity. But when you had a difference, it didn't quite fit; you had different allegiances. You couldn't just abandon those allegiances because they are fundamental to your identity. Fundamental to my identity was what it was to be a Jew'.[39]

There was antisemitism in the Women's Liberation Movement. Jews faced particular difficulties after Israel's invasion of Lebanon in 1982. The Marxist and feminist press got whipped up in the frenzy of anti-Israel sentiment. Jewish lesbians began to feel they needed greater representation. A Jewish Lesbian conference took place in London in 1982 and sparked off a wave of similar events throughout the mid-1980s. By the 1990s the Jewish feminist movement had blossomed.

After the first conference, Rabbi Elli joined a Jewish lesbian group and became part of an initiative to establish the Jewish feminist magazine *Shifra*. She started to read Jewish books extensively and was moved by a phrase used by Emil Fackenheim to describe the 614th commandment 'thou shalt not give Hitler posthumous victory'.[40] She felt that this commandment was directed to her personally and that being a Jew was not enough; she had to actively engage in her Judaism and to do what she could to contribute to the continuity of Jewish life after the Holocaust. She decided she wanted to be a rabbi for two main reasons – to thwart any posthumous victories for Hitler and to make Jewish life more egalitarian and inclusive.[41]

As an active radical feminist she began to explore her Jewishness, for despite her strong Jewish identity, her knowledge was patchy and she did not have a sense of what it meant to live as a Jew. The Jews she knew as a child were family members and friends, but the Jewish community was somewhere else. 'I knew it had nothing to do with me. My family was different and I was different'. She had no experience of the mainstream Jewish community before she embarked upon a career in the rabbinate.[42] Her immediate family, her parents and two siblings, were shocked when she told them she was going to study at Leo Baeck College, London. 'They had got around to accepting that I was a radical feminist lesbian but selling out and joining the Jewish establishment was a different matter'.[43] Her parents had never participated in Jewish communal life, apart from being members of a Reform synagogue when her brother was preparing for his barmitzvah. They saw the organised Jewish community as too narrow and conformist.

There would not be any lesbian rabbis without the ordination of women to the rabbinate, and her path was helped by the pioneering work of the women who had first broken the barriers against female rabbis.[44] They began a revolution and it did not take long for others to follow. Women rabbis, through their support, also led the way to the inclusion of lesbian rabbis who had kept their lesbianism a secret or were silent about their personal lives. For many, it seemed enough that women could enter the rabbinate. Silence about their sexual orientation was a small price to pay for the opportunity to serve the Jewish community. In the early years of women in the rabbinate, coming out as a lesbian was a dangerous proposition and could lead to a job loss.[45]

When Rabbis Elli and Sheila Shulman studied for the rabbinate at Leo Baeck in 1984 they were the first 'out' lesbians in the mainstream community. The combined progressive movements that funded the college were in a state of shock. In addition to being lesbians they were radical feminists.[46]

When they both went through the interview process at Leo Baeck they had two interviews to assess their psychological aptitude instead of one. From the moment they entered the College, the usual probation period of one year was extended to five and they were informed that they could be asked to leave at any time. There were concerns that their presence as lesbian rabbinic students might upset congregations and their members. As a result, instead of spending their third year in Israel, they had apprenticeships with the senior rabbis of two reform synagogues. Rabbi Elli was apprenticed to Rabbi Henry Goldstein of South West Essex Reform Synagogue.[47] Some rabbis were not keen to have a lesbian rabbi as 'there was a lot of homophobia'. After she and Sheila Shulman[48] were ordained in 1989 there was an extensive meeting to decide if they should be allowed to join the Assembly of Rabbis despite the fact that they were already active in the community and membership should be automatic. 'It was decided in our favour but shows you the atmosphere'.[49]

Following ordination, she served as a rabbi to Buckhurst Hill Reform Synagogue for five years followed by a three-year stint as director of programmes for the Reform Movement working alongside Rabbi Blue, the first rabbi to come out publicly in 1980. She wanted to help make Judaism more LGBT inclusive. In 1995 she established a working party on same sex commitment and the following year she appeared on the BBC programme *Heart of the Matter*[50] talking about LG commitment ceremonies.

In October 1996 Ellis caused a storm of protest when she spoke about commitment ceremonies in a sermon at a Yom Kippur (Day of Atonement) Kol Nidre service. There was an uproar and she resigned from her job in the Reform Movement in 1997. After her resignation the then executive director of the Liberal Movement invited her to join the Liberal Rabbinic Conference and in 1998 she became the first rabbi of the Leicester Progressive Jewish Congregation.[51] Since 2000 she has been the rabbi of Brighton and Hove Progressive Synagogue. She considers that due to her own personal experience the emphasis in her rabbinate has always been on enabling individuals to make Jewish choices, engage with Jewish heritage and realise their own ways of being Jewish.[52]

In 1998 the Working Party of the Rabbi's Assembly published a report to help Reform rabbis in deciding whether to conduct lesbian and gay commitment ceremonies. According to Rabbi Mark Solomons who was involved in the debate, gay marriage 'had become a very contentious issue and brought out a huge amount of latent homophobia that I don't think anyone realised was there'. It was not until 2000, when the Liberal Jewish Movement decided to draft a religious ceremony for same sex commitment ceremonies that the situation began to change. Rabbi Elli was chair of the publication and the text of this ceremony, published in December 2005, was called *Berit Ahava* (the Covenant of Love) . The ceremony modified a traditional Jewish wedding service for same sex couples. Its publication coincided with the Civil Partnership Act coming into effect in England and Wales in 2005. Rabbi Elli celebrated her own commitment ceremony with Jess Wood in 2006, the first rabbi to do so.[53] A civil partnership ceremony at Brighton Registry Office was followed by a blessing in the synagogue under a *chuppah*.[54]

Rabbi Elli knew when she decided she wanted to be a rabbi that she would face difficulties as a lesbian. She was determined to make a place for herself and overcome any obstacles. She wanted to do what she could to make Jewish life more inclusive, so that LGBT Jews could find a home within the Jewish community.[55] Early Jewish LGBT activists struggled for recognition against a backdrop of institutionalised homophobia and widespread misunderstanding. Today many are able to view their identities as a cause for celebration, but even so many LGBT Jews still struggle for acceptance within their communities and in themselves. Rabbi Elli notes that the most difficult issue today is around being transgender, and that the community must support trans people and recognise that there is gender variance and that there needs to be more of a debate about trans people within the Jewish world.

> I have been on a journey to enable and facilitate myself to be able to live in this world and find a place for myself. But at the same time I have been doing all I can to enable and facilitate other people – LGBT people and anybody who doesn't feel mainstream, feels on the margins and is excluded. There are so many people, the whole issue of who is Jewish, the whole Jewish identity. Ultimately what it means for me to be a lesbian Jew is to be somebody who enables others to be all of who they are and enables and facilitates the creation of community in which everybody with all their differences can find a place.[56]

While Rabbi Eli fought to overcome both gender bias and homophobia in order to become a rabbi, Dr Lindsey Taylor-Guthartz, in the liberal wing of mainstream orthodoxy, has faced battles as a female rabbi within the Orthodox Jewish world.

Lindsey Taylor-Guthartz (1959 -)

Lindsey Taylor-Guthartz's path to becoming a rabbi in an orthodox wing of Judaism is extraordinary considering her background. Born into an 'extremely assimilated family', Lindsey's Jewish mother and non-Jewish father divorced soon after her birth in Sydney, Australia in 1959. She came to England with her mother, spending time with her grandparents, until her mother remarried and settled in Liskeard, Cornwall.

Her mother came from an extremely assimilated Jewish background. Her grandparents married in a registry office in 1919 and the last synagogue marriage in the family was that of her maternal great-grandmother in the West London Reform synagogue in 1882. Her mother married in church and all her cousins married out. 'My grandparents lived in a Jewish area but were so traumatised by being Jewish they couldn't bring themselves to say the word. They would talk about people being 'J' and the only Jewish artefact that they owned was an early twentieth century cookbook called 'Dainty Dishes for Jewish Families' which was wrapped in brown paper presumably so that you couldn't see the title'.[57]

The family had been in England for a long time. 'Some were Spanish and Portuguese and others came over from Germany and Poland in the nineteenth century'. Her mother only found out she was Jewish when she was around 11. She was at South Hampstead High School where they had Jewish prayers. A girl came up to her and said she should be there because she knew that my mother's brother went to Jewish prayers. My mother came home and asked her mother if it was true that they were Jewish. 'She answered that she was afraid it was'.[58] Taylor-Guthartz explains that 'she and my uncle grew up with a most incredible complex. If she could have waived a magic wand and no longer been Jewish, she would have'. Taylor-Guthartz learnt she was Jewish by chance, at around seven, when she asked her mother if the family had come over with William the Conqueror. Her mother told her, rather bad temperedly, that they had not as they were Jewish.[59]

Growing up in Cornwall, she was sent to a Church of England boarding school and was confirmed in Truro Cathedral by the Bishop of Truro. 'After that in a *davka-ish*[60] sort of way, I started getting interested in things Jewish. The more I read, the more I liked'. She learnt biblical Hebrew from a teach-yourself library book and surreptitiously observed the festivals, not eating on Yom Kippur, reading the Book of Esther at Purim and at Chanukah, making herself a *chanukiah*[61] out of a large cork and wire covered in gold foil. At Passover she managed to buy a box of *matzas*, used water for wine and read the Haggadah. In the meantime her mother was making hot cross buns for Easter.[62] 'My family would have been horrified if they had known. I was an underground Jew'. Always fascinated by archaeology, she studied the subject, together with anthropology, at Cambridge University. It was there she met Jews for the first time. She started to go to synagogue and adopted an Orthodox lifestyle. Back in Cornwall on home visits she refused to eat non-kosher meat. She spent two summers on archaeological digs in Israel and subsequently emigrated and studied for an MA in archaeology at the Hebrew University. After graduation, she was an assistant librarian for the Israel Department of Antiquities and worked as a proofreader at the *Jerusalem Post* where she met her husband Norman Guthartz. One of the great things that Lindsey enjoyed about living in Jerusalem was the greater opportunities for self-expression for religious women.[63] She attended the innovative Orthodox congregation Kehillat Yedidya where women could read from the Torah.

When she returned to Britain with her husband and two daughters in 1997, she was 'amazed' to find herself being asked questions on Judaism. The first was from a woman in the United Synagogue who wanted to know 'are we allowed to pray outside the synagogue and are we allowed to pray in our own words'. Taylor-Guthartz was shocked that she had no idea. She enrolled in a programme at the London School for Jewish Studies (LSJS) to train women educators and subsequently taught there. She also completed a doctorate on the religious lives of Orthodox women in Britain. Her book *Challenge and Conformity: The Religious Lives of Orthodox Jewish women*[64] is the first academic study of this segment of the community. She considers these women are doubly 'invisible' both to the men in the community and to the wider world. Her study was not only about the struggle for women for greater religious self-expression, it was also about their creative adaptability in the face of the constraints male authority have put on them.[65]

She decided to study at the pioneering Yeshivat Maharat for women in New York (the only Orthodox institution outside Israel that grants rabbinic ordination to women) after attending the funeral of her LSJS colleague Maureen Kendler in 2018. The Reform Movement's senior rabbi, Laura Janner Klausner was standing behind her and said that she should do *semichah* (rabbinic ordination) for Kendler. She hoped it would help forge a path for others and that even if she did not become a communal rabbi, she would have done something that would help the next generation.[66]

When Taylor-Guthartz was about to receive her rabbinic ordination in 2021 she was told that she could no longer teach at LSJS. She had taught there for 16 years and had been considered one of the most popular teachers there and her courses included Jewish prayer, the bible and archaeology, the Mishnah, Midrash, world religions and Jewish history. She maintains that she enrolled at Yeshivat Maharat to enhance her Torah knowledge and develop her learning further so that she would develop skills and knowledge to teach at a higher level and provide needed leadership within the Orthodox Torah world in London and that she had never intended to seek a post as a communal rabbi.

The only formal notification she received about her dismissal was an email from the chief executive telling her that she could no longer use the title of LSJS Research Fellow and with the removal of the title she could no longer teach. Yet Taylor-Guthartz had told LSJS at the start of her rabbinical studies what she was doing and offered that once she graduated she would not use the title of 'rabba' (a feminised form of rabbi) whilst she was teaching.[67] Yeshivat Maharat is not recognised by the Orthodox authorities, including Ephraim Mirvis, Chief Rabbi of the United Synagogues of Great Britain and President of LSJS. The United Synagogue movement has been accused of lagging behind other mainstream denominations and wider society in opening itself up to women and it only allowed women to become trustees in 2014 after opening synagogue chairmanships to them two years earlier.[68]

The Chief Rabbi's office issued a statement that in this case it was clear that a continued formal affiliation with a person, whilst having contributed a great deal to the institution, had nonetheless stepped beyond the boundaries of mainstream Orthodoxy and this would have sent a misleading message about what LSJS stands for.[69] Around 1,500 Orthodox figures signed a letter in support of Mirvis and praised him for 'maintaining Torah standards in Jewish education from progressive activists'.[70]

The LSJS controversy kickstarted a conversation about how far British Orthodoxy is willing, or able, to adapt to women who want to see it move in a more egalitarian direction. A letter signed by 30 Liberal and Reform rabbis accused the Chief Rabbi of maintaining a 'glass ceiling of Torah above which half your community may not ascend'. Another research fellow at LSJS, Rabbi Michael Harris, resigned his fellowship and 300 people sponsored an advert in the *Jewish Chronicle* congratulating Taylor-Guthartz on her ordination. Mirvis did listen to criticism and sought a way to reach a solution. He reversed his decision after deciding that her role was academic rather than rabbinic and she would not use the title 'rabba'. Nonetheless, Taylor-Guthartz, who was reinstated at LSJS is confident that things are changing. Although she considers that Britain is 10-15 years behind Israel and the United States, the process has begun.[71]

Taylor-Guthartz appeared on BBC Radio 4's *Woman's Hour* where she voiced her view that there was a crying need in the UK for there to be women rabbis in the Orthodox community as many women felt the need to speak to women with knowledge of Jewish law when they seek advice on matters, such as miscarriage and fertility, and would rather not approach a male rabbi. She admitted that it was not an easy road and would take time. The title of rabbi is emotive but people will get used to it as they got used to having women doctors, lawyers and a prime minister. She looks forward to being this new emerging voice in Orthodoxy, serving as a resource and help for those that need.[72]

Conclusion

It was not until the emergence of reform movements in Judaism that Jewish women were able to challenge the patriarchal structures that had excluded them from both active participation in and education about their own religion. Beginning in the late nineteenth century, Jewish women in America began to question the exclusion of women from the rabbinate but it was not until the mid-twentieth century that the first women were ordained as rabbis in progressive religious communities in the USA and UK. This development has had profound impacts: the emergence of women rabbis defies years of male hegemony and control of public Jewish ritual life and female rabbis' very voices shatter the long-observed prohibition against Jewish women speaking or singing in public.

The four women profiled in this chapter came to rabbinical ordination from a variety of backgrounds, but all diverged from or even defied their upbringing by choosing the rabbinate as their career. Somewhat surprisingly, only one, Lily Montagu, was raised in an observant household, the other three coming from families that had complicated and ambivalent feelings about their Jewish heritage. Montagu broke from her orthodox background to become a founding member of Britain's Liberal Jewish community, while the families of both Julia Neuberger and Elli Tikva Sarah were shadowed by the Holocaust, with profound effects on their attitudes towards Judaism. This background was pivotal for Neuberger, who has made refugee issues the centrepiece of her pastoral activities. Rabbi Elli's embrace of feminism and Judaism set her apart from her culturally and religiously divided family and her awakening as a lesbian put her on the path of earning acceptance as a rabbi from the LGBT community. Taylor-Guthartz's career trajectory is perhaps the most surprising. The daughter of a mixed marriage, raised in a Church of England milieu, she chose to secretly and defiantly become Jewish and to challenge the remaining bastion of Jewish patriarchy by becoming a rabbi within the orthodox community.

These four women have all been pioneers in the movement towards inclusion of women into Jewish religious life. Their careers demonstrate the progress that has been made in welcoming a diversity of women rabbis including those from refugee, feminist and LGBT communities. Yet even today, the door remains closed to women rabbis in the British orthodox community, indicating that the battle for gender equity remains ongoing.

Conclusion

This book is about outstanding British Jewish women who became campaigners or entered the professions—science, medicine, law, politics, journalism, and religion between the late nineteenth and twenty-first centuries—a period of profound change for women that began with the Suffragette Movement and included both first and second-wave feminism. The women whose lives are explored in this study experienced the same discriminatory pressures and gender biases that had ignited these Movements and benefitted from the larger social and cultural changes in women's status and opportunities that followed. But the additional factor of their Jewishness set them apart from their female peers and often presented them with unique challenges as they pursued their careers.

In tracing their struggle to gain a foothold as campaigners, lawyers, doctors, writers, rabbis, scientists and politicians, it is often difficult to parse the distinction between the headwinds they faced as women and Jews. The earlier eras proved the most difficult for women in nearly all these careers, with the late twentieth century opening up much greater opportunities for all women. Yet, notably, the twenty-first century, with the rise of a new wave of social media driven antisemitism has proven particularly difficult for Jewish women in politics. Though many of the Jewish women profiled here experienced incidents of antisemitism and anti-Jewish bias in their lives, those who chose the professions of law, medicine, science and even religion found that their denial of equal educational opportunities, exclusion from professional organisations, and dismissal by their male colleagues were more likely to be based on gender than Jewish heritage. Writers and journalists encountered fewer impediments to entry either as women or Jews, especially after the Second World War, though they still struggled to rise to the top positions in their professions. Or all the fields covered in this book, it was undoubtedly the campaigners and agony aunts whose careers offered the greatest freedom for Jewish women. The former operated in a field that was more dynamic and organic than the tradition bound professions and addressed the issues of the oppression and social justice, while the latter was the most female-centric of all the professions discussed herein, and tackled the universal problems of interpersonal relationships and societal ills.

The women in this book came from backgrounds that span the entire hierarchical strata of British society, from the humblest working class to the most privileged aristocrats. They originated from all parts of the UK, London and the provinces, from the immigrant inner cities to the most elite of suburbs. Interestingly though, most came from immigrant families— indeed, some were immigrants themselves—though more commonly they were the first or second generation born of Eastern European Jewish immigrants of the late nineteenth and early twentieth century. This immigrant background was a profoundly important factor in many of these women's lives. Their parents' and grandparents' struggles as poor Jewish immigrants often imbued them with an exceptional drive to succeed and their families' expectations, encouragement and support were also motivating factors. For many, this immigrant legacy often provided deep insights into and sympathies for the struggles of the poor and oppressed, guiding them into helping professions or volunteer work as champions of social justice. The generationally close connection of those with immigrant backgrounds to relatives still in Eastern and Central Europe meant that the Second World War and the Holocaust were keenly felt in both their lives and careers. Some of their families took in Jewish refugees during the 1930s; a few were refugees from that period themselves. The younger generation of women often reconnected to the tragic legacy of the Holocaust through tracing their families' histories, travelling to sites of remembrance and participating in Holocaust memorial activities and many whose lives were touched by that cataclysm found ways to incorporate that legacy into their work.

Their background, their gender and their Jewishness also frequently conferred an outsider status on these exceptional Jewish women, motivating some to fit in at all costs, others to defiantly stand out. Many of their families from poor or modest means sacrificed to send their daughters to non-Jewish private and independent schools, where it was common for them to encounter overt and subversive antisemitism from both teachers and fellow pupils—often their first taste of the 'otherization' they would encounter in their chosen professions. The lesson some women took away from these experiences was a desire to assimilate—to look, speak and act as British as possible and to choose careers in which their 'otherness' could be overcome. Others boldly embraced their differences and utilised their outsider status to campaign for causes that championed the less privileged in society.

Though all of these women were Jewish by birth, their personal and professional relationships to their religious heritage varied enormously. Some, especially those born before the mid-twentieth century, came from orthodox or somewhat observant Jewish backgrounds, while others characterised their upbringing and themselves as secularly Jewish. A few were born to mixed marriages, in which the Jewish part of their lineage was discovered or embraced only later in life. Many of the women in this book, as a result of accumulated experiences at school and university, in mixed marriages of their own, and especially in their careers, moved away from orthodox or observant Jewishness to a secular Jewish identity or even a rejection of their religious heritage. Even among these, however, most preserved some sense, even a very strong sense of their Jewish background and heritage. None of them claimed that their Jewishness played no part in their lives. A few resolutely maintained their observant, even orthodox, beliefs and practices throughout their lives, even in careers in which such choices posed difficulties or sacrifices.

There is no question that the women featured in this volume lived lives of richness and accomplishment, made all the more remarkable for the fact that they were Jewish women attempting to break into male-dominated professions, some of which had traditionally barred both Jews and women. Some of the early pioneers of law, medicine, science, and religion were not recognised for their contributions and achievements in their lifetimes. Yet their efforts to forge meaningful and expansive careers in these fields undoubtedly prepared the path for those who followed, and some of those forerunners are now, belatedly, receiving the acknowledgement and acclaim they rightly deserve. The Jewish women who entered and became successful in the somewhat less hostile fields of journalism and politics nevertheless had to battle to attain positions as hard news reporters, editors, publishers, and cabinet ministers, and they, too paved the way for subsequent generations of ambitious Jewish writers and politicians. The campaigners built upon the legacy of Jewish activism from the nineteenth century and demonstrated in later years that even Jewish causes could garner widespread support throughout society. It is past time that all these women of determination, dedication and achievement receive recognition and admiration for their combined contributions to these varied professions.

Bibliography and Sources

Archival Material

British Library, London
Report of the Jewish Association for the Protection of Girls and Women 1925.
Ursula Owen, British Library Collection

The Women's Library, London
Jewish League of Woman Suffrage, FL227 7HFD/E/09.

Interviews with the Author
Blackman, Sandra, 7 October 2020, London.
Wedderburn, Lucy, 29 November 2020 (zoom).

Newspapers and Periodicals
Aberdeen Press and Journal
Big Issue
British Medical Journal
Daily Express
Daily Herald
Daily Mail
Daily Mirror
Daily Telegraph
Daily Worker
Dundee Courier
East London Advertiser
East London Observer
Elle
Evening Herald (Dublin)
Evening Standard
Evening Standard Magazine

Financial Times
Gloucestershire Echo
GQ Magazine
Guardian
Guardian Weekend
Ham & High
Independent
Independent on Sunday
Irish Independent
Irish Times
Jerusalem Post
Jewish Chronicle
Jewish Clarion
Jewish News
Jewish Renaissance
Jewish Telegraph
Jewish Telegraphic Agency
Liverpool Echo
Mail on Sunday
Manchester Jewish News
Mail on Sunday
Newcastle Evening Chronicle
Newcastle Journal
New Statesmen
New York Times
Observer
Observer Magazine
Oxford Mail
Portsmouth Evening News
Press Gazette
Reading Evening Post
Searchlight
Shifra
Sunday Mirror
Sunday Times
Sunday Tribune
Sunday Times Magazine
Sydney Morning Herald
The Cable
The London Gazette
Times of Israel
Transactions of the Jewish Historical Society of England
Tribune Magazine

The Vote
Uttoexeter Post and Times
Westminster Gazette
Yorkshire Post

Autobiographies

Edwina Currie, *Diaries 1987-1992* (London: Little Brown, 2002).
Olga Franklin, *Steppes to Fleet Street* (London: Victor Gollanz, 1968).
Ursula Owen, *Single Journey Only* ((London: Salt, 2019).
Esther Rantzen, *Esther* (London: BBC Worldwide Limited, 2001).
Claire Rayner, *How Did I Get Here From There?* (London: Virago, 2003).
Rudolf Rocker, *The London Years* (Nottingham: Five Leaves Publications, 2014).

Other Printed Primary Sources

Nicola Mendelsohn. Email correspondence to author, 24 January 2023.
Lucy Wedderburn. Email correspondence to author, 7 March 2021.
Alexandra Wright. Eulogy. A Farewell to Nina Wedderburn, 21 August 2020.
Alexandra Wright. Email correspondence to author, 26 October 2020.

Internet

Nancy Astor, *Woman's Hour,* archive clip, www.bbc.co.uk, 24 February 2002.
First Ladies of Fleet Street, www.bbc.co.uk, 6 December 2018
Antisemitism row: Labour MPs applaud after Commons speeches, www.bbc.co.uk, 17 April 2018.
Steven McIntosh, 'Why these Girlfriends stand out in British TV', www.bbc.co.uk, 3 January 2018.
BBC News, 'Key Quotes: Edwina Currie', 28 September 2002.
BBC News, '75 Years of Women Solicitors', 19 December 1997.
BBC News, 'Gender equality: No room at the top for women scientists', 6 September 2019.
Neil Bright, 'The Angel of Cable Street', www.blitzwalker.com, 18 December 2010.
Hilary Heilbron, 'Women at the Bar: An Historical Perspective', www.counselmagazine.co.uk
ITV News, 'MP for Stoke-on-Trent resigns from shadow cabinet post', 13 December 2019.
Sarah Jackson, 'Minnie Lansbury: Teacher, union activist, suffragette, rebel councillor, www.eastendwomensmuseum.org
David Katz, 'Review of Jewish Contribution to Medicine in the UK', www.jewishmedicalassociation.org.
Kate Murphy, '75 years of celebrating Woman's Hour', www.bbc.com

Sky News 'Labour's Ruth Smeeth described her party as 'racist' over antisemitism', 13 December 2019.
Rob Wilson, 'Luciana Berger on having to work harder than the rest', www.totalpolitics.com, 28 May 2012.

Youtube

Meet the most powerful woman in the tech industry - The Female Lead, 20 December 2021.
Ruth Smeeth: Meet the MPs, 10 August 2018.

Websites

www.ajrrefugeevoices.org.uk
www.ajwo.org
www.english-heritage.org.uk
www.biography.com
www.first100years.org.uk
www.historyrevealed.com
www.indexoncensorship.org
www.jewishlivesproject.com
www.jwa.org
www.nameberry.com
www.rainbowjews.com
www.rcseng.ac.uk
www.royalsociety.com.
www.ruthsmeeth.org.uk
www.sciencemag.org
www.susangreenfield.com
www.timeshighereducation.com
www.varsity.co.uk
www.victorianweb.org
www.womanshour.com

Radio

Desert Island Discs, 23 October 1977, BBC Radio 4.
Desert Island Discs, BBC Radio 4, 3 May 1991.
Desert Island Discs, BBC Radio 4, 2 March 1997.
Desert Island Discs, 19 September 1997, BBC Radio 4.
Desert Island Discs, 2 May 1999, BBC Radio 4.
Desert Island Discs, 11 December 2011, BBC Radio 4.
Desert Island Discs, 10 March 2019, BBC Radio 4.

Desert Island Discs, 29 October 2017, BBC Radio 4.
In the Psychiatrist's Chair, 90 by 90 The Full Set Clips 1988: Anthony and Claire: 13 November 2012, BBC Radio 4.
The House I Grew Up In, 9 August 2010, BBC Radio 4.
Woman's Hour, 17 June 2021, BBC Radio 4.

Secondary Sources

Lesley Abdela, *Women with X Appeal* (London: Optima, 1989).

Geoffrey Alderman, *Modern British Jewry* (Oxford: Clarendon Press, 1998).

Rebecca T. Alpert, Sue Levi Ewell and Shirley Idelson, *Lesbian Rabbis: The First Generation* (New Brunswick, NJ, Rutgers University, 2001).

Sarah Abrevaya Stein, *Ostrich Feathers, Jews and a Lost World of Global Commerce* (New Haven: Yale University Press, 2010).

Neil Belton, *The Good Listener: Helen Bamber: A Life Against Cruelty* (London: Faber and Faber, 2012).

Arnold Bennett, *Journalism for Women: A Practical Guide* (London: John Lane, 1898).

Gerry Black, *Lord Rothschild and the Barber* (London: Tymsder Publishing, 2000).

Gerry Black, *Service with a Smile: History of the League of Jewish Women* (London: Tymsder Publishing 2010).

Noreen Branson, *History of the Communist Party in Great Britain 1927-41*, (London: Lawrence & Wishart, 1985).

Rickie Burman, 'The Jewish Woman as Breadwinner: The Changing Value of Women's Work in a Manchester Immigrant Community', *Oral History* 10:2 (1982).

Rickie Burman, 'Jewish Women and the Household Economy in Manchester, c. 1890-1920', in David Cesarani (ed.), *The Making of Modern Anglo Jewry* (Oxford: Basil Blackwell, 1990).

Rickie Burman, 'Middle Class Anglo Jewish Lady Philanthropists and Eastern European Jewish Women', in Joan Grant (ed.) *Women, Migration and Empire* (Stoke-on-Trent: Trentham Books Ltd, 1996).

Nina Byers and Gary Williams, *Contributions of Twentieth Century Women to Physics* (Cambridge: Cambridge University Press, 2006).

Tabitha Carey, *Never Kiss a Man in a Canoe. Words of Wisdom from the Golden Age of Agony Aunts* (London: Boxtree, 2009).

Martin Conboy, *Journalism in Britain* (London: Sage Publications, 2011).

Rachel Cooke, *Her Brilliant Career. Ten Extraordinary Women of the Fifties* (London: Virago, 2013).

John Cooper, *Pride Versus Prejudice. Jewish Doctors and Lawyers in England 1890-1990* (Oxford: Littman Library of Jewish Civilization, 2003).

John Cooper, 'Jews Who Helped Make the Health Service', *British Journal of Medical Practice*, 69 (678), pp. 32-33 (2019).

Maurice Corina, *Pile It High, Sell It Cheap* (London: Weidenfeld and Nicholson, 1971).

Elizabeth Crawford, *The Women's Suffrage Movement: A Reference Guide 1866-1928* (London: Routledge, 2000).

Edwina Currie, *A Woman's Place* (London: Hodder & Stoughton, 1996).

Edwina Currie, *She's Leaving Home* (London: Warner Books, 1998).

David Dee, *The 'Estranged' Generation? Social and Generation Change in Interwar British Jewry* (London: Palgrave Macmillan, 2017).

Emil Fackenheim, *The Jewish Return into History. Reflections in the Age of Auschwitz and a New Jerusalem* (New York: Schocken Books, 1978).

William J. Fishman, *East End Jewish Radicals 1875-1914* (London: Gerald Duckworth & Co, 1975).

Olga Franklin, *Born Twice* (London: Peter Garnett, 1951).

Aileen Fyfe and Camilla Rostvik, 'How female fellows fared at the Royal Society', *Nature*, 6 March 2018.

Michael Galchinsky, *The Origin of the Modern Jewish Writer. Romance and Reform in Victorian England* (Detroit: Wayne State University Press, 1996).

Juliet Gardner, *Penguin Dictionary of British History* (London: Penguin, 2000).

Daphne Gerlis, *Those Wonderful Women in Black: The Story of the Women's Campaign for Soviet Jewry* (London: Minerva Press, 1996).

Susan Glenn, *Daughters of the Shtetl: Life and Labor in the Immigrant Generation* (New York: Cornell University Press, 1990).

Sarah Glynn, 'East End Immigrants and the Battle for Housing: A Comparative Study of Political Mobilisation in the Jewish and Bengali Communities', *Journal of Historical Geography*, 31 (2005), pp. 528-545.

Linda Gordon Kuzmack, *Woman's Cause: The Jewish Women's Movement in England and the United States 1881-1933* (Columbus: Ohio State University Press, 1990).

Frances Guy, *Women of Worth: Jewish Women in Britain* (Manchester: Manchester Jewish Museum, 1992).

Joe Haines, *Kick 'Em Back. Wilson, Maxwell and Me* (Guildford: Grosvenor House Publishing), 2019.

June Hannam, 'Women and Politics', in June Purvis (ed.), *Women's History: Britain 1850-1945* (London: UCL Press, 1995).

Hilary Heilbron, *Rose Heilbron. The Story of England's First Woman Queen's Counsel and Judge* (Oxford: Hart Publishing, 2012).

Andrew Hosken, *Nothing Like A Dame* (London: Granta Publications, 2006).

Mark Hurst, *British Human Rights Organizations and Soviet Dissent 1965-1985* (London: Bloomsbury Academic, 2016).

Richard Jaffa, *Letters from Oggi* (Sussex: Book Guild Publishing, 2015).

Laura Jefferson, Karen Bloor and Alan Maynard, 'Women in Medicine: Historical Perspectives and Recent Trends', *British Medical Journal*, 114: 5-15 (2015).

Norman Lebrecht, *Genius & Anxiety. How Jews Changed the World 1847-1947* (London: Oneworld Publications, 2009).

Brenda Maddox, *Rosalind Franklin: The Dark Lady of DNA* (New York: Harper Perennial, 2003).

Lara Marks, 'Dear Old Mother Levy's: The Jewish Maternity Home and Sick Room Helps Society 1895-1939', *Social History of Medicine*, Oxford University Press, Vol. 3 (1), April, 1990, pp., 61, 65-66, 76, 84-85.

Lara Marks, 'Race, Class and Gender: The Experience of Jewish Prostitutes and other Jewish Women in the East End of London at the Turn of the Century', in Joan Grant (ed.), *Women, Migration and Empire* (Stoke-on-Trent Trentham Books Ltd, 1996).

Kate Murphy, *Behind the Wireless: A History of Early Women at the BBC* (London: Palgrave Macmillan, 2016).

Eilat Negev and Yehuda Koren, *The First Lady of Fleet Street. The Life, Fortune and Tragedy of Rachel Beer* (London: Robson Press, 2012).

Julia Neuberger, 'Women in Judaism: The Fact and the Fiction', in Pat Holden (ed.), *Women's Religious Experience* (London: Croom Helm, 1983), pp. 135-139.

Hannah Neustatter, 'Demographic and Other Statistical Aspects of Anglo-Jewry', in Maurice Freedman (ed.), *A Minority in Britain: Social Studies of the Anglo-Jewish Community* (London: Valentine Mitchell, 1955).

Angela Patmore, *Marje. The Guilt and the Gingerbread* (London: Warner Books, 1993).

Phil Piratin, *Our Flag Stays Red* (London: Thames Publications, 1948).

Marjore Proops, *Dear Marje...* (London: Andre Deutsch 1976).

June Purvis, *Women's History: Britain 1850-1945* (London: UCL Press, 1995).

Erikca Rackley and Rosemary Auchmuty, *Women's Legal Landmarks. Celebrating the History of Women and Law in the UK and Ireland* (Oxford: Hart Publishing, 2019).

Rudolf Rocker, *Milly Witcop-Rocker* (Orkney: Cienfuegos Press, 1981).

Cathy Ross and John Clark, *London: The Illustrated History* (London: Penguin, 2008).

W. Rubinstein (ed.), *The Palgrave Dictionary of Anglo-Jewish History* (Basingstoke: Palgrave Macmillan, 2011).

C. H. Russell and H. S. Lewis, *The Jew in London* (London: Fisher Unwin, 1901).

Sarah Ryle, *The Making of Tesco* (London: Bantam Press, 2013).

Oliver Sacks, *On the Move* (London: Picador, 2015).

Oliver Sacks, *Uncle Tungsten* (London: Picador, 2001).

Elli Tikva Sarah, *Trouble Making Judaism* (London: David Paul, 2012).

Anna Sayre, *Rosalind Franklin and DNA* (New York: W W Norton & Co, 1978).

Joachim Schlor, *Escaping Nazi Germany: One Woman's Emigration from Heilbronn to England* (London: Bloomsbury Academic, 2021).

Evelyn Sharp, *Hertha Ayrton 1854-1923, A Memoir* (London: Edward Arnold & Co., 1926).

Naomi Shepherd, *A Price Below Rubies: Jewish Women as Rebels and Radicals* (Harvard: Harvard University Press, 1998).

Elaine Rosa Smith, *East End Jews in Politics, 1918-1939: A Study in Class and Ethnicity*, (Leicester: University of Leicester, 1990).

Bertha Sokoloff, *Edith and Stepney: The Life of Edith Ramsey* (London: Stepney Book Publications, 1987).

Henry Srebrnik, 'Class, Ethnicity and Gender Intertwined: Jewish Women and the East London Rent Strikes 1935-1940', *Women's History Review*, 1995, 4 (3), pp. 284-286.

Anne Summers, 'Gender, Religion and an Immigrant Minority: Jewish Women and the Suffrage Movement in Britain c. 1900-1920', *Women's History Review* 21: 3 (2012).

Rosemary Taylor, *Hannah Billig: The Angel of Cable Street* (London: Rosemary Taylor, 1996).

Lindsey Taylor-Guthartz, *Challenge and Conformity: The Religious Lives of Orthodox Jewish Women* (Oxford: Litman Library of Jewish Civilization, 2021).

Ellen M. Umansky, *Lily Montagu and the Advancement of Liberal Judaism: From Vision to Vocation* (New York: The Edwin Mellon Press, 1983).

Margaret Walters, *Feminism* (Oxford: Oxford University Press, 2005).

Ruth Watts, *Women in Science* (London: Routledge, 2007).

Joel H. Wiener, 'The Nineteenth Century and the Emergence of a Mass Circulation Press', in *Routledge Companion to British Media History*, ed. By Martin Conboy and John Steel (London: Routledge, 2015).

Julie Welch, *Fleet Street Girls: The Women Who Broke Down the Doors of the Gentlemen's Club* (London: Trapeze, 2020).

Leigh Ann Whaley, *Women's History as Scientists* (Oxford: ABC: Clio, 2003).

Stella Wills, 'The Anglo-Jewish Contribution to the Education Movement for Women in the Nineteenth Century', *Transactions* (Jewish Historical Society of England), Vol. 17 (1951-52).

Lisa Yount, *Twentieth-Century Women Scientists* (New York: Facts On File, 1996).

Endnotes

INTRODUCTION

1   Susan Tananbaum, 'Britain: Nineteenth and Twentieth Centuries', Jewish Women's Archive, jwa.org.

2   Rickie Burman, 'Middle Class Anglo Jewish Lady Philanthropists and Eastern European Jewish Women', in Joan Grant (ed.) *Women, Migration and Empire* (Stoke on Trent: Trentham Books Ltd, 1996), pp. 124-125.

3   Rickie Burman, 'The Jewish Woman as Breadwinner: The Changing Value of Women's Work in a Manchester Immigrant Community', *Oral History* 10:2 (1982), p. 35.

4   Susan Tananbaum, 'Britain: Nineteenth and Twentieth Centuries'.

5   Frances Guy, *Women of Worth* (Manchester: Manchester Jewish Museum, 1992), p. 3.

6   Geoffrey Alderman, *Modern British Jewry* (Oxford: Clarendon Press, 1998), p. 197.

7   Rickie Burman, 'Jewish Women and the Household Economy in Manchester, c. 1890-1920', in David Cesarani (ed.), *The Making of Modern Anglo Jewry* (Oxford: Basil Blackwell, 1990), p. 57.

8   Rickie Burman, 'The Jewish Woman as Breadwinner', pp. 27, 35.

9   Lara Marks, 'Race, Class and Gender: The Experience of Jewish Prostitutes and other Jewish Women in the East End of London at the Turn of the Century', in Joan Grant (ed.), *Women, Migration and Empire* (Stoke on Trent: Trentham Books Ltd, 1996), pp. 42-43.

10   Rickie Burman, 'The Jewish Woman as Breadwinner', p. 37.

11   C. H. Russell and H. S. Lewis, *The Jew in London* (London: Fisher Unwin, 1901), p. 186.

12   Rickie Burman, 'Jewish Women and the Household Economy in Manchester, pp. 71-72.

13   Rickie Burman, 'The Jewish Woman as Breadwinner', pp. 30-33.

14   Susan L. Tananbaum, 'Britain: Nineteenth and Twentieth Centuries', jwa.org

15   Anna Maria Goldsmid's father, financier Sir Issac Lyon Goldsmid was a

prominent British financier, philanthropist and social reformer. He was opposed to the divisions between Ashkenazi and Sephardi Jews and co-founded the West London Synagogue in 1842.

16   Michael Galchinsky, 'Anna Maria Goldsmid', jwa.org.

17   Louisa Goldsmid was the daughter of financier Moses Asher Goldsmid. She married her first cousin Francis Henry Goldsmid, who later became the first Jewish barrister in England.

18   Susan L. Tananbaum, 'Britain: Nineteenth and Twentieth Centuries', jwa.org

19   Stella Wills, 'The Anglo-Jewish Contribution to the Education Movement for Women in the Nineteenth Century', *Transactions* (Jewish Historical Society of England), Vol. 17 (1951-52), pp. 269-281.

20   Ibid.

21   Rickie Berman, 'Middle Class Anglo Jewry Lady Philanthropists', p. 126.

22   Ibid.

23   Susan Tanenbaum, 'Britain: Nineteenth and Twentieth Centuries' jwa.org.

24   Report of the Jewish Association for the Protection of Girls and Women 1925, British Library.

25   Rickie Burman, 'Middle Class Anglo Jewish Lady Philanthropists', pp. 129, 134.

26   Frances Guy, *Women of Worth*, p. 3.

27   Lara Marks, 'Race, Class and Gender', p. 47.

28   Rickie Berman, 'Middle Class Anglo Jewish Lady Philanthropists', p. 128.

29   Ibid., pp. 145-147.

30   June Purvis, *Women's History: Britain 1850-1945* (London: UCL Press, 1995), p. 251.

31   Frances Guy, *Women of Worth*, p. 11.

32   Anne Summers, 'Gender, Religion and an Immigrant Minority: Jewish Women and the Suffrage Movement in Britain c. 1900-1920', *Women's History Review* 21: 3 (2012), p. 400.

33   Linda Gordon Kuzmack, *Woman's Cause: The Jewish Women's Movement in England and the United States 1881-1933* (Columbus: Ohio State University Press, 1990), p. 134.

34   Anne Summers, 'Gender, Religion and an Immigrant Minority', p. 405.

35   Elizabeth Crawford, *The Women's Suffrage Movement: A Reference Guide 1866-1928* (London: Routledge, 2000), p. 310.

36   Linda Gordon Kuzmack, *Woman's Cause*, p. 142.

37   Jewish League of Woman Suffrage, The Women's Library, London FL227 7HFD/E/09.

38   Anne Summers, 'Gender, Religion and an Immigrant Minority', p. 412.

39   Linda Gordon Kuzmack, *Woman's Cause*, p. 141.

40   Gerry Black, *Service with a Smile: History of the League of Jewish Women* (London: Tymsder Publishing 2010), pp. 13, 17, 18.

41   Ibid.

42   Ibid., pp. 25-32.

43   Ibid., pp. 52-54.

44   Ibid. p. 77.

45   Ibid., p. 67.

46   Ibid., pp. 127, 145-148.

47   www.ajwo.org.

CHAPTER 1

1   Margaret Walters, *Feminism* (Oxford: Oxford University Press, 2005), pp. 56, 68.

2   Cathy Ross and John Clark, *London: The Illustrated History* (London: Penguin, 2008), p. 246.

3   Juliet Gardner, *Penguin Dictionary of British History* (London: Penguin, 2000), p. 646.

4   Cathy Ross and John Clark, *London*, pp. 246-247.

5   June Purvis, *Women's History: Britain, 1850-1945*, p. 251.

6   F Guy, Women of Worth: *Jewish Women in Britain* (Manchester: Manchester Jewish Museum, 1992), p. 11.

7   Linda Gordon Kuzmack, *Women's Cause: The Jewish Women's Movement in England and the United States 1881-1933* (Columbus: Ohio State University Press, 1990), p. 135.

8   The Women's Library, London. FL227 7HFD/E/09.

9   Anne Summers, 'Gender, Religion and an Immigrant Minority: Jewish Women and the Suffrage Movement in Britain c. 1900-1920', *Women's History Review* 21: 3 (2012), p. 412.

10   Linda Gordon Kuzmack, *Woman's Cause*, p. 141.

11   Margaret Walters, *Feminism*, p. 97.

12   Ibid., pp. 108-112.

13   'Women's Lib: The Second Wave of Feminism', www.historyrevealed.com.

14   Daphne Gerlis, *Those Wonderful Women in Black: The Story of the Women's Campaign for Soviet Jewry* (London: Minerva Press, 1996), p. xi.

15   Ibid., pp. 13-15.

16   Ibid., p. 16.

17   Ibid., pp. 17-18.

18   Mark Hurst, *British Human Rights Organizations and Soviet Dissent 1965-1985* (London: Bloomsbury Academic, 2016), p. 81.
19   Daphne Gerlis, *Those Wonderful Women in Black*, p. 27.
20   Ibid., pp. 28-30.
21   Mark Hurst, *British Humans Rights Organizations and Soviet Dissent 1965-1985*, pp. 82-85.
22   Ibid., pp. 86, 89.
23   Daphne Gerlis, *Those Wonderful Women in Black*, p. 43.
24   Mark Hurst, *British Humans Rights Organizations and Soviet Dissent 1965-1985*, p. 92.
25   Ibid., p. 94.
26   Ibid., p. 95.
27   Ibid. pp. 98-102.
28   Ibid., pp. 110-113.
29   Daphne Gerlis, Those *Wonderful Women in Black*, pp. 32-37
30   Mark Hurst, *British Human Rights Organizations and Soviet Dissent 1965-1985*, p. 114.
31   *Guardian*, 24 August 2014.
32   Neil Belton, *The Good Listener: Helen Bamber: A Life Against Cruelty* (London: Faber and Faber, 2012).
33   Ibid.
34   Ibid.
35   *Jewish Chronicle*, 10 January 1997, p. 8.
36   Neil Belton, *The Good Listener*.
37   *Daily Telegraph*, 22 August 2014.
38   *Desert Island Discs*, BBC Radio 4, 2 May 1999.
39   *Jewish Chronicle*, 12 February 1999, p. 33.
40   Ibid.
41   *Guardian*, 24 August 2014.
42   *Daily Telegraph*, 22 August 2014.
43   *Guardian*, 24 August 2014.
44   *Jewish Chronicle*, 12 July 1991, p. 5.
45   *Jewish Chronicle*, 10 January 1997, p. 8.
46   *Guardian*, 24 August 2014.
47   *Jewish Chronicle*, 17 May 1991, p. 1.
48   *Jewish Chronicle*, 14 April 1999, p. 10.
49   *Jewish Chronicle*, 12 February 1999, p. 33.
50   *New York Times*, 27 August 2014.
51   Guardian, 20 July 2001.
52   Ursula Owen, *Single Journey Only* ((London: Salt, 2019), Chapter 3.
53   AJR Refugee Voices, www.ajrrefugeevoices.org.uk
54   *Desert Island Discs*, BBC Radio 4, 19 September 1997.

55 Ibid.
56 *Guardian*, 20 July 2001.
57 *Desert Island Discs*, BBC Radio 4, 19 September 1997.
58 *Guardian*, 20 July 2001.
59 Ibid.
60 Ibid.
61 Ibid.
62 Ursula Owen, *Single Journey Only*, Chapter 16.
63 *Ham & High*, 12 November 2019.
64 *Guardian*, 20 July 2001.
65 *Ham & High*, 12 November 2019.
66 *Guardian*, 20 July 2001.
67 *Financial Times*, 20 September 2019.
68 *Jewish Chronicle*, 18 October 2019.
69 Ursula Owen, British Library Collection, www.bl.uk
70 *Guardian*, 20 July 2001.
71 Ibid.
72 *Jewish Chronicle*, 18 October 2019.
73 Ibid.
74 *Ham & High*, 12 November 2019.
75 Dietrich Bonhoeffer (1906-1945) was a German Lutheran pastor, theologian and anti-Nazi dissident. During the Nazi era, Bonhoeffer became an important contact for church and ecumenical leaders in the United States and Europe. His ties to the 20 July 1944 conspiracy to overthrow the Nazi regime led to his execution in 1945.
76 Martin Niemoller (1892-1984) was a prominent Protestant pastor who emerged as an outspoken public foe of Hitler and spent the last seven years of Nazi rule in concentration camps. He is remembered for the quotation: 'First they came for socialists and I did not speak out...'.
77 Ursula Owen, *Single Journey Only*, Chapter 5.
78 *Jewish Chronicle*, 1 November 2019.
79 *Jewish Chronicle*, 18 October 2019.
80 *Jewish Chronicle*, 1 November 2019.
81 *Guardian*, 20 July 2001.
82 AJR Refugee Voices.
83 *Desert Island Discs*, 19 September 1997.
84 AJR Refugee Voices.
85 *Jewish Chronicle*, 18 October 2019.
86 *Guardian*, 20 July 2001.
87 Mark Hurst, *British Human Rights Organizations and Soviet Dissent 1965-1983*.

CHAPTER 2

1   Adrian Lee, 'From ugly spouses to corset issues: 300 years of agony aunts', *Daily Express*, 6 March 2015.

2   Tabitha Carey, *Never Kiss a Man in a Canoe. Words of Wisdom from the Golden Age of Agony Aunts* (London: Boxtree, 2009), p. xiv.

3   *Daily Mail*, 10 February 2011.

4   *Jewish Chronicle*, 8 April 2016, p. 1.

5   *Jewish Chronicle*, 12 March 2015.

6   *Jewish Chronicle*, 13 March 2014, p. 43.

7   *Jewish Chronicle*, 8 April, 2016, p. 1.

8   *Jewish Chronicle*, 13 August 1976.

9   Adrian Lee, 'From ugly spouses to corset issues: 300 years of agony aunts', *Daily Express*, 6 March 2015.

10 *Independent*, 12 November 1996.

11 Angela Patmore, *Marje. The Guilt and the Gingerbread* (London: Warner Books, 1993).

12 *Jewish Chronicle*, 15 November 1996, p. 10.

13 *Independent*, 12 November 1996.

14 *Jewish Chronicle*, 26 September 1997, p. III.

15 *Independent*, 12 November 1996.

16 Marjore Proops, *Dear Marje…* (London: Andre Deutsch 1976).

17 Ibid.

18 *Jewish Chronicle*, 28 June 1991, p. 48.

19 Angela Patmore, *Marje*, p. 5.

20 Ibid., p. 70.

21 Leo Abse (1922- 2008) was the son of a Jewish solicitor and cinema owner in Cardiff. He was a Welsh Labour MP for nearly 30 years and became known as a campaigner to liberalise the laws on divorce and homosexuality.

22 *Independent*, 12 November 1996.

23 *Daily Mail, 10* February 2011.

24 *Jewish Chronicle*, 13 August 1976, p. 15.

25 *Jewish Chronicle*, 28 June 1991, p. 48.

26 *Jewish Chronicle*, 20 June 1969, p. 41.

27 *Jewish Chronicle*, 12 June 1970, p. 19.

28 Marjorie Proops, *Dear Marje,* pp. 7-8.

29 Tanith Carey, *Never Kiss A Man in a Canoe: Words of Wisdom from the Golden Age of Agony Aunts* (London: Boxtree, 2009).

30 Angela Patmore, *Marje,* p. 184.

31 *Daily Mail*, 12 October 2010, p. 10.

32   Claire Rayner, *How Did I Get Here From There?* (London: Virago, 2003), pp. 10-16.

33   The name Chetwynd has a long Anglo-Saxon heritage. It is derived from the old English compound word which means 'dweller at the winding ascent'.

34   Ibid., pp. 40, 81.

35   *Guardian*, 2 March 2003.

36   Ibid.

37   *Jewish Chronicle*, 14 March 2003, p. 37.

38   *Desert Island Discs*, BBC Radio 4, 23 October 1977.

39   Claire Rayner, *How Did I Get Here from There?*, p. 102.

40   *Guardian*, 10 October 2010

41   *Jewish Chronicle*, 7 June 1963, p. v.

42   *Jewish Chronicle*, 13 October 2010.

43   *Guardian,* 10 October 2010

44   Daphne Claff (1918-2022) was the daughter of Israel and Esther (Filschstein) Cohen. Her father, who died when she was young, had been secretary of Wellington Road Synagogue, Stamford Hill and her mother was an embroiderer. Daphne won a scholarship to St Martin's School of Art and then worked as a fashion artist and stage designer before joining *Woman's Own*. She managed a staff of 13 who were often faced with dealing with 2,000 letters a week. *Jewish Chronicle*, 25 November 2022.

45   *Daily Telegraph*, 12 October 2012.

46   *Guardian*, 10 October 2010.

47   *Jewish Chronicle*, 1 January 191, p. 26.

48   *Jewish Chronicle*, 18 May 1962, p. 27.

49   *Guardian*, 10 October 2010.

50   Claire Rayner, *How Did I Get Here From There?*, p. 102.

51   Ibid.

52   1988: Anthony and Claire: *In the Psychiatrist's Chair*, www.bbc.co.uk

53   *Guardian,* 2 March 2003.

54   *Jewish Chronicle*, 25 January 1980, p. 27.

55   *Jewish Chronicle*, 14 March 2003, p. 37.

56   *Jewish Chronicle*, 5 November 1965, p. v.

57   *Jewish Chronicle*, 8 April 2016, p. 41.

58   *Jewish Chronicle*, 11 September 2015, p. 83.

59   *Jewish Chronicle*, 11 April 2008, p. 30.

60   *Jewish Chronicle*, 15 February 1980, p. 17.

62   *Jewish Chronicle*, 2 October 1981, p. 15.

63   *Jewish Chronicle*, 4 April 2003, p. 33.

64   A street in central London where many homeless sleep out.

65   *Jewish Chronicle*, 3 April 1992, p. 8.
66   *Jewish Chronicle*, 5 October 2001, p. 10.
67   *Guardian*, 10 October 2010.
68   Claire Rayner, *How Did I Get Here From There?*, p. 335.
69   Angela Patmore, *Marje*, p. 164.
70   Ibid., p. 7.
71   Angela Patmore, *Marje*, p. 164.
72   Ibid., p. 7.
73   *Observer Magazine*, 20 June 2021.
74   www.jewishlivesproject.com
75   Clare Rayner, *How Did I Get Here From There*, pp. 15, 237, 267.

CHAPTER 3

1   June Hannam, 'Women and Politics', in June Purvis (ed.), *Women's History: Britain 1850-1945* (London: UCL Press, 1995), pp. 217-218.
2   Ibid., pp. 218, 225.
3   Nancy Astor, *Woman's Hour,* archive clip, www.bbc.co.uk, 24 February 2002.
4   Ibid.
5   Susan Glenn, *Daughters of the Shtetl: Life and Labor in the Immigrant Generation* (New York: Cornell University Press, 1990), p. 35.
6   Naomi Shepherd, *A Price Below Rubies: Jewish Women as Rebels and Radicals* (Harvard: Harvard University Press, 1998), p. 139.
7   Rudolf Rocker, *The London Years* (Nottingham: Five Leaves Publications, 2014), p. 26.
8   Rudolf Rocker, *Milly Witcop-Rocker* (Orkney: Cienfuegos Press, 1981), p. 12.
9   William J. Fishman, *East End Jewish Radicals 1875-1914* (London: Gerald Duckworth & Co, 1975), p. 300.
10   Linda Gordon Kuzmack, *Woman's Cause: The Jewish Women's Movement in England and the United States 1881-1933* (Columbus: Ohio State University Press, 1990), p. 111.
11   *Searchlight*, No. 136, October 1986.
12   *Chicken Soup with Barley* is about the emotional collapse of East End Jewish family Sarah and Harry Kahn and their children, from 1936-1956. The Kahns are Communists and the play traces their relationship with the Party from the high of Cable Street, when working men and women successfully forced Mosley's fascists into retreat, to the low of Soviet tanks rolling into Hungary. *Guardian*, 21 May 2011.
13   *Jewish Chronicle*, 13 April 2007, p. 6.

14   *Jewish Chronicle*, 5 April 2019, p. 42.

15   Eastendwomensmuseum.org.

16   *Jewish Chronicle*, 2 July 1965, p. 35.

17   Eastendwomensmuseum.org

18   *Jewish Chronicle*, 2 July 1965, p. 35.

19   *Guardian*, 10 June 2018.

20   Bertha Sokoloff, *Edith and Stepney: The Life of Edith Ramsey* (London: Stepney Book Publications, 1987), p. 43.

21   Ibid., pp. 43-46.

22   Ibid., pp. 81-82.

23   Ibid., pp. 79-81.

24   Henry Srebrnik, 'Class, Ethnicity and Gender Intertwined: Jewish Women and the East London Rent Strikes 1935-1940', *Women's History Review*, 1995, 4 (3), pp. 284-286.

25   Sarah Glynn, 'East End Immigrants and the Battle for Housing: A Comparative Study of Political Mobilisation in the Jewish and Bengali Communities', *Journal of Historical Geography*, 31 (2005), pp. 528-545.

26   Noreen Branson, *History of the Communist Party in Great Britain 1927-41* (London: Lawrence & Wishart, 1985), p. 197.

27   Henry Srebrnik, 'Class, Ethnicity and Gender Intertwined', p. 286..

28   Ibid., p. 288.

29   *Daily Worker,* 20 February 1939, p. 8.

30   Ibid.

31   Ibid.

32   Sarah Glynn, 'East End Immigrants and the Battle for Housing', pp. 528-545.

33   *Daily Worker*, 28 February 1939, p. 5.

34   Phil Piratin, *Our Flag Stays Red* (London: Thames Publications, 1948), p. 46.

35   Bertha Sokoloff, *Edith and Stepney*, p. 81.

36   Elaine Rosa Smith, *East End Jews in Politics, 1918-1939: A Study in Class and Ethnicity* (Leicester: University of Leicester, 1990), p. 211.

37   *East London Advertiser*, 20 April 1945, p. 4.

38   Henry Srebrnik, Henry, 'Class, Ethnicity and Gender Intertwined', p. 291.

39   *Jewish Clarion*, December 1946, p. 4.

40   Bertha Sokoloff, *Edith and Stepney*, pp. 126-127.

41   Ibid., pp 66-67.

42   Ibid., pp. 65-66.

43   *Guardian*, 10 June 2018.

44   Ibid.

45   Andrew Hosken, *Nothing Like A Dame* (London: Granta Publications,

2006), p. 1.

46   Ibid., pp. 6-7.

47   Ibid., pp, 7-8.

48   Maurice Corina, *Pile It High, Sell It Cheap* (London: Weidenfeld and Nicholson, 1971), p. 51.

49   Sarah Ryle, *The Making of Tesco* (London: Bantam Press, 2013), p. 6.

50   Ibid., pp. 14, 16.

51   Andrew Hosken, *Nothing Like a Dame*, p. 8.

52   Ibid., p. 18.

53   *Jewish Chronicle*, 9 March 1990, p. 2.

54   *Jewish Chronicle*, 17 May 1966, p. 28.

55   Andrew Hosken, *Nothing Like a Dame*, pp. 20, 25.

56   *Desert Island Discs*, BBC Radio 4, 3 May 1991.

57   *Jewish Chronicle*, 31 July 1981, p. 3.

58   *Jewish Chronicle*, 12 March 1982, p. v.

59   *Jewish Chronicle*, 31 October 1988, p. 32

60   *Jewish Chronicle*, 31 May 1991, p. 8.

61   *Times,* 27 September 1985, p. 11.

62   Andrew Hosken, *Nothing Like a Dame*, p. 36-37.

63   Lesley Abdela, *Women with X Appeal* (London: Macdonald Optima, 1989), p. 189.

64   *Jewish Chronicle*, 17 May 1966, p. 28.

65   Hosken, *Nothing Like a Dame*, pp. 42-43, 47.

66   Ibid., p. 68.

67   *Independent*, 16 December 2001.

68   Andrew Hosken, *Nothing Like a Dame*, p. 2.

69   *Guardian*, 14 December 2001.

70   *Jewish Chronicle*, 17 May 1996, p. 28. Gerrymandering is a practice intended to establish an unfair political advantage for a particular party or group by manipulating district boundaries.

71   *Guardian*, 22 May 2018.

72   *Jewish Chronicle*, 10 May 2019, p. 33.

73   *Jewish Chronicle*, 17 May 1966, p. 28.

74   *Jewish Chronicle*, 18 March 1960, p. 12.

75   Andrew Hosken, *Nothing Like a Dame,* pp. 18-19.

76   *Jewish Chronicle*, 31 July 1981, p. 3.

77   Kol Nidre is recited in the synagogue before the beginning of the evening service on Yom Kippur (Day of Atonement).

78   *Desert Island Discs*, BBC Radio 4, 3 May 1991.

79   *Jewish Chronicle*, 22 February 1991, p. 36.

80   *Jewish Chronicle*, 30 March 2007, p. 33.

81 Lesley Abdela, *Women with X Appeal*, p. 187.

82 *Evening Standard*, 13 October 2004.

83 Lesley Abdela, *Women with X Appeal*, p. 1.

84 Edwina Currie, *Diaries 1987-1992* (London: Little Brown, 2002).

85 BBC News, 28 September 2002.

86 Lesley Abdela, *Women with X Appeal*, pp. 6-7.

87 *Jewish Chronicle*, 26 September 1997, p. 47.

88 www.jewishlivesproject.com

89 *Jewish Renaissance*, January 2008, p. 19.

90 Lesley Abdela, *Women with X Appeal*, p. 5.

91 *Jewish Chronicle*, 19 March 1993, p. 19.

92 Lesley Abdela, *Women with X Appeal*, p. 7.

93 Ibid.

94 *Jewish Chronicle*, 16 December 1994, p. 22.

95 *Jewish Chronicle*, 12 October 2012, p. 29.

96 *Jewish Chronicle*, 19 March 1993, p. 19.

97 *Jewish Chronicle*, 27 March 1998.

98 *Jewish Chronicle*, 27 April 2001, p. 33.

99 *Jewish Chronicle*, 8 July 1988, p. 12.

100 *Jewish Chronicle*, 24 March 1995, p. 32.

101 *Jewish Chronicle*, 19 April 1996.

102 *Guardian*, 27 October 2012.

103 Edwina Currie, *She's Leaving Home* (London: Warner Books, 1998).

104 *Jewish Chronicle*, 26 September 1997, p. 46.

105 Ibid.

106 *Jewish Chronicle*, 10 October 1997, p. 27.

107 Lesley Abdela, *Women with X Appeal*, p. 2.

108 *Jewish Chronicle*, 23 September 1999, p. 20.

109 Leon Brittan, son of Lithuanian Jews, resigned as Trade and Industry Secretary in January 1986. Brittan had authorised the leaking of a letter from the Solicitor General that had accused Michael Heseltine of inaccuracies in his campaign for Westland Helicopters to be rescued by a consortium of European investors.

110 Conservative peer Lord Young resigned in 2010 as an adviser to the government in the wake of his controversial remarks about the Government. He had said that the vast majority of 'people had never had it so good' because of low interest rates. BBC News, 19 November 2010.

111 *Jewish Chronicle*, 10 November 1989, p. 7.

112 *Jewish Chronicle*, 12 March 2004, p. 6.

113 *Jewish Chronicle*, 24 March 1995, p. 32.

114 William D. Rubinstein, Michael Jolles, Hilary L. Rubinstein, *The Palgrave Dictionary of Anglo-Jewish History* (London: Palgrave Macmillan, 2011), p. 189.

115 *Jewish Chronicle*, 26 September 1997, p. 47.

116 *Jewish Chronicle*, 27 March 1998.

117 *Jewish Renaissance*, Winter 2003, p. 10.

118 *Jewish Chronicle*, 30 October 2020, p. 37.

119 Edwina Currie, *Diaries 1987-1992* (London: Time Warner, 2003). p. 182.

120 *Jewish Chronicle*, 24 June 1994, p. 1.

121 *Jewish Chronicle*, 3 June 1988, p. 9.

122 *Yorkshire Post*, 13 February 1987.

123 Daily Mirror, 28 December 2015.

124 Ibid.

125 *Mail on Sunday*, 26 December 2015.

126 Edwina Currie, *A Woman's Place* (London: Hodder & Stoughton, 1996).

127 *Jewish Chronicle*, 26 January 1986, p. 28.

128 'Lunch with the FT: Margaret Hodge', *Financial Times*, 6 December 2013.

129 *Evening Standard*, 28 January 2022, p. 11.

130 Ibid.

131 *Jewish Chronicle*, 17 June 1994, p. 9.

132 *Guardian*, 15 March 2015.

133 *Guardian*, 21 November 2003.

134 *Jewish Chronicle*, 17 June 1994, p. 9.

135 Ibid.

136 *Guardian,* 21 November 2003.

137 *Guardian* 15 March 2015.

138 *Jewish Chronicle*, 25 May 2007, p. 9.

139 *Jewish Chronicle*, 1 June 2007, p. 12.

140 *Jewish Chronicle*, 7 December 2012, p. 25.

141 *Jewish Chronicle*, 16 April 2010, p. 6.

142 *Jewish Chronicle*, 20 November 2009, p. 1.

143 *Jewish Chronicle*, 19 July 2013, p. 29.

144 Ibid.

145 *Jewish Chronicle*, 7 December 2012, p. 25.

146 Ibid.

147 *Telegraph*, 12 December 2012.

148 *Guardian*, 18 July 2018.

149 *Jewish Chronicle*, 27 July 2018, p. 1.

150 *Jewish Chronicle*, 22 February 2019, p. 5.

151 *Jewish Chronicle,* 20 July 2018, p. 4.

152 *Jewish Chronicle*, 10 August 2018, p. 6.

153   *Jewish Chronicle,* 24 August 2018, p. 7.
154   *Jewish Chronicle,* 21 September 2018, p. 4.
155   *Jewish Chronicle,* 14 November 2014, p. 10.
156   *Jewish Chronicle,* 14 November 2014, p. 10.
157   *Jewish Chronicle,* 20 April 2018, p. 6.
158   *Jewish Chronicle,* 17 June 1994, p. 9.
159   Ultra-orthodox Jewish sect.
160   *Jewish Chronicle,* 5 March 2004.
161   *Jewish Chronicle,* 7 November 2003, p. 2.
162   *Jewish Chronicle,* 29 January 2010, p. X06.
163   *Jewish Renaissance,* April 2010, p. 5.
164   *Jewish Chronicle,* 7 December 2018, p. 5.
165   *Jewish Chronicle,* 10 December 2021, p. 11.
166   *Liverpool Echo,* 30 September 1997, p. 19.
167   *Jewish Chronicle,* 5 August 2018, p. 7.
168   *Jewish Chronicle,* 17 September 2004, p. 26.
169   *Jewish Chronicle,* 5 August 2018, p. 7.
170   *Liverpool Echo,* 15 March 1983, p. 10.
171   *Jewish Renaissance,* April 2020, p. 12.
172   *Jewish Chronicle,* 30 June 1995, p. 9.
173   *Jewish Chronicle,* 5 August 2018, p. 7.
174   *Liverpool Echo,* 31 December 1997, p. 7.
175   The Jewish Labour Movement, known as Poale Zion from 1903-2004, is one of the oldest socialist societies affiliated to the UK Labour Party.
176   *Jewish Chronicle,* 5 August 2018, p. 7.
177   *Jewish Chronicle,* 3 July 1998, p. 11.
178   *Jewish Chronicle,* 3 July 1998, p. 11.
179   *Times of Israel,* 12 May 2017.
180   *Jewish Chronicle,* 3 November 2000, p. 10.
181   *Jewish Chronicle,* 19 July 2002, p. 10.
182   *Jewish Chronicle* 23 January 2009, p. 7.
183   *Jewish Chronicle,* 28 May 2004, p. 20.
184   *Jewish Chronicle,* 20 December 2002, p. 4.
185   *Jewish Chronicle,* 11 April 2003, p. 4.
186   *Jewish Chronicle,* 23 July 2004, p. 4.
187   *Jewish Chronicle,* 7 October 2005, p. 4.
188   *Jewish Chronicle,* 13 October 2006, p. 12.
189   *Jewish Chronicle,* 11 January 2019, p. 2.
190   *Jewish Chronicle,* 6 April 2012, p. 1.
191   *Jewish Chronicle,* 16 April 2010, p. 5.
192   *Jewish Chronicle,* 23 February 2018, p. 12.

193   *Times of Israel*, 12 May 2017.
194   *Jewish Chronicle*, 5 August 2018, p. 7.
195   *Jewish Chronicle*, 8 April 2016, p. 1.
196   *Jewish Chronicle*, 1 March 2019, p. 6.
197   *Times of Israel*, 12 May 2017.
198   *Jewish Chronicle*, 20 April 2018, p. 6.
199   *Mail on Sunday*, 4 August 2018.
200   *Jewish Chronicle*, 10 August 2018, p. 11.
201   *Jewish Renaissance*, January 2017, p. 9.
202   *Times*, 16 October 2019.
203   *Jewish Renaissance*, April 2020.
204   *Guardian*, 17 October 2019.
205   *Daily Mail*, 16 October 2019.
206   *Jewish Chronicle*, 16 June 2006, p. 3.
207   BBC News, 27 September 2021.
208   Totalpolitics.com 28 May 2012.
209   Ibid.
210   *Sunday Times Magazine*, 7 December 2019.
211   *Jewish Renaissance*, April 2015, p. 12.
212   *Observer*, 28 August 2016.
213   Ibid.
214   Totalpolitics.com. 28 May 2012.
215   Jewish Telegraphic Agency, 18 April 2005.
216   *Guardian*, 15 April 2005.
217   *Times of Israel*, 18 February 2019.
218   *Jewish Chronicle*, 29 January 2010, p. 5.
219   *Jewish Chronicle*, 16 April 2010, p. 5.
220   *Jewish Chronicle*, 21 June 2013, p. 1.
221   *Jewish Renaissance*, April 2015, p. 13.
222   *Jewish Chronicle*, 20 November 2015, p. 24.
223   *Jewish Chronicle*, 31 October 2014, p. 4.
224   *Jewish Chronicle*, 24 October 2014, p. 10.
225   *Sunday Times Magazine*, 7 December 2019.
226   *Jewish Chronicle*, 7 April 2017, p. 1.
227   *GQ Magazine*, 18 February 2019.
228   *Jewish Chronicle*. 28 December 2018, p. 26.
229   *GQ Magazine*, 18 February, 2019.
230   Momentum is a British left-wing political organisation, founded in 2015,
       that is a grassroots movement supportive of Jeremy Corbyn and the
       Labour Party.
231   *Sunday Times*, 1 April 2018.

232 *Jewish Chronicle,* 7 August 2015, p. 6.
233 *Jewish Chronicle,* 9 December 2018, p. 1.
234 *Jewish Chronicle,* 9 December 2015, p. 1.
235 *Jewish Chronicle,* 14 July 2017, p. 10.
236 *Sunday Times Magazine,* 7 December 2019.
237 *Jewish Chronicle,* 13 January 2017, p. 18.
238 *Jewish Chronicle,* 19 January 2018, p. 6.
239 *Jewish Chronicle,* 26 May 2017, p. 8.
240 *Jewish Chronicle,* 14 September 2018, p. 5.
241 *GQ Magazine,* 18 February 2019.
242 *Jewish Chronicle,* 21 June 2013, p. 7.
243 *Jewish Chronicle,* 29 February 2014, p. 12.
244 *Jewish Chronicle,* 18 September 2015.
245 *Jewish Chronicle,* 9 December 2016, pp. 1, 4, 5.
246 *Jewish Chronicle,* 22 February 2019, p. 1.
247 *Jewish Chronicle,* 30 November 2018, p. 4.
248 Totalpolitics.com. 28 May 2012.
249 *Times,* 14 December 2019, p. 12.
250 www.bbc.co.uk, 17 April 2018.
251 *Jewish Chronicle,* 2 March 2018, p. 38.
252 *Evening Standard,* 20 September 2016.
253 Jewish coming of age ceremony for girls.
254 *Jewish Chronicle,* 15 May 2015, p. 7.
255 Meet the MPs, 10 August, 2018, youtube.
256 Ruthsmeeth.org.uk
257 A British charity whose purpose is to provide safety, security and advice to the Jewish community in the UK.
258 *Uttoexeter Post and Times,* 5 April 2015.
259 *New Statesman,* 28 July 2016.
260 National Leasehold Campaign, youtube 24 July 2018.
261 *Jewish Chronicle,* 14 October 2016, p. 10.
262 *Jewish Chronicle,* 21 March 2008, p. 1.
263 BBC News, 30 June 2016.
264 *Evening Standard,* 20 September 2016.
265 *Guardian,* 2 September 2016.
266 *Jewish Chronicle,* 23 September 2016, p. 16.
267 *Evening Standard,* 20 September 2016.
268 ITV News, 27 June 2016.
269 *Jewish Chronicle,* 12 April 2019, p. 8.
270 *Jewish Chronicle,* 25 January 2019, p. 16.
271 *Jewish Chronicle,* 5 May 2019, p. 9.

272   Meet the MPs, 10 August 2018, youtube.

273   *Jewish Chronicle,* 1 February 2019, p. 5.

274   Sky News, 13 December 2019.

275   *Evening Standard,* 20 September 2016.

276   Indexoncensorship.org

277   *Jewish Chronicle,* 6 January 2023.

CHAPTER 4

1   Joel H. Wiener, 'The Nineteenth Century and the Emergence of a Mass Circulation Press', in *Routledge Companion to British Media History,* ed. By Martin Conboy and John Steel (eds), p. 206.

2   Cathy Ross & John Clark, *London: The Illustrated History* (London: Penguin, 2008), p. 240.

3   First Ladies of Fleet Street, www.bbc.co.uk, 6 December 2018

4   Eilat Negev and Yehuda Koren, *The First Lady of Fleet Street. The Life, Fortune and Tragedy of Rachel Beer* (London: Robson Press, 2012), pp. viii-ix.

5   Julie Welch, *Fleet Street Girls: The Women Who Broke Down the Doors of the Gentlemen's Club* (London: Trapeze, 2020).

6   Olga Franklin, *Steppes to Fleet Street* (London: Victor Gollanz, 1968), pp. 157-158.

7   Julie Welch, *Fleet Street Girls.*

8   Martin Conboy, *Journalism in Britain* (London: Sage Publications, 2011), p. 46.

9   Ibid., p. 76.

10   Eilat Negev and Yehuda Koren, *The First Lady of Fleet Street,* pp. viii-ix.

11   *Ridley Road* focuses on the 62 Group, a collection of Jewish anti-fascists who infiltrated the neo-Nazi Nationalist Socialist Movement run by Colin Jordan in the 1960s.

12   *Jewish Chronicle,* 1 October 2021, p. 34.

13   Julie Welch, *Fleet Street Girls.*

14   Ibid.

15   Her father David Sassoon had been very involved in local Jewish communal affairs. He had been a member of the council of Jews' College and Jews' Free School and a warden of the Spanish and Portuguese synagogue. Her mother Flora was a scholar of Hebrew. She could engage in abstruse discussion on the Talmud. She had an interest in local Jewish welfare organisations and laid the foundation stone for the London Jewish Hospital in 1915. W. Rubinstein (ed.), *The Palgrave Dictionary of Anglo-Jewish History* (Basingstoke: Palgrave Macmillan, 2011).

16   Eilat Negev and Yehuda Koren, *The First Lady of Fleet Street*, p. x.
17   Ibid., p. 137.
18   Julie Welch, *Fleet Street Girls*.
19   *Jewish Chronicle*, 6 May 2011, p. 21.
20   *Jewish Chronicle*, 9 March 2012, p. 5.
21   Eilat Negev and Yehuda Koren, *First Lady of Fleet Street*, p. 203.
22   *Jewish Chronicle*, 6 May 2011, p. 21.
23   Arnold Bennett, *Journalism for Women: A Practical Guide* (London: John Lane, 1898), p. 10.
24   *Daily Mail*, 14 May 2015.
25   Richard Jaffa, *Letters from Oggi* (Sussex: Book Guild Publishing, 2015), p. x.
26   *Daily Mail*, 14 May 2015.
27   Olga Franklin, *Steppes to Fleet Street*, pp. 157-158.
28   Ibid., pp. 211-212, 236.
29   *Jewish Chronicle*, 31 May 1957, p. 25.
30   Olga Franklin, *Steppes to Fleet Street*, p. xi.
31   Ibid, p. 33.
32   Olga Franklin, *Born Twice* (London: Peter Garnett, 1951), pp. 18-19.
33   Olga Franklin, *Steppes to Fleet Street*, p. 9.
34   *Jewish Chronicle*, 15 February 1985, p. 21.
35   Olga Franklin, *Steppes to Fleet Street*, p. 11.
36   Ibid., pp. 235-236.
37   Ibid., pp. 235-236.
38   www.jewishlivesproject.com
39   Desert Island Discs, 11 December 2011, www.bbc.co.uk
40   Ibid.
41   Ibid.
42   Lisa Katz, 'The effect of the Holocaust on children of survivors', www.thoughtco.com
43   *Jewish Chronicle*, 23 September 1988, p. 20.
44   Joe Haines, *Kick 'Em Back. Wilson, Maxwell and Me* (Guildford: Grosvenor House Publishing 2019), p. 233.
45   *Jewish Chronicle*, 10 July 1987, p. 40.
46   *Guardian*, 16 June 2005.
47   Ibid.
48   *Newcastle Journal*, 13 June 1995, p. 31.
49   *Irish Independent*, 8 September 1995, p. 11.
50   *Desert Island Discs*, 11 December 2011.
51   *Sunday Tribune*, 9 April 2000, p. 29.
52   *Jewish Chronicle*, 30 June 1995, p. 33. The Dalkon Shield was an

intrauterine birth control device sold in the early 1970s that was responsible for a high number of reported incidents of inflammatory pelvic infections, uterine perforations and spontaneous septic abortions.

53   *Sunday Mirror*, 16 November 1980, p. 17.
54   The Media, BBC Radio 4, 14 December 2014, www.bbc.co.uk
55   *Jewish Chronicle*, 30 June 1995, p. 33.
56   *Desert Island Discs*, 11 December 2011.
57   *Jewish Chronicle*, 19 May 1989, p. 7.
58   *Jewish Chronicle*, 17 November 1995.
59   *Jewish Chronicle*, 28 March 2008, p. 48.
60   *Jewish Chronicle*, 8 August 2008. p. 36.
61   *Jewish Chronicle*, 12 September, 2003, p. 2.
62   *Press Gazette*, 10 June 2019.
63   Ibid.
64   Kate Murphy, *Behind the Wireless: A History of Early Women at the BBC* (London: Palgrave Macmillan, 2016).
65   *Desert Island Discs*, 10 March 2019.
66   *Guardian*, 16 March 2021.
67   Esther Rantzen, *Esther* (London: BBC Worldwide Limited, 2001), pp. 9-12.
68   Ibid., pp. 14-17.
69   Ibid., p. 30.
70   Ibid., pp. 97-98, 352, 357.
71   *Desert Island Discs*, 10 March 2019.
72   *Daily Mail*, 30 January 2015.
73   *Desert Island Discs*, 10 March 2019.
74   Ibid.
75   Ibid.
76   Ibid.
77   *Daily Telegraph*, 19 November 2013.
78   *Daily Express,* 29 December 2018.
79   *Desert Island Discs,* BBC Radio Four, 29 October 2017.
80   *The House I Grew Up In,* BBC Radio 4, 9 August 2010.
81   *Guardian*, 29 December 2017.
82   *The House I Grew Up In.*
84   *Guardian*, 29 December 2017.
85   Gaynor Faye is an actress and writer, best known for playing Judy Mallett in *Coronation Street* (1995-99) and Megan Macey in *Emmerdale* (2012-2019). Yvonne Francas is a television producer.
86   *Jewish Chronicle*, 31 December 1993, p. 30.
87   *Jewish Chronicle*, 8 August 2014, p. 34.

88   *Jewish Chronicle*, 9 December 1994.
89   *Jewish Chronicle*, 17 October 1997, p. 28.
90   *Big Issue*, 6 March 2021.
91   *Jewish Chronicle*, 8 August 2014, p. 33.
92   *Yorkshire Post*, 29 December 2017.
93   *Jewish Chronicle*, 10 June 2016, p. 36.
94   *Jewish Chronicle*, 8 August 2014, p. 34.
95   *The House I Grew Up In.*
96   *Jewish Chronicle*, 8 August 2014, p. 34.
97   *The House I Grew Up In.*
98   *Jewish Chronicle*, 31 December 1993, p. 30.
99   *The House I Grew Up In.*
100   *Jewish Chronicle*, 8 August 2014, p. 34.
101   *Jewish Chronicle*, 19 July 2002, p. 33.
102   *Jewish Chronicle*, 10 June 2016, p. 36.
103   *Jewish Chronicle*, 30 January 2004, p. 17.
104   *Jewish Chronicle*, 27 October 2000.
105   *Jewish Chronicle*, 13 September 2002, p. 51.
106   A canopy under which a Jewish couple stand during their wedding ceremony.
107   *Jewish Chronicle*, 1 December 2017, p. 14.
108   Steven McIntosh, 'Why these girlfriends stand out in British TV', www.bbc.co.uk, 3 January 2018.
109   *Desert Island Discs*, 29 October 2017.
110   *The House I Grew Up In.*
111   *Times*, 19 May 2022, p. 55.
112   Dr Jacob Maitlis is an authority on Yiddish literature and Jewish history. *Jewish Chronicle*, 13 August 1971, p. 16.
113   *Daily Mail*, 14 April 2019.
114   *Guardian*, 20 April 2019.
115   *Jewish Chronicle*, 14 September 2014, p. 14.
116   *Evening Standard Magazine*, 8 March 2013.
117   Ibid.
118   *Jewish Chronicle*, 29 November 2002, p. 10.
119   bbc.co.uk, 20 March 2019.
120   www.tatler.com, 27 February 2020.
121   www.eveningexpress.co.uk, 26 February 2020.
122   *Guardian*, 24 November 2019.
123   *Jewish Chronicle*, 29 November 2002, p. 10.
124   *Guardian*, 18 January 2018.
125   *Express*, 23 October 2019.

126   *Jewish Chronicle*, 19 April 2017.
127   *Jewish Chronicle*, 1 December 2006, p. 22.
128   *Evening Standard Magazine*, 8 March 2013.
129   *Jewish Chronicle*, 16 September 2009, p. 7.
130   *Jewish Chronicle*, 19 April 2017.
131   *Guardian*, 21 April 2019.
132   *Express*, 30 May 2020.
133   *Elle*, 9 April 2020.
134   *Jewish Chronicle*, 30 November 2012, p. B001.
135   *Jewish Chronicle*, 13 February 2015, p. 20.
136   *Jewish Chronicle*, 29 November 2002, p. 10.
137   *Guardian*, 18 April 2019.
138   *Guardian*, 24 November 2019.
139   *Sunday Times Magazine*, 3 January 2021, p. 23.
140   *Daily Express*, 28 November 2017.
141   A Radio 5 chat show where a range of guests talk about challenges and hurdles that they have faced in their lives. 22 September 2020.
142   *Daily Mail*, 10 December 2020.
143   *Daily Express*, 28 November 2017.
144   *Sunday Times Magazine*, 3 January 2021, p. 20
145   Ibid., p. 23.
146   *Jewish Chronicle*, 22 February 2008, p. 7.
147   *Jewish Chronicle*, 12 November 2010, p. 12.
148   *Manchester Jewish News*, 19 April 2010.
149   *Jewish Chronicle*, 4 February 2011, p. 10.
150   *Daily Mail*, 11 June 2016.
151   Ibid.
152   *Daily Express*, 28 November 2017.
153   *Evening Standard*, 7 September 2020.
154   *Sunday Times Magazine,* 3 January 2021, p. 20.
155   It is now aired at 10am, Monday-Friday and Saturday at 4pm.
156   Kate Murphy, '75 Years of Celebrating Women's Hour', www.bbc.com.
157   www.bbc.co.uk, 4 January 2021.
158   *Sunday Times Magazine*, 3 January 2021, p. 23.
159   *Jewish Chronicle*, 28 October 2016, p. 36.
160   *Jewish Chronicle*, 10 June 2016, p. 40.
161   *Jewish Chronicle*, 3 May 2013, p. 12.
162   She met her husband at university. She never discloses his name nor the name of their son who was born in 2018.
163   *Jewish Chronicle*, 10 June 2016, p. 40.
164   Ibid., p. 40.

165   *Jewish Chronicle*, 16 September 2016, p. 17.
166   *Jewish Chronicle*, 30 November 2018, p. 4.
167   *Sunday Times Magazine*, 3 January 2021, p. 23.
168   *Guardian Weekend*, 20 February 2021, p. 8.
169   Wiley's Twitter account was temporarily locked while Instagram deleted some of his content after a series of posts that included comparing Jews to the Ku Klux Khan.
170   *BBC News*, 27 July 2020.
171   *Independent*, 27 July 2020.
172   *Guardian*, 8 January 2021
173   *Times*, 4 January 2021.
174   *Guardian*, 1 September 203.
175   *Jewish Chronicle*, 10 May 2013, p. 29.
176   *Evening Standard*, 1 July 2014.
177   *Mail*, 18 November 2022.
178   *Jewish Telegraph*, 4 December 2020.
179   *Times*, 27 June 2021.
180   *Mail*, 18 November 2022.
181   Email correspondence with Isabelle Seddon, 24 January 2023.
182   Ibid.
183   The Female Lead, 20 December 2021, youtube.
184   *Jewish Telegraph*, 4 December 2020.
185   Ibid.
186   *Jewish Chronicle*, 25 August 2022.
187   *Mail*, 18 November 2022.
188   Ibid.
189   Email correspondence with Isabelle Seddon, 24 January 2023.
190   *Times*, 27 June 2021.
191   *Jewish Chronicle*, 21 November 2014, p. 20.
192   *Guardian,* 27 June 2005.
193   Eilat Negev and Yehuda Koren 'The First Lady of Fleet Street', 1

CHAPTER 5

1   '75 Years of Women Solicitors'. BBC News, 19 December 1997.
2   Erikca Rackley and Rosemary Auchmuty, *Women's Legal Landmarks. Celebrating the History of Women and Law in the UK and Ireland* (Oxford: Hart Publishing, 2019), pp. 258-259.
3   John Cooper, 'How Jews Broke into the Professions', *Jewish Chronicle*, 7 November 2012.
4   *Times*, 13 December 2015.

5   Hilary Heilbron, *Rose Heilbron. The Story of England's First Woman Queen's Counsel and Judge* (Oxford: Hart Publishing, 2012), p. 4.

6   Rachel Cooke, *Her Brilliant Career. Ten Extraordinary Women of the Fifties* (London: Virago, 2013), p. 272.

7   Hilary Heilbron, *Rose Heilbron*, p. 4.

8   Ibid., p. 14.

9   Hannah Neustatter, 'Demographic and Other Statistical Aspects of Anglo-Jewry', in Maurice Freedman (ed.), *A Minority in Britain: Social Studies of the Anglo-Jewish Community* (London: Valentine Mitchell, 1955).

10   Ibid., p. 6.

11   Rachel Cooke, *Her Brilliant Career*, p. 273.

12   Ibid., p. 274.

13   Hilary Heilbron, *Rose Heilbron*, p. 13.

14   It was particularly popular between 1896-1921, the early heyday of flower names, when it was in the Top 20. www.nameberry.com.

15   Hilary Heilbron, 'Women at the Bar: An Historical Perspective', www.counselmagazine.co.uk.

16   *Jewish Chronicle*, 2 November 2012, p. 35.

17   Rachel Cooke, *Her Brilliant Career*, p. 276.

18   Heilbron, *Rose Heilbron*, p. 25.

19   The existence of the Harrogate Jewish community is linked to the town becoming a fashionable spa and the subsequent expanse of the railways.

20   Rachel Cooke, *Her Brilliant Career*, p. 279.

21   *Daily Herald*, 24 September 1955.

22   *Jewish Chronicle*, 3 January 2020, p. 11.

23   Ericka Rackley and Rosemary Auchmuty, *Women's Legal Landmarks*, p. 258-259.

24   Rachel Cooke, *Her Brilliant Career*, p. 284.

25   *Telegraph*, 10 December 2005.

26   *Guardian*, 13 December 2015.

27   *Times*, 13 December 2005.

28   Hilary Heilbron, 'Women at the Bar'.

29   Rachel Cooke, *Her Brilliant Career*, pp. 296-7.

30   *Times*, 13 December 2005.

31   Rachel Cooke, *Her Brilliant Career*, p. 270.

32   Ibid., p. 271.

33   *Guardian*, 13 December 2015.

34   *Liverpool Echo*, 26 October 2012.

35   *Jewish Chronicle*, 10 September 1954, p. 20.

36   Jewishlivesproject.com

37   *Daily Mirror*, 27 March 1952.

38   *Times*, 13 December 2005.

39   Hilary Heilbron, *Rose Heilbron*, p. 5, 9.

40   *Jewish Chronicle*, 8 October 1954, p. 16.

41   *Jewish Chronicle*, 30 December 2005, p. 20.

42   *Jewish Chronicle*, 2 November 2012, p. 35.

43   Hilary Heilbron, *Rose Heilbron*, pp. vii-viii.

44   *Telegraph*, 10 December 2005.

45   Heilbron, *Rose Heilbron*, pp. x-xi.

46   *Jewish Chronicle*, 2 November 2012, p. 35.

47   *Jewish Chronicle*, 8 July 1949, p. 8.

48   *Jewish Chronicle*, 3 January 2020, p. 11.

49   Jewishlivesproject.com

50   *Jewish Chronicle*, 17 November 1995, p. 16.

51   *Jewish Chronicle*, 21 September 1979, p. 5.

52   Judge Dawn Freedman was the youngest person, at the age of 37, to have been appointed a stipendiary magistrate. She grew up in Westcliff and was called to the Bar in 1966. She was the first woman in her chambers which was headed by the writer and broadcaster John Mortimer and was a member of the Board of Deputies until her appointment as a circuit judge in 1991.   Her Judaism was important to her and she considered being Jewish meant living her heritage; being respected by her colleagues for adhering to the principle of her faith, her love for Israel and running a traditional Jewish home whilst at the same time being afforded respect by rabbis who sit in the religious courts for her role as a judge. *Jewish Chronicle*, 8 February 2002, p. 2.

53   John Cooper, *Pride Versus Prejudice. Jewish Doctors and Lawyers in England 1890-1990* (Oxford: Littman Library of Jewish Civilization, 2003), p. 392.

54   Jewsishlivesproject.com

55   The Cleveland child abuse scandal was a 1987 wave of suspected child sexual abuse cases, many of which were later discredited, in Cleveland, England.

56   *Times*, 6 November 2002.

57   *Jewish Chronicle*, 17 November 1995, p. 16.

58   *Newcastle Evening Chronicle*, 26 July 1989, p. 12.

59   *Newcastle Journal*, 18 May 1970, p. 6.

60   *Newcastle Evening Chronicle*, 26 July 1989, p. 12.

61   *Newcastle Journal*, 18 May 1970, p. 6.

62   *Times*, 6 November 2002.

63   *Jewish Chronicle*, 30 March 2001, p. 23.

64   *Jewish Chronicle*, 12 November 1999, pp. 1, 35.

65   Interview with Sandra Blackman, London. 7 October 2020.

66   *Jewish Chronicle*, 21 September 2001.

67   Interview with Sandra Blackman, London. 7 October 2020.

68   *Times*, 6 November 2002.

69   *Jewish Chronicle*, 1 November 2002, p. 26.

70   *Jewish Chronicle*, 26 July 2002, p. 24.

71   *Jewish Chronicle*, 28 February 2003, p. 9.

72   *Newcastle Journal*, 18 May 1970, p. 6.

73   *Jewish Chronicle*, 14 January 1972, p. 8.

74   *Jewish Chronicle*, 20 January 1989, p. 25.

75   *Jewish Chronicle*, 17 November 1995, p. 16.

76   'First   Hundred   Years.   Celebrating   Women   in   Law',
       www.first100years.org.uk.

77   *Newcastle Journal*, 18 May 1970, p. 6.

78   Some people choose to be buried in Jerusalem out of Zionist motives.
       For others, an Israeli burial is linked to the belief that a burial in Israel
       ensures that they will be first to rise from the grave when the Messiah
       comes.

79   *Jewish Chronicle*, 1 November 2002, p. 6.

80   Erika Rackley and Rosemary Auchmuty, *Women's Legal Landmarks*, p.
       260.

81   *Jewish Chronicle*, 1 November 2002, p. 6.

82   Hilary Heilbron, *Rose Heilbron*, p. xi.

CHAPTER 6

1   Laura Jefferson, Karen Bloor and Alan Maynard, 'Women in Medicine:
       Historical Perspectives and Recent Trends', *British Medical Journal*, 114:
       5-15 (2015).

2   Ibid.

3   David Katz, 'Review of Jewish Contribution to Medicine in the UK',
       www.jewishmedicalassociation.org.

4   David Dee, *The 'Estranged' Generation? Social and Generation Change
       in Interwar British Jewry* (London: Palgrave Macmillan, 2017), pp. 106,
       108-110.

5   John Cooper, 'Jews Who Helped Make the Health Service', *British
       Journal of Medical Practice*, 69 (678), (2019), pp. 32-33.

6   Gerry Black, *Lord Rothschild and the Barber* (London: Tymsder
       Publishing, 2000), p. 97.

7   p. 98.

8   www.rcseng.ac.uk

9   Oliver Sacks, *Uncle Tungsten* (London: Picador, 2001), pp. 8-9.

10   Ibid.

11   Livesonline, rcseng.ac.uk

12   The London Jewish Hospital also served the Jewish medical community. Jewish doctors had the opportunity of securing a post if they did not want to go into general practice or take a position in a comparatively small obscure hospital that had difficulty in attracting candidates. The Hospital presented an alternative. Gerry Black, *Lord Rothschild and the Barber*, p. 97.

13   Oliver Sacks, *Uncle Tungsten*, p. 240.

14   *East London Observer*, 19 May 1928, p. 6.

15   Lara Marks, 'Dear Old Mother Levy's: The Jewish Maternity Home and Sick Room Helps Society 1895-1939', *Social History of Medicine*, Oxford University Press, Vol. 3 (1), April, 1990, pp., 61, 65-66, 76.

16   *The Cable* (16), 2011, p. 31.

17   Lara Marks, 'Dear Old Mother Levy's: The Jewish Maternity Home and Sick Room Helps Society 1895-1939', *Social History of Medicine*, Oxford University Press, Vol. 3 (1), April, 1990, pp. 84-85.

18   Gerry Black, *Lord Rothschild and the Barber*, p. 127.

19   *Jewish Chronicle*, 29 July 1910, p. 17.

20   *Jewish Chronicle*, 16 June 1972, p. 18.

21   *Irish Times*, 5 September 2015.

22   Oliver Sacks, *Uncle Tungsten*, p. 33.

23   *Jewish Chronicle*, 1 December 1972, p. 34.

24   www.livesonline.rcseng.ac.uk

25   Oliver Sacks, *Uncle Tungsten*, p. 237.

26   Ibid., p. 173.

27   Oliver Sacks, *On the Move* (London: Picador, 2015), pp. 192-193.

28   *Jewish Chronicle*, 1 December 1972, p. 34.

29   *Guardian*, 26 September 2016.

30   Neil Bright, 'The Angel of Cable Street', www.blitzwalkers.com, 18 December 2010.

31   *British Medical Journal*, 29 August 1987, p. 558.

32   *The London Gazette*, 26 February 1943, p. 988, 29 December 1944, p. 13.

33   *British Medical Journal*, 29 August 1987, p. 558.

34   Gerry Black, *Lord Rothschild and the Barber*, p. 96.

35   Rose Henriques (Loewe) was born into an Orthodox Jewish family in Stoke Newington in 1889. In 1917 she married Basil Henriques and together they established and ran the Bernhard Baron Settlement in

Berners Street pursuing philanthropic work among the Jewish community in the East End for more than half a century. She produced paintings that document the times she lived in intimate human detail, exhibiting her work at the Whitechapel Gallery from 1934 onwards.www.spitalfieldslife.com. The sketches that she made of Stepney during the Second World War provided a unique and significant document of the War's impact on the area.

36   *Jewish Chronicle*, 3 April 1964, p. 8.

37   Rosemary Taylor, *Hannah Billig: The Angel of Cable Street* (London: Rosemary Taylor, 1996), p. 15.

38   www.eastendtalking.org.uk.

39   *Guardian*, 26 September 2016.

40   The Sex Discrimination Act 1975 was an Act of Parliament which protected men and women from discrimination on the grounds of sex or marital status. The Act concerned employment, training, education, harassment, the provision of goods and the disposal of premises.

41   Jefferson, Bloor and Maynard, Women in Medicine. Historical Perspectives and Recent Trends *British Medical Bulletin*, 114:1, 2015.

42   *Jewish Renaissance*, July 2008, p. 8.

43   *Daily Mail*, 8 March 2019.

44   *Daily Mail*, 24 February, 2017.

45   *Irish Independent*, 2 July 1994, p. 34.

46   *Tribune Magazine*, 2 July 1995, p. 40.

47   *Daily Mail,* 27 November 2016.

48   *Irish Independent*, 2 July 1994, p. 34.

49   *Don't Ask Me* was a popular British television show made by Yorkshire Television from 1974-78.

50   *Tribune Magazine*, 2 July 1995, p. 40.

51   *Aberdeen Press and Journal*, 24 April 1986, p. 7.

52   *The Times*, 23 November 2020, p. 29.

53   *Aberdeen Press and Journal*, 8 February 1988, p. 4.

54   *Guardian*, 10 October 2010.

55   *Reading Evening Post*, 31 March 1982, p. 2.

56   *Jewish Chronicle*, 8 March 1996, p. 26.

57   *Independent*, 3 November, 2003.

58   Oona King, Baroness King of Bow, was a Labour Member of Parliament for Bethnal Green and Bow (1997-2005) and the second Black Member of Parliament. She is currently Google's Director of Diversity Strategy.

59   *Jewish Renaissance*, July 2008, p. 8.

60   *Sydney Morning Herald*, 22 November 2006.

61   *Jewish Chronicle*, 8 March 1996, p. 26.

62   *Sydney Morning Herald*, 22 November 2006.

63   *Jewish Chronicle*, 17 January 1997, p. 10.

64   *Jewish News*, 23 February, 2017, p. 23.

65   *Jewish Chronicle*, 17 January 1997, p. 10.

66   *The Real Marigold Hotel* is a British travel documentary series that follows famous elderly celebrities as they travel around India and experience the culture.

67   *Shiva* is the week-long mourning period following burial.

68   The raised platform in the synagogue where the Torah (the first five books of the Hebrew bible) is read.

69   *Jewish News*, 23 February 2017, p. 23.

70   Irish Independent, 1 May 1993, p. 35.

71   Rosemary Taylor, *Hannah Billig: The Angel of Cable Street*, p. 15.

CHAPTER 7

1   Ruth Watts, *Women in Science* (London: Routledge, 2007), pp. 141-142.

2   Leigh Ann Whaley, *Women's History as Scientists* (Oxford: ABC: Clio, 2003), p. viii.

3   Kathleen Lonsdale (1903-1971) was a British crystallographer who developed several X-ray techniques for the study of crystal structure. She was the first woman to be elected (1945) to the Royal Society of London.

4   Ruth Watts, *Women in Science*, pp. 156-157, 166, 194.

5   *Dundee Courier*, 29 August 1923, p. 7.

6   Evelyn Sharp, *Hertha Ayrton 1854-1923, A Memoir* (London: Edward Arnold & Co., 1926), pp. 1, 3, 9.

7   Michael Galchinsky, *The Origin of the Modern Jewish Writer. Romance and Reform in Victorian England* (Detroit: Wayne State University Press, 1996), pp. 105, 107.

8   *Jewish Chronicle*, 16 May 1913, p. 16.

9   *Jewish Chronicle*, 9 April 1923, p. 20.

10   Frederika Bremer (1801-1865) was a Swedish writer, reformer and champion of women's rights and introduced the domestic novel into Swedish literature. Her novel *Hertha* (1856) is about a woman whose father embezzled her money and refused to let her sister marry the man of her choice.

11   Nina Byers and Gary Williams, *Contributions of Twentieth Century Women to Physics* (Cambridge: Cambridge University Press, 2006), p. 15.

12   Louisa Goldsmid (1819-1908) was born into a privileged Anglo-Jewish

family. She married her cousin Francis Henry Goldsmid, an Anglo-Jewish barrister, politician and a member of the Goldsmid banking family. She was a philanthropist and education activist concerned with improving education provision for women. She sat on committees at the Governesses' Benevolent Institution; Queen's College, Harley Street; Girton College, Cambridge and College Hall, the first female hall of residence to be opened at University College, London after women were admitted to full degree status in 1878. She was a founder of the International Federation of University Women in 1919 and of the National Union of Scientific Workers in 1920.

13   Jewish Women's Archive, jwa.org

14   Israel Zangwill (1864-1926) was a novelist, playwright and Zionist leader and one of the earliest English interpreters of Jewish immigrant life.

15   Jewish Women's Archive, jwa.org

16   Evelyn Sharp, *Hertha Ayrton 1854-1923*, p. vii.

17   Jewish Women's Archive, jwa.org

18   Nina Byers and Gary Williams, *Contribution of Twentieth Century Women to Physics*, pp. 21-22.

19   www.english-heritage.org.uk

20   Jewish Women's Archive, jwa.org

21   *Westminster Gazette*, 28 August 1923, p. 1.

22   *Dundee Courier*, 29 August 1923, p. 7.

23   Jewish Women's Archive, jwa.org

24   *Gloucestershire Echo*, 28 August 1923, p. 5.

25   Barbara Ayrton Gould (1886-1950) was one of the founding members of the United Suffragists and a member of the national executive of the Labour Party for over 20 years. She became Labour Member of Parliament for Hendon North in 1945.

26   Nina Byers and Gary Williams, p. 22.

27   www.english-heritage.org.uk

28   *The Vote*, 7 September 1923, p. 1.

29   *Jewish Chronicle*, 9 April 1923, p. 20.

30   Evelyn Sharp, *Hertha Ayrton 1854-1923*, pp. 9, 26.

31   *Portsmouth Evening News*, 24 October 1923, p. 5.

32   Jewish Women's Archive, jwa.org.

33   Nina Byers and Gary Williams, pp. 23-24.

34   Lisa Yount, *Twentieth-Century Women Scientists* (New York: Facts On File, 1996), pp. xi-xiv.

35   Ibid., p. 62.

36   Ibid., p. 61.

37 *Jewish Chronicle*, 23 September 2005, p. 35.
38 Brenda Maddox, *Rosalind Franklin: The Dark Lady of DNA* (New York: Harper Perennial, 2003), Chapter 1.
39 Anna Sayre, *Rosalind Franklin and DNA* (New York: W W Norton & Co, 1978), pp. 33-34.
40 Ibid., p. 34.
41 Ibid., pp. 29-30.
42 Ibid., p. 35.
43 *Jewish Chronicle,* 14 February 1992, p. 16.
44 Brenda Maddox, *Rosalind Franklin:The Dark Lady of DNA* Chapter 1.
45 Ibid., Chapter 2.
46 *Jewish Chronicle*, 5 July 1968, p. 7.
47 *Anna Sayre, Rosalind Franklin and DNA*, pp. 36, 41-43.
48 *Jewish Chronicle*, 2 August 2002, p. 30.
49 www.varsity.co.uk, *Rosalind Franklin: The Dark Lady of DNA* 15 March 2019.
50 Brenda Maddox, *Rosalind Franklin: The Dark Lady of DNA* Chapter 4.
51 www.biography.com
52 Ibid.
53 *Evening Herald* (Dublin), 21 June 2002, p. 30.
54 www.biography.com
55 *Jewish Chronicle*, 2 August 2002, p. 30.
56 *Times*, 5 June 2013.
57 Brenda Maddox, *Rosalind Franklin: The Dark Lady of DNA* Prologue
58 Ibid., Chapter 9.
59 *Jewish Chronicle*, 2 August 2002, p. 30.
60 Brenda Maddox, *Rosalind Franklin: The Dark Lady of DNA*, Chapter 9.
61 *Jewish Chronicle*, 5 July 1968, p. 7.
62 Brenda Maddox: *Rosalind Franklin: The Dark Lady of DNA* Epilogue
63 Norman Lebrecht, *Genius & Anxiety. How Jews Changed the World 1847-1947* (London: Oneworld Publications, 2009), p. 382.
64 *Jewish Chronicle*, 5 July 1968, p. 7.
65 *Sunday Tribune*, 30 June 2002, p. 60.
66 Organised rescue effort (1938-40) which brought thousands of refugee Jewish children to Great Britain from Nazi Germany.
67 Anna Sayre, *Rosalind Franklin and DNA*, p. 35.
68 *Jewish Chronicle*, 5 July 1968, p. 7.
69 Norman Lebrecht, *Genius & Anxiety*, p. 380.
70 *Times*, 5 June 2013.
71 Norman Lebrecht, *Genius & Anxiety*, p. 381.
72 *Jewish Chronicle*, 5 July 1968, p. 30.

73   Ibid., p. 7.

74   Norman Lebrecht, *Genius & Anxiety*, p. 381.

75   Brenda Maddox, *Rosalind Franklin: The Dark Lady of DNA* Chapter 6.

76   *Jewish Chronicle*, 5 July 1966, p. 7.

77   *Jewish Renaissance,* January 2020, p. 41.

78   *Evening Herald (Dublin),* 21 June 2002, p. 30.

79   Brenda Maddox, *Rosalind Franklin: The Dark Lady of DNA* Prologue

80   *Jewish Chronicle*, 3 March 1995, p. 19.

81   *Independent*, 23 October 2011.

82   Sarah Abrevaya Stein, *Ostrich Feathers, Jews and a Lost World of Global Commerce* (New Haven: Yale University Press, 2010), p. 180.

83   Jewish Historical Studies, *Transactions of the Jewish Historical Society*, Vol. 18, 1953.

84   Jewish Historical Studies, *Transactions of the Jewish Historical Society*, Vol. 11, 1924.

85   www.jewishlivesproject.com

86   *Transactions of the Jewish Historical Society*, Vol. 11, 1924.

87   Zoom interview with Lucy Wedderburn, 29 November 2020.

88   Email correspondence from Lucy Wedderburn to Isabelle Seddon, 7 March 2021.

89   Zoom interview with Lucy Wedderburn, 29 November 2020.

90   Newnham was established in 1871 as house in which young women could reside while attending lectures at Cambridge, long before they were allowed to become full members of the university with the granting of degrees to women in 1948.

91   Email correspondence from Lucy Wedderburn to Isabelle Seddon, 7 March 2021.

92   Ibid.

93   Ibid.

94   Ibid.

95   Zoom interview with Lucy Wedderburn, 29 November 2020.

96   Email correspondence from Lucy Wedderburn to Isabelle Seddon, 7 March 2021.

97   Email correspondence from Rabbi Alexandra Wright to Isabelle Seddon, 26 October 2020.

98   A Farewell to Nina Wedderburn, Eulogy by Rabbi Alexandra Wright, 21 August 2020.

99   Email correspondence from Lucy Wedderburn to Isabelle Seddon, 7 March 2021.

100   Ruth Watts, *Women in Science*, pp. 200-201.

101   *Guardian*, 30 April 2004. Greenfield gives talks across a wide variety of

sectors including finance, technology, human resources, media and education. Organisations include McKinsey's, Investec, Deutsche Bank, Barclays, CoreNet Global, KION group and Newcastle University. Susangreenfield.com.

102   *Jewish Chronicle*, 25 November 2011, p. 19.

103   A non-Jewish person who performs certain tasks prohibited for a Jewish person on the Sabbath.

104   *Jewish Chronicle*, 9 January 2004, p. 25.

105   *Jewish Chronicle,* 25 November 2011, p. 19.

106   Susangreenfield.com

107   *Guardian*, 30 April 2004.

108   Sciencemag.org, 11 January 2010.

109   The Christmas lectures were started by Michael Faraday ('the father of electrical engineering' who launched the modern world by demonstrating the power of electricity) in 1825 and are now broadcast on television every year. The lectures present scientific subjects to a general audience, including young people, in an informative and entertaining manner.

110   *Independent on Sunday*, 11 May 2008.

111   *Guardian*, 10 January 2010.

112   Sciencemag.org, 11 January 2010.

113   *Guardian*, 10 January 2010.

114   *Oxford Mail*, 9 August 2013.

115   www.royalsociety.com.

116   Aileen Fyfe and Camilla Rostvik, 'How female fellows fared at the Royal Society', *Nature*, 6 March 2018.

117   *Jewish Chronicle*, 25 November 2011, p. 19.

118   *Guardian*, 30 April 2004.

119   *Jewish Chronicle*, 24 November 2011.

120   'Gender equality. No room at the top for women scientists'. BBC News, 6 September 2019.

121   Timeshighereducation.com, 15 May 2020.

122   *Jewish Chronicle*, 25 November 2011, p. 19.

123   *Jewish Chronicle*, 9 January 2004, p. 25.

124   *Jewish Chronicle*, 25 November 2001, p. 20.

125   *Jewish Chronicle*, 9 January 2004, p. 25.

126   *Jewish Chronicle,* 25 November 2011, p. 19.

127   *Desert Island Discs*, BBC Radio 4, 2 March 1997.

128   *Jewish Chronicle*, 9 January 2004, p. 25.

129   Ibid.

130   *Guardian,* 31 December 2000.

131   *Independent,* 29 June 2013.

CHAPTER 8

1   Julia Neuberger, 'Women in Judaism: The Fact and the Fiction', in Pat Holden (ed.), *Women's Religious Experience* (London: Croom Helm, 1983), pp. 135-139.
2   Jewish Women's Archive, jwa.org.
3   Rabbiting On, Episode 20, podcast 3 March 2022, reformjudaism.org.uk.
4   www.theconversation.com, 27 May 2022.
5   Jewish Women's Archive, jwa.org.
6   Ellen M. Umansky, *Lily Montagu and the Advancement of Liberal Judaism: From Vision to Vocation* (New York: The Edwin Mellon Press, 1983), p. 137.
7   Victorianweb.org.
8   Jewish Women's Archive, jwa.org.
9   Ibid.
10 *Jewish Chronicle,* 16 March 2002, p 34.
11 *Jewish Chronicle,* 21 June 1996, p. 25.
12 Joachim Schlor, *Escaping Nazi Germany: One Woman's Emigration from Heilbronn to England* (London: Bloomsbury Academic, 2021).
13 *Jewish Chronicle,* 21 June 1996, p. 25.
14 *Independent,* 6 March 2005.
15 Ibid.
16 Tzedakah: The Rest is Commentary, jdov.com
17 Jewish Volunteering Network, 3 March 2011.
18 Interview with *Examined Life,* West London Synagogue, 2017.
19 *Jewish Chronicle,* 4 July 1980, p. 12.
20 *Times of Israel,* 23 July 2019.
21 *Jewish Chronicle,* 31 May 2019. p. 13.
22 *Independent,* 6 March 2005.
23 Jewish Women's Archive, youtube, 16 June 2016.
24 *Guardian,* 15 November 2016.
25 *Independent,* 6 March 2005.
26 Interview with *Examined Life,* West London Synagogue, 2017.
27 She took her middle name 'Sarah' as her surname instead of her original surname Klempner.
28 Interview with Suzanne Paginton, Rainbow Jews exhibition, www.rainbowjews.com.
29 Elli Tikva Sarah, *Trouble Making Judaism* (London: David Paul, 2012), p.14.

30   Ibid., p. 15.
31   Interview with Suzanne Paginton.
32   *Shifra*, December 1984 (1), p. 9.
33   Elli Tikva Sarah, *Trouble Making Judaism*, p. 15.
34   Ibid., p. 17.
35   Interview with Suzanne Paginton.
36   Ibid.
37   Rebecca T. Alpert, Sue Levi Ewell and Shirley Idelson, *Lesbian Rabbis: The First Generation* (New Brunswick, NJ, Rutgers University, 2001), p. 77.
38   Rainbowjews.com.
39   Interview with Suzanne Paginton.
40   Emil Fackenheim, *The Jewish Return into History. Reflections in the Age of Auschwitz and a New Jerusalem* (New York: Schocken Books, 1978).
41   Elli Tikva Sarah, *Trouble Making Judaism*, pp. 17-19.
42   Alpert, Ewell and Idelson, *Lesbian Rabbis*, p. 77.
43   Elli Tikva Sarah, *Trouble Making Judaism*, p. 20.
44   *Lesbian Rabbis*, p. 13.
45   Ibid., p. 21.
46   Ibid., pp. 75-76.
47   Elli Tikva Sarah, *Trouble Making Judaism*, pp. 22-23.
48   Rabbi Sheila Shulman was the founder of London's gay and lesbian synagogue Beit Klal Yisrael.
49   Interview with Suzanne Paginton.
50   A debate series (1979-2000) whose subject matter was often concerned with religious or ethical issues.
51   Elli Tikva Sarah, *Trouble Making Judaism*, p. 27.
52   Ibid., p. 19.
53   Rainbowjews.com.
54   A canopy beneath which Jewish marriage ceremonies are performed.
55   Elli Tikva Sarah, *Trouble Making Judaism*, p. 27.
56   Rabbi Elli Tikva Sarah: Troublemaking Judaism, rainbowjews.com
57   *Jewish Chronicle*, 1 December 1995, p. 27.
58   *Jewish Telegraph*, 2010.
59   *Jewish Chronicle*, 1 December 1995, p. 27.
60   A Hebrew word, derived from Aramaic, that means to be contrary; out of spite in a childish way. www.hebrewpod101.com.
61   A nine branched candelabrum usually made out of metal or stone.
62   *Jewish Chronicle*, 1 December 1995, p. 27.
63   'Religious Lindsey was seven before she knew she was Jewish' *Jewish Telegraph*, 2010.

64   Lindsey Taylor-Guthartz, *Challenge and Conformity: The Religious Lives of Orthodox Jewish Women* (Oxford: Litman Library of Jewish Civilization, 2021).

65   *Jewish Chronicle*, 19 March 2021, p. 45.

66   *Jewish Chronicle*, 1 January 2021, p. 4.

67   *Jewish Chronicle*, 11 June 2001, p. 2.

68   *Times of Israel*, 4 October 2021.

69   *Jewish Chronicle*, 18 June 2021, p. 2.

70   *Jewish Chronicle*, 2 July 2021, p. 7.

71   *Times of Israel*, 4 October 2021

72   *Woman's Hour*, www.bbc.co.uk, 17 June 2021.

Index

Note: Page numbers in italics are illustrations. References to notes are indicated by 'n' after the page number (287n90).